THE JOHN HARVARD LIBRARY

Bernard Bailyn
Editor-in-Chief

THE

INDEPENDENT REFLECTOR

OR

Weekly Essays on Sundry Important Subjects

More particularly adapted to the

Province of New-York

By

WILLIAM   LIVINGSTON

and Others

Edited by Milton M. Klein

THE BELKNAP PRESS OF
HARVARD UNIVERSITY PRESS
Cambridge, Massachusetts
1 9 6 3

Distributed in Great Britain by Oxford University Press, London

Library of Congress Catalog Card Number 62–13268

Printed in the United States of America

CONTENTS

THE

INDEPENDENT REFLECTOR

CONTENTS

CONTENTS

vii

CONTENTS

CONTENTS

ix

INTRODUCTION

1

The appearance of the *Independent Reflector* on November 30, 1752, should have created a stir in colonial New York. Until then, the province had never had a periodical publication other than its regular newspapers; it would not have another until 1787.[1] The *Reflector* gave New York City a kind of literary parity with Philadelphia and Boston, which had entered the magazine-publishing field about ten years earlier. Since the Pennsylvania and Massachusetts experiments had failed, New York, with the *Reflector* (and the other journals it sired), was for the time the center of periodical-publishing in the English colonies of North America. The preëminence was to endure for five years: in 1757 Philadelphia made a second attempt to produce a literary periodical.[2] The distinction of the *Independent Reflector*, however, lay not merely in its priority of publication but in its style, its content, and its impact on the political, religious, and educational history of New York.

Strictly speaking, the *Reflector* was not a magazine in the eighteenth-century sense. To its English originators and its American imitators, a magazine was literally a "storehouse" or "miscellany" of writings sometimes original but more often excerpted from other publications. It was a "Repository of Ancient and Modern Fugitive Pieces, Prose and Poetical" — the self-characterization of the Philadelphia *American Museum*; or a collection of "curious and entertaining pieces in Prose and Verses, . . . the

[1] New York's second experiment in periodical literature was Samuel Loudon's *American Magazine* (December, 1787–November, 1788).

[2] *The American Magazine, or Monthly Chronicle*, published by William Bradford and edited by Rev. William Smith, Provost of the Philadelphia College. The earliest American magazines are analyzed comprehensively in Lyon N. Richardson, *A History of Early American Magazines, 1741–1789* (New York, 1931) and discussed more generally in Frank Luther Mott, *A History of American Magazines, 1741–1780* (New York and London, 1930). (This is Vol. I of the 4 vol. ed. published by Harvard University Press, 1957).

1

most recent Occurrences, . . . and several Advertisements," as the *New-Jersey Magazine* described itself. Appearing monthly, the magazine usually included instructive or moral essays; entertainment in the form of poetry, fiction, riddles, etc; feature articles on scientific discoveries or experiments; public notices; summaries of foreign and domestic news; climatological information; and lists of books recently published.[3] The pattern was set in England in 1731 by the *Gentleman's Magazine,* and American periodicals strove to imitate this model. They succeeded so well that the historian of American magazines can say of the Boston *American Magazine and Historical Chronicle* that "except for the imprint it might have been printed in London." [4]

Like their English exemplars, the early American magazines were largely eclectic. About ninety per cent of Benjamin Franklin's Philadelphia *General Magazine, and Historical Chronicle* (1741) consisted of material copied from other publications. Authors were less disturbed at pirating than at distortions, which were often so egregious that the "natural Parent" could not recognize the pilfered compositions in their new dress. Editors and publishers made no apologies for their imitative proclivities. The *New-England Magazine* confessed that it was less interested in presenting essays on *new* subjects than in "giving Things that *are known* an applicable or agreeable Turn." "A *new* Author's *Expression* and *Application*," it added, "is what we are chiefly to admire," not his originality.[5]

The editorial ideal was an article of timeless rather than timely quality. The aim of the publisher was to offer a collection of "entertaining" and "useful" compositions that would comprise "a Piece of valuable Furniture in the Library of a Gentleman." The publication should also give persons "at a distance a just idea of the public state of these *American* colonies," and "enable Posterity to form an Idea of the Learning, Wisdom, . . . abilities, . . . Temper, Taste, . . . Customs, Manners, Morals, Religion

---

[3] For the earliest English prototypes of American magazines, see Walter Graham, *English Literary Periodicals* (New York, 1930), chap. 5.

[4] Mott, *American Magazines,* pp. 40, 79; see also Richardson, *Early American Magazines,* pp. 34, 37–46.

[5] *The New-England Magazine* (Boston), I (August, 1758), 8.

and Politics of their Forefathers." [6] The earliest magazines sought to be comprehensive, not selective; English, not American; entertaining, not didactic.

Before 1752 there had been five attempts at magazine publishing in the American colonies. None had proved either a literary or financial success. Philadelphia gave birth to two periodicals in 1741, the *American Magazine* and the *General Magazine,* but the first lasted only three issues and the other, six.[7] Two years later Boston erupted with three journals: *The Christian History,* the *Boston Weekly Magazine,* and *The American Magazine and Historical Chronicle.* The first was less a magazine than an extended chronicle of the Great Awakening; the second did not survive beyond three numbers; the last was most successful, running for three years, but it was so deliberately imitative of English periodicals as scarcely to be called American. Neither its inception nor its demise created any ferment in Boston, and it made little impress on the literary history of America.[8]

The *Independent Reflector* differed singularly from its predecessors. Its model was the single-essay journal of original composition which Joseph Addison and Richard Steele had elevated to literary art in the *Tatler* and the *Spectator.* Where earlier magazines sought to amuse and please, the *Reflector* purposed to expose, attack, and reform. The journal's excursions into politics were not intended to explain New York public affairs to its neighbors but to enlighten New Yorkers about their own. Its didactic essays were not directed at posterity but at readers in its own day; the topics it discussed were not those of universal interest but those "More particularly adapted to the Province of New-York." [9]

[6] *The Boston Weekly Magazine,* March 2, 1743; *The American Magazine, or Monthly Chronicle* (Philadelphia), I (October 1757), Preface, 4; announcement of Bradford's *American Magazine* (Philadelphia) in his newspaper, *The American Weekly Mercury,* November 6, 1740, quoted in Anna J. DeArmond, *Andrew Bradford: Colonial Journalist* (Newark, Delaware, 1949), p. 225.

[7] Richardson, *Early American Magazines,* chap. 2; DeArmond, *Andrew Bradford,* pp. 223–239. Andrew Bradford was the publisher of the *American Magazine* and Benjamin Franklin of the *General Magazine.* Franklin thought so little of his journal that he did not mention it in his *Autobiography.*

[8] Richardson, *Early American Magazines,* pp. 45, 58–73; Elizabeth C. Cook, "Colonial Newspapers and Magazines," in *The Cambridge History of American Literature,* 4 vols. (Cambridge and New York, 1918–1921), I, 121.

[9] The subtitle of the journal, in the *Preface* published early in 1754, was

INTRODUCTION

The *Reflector* lacked neither wit nor caustic humor, but these were employed to satirize and burlesque rather than to please and amuse. The frivolous discourses on female fashions, love, courtship, marriage, the weather, and human frailties which entertained readers of the *Tatler* were missing from the *Reflector*. Its tone was serious rather than sportive, its contents reflective rather than diverting; and while other periodicals were circumspect in their observations on controversial matters like religion and politics, the *Reflector* aimed boldly, as its first number declared, at exposing "the Abuses and Encroachments" of both priests and politicians and at vindicating the *"civil and religious* RIGHTS" of countrymen from enemies of "whatever dignified Shape."

The expectation of most editors and publishers of early American magazines was first to make money and second to improve and promote culture. The editor of the *Reflector* earned nothing by his literary efforts. Indeed, his law practice suffered because he devoted so much energy to his journalistic interests. His was a labor of love, not of advantage. The printer, although paid for his efforts, undertook the project at the solicitation of the editor and as an accommodation. Both editor and publisher undoubtedly hoped that the *Reflector* would enhance the reputation of New York for culture and learning; but when the paper, in its second issue, assailed the inequitable excise system of the province and, in the third, lashed out at municipal road repair and police protection, it became obvious that culture yielded to civic improvement among its objectives.

Other magazines steered clear of controversy for fear of losing subscribers. The ironic price paid for attention to popularity was historic oblivion. Expecting to interpret their age for posterity, they succeeded only in obscuring it. The *Reflector,* by contrast, reveled in controversy. Its most forceful essays were born of contention. Its pungent and passionate language and its timely observations on New York problems provide grist for the historian's mill; and its appearance excited the attention of contemporary readers and excites that of latter-day chroniclers. Literary historians have praised the *Reflector* for raising American essay-writing

"Weekly Essays on Sundry Important Subjects. More particularly adapted to the Province of New-York."

4

to a new height in exposition and argument and for infusing into eighteenth-century English periodical literature needed vigor and trenchancy.[10] Political scientists searching for roots of American political thought have found in the *Reflector* essays on religion and government clues to the colonial mind of the mid-eighteenth century; and historians concerned with the more prosaic task of describing the pattern of municipal life in colonial New York have mined the columns of the *Reflector* for their material.[11]

Contemporaries paid the journal the compliment of denouncing its boldness before the third issue had appeared. The essay on the excise system was assailed by a number of "wrathful Gentlemen" who accused the editor of writing "contemptuously" about government. Rather than deterring the editor, the charge spurred him to enter other forbidden pastures. In the sixth issue he shocked the orthodox by a defense of the Moravian Brethren, a heterodox sect, and by an attack on the dogmas of all denominations. In the seventeenth number he launched a full-scale assault on the proposal for a college in New York under Church of England auspices. The "clamour" that erupted after the college essays relegated the excitement over the Moravians to a mere flurry; and, as the Loyalist historian of New York recalled some years later, these essays

produced answers, a paper war was the consequence, and persons of all degrees, of all denominations, of all religions, and almost of all ages, joining either the one side or the other, the Colony, in a short time, . . . became a scene of confusion, of uproar, and disorder, thanks to the triumvirate Livingston, Scott, and Smith, and to them only.[12]

2

The triumvirate to whom Jones paid his unintended compliment were William Livingston, William Smith, Jr., and John Morin Scott, and the *Independent Reflector* was their handiwork.

[10] Richardson, *Early American Magazines*, pp. 74, 77; Robert Spiller *et al.*, *The Literary History of the United States*, 3 vols. (New York, 1948–1949), I, 94.

[11] Clinton Rossiter quotes liberally from the *Reflector* in his *Seedtime of the Republic* (New York, 1953); and George W. Edwards draws heavily on the *Reflector* in *New York as an Eighteenth Century Municipality, 1731–1776* (New York, 1917).

[12] Thomas Jones, *History of New York during the Revolutionary War*, 2 vols., Edwin Floyd De Lancey, ed. (New York, 1879), I, 7.

All three shared in planning the journal; all three contributed essays to it; and when it came under attack, each defended it. Yet when defenders and detractors rendered their differing respects to *the* editor of the *Reflector,* they directed them always to the senior member of the trio, the principal author of its essays, William Livingston.

In 1752 Livingston was twenty-nine years old. By accident or design, the first issue of the periodical came off the press on his birthday, November 30.[13] The youngest of the six sons of Philip Livingston, second lord of the Livingston Manor, William was already a more prominent public figure than his older brothers. His youth had been spent in Albany, where his father maintained his business and one of his many residences. Here William was reared in circumstances which he later recalled as those of "ease and affluence." [14] After the customary "grammatical education," he was sent to Yale, which three of his brothers — Peter, John, and Philip — had already attended; [15] but at this point his career diverged sharply from theirs. The three Livingston sons who were graduated from Yale, together with brothers Robert and Henry, entered the mercantile field; but commerce was neither to William's liking nor in the interest of the family. The Livingston Manor was more than a system of agricultural landholding; it was a vast complex of ships, stores, warehouses, mills, mines, forges, and farmlands, with centers in Albany, New York City, and the manor on the Hudson, and appendages in New England, old England, and the West Indies. The first two manor lords, Robert and Philip, had directed these extensive enterprises each almost alone, as landlord, merchant, storekeeper, manufacturer, ironmaster, and lawyer; but by 1741, when William left Yale, the family's economic interests had become too varied for such unsystematic management.[16] Philip

[13] Livingston was born in Albany on November 30, 1723. Theodore Sedgwick, Jr., *A Memoir of the Life of William Livingston* (New York, 1833), p. 45 note. Sedgwick gives this as the "probable" date. It is confirmed by an entry in the Family Bible of Mrs. Catherine Livingston, Livingston's daughter, in the Massachusetts Historical Society (hereafter cited as MHS).

[14] Livingston to Alida Hoffman, October 29, 1782, Livingston Papers, Box 13, MHS.

[15] Franklin B. Dexter, ed., *Biographical Sketches of the Graduates of Yale College,* 6 vols. (New York and New Haven, 1885–1912), I, 422, 474, 521.

[16] The sole biography of the founder of the family in America, Lawrence H.

INTRODUCTION

Livingston educated each of his six sons for his specialized role in the family's economic empire clearly in view; and William's destiny lay in the law. The decision was not his, but his father's; and before he completed the required apprenticeship Livingston demonstrated his disapproval in a variety of ways, some of which shocked his family and all of which evidenced the strain of quixoticism and intemperance characteristic of his career.

Three-quarters of the way through his clerkship in the office of James Alexander, dean of the New York bar and a friend of the family, Livingston impetuously dispatched to the press a scathing indictment of the system of legal apprenticeship, including some harsh words for masters who made a "young Fellow trifle away the Bloom of his Age" in the endless drudgery of copying forms, cases, statutes, and precedents.[17] Only the use of a pseudonym saved him from the irate Alexander's reprimand. Less than a year later Livingston touched his master in a rawer spot, by publicly attacking Mrs. Alexander, the dowager of New York society, for excessive vanity and social pretentiousness. The penalty was quick: Livingston was dismissed from Alexander's law office.[18]

Livingston completed his apprenticeship in the office of another distinguished New York attorney, William Smith, Sr. He devoted himself seriously to the practice of law for the next twenty-five years, but he never developed any genuine affection for it.[19] His first love remained belles-lettres, of which he had become a devotee at Yale. His greatest pleasure came not from pleading or even winning law suits, but from writing. He was a facile and an inveterate penman. His youthful literary forays were merely exordiums to his long and successful career as essay-writer, versifier, and political pamphleteer-extraordinary. "Never . . . expect from me what they call fine letters," he cautioned Noah Welles, his Yale classmate, at the commencement of their long correspond-

---

Leder's *Robert Livingston and the Politics of Colonial New York* (Chapel Hill, N.C., 1961) deals only incidentally with the manor and its management. There is no biography of Philip, the second manor lord.

[17] The composition was published in the *New-York Weekly Post-Boy*, August 19, 1745.

[18] The second essay appeared in the *Post-Boy* on March 3, 1746.

[19] See Milton M. Klein, "The Rise of the New York Bar: The Legal Career of William Livingston," *William and Mary Quarterly*, XV (1958), 334-358.

ence, "for we will not dispute the field with weapons of witt and Eloquence." "Witt," he added, "is not my Talent, nor Eloquence my property."[20] The modesty was feigned — both wit and eloquence flowed from his pen, and he cultivated each talent deliberately.

Livingston's fondness for writing is at least partly explained by his limitations as a speaker. Though forthright to the point of imprudence as a writer, he was reserved, almost shy, as a public speaker, and uncomfortable in large gatherings. Tall, lean, awkward, and unhandsome, he shunned balls and theaters, preferring the company of a few close friends to the crowded assemblies of New York high society or the press of political meetings. He once ruefully described himself as one of those "ordinary fellows . . . whose noses hang parallel with their chins." On another occasion he called himself "spindle Shanks." He early became accustomed to the rebuffs of young ladies "who are tickled with an handsome appearance"; and while the experience did not distort his personality, it encouraged him to cultivate his literary skills.[21] He compensated for taciturnity in conversation by "being the more garrulous . . . with the quill," and the consequence was the extravagant ornamentation and the diffusiveness which marred his literary style.[22]

The *Independent Reflector* was Livingston's most important early publishing venture, but he did not emerge into literary maturity full-blown in 1752. He had served his literary apprenticeship simultaneously with his law clerkship. In addition to the two intemperate essays he sent to the press while he was in Alexander's office, Livingston managed to complete two short poems, attempt a play, write a treatise on the history of the drama, and publish a long pastoral. Neither of the two bits of verse appeared in print at

[20] Livingston to Welles, May, 1742, Livingston-Welles Correspondence, Johnson Family Papers, Yale University (hereafter cited as JFP, Yale).

[21] Livingston to Welles, June 16, 1747, April 16, 1748, JFP, Yale. Stopping in New Jersey in 1774, en route to the First Continental Congress, John Adams was told that Livingston even then was regarded as a good writer but a "bad speaker." John Adams, "Diary," in *The Works of John Adams*, 10 vols., C. F. Adams, ed. (Boston, 1856–1866), II, 356.

[22] Livingston to James Pemberton, December 21, 1788, Etting Papers, "Washingtonia," Historical Society of Pennsylvania. Long before, Livingston had admitted his "prolixity" in a letter to Welles (July 26, 1745, JFP, Yale).

the time. One was a poetic paraphrase of the Lord's Prayer. The other was a conventional panegyric to "Eliza." [23] The dissertation on the drama was sent to Noah Welles, who was so impressed, he proposed submitting it to the *American Magazine and Historical Chronicle* in Boston, but Livingston demurred — the piece was "too incorrect and superficial to obtrude on the Publick." [24] He did not often display such modesty.

The young law clerk-turned-versifier demonstrated less reluctance in sanctioning in 1747 the publication of a longer poem, *Philosophic Solitude, or The Choice of a Rural Life.* Unoriginal in form and content, this extended eclogue is patterned after an English work by the Reverend John Pomfret, *The Choice*, which had a wide vogue in England among those pretending to taste and knowledge. In 684 lines of rhymed couplets imitative of Pope, *Philosophic Solitude* rhapsodizes the life of rural retirement, moderate elegance, and intelligent idleness — the aristocratic ideal of the age.[25] Twentieth-century critics have seen in it nothing but a "faint echo" of Pomfret,[26] but Livingston's contemporaries were more impressed. Fellow Yalensians hailed it as the first contribution to "polite" literature by a graduate of the New Haven college, and Noah Welles introduced it with a prefatory eulogy:

> Yalensis smiles the finished piece to view,
> And fondly glories in a Son like you.[27]

Dr. Benjamin Colman, the prominent Boston clergyman, was

[23] The MS of the prayer is in the Livingston Papers, Box 6, MHS. Sedgwick, Livingston's biographer and great-grandson, discovered the original among some old family papers. He indorsed it: "I have never met with it before but often seen and heard it mentioned." Livingston's son William, Jr., identified it as his father's. Livingston, Jr., to William Paterson, May 29, 1801, New York Historical Society. The poem to Eliza appears, in part, in Sedgwick, *A Memoir*, pp. 117–118. The complete manuscript is in the Livingston Papers, Box 6, MHS. The playwriting effort was disclosed to Miss E— T—, November 17, December 29, 1744, Letter Book, 1744–1745, Sedgwick Papers, Box 19, MHS.

[24] Livingston to Welles, March 17, April 12, 1746, JFP, Yale.

[25] See the article by Edwin T. Bowden, "Benjamin Church's *Choice* and American Colonial Poetry," *New England Quarterly*, XXXII (1959), 170–184.

[26] For uncomplimentary estimates see Spiller, *Literary History*, I, 94; Moses C. Tyler, *A History of American Literature*, 2 vols. (New York, 1878), II, 219; and Charles Angoff, *Literary History of the American People*, 2 vols. (New York, 1931), I, 358–359.

[27] *Philosophic Solitude* (New-York, 1747), vi.

sufficiently interested to ask New Jersey friends about the author. Jonathan Belcher, governor of the colony, read the poem and sent several copies to England in order to "disabuse" the authorities at home "in the wrong opinion they entertain of our Ignorance and barbarism, and to shew them that America produces some Geniusses little inferior to the most Eminent Europeans." [28]

Whatever its shortcomings, *Philosophic Solitude* achieved an uncommon popularity during the author's lifetime; and its repute survived his death. If by 1833 it rested in oblivion — in the words of a critic of that day — it had endured remarkably up to that time.[29] As a separate publication it went through thirteen editions, the last in 1790. It was a favorite of magazine editors and anthologists during the Revolution and the early years of the Republic; [30] and it made its author colonial New York's first and principal poet.

Despite his fondness for versifying, Livingston's most effective literary medium was prose; and by 1752 he had already received his baptism as an essayist and political pamphleteer. In 1749, only a year after his entrance to the bar, he published an appeal for speedier legislative action on the college then under public discussion, *Some Serious Thoughts on the Design of Erecting a College in the Province of New-York*, under the enigmatic pseudonym, "Hippocrates Mithridate. Apoth." [31] It was prompted by

[28] Livingston to Welles, Sept. 19, 1747, JFP, Yale.

[29] The unkind comment appeared in a review of Sedgwick's *A Memoir*, in *American Quarterly Review*, XIV (1833), 5–6. A more recent estimate is in Max Savelle, *Seeds of Liberty: The Genesis of the American Mind* (New York, 1948), pp. 408, 417.

[30] A partial investigation reveals, in addition to New York editions of 1747, 1769, and 1790, a Boston edition of 1762 and a Trenton edition of 1782. The poem was reproduced in part in *The New-England Magazine*, I (August, 1758), 50–51; reprinted serially in the *Boston Magazine*, II (March–June, 1785), 107–109, 147–148, 189–190, 227–228; and included in the *Columbian Muse, A Selection of American Poetry, from Various Authors of Established Reputation* (New York, 1794), pp. 16–33; *American Poems, Selected and Original* (Litchfield, 1793), pp. 154–175; and the *Young Gentleman and Lady's Monitor. . .* (New York, 1790), pp. 325–342.

[31] This extremely rare pamphlet, printed by John Zenger, Jr., was advertised for sale in the *New-York Weekly Journal*, March 20, 1749. There is a copy in the Columbia University Library. The essay has not previously been identified as Livingston's. Livingston disclosed his authorship in a letter to Noah Welles, February 18, 1749, JFP, Yale. It does not appear to have sold well. Six months after its appearance, the printer was still advertising copies for sale. See *New-York Weekly Journal*, September 25, 1749.

his concern over lagging popular interest in a project which had been initiated by a public lottery under the Assembly's sponsorship three years earlier.[32] King George's War and the "perplexity" of public affairs threatened to relegate the college project to a legislative side-show. Livingston was determined to keep the issue alive; and in the pamphlet he expounded, with a judicious mixture of humor and earnestness, the "numberless Advantages" of a "publick Seminary of Learning." This nine-page publication was one of the rare Livingston fabrications that did not provoke controversy, principally because it was non-political in tone.

A year earlier, Livingston had demonstrated that he could wield a sharper quill when he concentrated his efforts on a political target. Neither the circumstances nor the publications themselves are known precisely, but two pamphlets appear to have been written by him late in 1748 burlesquing the political aspirations of one of Governor George Clinton's closest aides. A brief literary skirmish ensued. The maligned politico was publicly defended by one of his associates; Livingston prepared a rejoinder; literary honors appear to have been about even.[33]

Such political pamphleteering was exceptional during Livingston's clerkship period. New York politics were too confused and Livingston's political loyalties as yet too imprecise to permit him to embark on the sea of political journalism with any sense of direction. His friends and future coadjutors on the *Reflector* and his law tutors were all in the camp of Governor Clinton. The Governor considered the Livingstons a "vile family." William's father returned the compliment by declining to have any "Concern" with Clinton and by denouncing him for having "abuzd" all those who would not do his bidding.[34] New York politics were a

<hr>

[32] *The Colonial Laws of New York*, 5 vols. (Albany, 1894), III, 607–616, 679–688, 731–732.

[33] The target of Livingston's attack was camouflaged as "Selyn Molouck," and Livingston's own pseudonym was "Solomon Bensirach." The pamphlets are referred to in the *New-York Evening Post*, November 14, 1748. A manuscript version of one is in the Livingston Papers, Box 6, MHS. For his rejoinder Livingston selected another pseudonym, "Don John Ferdinando Scribblous." The defense, signed "G. B.," appeared in the *Evening Post*, November 14; the author may have been Goldsbrow Banyar, Governer Clinton's secretary. Livingston's "Answer to a paper signed G. B." is in the Livingston Papers, Box 3, MHS.

[34] Clinton to the Duke of Newcastle, November 18, 1745, in E. B. O'Callaghan,

weird mixture of economic rivalries, ethnic-religious factionalism, family feuds, personal enmities, and sectional differences; and the reason for the shifting allegiance of families like the Smiths, Alexanders, Livingstons, De Lanceys, and Morrises is not always clear. What is evident in 1750, however, is the continued hostility between the Livingstons and Governor Clinton, despite the demise in 1749 of the second manor lord, Philip Livingston. In the provincial elections of that year the Livingstons fought to defeat the Clinton candidates for the Assembly; and in New York City William contributed a small pamphlet to the effort.

This was a twelve-page *Letter to the Freemen and Freeholders of the Province of New-York*, which appeared over a characteristic pseudonym, "Tribunus Populi." [35] The content of the publication is of less interest than its style. Abounding in abusive satire, sparked by pungent witticisms, replete with classical allusions, and written in language both florid and eloquent, it foreshadowed the manner of the *Independent Reflector*.

Livingston's pen was not idle during the next two years. He wrote another political tract satirizing Governor Clinton and Chief Justice James De Lancey for engaging in an absurd jurisdictional feud over the right to try one of His Majesty's sailors for an alleged homicide committed in New York harbor; [36] he celebrated the defeat of the Clintonites at the polls in 1750 in a brief valedictory

---

ed., *Documents Relative to the Colonial History of the State of New York*, 15 vols. (Albany, 1853–1887), VI, 286; Philip Livingston to Jacob Wendell, February 13, 1747, Livingston Papers, Museum of the City of New York.

[35] The pamphlet was dated August 22, 1750. The only copy located is that of the Library of Congress. The attribution of authorship is somewhat circuitous. In October, 1750, there appeared a publication titled *A Reply to A Letter from a Gentleman in New-York, To his Friend in Brunswick* ([New York, October] 1750), also signed "Tribunus Populi." The writer acknowledged himself to be the author of the earlier *Letter to the Freemen*. James Alexander identified the author of the *Reply*, in private correspondence, as "W—— L——." See Alexander to Robert Hunter Morris, October 26, 1750, Stevens Papers, Stevens Institute of Technology, Hoboken, N. J.; and Alexander to Cadwallader Colden, January 2, 1751, *The Letters and Papers of Cadwallader Colden, 1711–1775* (New York Historical Society, Collections, 1917–1923, 1934–1935 [New York, 1918, 1937]), IV, 249–250.

[36] Political Bill of Mortality for the Month of August in the Year 1750, in a Certain Quarter of the Town near the Bowling-green," printed in Sedgwick, *A Memoir*, p. 65. The MS is in the Livingston Papers, Vol. A, MHS. For the facts in this case, see Julius Goebel, Jr. and T. Raymond Naughton, *Law Enforcement in Colonial New York* (New York, 1944), pp. 304–306.

for the newspapers; he penned another *Letter to the Freemen and Freeholders* in the election of 1752; [37] and he engaged in a heated pamphlet exchange with some Jersey landowners over the disputed boundary between that province and New York. When politics did not engage him, he joined with his colleague, William Smith, Jr., to press for higher standards of admission to the bar and to prepare a much-needed codification of the laws of the colony.[38]

3

It was therefore no literary novice who commenced the editorship of the *Independent Reflector* late in 1752. The planning of the new journal was a collaborative effort representing over three years of cerebration among its founders. The scheme was conceived early in 1749, and Livingston wrote to Noah Welles of the project on February 18:

I Begg leave to inform you that the two Mr. Smiths, Scot[t] and myself have form'd a Design of publishing weekly Essays as soon as possible upon the plan of The Spectator, for correcting the taste and improving the Minds of our fellow Citizens. We propose to write a paper a month respectively till we have about 150 and then publish our Scheme, and when the printer has a sufficient number of Subscr [ibers?], print 1 or 2 a week according to the Encouragement we meet with. But we are apprehensive that we shall stagger under the Burden unless we engage you in the Design, and we doubt not but so generous, and (if well managed) useful an Undertaking will meet with your approbation and assistance. Essays on Religion and Molarity [Morality] are your peculiar province. Nor are you a Stranger to the fashionable vices and foibles of the age, and your pen is able to rally them. One paper a Month can scarcely interfere with the Duties of

[37] *New-York Gazette*, September 3, 1750; *A Letter to the Freemen and Freeholders. . .* ([February, 1752]). No copy of the latter publication has been located, but it was advertised in the *New-York Gazette* for February 10 and 17, 1752. Livingston's authorship is suggested by the similarity in title to the *Letter* of 1750 and by Philip Livingston's broad hint to his brother Robert that the pamphlet was "wrote . . . by a relation of ours." Philip to Robert Livingston, February 15, March 25, 1752, Livingston-Redmond Collection, Franklin D. Roosevelt Library, Hyde Park, N. Y.

[38] *New-York Gazette*, February 18, April 1, 1751; *Laws of New-York, from the Year 1691, to 1751, Inclusive* (New York, 1752). Livingston also wrote a humorous poetic attack on malpractitioners of the law, *The Art of Pleading, In Imitation of Horace's Art of Poetry* (New York, 1751).

your function. Part of a Sermon thrown into a somewhat different form, may often make a beautiful Speculation.

The quadrumvirate named in Livingston's letter represented a combination of talents formidable enough to realize the ambitious project even without Welles's assistance. Of the four, William Peartree Smith proved ultimately to be the least active contributor. Like the others, a graduate of Yale, Peartree Smith studied law but never practised it. A bountiful inheritance from his father and a profitable marriage freed Smith from putting his law studies to use. Apart from his collaboration with the triumvirate on the *Reflector* and its successor, "The Watch-Tower," little is known of his New York career. He was active in the city's Presbyterian Church, helped to found the College of New Jersey (Princeton), and served on its board of trustees. He moved to Elizabethtown, New Jersey, in 1757, where he served as mayor for many years.[39]

William Smith, Jr., and John Morin Scott were Livingston's closest collaborators not only on the *Reflector* but also in the many other projects which engrossed his attention for over twenty years. In fact, in few New York projects of any significance from 1750 to the eve of the Revolution did the triumvirate fail to play a major and often a decisive role. Did New York need a public library? The trio would found one — the New York Society Library. Was the city lacking a serious discussion group? The three sons of Eli would organize a Society for the Promotion of Useful Knowledge. Did the law require reform? The three young attorneys would organize a primitive bar association, The Moot, at which legal problems could be discussed and the law professionalized. Were the tenure of judges and the jury system endangered by the highhandedness of a provincial governor? The triumvirate would lead the attack on Lieutenant Governor Cadwallader Colden and come to the court's defense. Was New York lukewarm in supporting the war against France? The trio would

[39] Peartree Smith was graduated from Yale in 1742, one year after Livingston. He was related to William Smith, Jr., through his grandfather, the elder Smith's uncle. See Dexter, *Biographical Sketches of Yale Graduates*, I, 719–720; Maturin L. Delafield, "William Smith, Judge of the Supreme Court of the Province of New York," *Magazine of American History*, VI (1881), 264–282, especially pp. 264, 271, 273–274; Thomas J. Wertenbaker, *Princeton, 1746–1896* (Princeton, N.J., 1946), pp. 14–15.

rush into print to arouse the war spirit. Had the mother country gone mad after 1763 and begun to load New Yorkers with intolerable taxes? The Assembly would call on Livingston, Smith, and Scott to pen the colony's remonstrance. Was America about to receive the dreaded Episcopal establishment? The three Presbyterian lawyers would found a new paper to sound the alarm.[40]

By 1765 their steady espousal of "independent principles" in politics and religion had earned for them the suspicion of Episcopal churchmen and the enmity of arch-royalists. Tories who saw in the three "popular lawyers" the harbingers of republicanism and freethinking were consistently astigmatic. The triumvirate's bold assertions of civil and religious liberty were not much more than sound English Whiggism; but to British officialdom their opposition to "encroaching" prerogative and religious authoritarianism appeared as pure radicalism. The trio enjoyed the compliment; they relished shocking the sensibilities of traditionalists and delighted in controversies which would permit them to use their collective pen. In literary warfare the three excelled. "The Press is to them what the Pulpit was in times of Popery," was the bitter plaint of their most persistent foe, Cadwallader Colden.[41] Reverend Samuel Johnson, another of the trio's opponents, conceded grudgingly that it was "indeed fencing against a flail to hold any dispute with them," so artful had they become in press warfare.[42]

The *Independent Reflector* was born of the same motivations that impelled the trio to embark on their other civic enterprises;

[40] The only book that treats the three as a group is Dorothy R. Dillon, *The New York Triumvirate: A Study of the Legal and Political Careers of William Livingston, John Morin Scott, William Smith, Jr.* (New York, 1949). Its emphasis is on the trio's later collaboration rather than on their activities in the mid-eighteenth century. For separate sketches of Smith and Scott, see Dexter, *Biographical Sketches*, II, 55–60, 85–89; *Dictionary of American Biography*, XVI, 495–496, and XVII, 357–358; Maturin L. Delafield, "William Smith — The Historian," *Magazine of American History*, VI (1881), 418–439; Roger Wines, "William Smith, the Historian of New York," *New York History*, XL (1959), 3–17.

[41] Colden to the Secretary of State and the Board of Trade, December 6, 1765, *The Colden Letter Books, 1760–1775* (New York Historical Society *Collections*, IX–X [New York, 1877–1878]), II, 71.

[42] Johnson to Thomas Secker, March 1, 1759, *Samuel Johnson, President of King's College: His Career and Writings*, Herbert and Carol Schneider, eds., 4 vols. (New York, 1929), I, 283.

but the links that bound them in such intimate association were forged before 1752. Like Livingston, Smith and Scott were educated at Yale. All three young men served all or part of their apprenticeship in the law office of Smith's father, William Smith, Sr. Livingston was admitted to the bar in 1748; Smith, two years later. The two legal tyros quickly formed a partnership; Scott joined them upon his own entrance into the profession in 1752.

Livingston shared not only the professional interests of his fellow Yalensians but also their aspirations to intellectual sophistication. Livingston had not been long out of Yale before he complained of the sterility of learning in New York City and the necessity of associating with sturdy "bumper men" unless he chose to live in "hermitage." [43] The arrival of Smith and Scott from New Haven obviated the necessity of retirement; and the three Yale graduates, together with Peartree Smith and William Alexander, the son of Livingston's former law teacher, made up a company of youthful "philosophers" who regarded themselves as above the level of the majority of the younger set.

William Smith, Jr., shared Livingston's fondness for scribbling. He had begun writing at the precocious age of sixteen, and before the appearance of the *Reflector* he had published a full-length work of literary criticism.[44] Five years younger than Livingston, Smith did not always pay his older colleague the deference that his years commanded. He sharply criticized the first draft of *Philosophic Solitude* and reproached Livingston for intemperate drinking when at Yale. Livingston heatedly denied the charge as a "malevolent aspersion" — "Drunkenness I really think is the last Vice that ever I shall fall into" — and alluded unflatteringly to "Billy Smith's ministerial Severity" and his priggish "Compunction of Conscience" in joining his friends around the punch bowl.[45]

[43] Livingston to Welles, October 6, 1745, February 10, 1746, JFP, Yale; Livingston to Chauncey Whittelsey, August 23, 1744, Letter Book, 1744–1745, Sedgwick Papers, Box 19, MHS.
[44] *Some Critical Observations upon A late Poem, entitled The Breeches . . .* (New York, 1750). For this and Smith's other early writings, see Beverly McAnear, "American Imprints Concerning King's College," *Papers of the Bibliographical Society of America*, XLIV (1950), 306–307 note.
[45] Livingston to Welles, November 27, 1746, January 27, 1747, JFP, Yale.

INTRODUCTION

Smith bore a reputation for piety and seriousness throughout his life. A devout Presbyterian, "rigid" in his orthodoxy, and regular in church attendance, he shunned drinking and card playing. His enemies saw in his "steady, demure, puritanical countenance" only the disguise of "a most profound dissembler . . . a noted flatterer, [and] a great sycophant," but more sympathetic observers were impressed with his charm, grace, and urbanity.[46]

In contrast to the earnest, subtle, and cool Smith, John Morin Scott was bluff, hearty, and jovial; as fluent in conversation as Smith but less smooth; always at ease in company and warm in his personal relationships. His humor, candor, and generosity earned him the admiration even of political foes, who thought his only error of judgment was his naïveté in joining the crafty Smith-Livingston combination and allowing himself to be "duped" by them. Less adroit with the pen than his friends, Scott could yet write with vigor and clarity; and he lacked neither intelligence nor learning. His inclusion in the trio completed the assortment of talents the group required to achieve its ends. Smith's aristocratic bearing permitted him to move easily in New York high officialdom; Scott's rough, ingenuous manner made him an ideal manager of popular meetings held in the taverns and in "the fields"; Livingston, always uncomfortable in the salons and on the streets, and lacking both Smith's suavity and Scott's geniality, provided the intellectual leadership and the literary energy.

Either his age — he was five years older than both Smith or Scott — or his talent earned Livingston the sobriquet of "boss" early in their association; and the title remained throughout their joint career. The heart of their association was their shared affection for belles-lettres and their common concern for "popular" rights against the infringements of governors at home or Crown and Parliament abroad; but kinship and religion added new links to their friendship.

Scott's forebears came from Ancrum, Scotland, the ancestral home of the Livingstons; and a sister of the first Livingston in America had married the Reverend John Scott. Smith's sister was

[46] See for the critical view, Thomas Jones, *History*, I, 4. See also Wines, "William Smith," *New York History*, XL, 5–6.

1 7

the wife of one Livingston, and he himself married another.[47] All three men were Presbyterians. Smith's attachment to the denomination was more earnest and more doctrinaire than Livingston's and Scott's, who were newcomers to the fold, having shifted from the Dutch and French Reformed Churches about the time of the founding of the *Independent Reflector*. More casual in observance than the "rigid" Smith, they were no less suspicious of the Church of England nor less zealous in opposing Anglican encroachments on the religious liberties of dissenting sects in New York.[48]

Their common conviction that New York was an intellectual wasteland led the three to organize an informal literary club which by 1748 bore the title, "Society for the Promotion of Useful Knowledge" but was dubbed by its critics as the "Society of Sage Philosophers." [49] It was probably at one of its meetings that the idea of launching the *Independent Reflector* was born. Despite contemporary charges that the society was a "Whig Club" or a hotbed of atheism and that the *Reflector's* objective was the formation of a new Livingston Party, there appears to have been no political or religious motivation behind either. The club was divided in political loyalty and religious affiliation in 1748. James Alexander and William Smith, Sr., the society's senior members, were confidantes of Governor Clinton; the Livingstons in its ranks were anti-Clinton. Alexander and his son were Anglicans; the Smiths, Presbyterians; others among the members, Quakers and Dutch Reformed. The three future editors of the *Reflector* were themselves in dif-

[47] Edwin B. Livingston, *The Livingstons of Livingston Manor* (New York, 1910), pp. 19–20, 54–55, 540; Maria S. B. Chance and Mary A. E. Smith, eds., *Scott Family Letters* (Philadelphia, 1930), pp. 11, 318, 335; Delafield, "William Smith, Judge," *Magazine of American History*, VI, 276, "Wiliam Smith — The Historian," *ibid.*, p. 431.

[48] On the religious affiliations of the triumvirate, see Jones, *History*, I, 4, 41 note; "Memoir of the Honourable William Smith," in William Smith, Jr., *The History of the Late Province of New-York* (New York Historical Society *Collections*, 1829 [New York, 1830]), I, x, xiv–xv; Livingston to Rev. Aaron Burr, May 29, 1754, Letter Book A, 1754–1770, Livingston Papers, MHS; Dillon, *The New York Triumvirate*, p. 18 note.

[49] The club's existence was disclosed by a newspaper controversy with its critics. See *New-York Weekly Journal*, February 13, 27, March 20, April 3, 1749, October 8, 1750; "To the Publick," n.d., William Smith Papers, No. 203, New York Public Library.

ferent political camps in 1749 when the journal was conceived. It seems clear from their letter to Welles of that year that the aim of the periodical — as of the Philosophic Society — was simply "improving the Minds of our Fellow Citizens." [50]

Moreover, it is highly unlikely that James Parker, the *Reflector's* printer, would have chosen to become associated with a partisan journal. As the colony's official printer, he could not afford to offend either the civil or the religious authorities. A few years earlier, he had irritated the Assembly by declining to publish one of its "Remonstrances" against the Governor; and only a few month's before the *Reflector's* appearance, he had been indicted for a "blasphemous libel" against Christianity in his newspaper, the *Gazette*. Only Benjamin Franklin's intercession and a promise to be more "circumspect" in the future kept him from jail.[51] The *Reflector's* bland announcement in its first two numbers that it would eschew political controversy and decline contributions with too strong a "Tincture of Party-Spirit" must have been reassuring to Parker. There seems little reason for questioning his explanation, made some years later, that he undertook to publish the *Reflector* because "all the Printing done here was very poor, and in some Measure a Disgrace to the Country." [52]

Neither the printer nor the editors could have foreseen how quickly the *Reflector* would change its tone and character, how

[50] Livingston to Welles, February 18, 1749, JFP, Yale. Thomas Jones' characterization of the Philosophic Society as a Whig Club (*History*, I, 5–6, 221) is repeated in Charles H. Levermore, "The Whigs of Colonial New York," *American Historical Review*, I (1896), 242; Carl Becker, "Nominations in Colonial New York," *ibid.*, VI (1901), 273; Wilbur C. Abbott, *New York in the American Revolution* (New York and London, 1929), p. 44; and Richard B. Morris, ed., *The Era of the American Revolution* (New York, 1939), pp. 269–270. The charge that the *Reflector* was launched to inaugurate a new political party appears in Beverly McAnear's writings: "Politics in Provincial New York, 1689–1761" (unpublished Ph.D. dissertation, Stanford U., 1935), pp. 775–777; "Mr. Robert R. Livingston's Reasons against a Land Tax," *Journal of Political Economy*, XLVIII (1940), 68 note; and "American Imprints Concerning King's College," *Papers of the Bibliographic Society*, XLIV, 307.

[51] On Parker's difficulties in 1747, see *Journal of the Votes and Proceedings of the General Assembly of . . . New-York*, [1691–1765], 2 vols. (New York, 1764–1766), II, 173–180, 192–193, 202, 272; on the 1752 incident, *New-York Gazette*, April 27, May 11, 1752; Goebel and Naughton, *Law Enforcement*, pp. 153–154; Franklin to Cadwallader Colden, May 14, 1752, *Colden Papers*, IV, 324–325.

[52] *New-York Gazette*, January 6, 1755.

soon it would become embroiled in heated controversies of both a religious and a political nature, and how out of these contests a new political combination of Livingstons and former Clintonites would be formed. It was only after the *Reflector* itself was dead that some color would be given to the frenetic accusation of the Loyalist, Thomas Jones, that its three editors,

. . . presbyterians by profession, and republicans in principle, being all of the law, nearly of an age, and linked together in friendship, in politics, and religion, . . . formed themselves into a triumvirate, and determined . . . to pull down Church and State, to raise their own Government and religion upon its ruins, or to throw the whole province into anarchy and confusion.[53]

4

Three years elapsed between the germination of the idea and the appearance of the *Reflector*. During the interval it underwent a change in character. When the paper emerged it was not merely a pale imitation of the English *Tatler* and *Spectator*, nor were its editors content to fill its pages with literary and philosophic speculations. By the time of its publication the *Reflector* had been refashioned into a crusading as well as a speculative journal, a change that reflected the growing concern of the editors with the extension of Anglican clerical power in the American colonies. The three-year delay was unintentional. Livingston's interest had remained undiminished, but his colleagues had become too absorbed in their legal and business affairs to render him much assistance. Since the original plan contemplated deferring publication until at least 150 essays were ready, the founders obviously anticipated a long life for their brain child; and, confined to the literary essays of the *Tatler* and *Spectator* variety, the journal might have run on for years. The title first selected, "The New-York Guardian," suggests the degree to which the New Yorkers intended to emulate Addison and Steele: *The Guardian* was the successor to the *Tatler* and *Spectator*.[54] By the time the *Reflector*

[53] Jones, *History*, I, 6.
[54] The draft of the first issue of the *Reflector*, bearing the "Guardian" title, is in the William Smith Papers, No. 212, New York Public Library. *The Guardian* in

appeared, however, Livingston had developed an even warmer admiration for two other English essayists, Thomas Gordon and John Trenchard.

Trenchard was a wealthy lawyer and country squire; Gordon, an obscure and poor Scotsman who became Trenchard's companion and amanuensis. Both were staunch Whigs who shared a common suspicion of standing armies, Tory politicians, divine right theorists, and High Churchmen. In 1720 they began writing two series of essays for the press which became known, collectively, as *The Independent Whig* and *Cato's Letters*. The Cato series was launched as an attack on the political malefactors who engineered the infamous South Sea Bubble speculation, but it soon took a wider range. The *Whig* was narrower in focus, concentrating on the dangers of a Catholic revival and the threat of Popery to English civil and religious liberties.[55]

These two essay-series achieved a phenomenal popularity in the American colonies. Fifty-three of the *Whig* papers were collected in a single volume and published in 1721. By 1750 the book had gone through seven editions in England, two in America, and one in France.[56] In collected form the essays bore the subtitle: "A Defence of Primitive Christianity . . . against the exorbitant claims of fanatical and disaffected clergymen." *Cato's Letters*, somewhat less mordant in their anticlericalism, also discussed

---

England began in March, 1713, three months after the demise of the *Spectator*, and continued until October.

[55] These two enormously influential English pamphleteers deserve full-length biographical treatment. They have received more attention from literary than political historians. Only a detailed reading of the *Whig* and *Cato's Letters* can reveal adequately the reason for their warm reception in the American colonies. The best recent treatment of Gordon and Trenchard is in Caroline Robbins, *The Eighteenth Century Commonwealthmen* (Cambridge, Massachusetts, 1959), pp. 115–125. Biographical material may be found in the *Dictionary of National Biography*, VIII, 230–231, and XIX, 1125–1126; and in Charles B. Realey, *The London Journal and Its Authors, 1720–1723* (Bulletin of the University of Kansas Humanistic Studies [Lawrence, Kansas], 1935, V, No. 3), pp. 237–274.

[56] There is some disagreement about the dates of these editions. The *D.N.B.* (VIII, 230–231) dates the seventh English edition at 1743; Robbins (*op. cit.*, p. 392) says there were six editions before 1754, but the Harvard Library copy of the eighth edition is dated 1752. The figures given in the text are from Realey. The first American edition of the *Whig* was a Philadelphia printing in 1724. See Charles R. Hildeburn, *A Century of Printing*, 2 vols. (Philadelphia, 1885), I, 68. A one-volume edition of *Cato's Letters* appeared in 1721, a four-volume collection in 1724, which by 1753 had gone through eight editions.

freedom of speech, the importance of education, the right of resistance, and limited versus unlimited sovereignty. They were republished in book form but never in an American edition. American newspapers simply pirated the work by extensive and frequent republication of the essays. The Philadelphia *American Weekly Mercury* began reprinting the *Cato* letters in 1722, while they were still running serially in the British press, and the New York, Boston, and South Carolina papers quickly followed suit.[57] By the middle of the eighteenth century American newspapers were referring to Gordon and Trenchard in adulatory terms as "that incomperable [*sic*] Lay Author" and "the Divine English Cato." [58] Only Anglican clergymen were disturbed by the extensive popularity of such "pernicious" writers.[59]

Livingston and his colleagues joined in the general acclaim accorded to the *Whig* authors, who were "invincible Writers," "Geniusses sublime and inimitable," and those "Great and . . . Good" essayists; and when early issues of the *Reflector* were dismissed by Anglican critics as mere imitations, William Smith, Jr., responded:

> You could not, Sir, have done greater Honour to the Abilities of the *Independent Reflector*, than by allowing him a Capacity to imitate the *Independent Whigg*, who had one of the finest Pens in Europe, and is justly esteem'd, a signal Ornament to the Republic of Letters.[60]

[57] DeArmond, *Andrew Bradford*, pp. 16–17, 166–170; Elizabeth C. Cook, *Literary Influence in Colonial Newspapers, 1704–1750* (New York, 1912), pp. 81–83 and *passim*; Hennig Cohen, *The South Carolina Gazette* (Columbia, S.C., 1953), pp. 217–218.

[58] DeArmond, *Andrew Bradford*, p. 166 note; *New-York Weekly Journal*, December 10, 1733. Miss Robbins properly calls the essays of Gordon and Trenchard "the most famous" occasional political papers of the early eighteenth century (p. 392). Clinton Rossiter (*Seedtime of the Republic*, p. 141) says that Gordon and Trenchard were more often invoked in defense of colonial liberties than was John Locke.

[59] Reverend Samuel Johnson to the Archbishop of Canterbury, June 29, 1753, *N. Y. Col. Docs.*, VI, 777.

[60] *New-York Gazette*, February 19, 1753; *The Craftsmen: A Sermon from the Independent Whig* . . . (New York, 1753). The latter was a republication by the triumvirate of a work by Gordon, to which they added a new preface "Suitable to the peculiar malignity of the present Day." The allusions to Gordon and Trenchard are in the preface, pp. ii, xxvi. Livingston quoted *Cato's Letters* in the *Reflector*, No. XLIII, and made more frequent complimentary references to Gordon and Trenchard in his later newspaper series, "The Watch-Tower," *New-York Mercury*,

INTRODUCTION

The anticlericalism of the *Independent Whig* coincided almost perfectly with Livingston's own religious views. Reared in the easy, liberal religious atmosphere of Dutch Albany, Livingston had known neither the zealotry of the enthusiast nor the rigid conformity of the doctrinaire. He had experienced both at Yale and recoiled from each. He was shocked by the narrow formalism of Connecticut Congregationalism, to which he was subjected as a student. When he wrote caustically in the *Reflector* of sermons that were "so replete with abstruse *Erudition*" as to be "unintelligible to forty-nine in fifty" of the congregation and more calculated to make one a "Critic or Pedagogue than a good Man or a Christian," he was undoubtedly thinking of the dry oratory of New Haven preachers.[61]

Searching for a religious philosophy that avoided the evils both of enthusiasm and of rigid conformity, Livingston early arrived at the spiritual position he held for the rest of his life. Rejecting all orthodoxy as irrational — "every Man is *orthodox* to himself, and *heretical* to all the World besides" — Livingston adopted a "pure and simple" Christianity, shorn of doctrinal rigidity and ritualistic complexity. If this placed him outside the bounds of denominational religion, he would be content, "with a set of sound principles and a good heart, to pass almost for any thing." Publicly and privately he insisted that since "true piety" had never been agreed upon by mankind, he would not permit "any human tribunal" to "settle its definition" for him.[62]

In such a latitudinarian mood Livingston became increasingly receptive to the anticlericalism of Gordon and Trenchard; but these authors merely reinforced the prejudices toward the clergy that Livingston already had developed. The Great Awakening, with the fratricidal strife it engendered among New England Congregationalists and Middle Colony Presbyterians, shocked Livingston into a recognition of the dangers of hard doctrinal

---

January 13, March 3, September 15, 1755. See also *Reflector*, No. XL, note 1, below, and Appendix III.

[61] No. LI.

[62] See No. VI, and *Preface*, p. 3; Livingston to Rev. James Mason, May 29, 1778, in Sedgwick, *A Memoir*, pp. 228–290; Livingston to Henry Laurens, February 5, 1778, Laurens Papers, South Carolina Historical Society.

positions. In his view not only were disputations on matters of organization, ritual, and doctrine irrational, they weakened all the dissenting churches in their larger struggle against the common foe, Episcopacy. He was particularly disturbed at the large number of Dissenters who, disillusioned with the excesses of the revivalists, turned to the stability of the Anglican Church. The process was occurring in Livingston's own Dutch Church, where he could observe its baneful effects at first hand. Although the dispute in the Reformed Church was not entirely the product of the Great Awakening, it was related to the revival. The issues that split conservatives and liberals among the Dutch were the proposals for introducing English as the language of the service and the organization of a separate American "Classis" or church council. The inflexibility of the traditionalists in retaining both the Dutch language and the organizational connection with the Amsterdam Classis drove many younger, more liberal members out of the Reformed Church directly into the Anglican.[63]

While Livingston's own rational theology made him suspicious of every "little Flutterer in a Gown and Cassock" and hostile to the "Popes and Persecutors of all Churches, whether . . . of Rome, England, Holland or Geneva," in practice the brunt of his biting attacks on "priestcraft" was borne by the Church of England. Its "ridiculous Ceremonies Idolatries and Superstitions" were of a piece with Roman Catholicism; it had

too many popish relicks, not to say, gross Superstitions, to approve itself to the Judgment of any person who knows that true Religion consists in the internal purity of the heart, and the soul's being as it

[63] Livingston to Welles, July 23, 1747, December 15, 1753, JFP, Yale. See Alexander J. Wall, "The Controversy in the Dutch Church in New York concerning Preaching in English," New York Historical Society *Quarterly Bulletin*, XII (1928), 39–58; and Nelson R. Burr, "The Episcopal Church and the Dutch in Colonial New York and New Jersey, 1664–1784," *Historical Magazine of the Protestant Episcopal Church*, XIX (1950), 90–109, especially, pp. 103–107. Livingston himself left the Dutch Church because he could no longer understand the sermons preached in Dutch, even though still able to read the language. As a Presbyterian, he continued to lament the decline of the Dutch Church and to urge the appointment of an English-speaking minister. Livingston to Rev. Aaron Burr, May 29, 1754, Letter Book A, 1754–1770, Livingston Papers, MHS; *Independent Reflector, Preface*, p. 23; *Occasional Reverberator*, III, September 21, 1753. On the controversy in the Dutch Church, see also E. T. Corwin, ed., *Ecclesiastical Records of the State of New York*, 6 vols. (Albany, 1901–1905), IV, 2582–2583, 3037–3038.

were moulded into the image of God, . . . and not in a multitude of ridiculous fantastical rites, that seem to make religion more cumbersom[e], and often betray a Man into many Sins of Omission by neglecting what (tho indifferent in itself) he has been taught to look upon as a matter of Duty.[64]

This sentiment Livingston expressed when still a law clerk. By 1752 he had added to his suspicion of "ecclesiastical trumpery" a compelling fear of "ecclesiastical tyranny" in the form of an official establishment of the Church of England in the colonies. His letters to Noah Welles were increasingly filled with aspersions upon the Anglican Church and its clergymen. When, in 1747, New England Dissenters and Episcopal churchmen became embroiled in a brief, hot paper war over the relative merits of episcopal as against presbyterian ordination, Livingston gladly lent a hand, sponsoring a republication in New York of one of the anti-Anglican pamphlets. Its virtue, Livingston decided, was that it perfectly confuted all the "glib Nonsense" Anglicans had invented "to palliate superstition and bigotry." [65]

As additional polemics poured from the press, Livingston purchased or borrowed them all, read them, and rejoiced at every Dissenting literary victory.[66] Absorbed in the controversy, he began to study the question of Episcopal claims to jurisdiction in the colonies and prepared a lengthy paper on the extent of the Crown's prerogative in ecclesiastical matters. He noted with alarm every sign of Anglican "bigotry" in New York City. One such was church pressure to compel strict observance of Good

[64] Livingston to Welles, July 23, December 18, 1747, JFP, Yale; No. VI, *Reflector*. Like his contemporaries, Livingston was intensely anti-Catholic, but his hostility was expressed in political (anti-French) form more often than in direct attacks on Catholic theology or ritual. See Sister Mary Augustina (Ray), *American Opinion of Roman Catholicism in the Eighteenth Century* (New York, 1936).

[65] Livingston to Welles, July 23, September 19, December 18, 1747, March 12, April 16, 1748, JFP, Yale. The pamphlet was an English publication, Micaiah Towgood, *The Dissenting Gentleman's Answer to the Reverend Mr. White's Three Letters; in which The Church of England and the Church of Jesus Christ, are . . . found to be . . . of a quite Different Nature* (New York, 1748). The London edition had been published in 1746. The exchange in England was being carried on with Rev. John White, Fellow of St. John's College, Cambridge.

[66] Livingston to Welles, February 18, 1749, [March, 1751?], JFP, Yale. The second phase of this literary warfare was carried on between Noah Hobart, the Congregationalist minister at Fairfield, Conn., and James Wetmore, the Episcopal rector at Rye, New York. On this controversy, see No. XLIV, note 6, below.

Friday; and while he did not want to exaggerate isolated incidents of clerical power, he was fearful that "Great Things rise from small Beginnings." Unless the "monster Tyranny" were nipped in the bud, it might proliferate beyond the capacity of Dissenters to curb it. Then New York's highly prized liberty of conscience would be irretrievably lost.[67]

Livingston's transfer of religious allegiance from the Dutch to the Presbyterian Church sometime in 1752 provided him with another vantage point for his view of the Church of England. The Anglican Trinity Church in New York City not only possessed a royal charter but also received financial support from the taxpayers under a law passed in 1693. The aim of the law had been to provide public support of "a good sufficient Protestant Minister" in the four southern counties of the colony, but interpretation by royal governors had resulted in Trinity's drawing to itself the exclusive benefits of the act.[68] The Presbyterians were disturbed because, while Trinity enjoyed both financial and legal privileges, their own church in New York City had repeatedly failed to secure a royal charter of incorporation. They attributed their precarious position to the opposition of Trinity Church. To acquire some legal status it had become necessary for the Presbyterian Church to vest title to its property in the Church of Scotland.[69]

Livingston shared the resentment of his co-religionists against Trinity Church, but both he and William Smith, Jr., had still another basis for their mistrust of the Anglicans: indignation over the labors of the missionary arm of the Church in America, the Society for the Propagation of the Gospel in Foreign Parts. The missionaries, Livingston and Smith charged, were more bent on the advancement of "Prelacy" than of Christianity and spent

[67] Livingston to Welles, [March, 1751?], JFP, Yale. The paper, dated April 7, 1751, was sent to Welles.

[68] See No. XLIV, note 3, below.

[69] N. Y. Ecclesiastical Records, IV, 2392, 2547, 2565, 2601, 2624, 2635–2636, 2645–2646; Richard Webster, History of the Presbyterian Church in America (Philadelphia, 1857), pp. 328–329; Ezra Hall Gillett, History of the Presbyterian Church in the United States of America (Philadelphia, 1864), I, 10–16, 38; Samuel Miller, Memoirs of Rev. John Rodgers (New York, 1813), pp. 136, 141–142; Charles W. Baird, "Civil Status of the Presbyterians in the Province of New York," Magazine of American History, III (1879), 593–628.

more energy seducing Dissenters into the Anglican fold than in bringing the Gospel to the Indians, which was the work the Society was formed to do.[70]

The *Reflector* thus mirrored the new orientation Livingston acquired as a result of his preoccupation with Anglican power; its contents revealed the heavy debt of its editor to the English anticlericals, Gordon and Trenchard. Of the fifty-two numbers of the *Reflector* only five dealt with "the fashionable vices and foibles" of the day. Twelve were on religion and related topics, most of them heavily tinged with Livingston's anticlericalism. And the first issue of the *Reflector* was strikingly patterned after the *Independent Whig*.

The first two numbers of the *Independent Whig* were "The Introduction" and "The Design of this Paper." Livingston labeled his own first issue: "The Introduction, or Design of this Paper." Gordon and Trenchard had stated that "Whoever goes about to reform the World, undertakes an Office obnoxious to Malice, and beset with Difficulties." Livingston parroted the sentiment: "Whoever sets up as a Reformer of public Abuses, must expect to encounter innumerable Difficulties." The *Whig* announced that "neither these, nor any other Difficulties or Discouragements, shall hinder me from the generous Attempt of endeavouring to reform Mankind. I have the Magnanimity to face them all." The *Reflector* duplicated this warning: "None of these Discouragements shall, however, deter me from vindicating the *civil and religious Rights* of my Fellow-Creatures. . . . I have the Magnanimity to attack the Enemies of [the] human Race, in whatever . . . Shape they appear." The *Whig* disavowed political partisanship: "For my self, who have no manner of Attachment to any Party, I shall not be afraid to speak my Mind of All." The *Reflector* reiterated the same sentiment: "The Author, being under no Attachment to any Party, thinks himself the better qualified to make impartial Remarks on the Conduct of every Party." The *Whig* modestly disclaimed any particular talent for its authors: "I . . . have long wished some abler Genius would have undertaken it." The *Reflector* echoed the humility: ". . . 'tis to be hoped a Design so gener-

[70] Livingston to Welles, January 3, 1756, JFP, Yale; Smith, *History*, I, 56.

ous and humane . . . might be carried on by an abler Genius." [71]

Despite these similarities, the *Independent Reflector* was no more a carbon copy of the *Whig* than of the *Tatler* and *Spectator*. Gordon and Trenchard were too narrowly religious in their interest to suit Livingston's mood in 1752; and while anticlericalism weighed heavily on his mind, he desired the freedom to discuss "sundry" other subjects relating to the province of New York.

The choice of a title for his journal reflected Livingston's enlarged outlook. Borrowing from the *Reflector*, an English literary magazine of 1750 modeled on the *Tatler* and *Spectator*, as well as the *Whig*, Livingston arrived at the happy compromise, the *Independent Reflector*. The new periodical would adopt the politico-religious liberalism of the *Independent Whig* and employ the didactic style of the Addisonian *Reflector*. The name was thus a felicitous characterization of the paper's dual character.[72]

5

The *Reflector's* one-year existence proved to be stormy, but its demise was more spectacular than its birth. Parker advertised its appearance by reproducing the entire first number in his weekly newspaper, but surplus copies continued to pile up in his office during the first month of publication.[73] By the fifth week, however, New Yorkers began to warm to the new periodical. New subscriptions came in so rapidly that back copies of the first six issues were exhausted, and such subscribers were informed that they would have to wait until the following spring before a new printing would permit them to complete their

[71] The quotations from the *Whig* are all from Numbers I and II; from the *Reflector*, No. I. For further parallels between the two periodicals, see Appendix III.

[72] The full title of the English periodical was *The Reflector: representing human affairs, as they are; and may be improved.* It was edited by a physician, Peter Shaw. Articles from the *Reflector* were reprinted in the *New-York Evening Post* on March 25, April 15, June 24, September 2, 1751; and one appeared in the *New-York Gazette* on February 10, 1755. Selections from it also ran in the *Boston Evening-Post* late in 1752 and early in 1753.

[73] The first number of the *Reflector* was reproduced in the *New-York Gazette*, December 4, 1752.

sets.[74] Critics disparaged these claims as the fabrications of the editors, insisting that the subscribers constituted only a "scanty Number" and the paper lay "by Fifty's" in Parker's office.[75] It is unlikely that the business-minded printer would have been a party to such deception; and there is typographical evidence that in March, 1753, Parker did reprint the first six issues as promised.[76] In any case, within a few years after its demise, the *Reflector* was a scarce item in the New York literary market, prospective American purchasers being unable to secure copies to satisfy the curiosity of English readers.[77]

The precise circulation of the *Reflector* is unknown. Weekly newspapers of the time averaged about 600 copies, which was the minimum required by a publisher to achieve even a modest profit. Monthly magazines, much fuller in content and more expensive to print, required only a circulation of 400 to remain self-supporting.[78] The *Reflector's* circulation probably approximated that of the weekly newspaper. If the journal had 500 subscribers, it provided about one copy for every ten potential adult readers in New York City. This would make it an influential organ of public opinion in the city.[79] Besides, the influence of both newspapers and magazines in mid-century America was far out of proportion to the actual number of copies printed. Reading matter was not a common article of the daily mail, and every page of every newspaper and periodical was usually read with care by many persons other than the subscriber.

[74] See printer's notices in Nos. V, IX.

[75] The disparaging remarks appeared in the *New-York Mercury*, April 30, 1753.

[76] The differences in the two printings may be readily observed by comparing the two sets of the *Reflector* at the Henry E. Huntington Library, San Marino, California (107794 and 107797). They include variations in ornamentation in Nos. III, IV, and VI, the colophon at the end of No. IV, and the pagination of No. III. See McAnear, "American Imprints Concerning King's College," *Papers of the Bibliographical Society*, XLIV, 308 note.

[77] Samuel Johnson to Archbishop of Canterbury, October 20, 1759, in *Samuel Johnson Writings*, IV, 51.

[78] Clarence S. Brigham, *Journals and Journeymen: A Contribution to the History of Early Newspapers* (Philadelphia, 1950), pp. 19–20; Arthur M. Schlesinger, *Prelude to Independence: The Newspaper War on Britain, 1764–1776* (New York, 1958), pp. 54, 303–304; Mott, *History of American Magazines*, p. 14.

[79] The population of New York City in 1749 was 10,926 whites and 2,368 Negroes. It is estimated that half of the white population was adult. E. B. O'Callaghan, *The Documentary History of the State of New York* (Albany, 1849–1851), I, 695.

The subscription price of ten shillings a year was somewhat less than that of earlier magazines and was fixed largely to cover the cost of publication. The *Reflector* was not intended as an addition to Livingston's income; "his Circumstances," he informed his readers in the first issue, "put him above the Aids of this Paper for Subsistence."

The ringing statement of purpose with which Livingston introduced the paper should have warned New Yorkers that a new element had been added to its seething political and religious situation. The equanimity of local politicians was shaken when Livingston indicted the tax-farming system in the second issue and followed in the third with a slashing indictment of the local police and road-repair apparatus. The city fathers took alarm. If the *Reflector's* crusades against inefficient fire-fighting, medical quackery, and extravagant funerals left them undisturbed, the paper's criticism of tax-farming, the sale of public offices, and electoral corruption stung them sharply. They began denouncing the publication, hinting that the authors were political "levellers." Undaunted, in the third number Livingston promised these "Wretches" he would make them "the marks of the public Resentment," and in the tenth issue he printed a sensational exposé of a shady land deal by which some local businessmen, in collusion with the City Council, planned to get valuable shoreline property for a song.

The anguished cries of politicians were shortly augmented by the agonized protestations of clergymen. In his defense of the Moravians in the sixth issue, Livingston denounced the "little Popes" of all denominations. The pulpits were now employed to impugn him as an atheist; clergymen demanded that the *Reflector* be recommended to the grand jury as libelous; and Anglican priests began marshaling a corps of penmen to mount a counterattack. The *Reflector's* indiscriminate disparagement of clergymen and churches offended not only Anglicans but also Congregationalists and Dutch Reformed churchmen; and the latter were Livingston's prospective supporters and allies in any full-scale assault launched against the Church of England. Livingston himself preferred to believe that the "prodigious Noise" provoked by the

Moravian essay was confined to "High Church of all kinds." Nevertheless, he was given pause by a suggestion from his friend Welles that he moderate his anticlericalism or at least differentiate between worthy and unworthy clerics; and the warning was reinforced by a public admonition to the *Reflector* from a Dutch divine. Since the author of the public rebuke was a member of the liberal wing of the Dutch Reformed Church with which Livingston was most closely allied, the advice could not be ignored.[80] For the next month Livingston checked his natural inclination to lock horns with his ministerial critics, but in the eleventh issue, he returned to the attack. Anglicans responded, Smith defended Livingston, and "paper war" commenced in earnest.[81]

In the press warfare that now reached its zenith, the Anglicans had a powerful advantage. The *Gazette,* Parker's paper, was effectively closed to the triumvirate; the *Mercury,* the city's other regular newspaper, was the Anglicans' exclusive preserve. Livingston could either utilize the *Reflector* itself or remain silent. He was not, however, without other weapons to continue the contest with the Episcopal clergy. One technique was the use of pamphlets. The Anglicans initiated this mode of warfare during the summer of 1753 with two satirical commentaries on Livingston's notions of pristine religion.[82] Livingston and his friends responded by republishing an old anticlerical tract of Gordon, *The Craftsmen,* to which they added a new preface reminding the public of the revival of "Priestianity" in New York with all its "violent Thirst for Persecution and Dominion." [83]

The *Reflector,* however, was still Livingston's big gun, and

[80] Livingston to Welles, January 17, February [19?], 1753, JFP, Yale; David Marin Ben Jesse, *A Letter to the Independent Reflector* (New York, 1753). The author's name was a pseudonym for the Reverend Theodore Frelinghuysen. For this identification, see McAnear, "American Imprints Concerning King's College," *Papers of the Bibliographical Society,* XLIV, 327–328 note.

[81] See *Reflector,* Nos. XI, note 3; XV, note 4; and XXXI, note 1.

[82] See again No. XXXI, note 1. On this and the other pamphlets issued during this phase of the contest, see McAnear, "American Imprints," pp. 311–313.

[83] *The Craftsmen: A Sermon from The Independent Whig. Suitable to the peculiar Malignity of the present Day* . . . (New-York, 1753). The preface was dated August 22, and the publication appeared in September. The manuscript of the preface is in the William Smith Papers No. 212, New York Public Library. It was written by Livingston and Smith and corrected by Scott. See also *Reflector,* No. XL, note 1.

while he engaged in scattered fire with Anglican clergymen on theological matters, he prepared to destroy them with a more powerful salvo. The opportunity was provided by an Anglican proposal for a college in New York to be chartered by the Crown and placed under the supervision of an Episcopal clergyman. Livingston gleefully planned his new barrage. "The Town," he wrote Welles in jubilant anticipation, "is not yet ripe for loosing plainer Truth. The Veil must be removed from their eyes by slow degrees." [84] The unveiling process commenced on March 22, 1753, when Livingston published the first of six essays on the subject of the projected college.

6

The controversy between Livingston and his clerical critics reached its climax in their irreconcilable differences over the constitution of the proposed New York college. Anglican sponsors of the project contended for a royally chartered, private institution in which the Episcopal Church should have "a preference." Livingston countered with a vigorous plea for a legislatively incorporated and publicly-controlled school under the management of no particular religious denomination but with an "equality" of privilege accorded to all Protestants. Despite its theological and political repercussions, the college controversy was not simply a clash between contending religious sects nor a contest between rival political factions. It was largely Livingston's one-man crusade for a more liberal system of higher education; and despite the political and religious overtones of the affair, Livingston's own role remained peculiarly and often quixotically personal. There was no cant in his public defense, early in 1754, of the anti-Anglican stand he took in the *Reflector* on the college issue:

The affair of the College, I considered as one of the most important matters, that ever fell under the consideration of our Legislature. It will either prove one of the greatest blessings, or an execrable source of the keenest and most complicated disasters. If it is constituted upon a foundation generous and catholic, there is nothing we can fall upon,

[84] Livingston to Welles, February [19?], 1753, JFP, Yale.

that will spread more real felicity thro' the Province. But should it on the other hand, be made the tool of a faction, and an instrument in the hand of one sect, for the advancement of itself, and the oppression of the rest, what can we expect . . . but either the deprivation or the abridgment of our civil and religious liberties? [85]

The idea of a college in New York was not Livingston's, but few could deny the persistence or the sincerity of his interest. As early as 1749 he had complained:

The want of a liberal Education has long been our Reproach and Misfortune. Our Neighbours have told us in an insulting Tone, that the Art of getting Money, is the highest Improvement we can pretend to: That the wisest Man among us without a Fortune, is neglected and despised; and the greatest Blockhead with one, caress'd and honour'd: That, for this Reason, a poor Man of the most shining Accomplishments, can never emerge out of his Obscurity; while every wealthy Dunce is loaded with Honours. . . .[86]

From this intellectual discontent arose his activity on behalf of a New York college and his *Reflector* essays on the subject — not from political motivations.

The movement for a college in New York was part of the "college enthusiasm" which stirred all the northern colonies in the decade after 1740.[87] To some degree, the revived interest in higher education was an outgrowth of the Great Awakening, old and new churches vying with each other in founding seminaries for the training of ministers. To a larger degree, however, the college movement represented a stage in the maturation of the colonies as prosperity, leisure, and stability led men to divert some of their energies from mere physical existence to building an American culture.

[85] *Independent Reflector*, Preface, p. 14.

[86] Livingston to Welles, January 13, 1746, JFP, Yale; *Some Serious Thoughts on the Design of erecting a College in the Province of New-York* (New York, 1749), p. 1. (On this pamphlet, see *Reflector*, XVII, note 2.) Livingston's complaint was reiterated by men like Cadwallader Colden, who informed the English authorities that nothing had been more neglected in New York than education and that the "only Principle of Life propagated among the young People is to get money," men being "esteemed only according to what they are worth, that is, the money they are possessed of." [Cadwallader Colden] to [Rev. Hezekiah Watkins], [December 12, 1748], SPG MSS, B–20, pp. 86–88, Archives of the Society for the Propagation of the Gospel in Foreign Parts, London.

[87] See Beverly McAnear, "College Founding in the American Colonies, 1745–1775," *Mississippi Valley Historical Review*, XLII (1955), 24–55.

INTRODUCTION

The efforts at college building bore first fruit in New Jersey and Pennsylvania, with the founding of the College of New Jersey (later Princeton) in 1746 and the Philadelphia Academy (later the University of Pennsylvania) in 1749. "A jealousy of our neighbors," Livingston observed later, "at length gave a spring to our ambition." [88] The result was a series of public lotteries, beginning in 1746, authorized by the New York legislature for "the Advancement of Learning." By 1751, £3,443 had been raised, the money vested in a board of ten trustees, empowered to lend the funds at interest and receive proposals for the site of the college.[89] Of the ten trustees, seven were members *ex officio*; of the three appointed by name, Livingston was one. The religious composition of the members of the board was similarly uneven: seven Episcopalians, two Dutch Reformed, and Livingston, Presbyterian.

The disproportionate strength of the Episcopalians on the board did not reflect their numbers in the colony's population; only about ten per cent of New York's inhabitants were Anglicans. It did, however, reflect the intense interest of Episcopal churchmen who had long complained of Harvard and Yale as "nurseries of sedition." The success of the Presbyterians in founding the New Jersey College irritated them even more. There was all the more reason, then, in the Anglican view, that the proposed New York school should be "an Episcopal College" established "upon a Foundation, that may give a Prospect of promoting religion in the way of the National Ch[urch]." [90]

The Anglican proposal represented the fulfillment of a scheme that had been at least a half-century in the making. The idea had first been broached when Trinity Church received a grant of

[88] "The Watch-Tower," XLII, *New-York Mercury*, September 8, 1755.

[89] *Colonial Laws of New York*, III, 607–616, 679–688, 731–732, 842–844. The trustees announced that they would meet regularly at the City Hall to receive requests for loans and proposals for the location of the college. *New-York Gazette*, January 20, March 23, 1752.

[90] Samuel Johnson to Cadwallader Colden, April 15, 1747, *Colden Papers*, III, 374–375; Johnson to Bishop George Berkeley, September 10, 1750, Thomas B. Chandler to Johnson, February 6, 1753, *Samuel Johnson Writings*, I, 137, 166; James Wetmore to the SPG, June 25, 1753, quoted in W. W. Kemp, *The Support of Schools in Colonial New York by the Society for the Propagation of the Gospel in Foreign Parts* (New York, 1913), p. 42 note.

valuable Crown property in New York City in 1705 — some thirty-two acres west of Broadway and south of Warren Street and known as the "Queen's Farm." In petitioning for the land, Anglicans had noted that it would be "a Proper Place for a Colledge." [91] They never changed their opinion; and their support of the lottery legislation of the 1740's was conditioned by their understanding that the prospective college would be the Episcopal seminary of their studied contemplation. They had already settled upon the Reverend Samuel Johnson, Episcopal pastor at Stamford, Connecticut, as the president. Their control of the lottery trustees seemed to insure success.

On March 5, 1752, the Vestry of Trinity Church officially tendered part of the Queen's (now the King's) Farm to the trustees as a site for the proposed college.[92] No conditions were attached to Trinity's offer. None were necessary. "We always expected," Trinity's vestrymen said some years later, "that a Gift so valuable in itself . . . would be a Means of obtaining some Priviledges to the Church." [93]

Livingston was not taken into Trinity's confidence, and as a member of the trustees of the lottery funds, he offered no objections to receiving the church's offer or to viewing the proffered property. The composition of the trustees he regarded as "so partial as could not but excite the Jealousy of every unbiased

[91] Lewis Morris to the Secretary of the SPG, [1702], SPG Archives, I, 171 (transcript), College Papers, I, Columbia University; Morgan Dix, *A History of the Parish of Trinity Church in the City of New York*, 4 vols. (New York, 1898), I, 141, 145. The Queen's Farm property was first leased to Trinity by Governor Benjamin Fletcher in 1697 and finally deeded to the church by Lord Cornbury eight years later.

[92] Dix, *Trinity Church*, I, 258. The value of the property has been estimated at £7–8,000. See Arthur P. Middleton, "Anglican Contributions to Higher Education in Colonial America," *Pennsylvania History*, XXV (1958), 259.

[93] Vestry of Trinity Church to the SPG, November 3, 1755, SPG MSS, B–2, No. 315, SPG Archives, London. Trinity's expectation of preferential status in the college in the light of its offer is plainly conceded by historians of the college. See, for example, Nathaniel F. Moore, *An Historical Sketch of Columbia College* (New York, 1846), pp. 8–9; John B. Pine, "King's College and the Early Days of Columbia College," *New York State Historical Association Proceedings*, XVII (1919), 110; John B. Langstaff, "Anglican Origins of Columbia University," *Historical Magazine of the Protestant Episcopal Church*, IX (1940), 257–260. There was certainly no question in Samuel Johnson's mind that the school over which he was asked to preside was to be an "Episcopal College" and "a Seminary of the Church." See *Samuel Johnson Writings*, I, 137; *N. Y. Col. Docs.*, VI, 777.

mind"; [94] but this observation was made two years later, with the benefit of hindsight. In 1752 he was less disturbed about the possibility of Anglican control than by the prospect of the college's stillbirth because of public apathy. Six months later, however, he found more substantial cause for alarm, as the Anglicans made public their intentions. William Smith, later Provost of the Philadelphia Academy, in November, 1752, wrote a letter to both city newspapers proposing that the intended college be established by royal charter, that Dr. Samuel Johnson of Stamford become its president, and that Johnson be named as a rector of Trinity Church simultaneously in order to permit him to "subsist honourably upon a less Salary from the College." [95]

The arrangement, a most "convenient" economy to the Anglicans, horrified Livingston; and he turned to the *Independent Reflector* for airing his suspicions. The arguments he expounded in detail in six issues of the *Reflector* were foreshadowed almost perfectly in a letter to Welles a month in advance. In mid-February he wrote his classmate: [96]

There is a thing . . . which has long been the Subject of my thoughts and which I should be glad to transmit to the Reflector in a course of Letters. . . . The case is this — Our future College will undoubtedly be of great Importance to this Province, and is like to fall without a vigorous opposition, under the sole management of Churchmen. The Consequence of which will be universal Priestcraft and Bigotry in less than half a Century. The Trustees lately proposed were every one Churchmen, and many of them the most implicit Bigots. The Church can assign no colour of Reason to have the Direction of the Affair in preference of any other Sect, but I would not have it managed by any Sect. For that reason I would have no Charter from the Crown, but an Act of Assembly for the Purpose. Nor, for the same Reason should Divinity be taught at College because whoever is in the Chair will obtrude his own Notions for Theology. Let the Students follow their own Inclinations in the Study of Divinity and read what Books they please in their Chambers or apply themselves to it after they leave the College. Their religious Exercises should consist of reading the Scriptures, and hearing a Prayer in which all Protestants may join. I

[94] "The Watch-Tower," I, *New-York Mercury*, November 25, 1754.
[95] *New-York Mercury*, November 6, 1752; *New-York Gazette* (Supplement), November 7, 1752.
[96] Livingston to Welles, February [19?], 1753, JFP, Yale.

know that if it falls into the hands of Churchmen, it will either ruin the College or the Country, and in fifty Years, no Dissenter however deserving, will be able to get into any office.

If Livingston's crusade against an Anglican college had any political motivations, as was later charged, he concealed them from his most intimate correspondent, and no political overtones are apparent in the six issues of the *Reflector* in which Livingston expounded his views (March 22 to April 26, 1753). His overriding objection to the Anglican scheme was that it would make the college "a contracted Receptacle of Bigotry," unduly strengthen the Anglican Church, and even lead to a full Episcopal establishment. Aware of popular sensitivity about the Assembly's power, he argued his case on political as well as religious grounds: a royal charter would represent a gubernatorial encroachment on a legislative preserve. Cloaked in the trenchant exposition and the florid rhetoric of the *Reflector*, Livingston's essays transformed the college question into a burning issue of broad political and religious consequence.

"Had a new government, tyrannical, arbitrary, and despotic, been erected, the popish religion established, the presbyterians burned at the stake and the Episcopalians their persecutors," Thomas Jones recalled in amazement, "more noise could not have been made, than was now excited about this charter." For the next two years, the coffee houses and taverns were alive with the subject, and only the imminent war with France competed with the college controversy as the "Grand topheck" of public discussion.[97] The followers of James De Lancey, who comprised the party in power in the legislature, were placed in an embarrassing position. Their leader, Chief Justice De Lancey, became acting Governor in October; and since his strongest patrons in England were members of the Episcopal hierarchy, the De Lanceyites were compelled to support the Anglican charter proposal. Secretly, however, they cursed the *Reflector* for raising the issue, since the De Lanceyites in the Assembly were largely Dissenters and in sympathy with the *Reflector's* stand. The Chief Justice's

[97] Jones, *History*, I, 12; Robert Livingston to Jacob Wendell, December 13, 1754, Livingston Papers, Museum of the City of New York.

own ambivalent behavior weakened his hold on his followers and helped ultimately to bring about his downfall; but this was not until 1758. Meanwhile, Anglican clergymen carried on the war against the *Reflector* with great vigor.

The *New-York Mercury* remained the Anglican forum, and from April to October, 1753, its pages were filled with the lucubrations of the "anti-Reflectors." When they were not assailing Livingston and his co-editors as "furious" bigots, "Champions of Ribaldry," and "a sly insidious, restless Set of Men," they were actively defending the charter plan as legitimate, justifiable, and financially desirable. While they insisted on the necessity for a "Church-college," they assured Dissenters that their religious liberties would not be endangered. Paradoxically, the Anglicans simultaneously denied that any "perfect Equality" of religious privilege existed in either New York or England. The triumvirate's real motive, it was alleged, was to prevent the establishment of *any* New York college in order to assure the prosperity of the Presbyterian College of New Jersey. Again in a confusion of allegations, they charged Livingston with seeking to destroy both the Anglican and Dutch Churches in order to raise the Presbyterian on the ruins, and to organize a new party — a "most abject Republican Party, both in Politics and Religion" at that.[98]

"Madd[en]ed . . . not a little" by these Anglican insinuations, Livingston hewed to the line he had announced in No. XV of not engaging his opponents in face-to-face combat in the columns of the *Reflector*. This did not prevent him, however, from using its pages to respond to the Anglican position indirectly. The essays on priestcraft, church establishments, natural rights, the compact theory of government, and the right of resistance all dealt with subjects raised by his Anglican critics, and the *Reflector's* burlesques of orthodoxy and religious credulity were grist for his mill in arguing the anti-Anglican case.[99] Despite this,

[98] Samuel Johnson to the Bishop of London, June 25, 1753, King's College, Letters and Documents, 1753–1762, Columbia University. See particularly the following issues of the *New-York Mercury*: April 30, June 4, 11, July 9, 23, 30, September 10, 24, October 8, 15, 22, 1753.

[99] *Samuel Johnson Writings*, I, 169. The numbers of the *Reflector* dealing with these topics were XXXI, XXXIII, XXXIV, XXXVI, XXXVII, XXXVIII, XXXIX, XLIV, XLVI, and XLVII.

the triumvirate was at a disadvantage in the continuing press warfare in the lack of a regular outlet. To solve their dilemma, they launched a new periodical.[100]

7

The new journal, *The Occasional Reverberator*, first appeared in September, 1753. Its title described with considerable accuracy its character and purpose. It was not conceived with the forethought and care that went into the *Reflector*, and it is not likely that the editors expected it to last very long. They probably hoped it would prod Hugh Gaine, printer of the *Mercury*, or Parker, of the *Gazette*, into opening their papers to the *Reflector's* supporters; it could then die a quiet death. Only the latter expectation was realized. The *Reverberator* expired after its fourth number. Its reverberations proved even more offensive to Anglican clergymen than the *Reflector*. William Smith, Jr., was its nominal editor, and his pen was more vituperative and more personal than Livingston's.

Livingston employed the paper's columns to answer directly the "foul-mouthed Invectives" which were "perpetually disgorged" against him in the *Mercury*. In the *Reverberator* he assumed the role of polemicist, permitting himself a style less impersonal and more abusive than he employed in the *Reflector*. In stigmatizing his Anglican opponents as "wilful Calumniator[s]" and "fulminating Ecclesiastic[s]," Livingston did little to clarify the issues in dispute and only provoked the clergymen to direct action. Their pressure on Parker, the printer of the *Reverberator*, brought about its demise on October 5, 1753. Incensed, Livingston denounced the printer for his "irresolution or corruption" and returned to the *Reflector* for his literary cannonading.[101]

---

[100] For the triumvirate's inability to secure space in the regular press, see *Reflector*, No. XL, note 1.

[101] *Independent Reflector*, Preface, p. 14. For a literary evaluation of the *Reverberator*, see Richardson, *Early American Magazines*, pp. 89–91. The *Reverberator* appeared on September 7, 14, 21, and October 5, 1753. The manuscript of the first issue is in the William Smith Papers, No. 212, New York Public Library.

INTRODUCTION

The most effective of the remaining essays, No. XLVI, was a caustic burlesque on all clerical pretensions to theological infallibility, to which Livingston added a personal religious "creed" in mock imitation of those for which he had repeatedly professed his repugnance. The language of this number, however entertaining to the triumvirate, proved too strong for either Parker or the Episcopal clergy. Six weeks later, the printer discontinued publication without notice to either Livingston or his associates. Their surprise is attested by the fifty-second and last issue of the journal, which contained no hint of its prospective demise; indeed, the next week's issue was already written.[102]

William Smith, the Anglican penman, celebrated the *Reflector's* end with a jubilant epitaph, but Livingston was infuriated. Parker's "singular" action he found reprehensible: "it shewed that some of those who ought to be the guardians of our liberties, were ready to become the authors of our vassalage, when ever a spirit of freedom interfered with their politics." Two months earlier Livingston had received the printer's promise to continue publishing at least until June, 1754, or to provide timely notice to the editors if financial considerations dictated an earlier discontinuance. In quitting, Parker had honored neither promise. He had informed subscribers of the paper's forthcoming demise only through the newsboy who delivered it.[103]

Asked for an explanation, Parker admitted that "he had been threat[e]ned with the loss of the public business" unless he ceased publication of the offending periodical. To Livingston this appeared as a plain case of suppression arising from "a villainous Collusion" between the printer and the Anglican-De Lanceyite coalition. De Lancey's role was enacted in the Assembly, which his party controlled. Parker's danger was loss of position as public printer, a position determined by the Assembly.[104] De Lancey was

[102] The manuscript, entitled "On the Importance Privileges and Duty of Gran[d] Juries," is in the William Smith Papers, No. 212, New York Public Library.

[103] William Smith, "An Epitaph on the Independent Reflector," n.d., in "List of old Papers written by W[illiam] S[mith]," William Smith Papers, Historical Society of Pennsylvania; *Independent Reflector, Preface*, pp. 2, 26.

[104] Livingston to Welles, December 15, 1753, JFP, Yale; *Independent Reflector, Preface*, pp. 2–3. By 1753, colonial printers were relatively immune to all threats except that of legislative action. Financial pressure, as in the case of the *Reflector*, was

happy to assist the Anglicans in suppressing the *Reflector,* whose death restored his political peace. Its campaign against a charter college had placed him in the awkward position of having to take sides on the delicate question of royal versus legislative incorporation when he was simultaneously leader of the Assembly and acting Governor.

The pressure on Parker was so severe that he even declined to print for the triumvirate a supplement to the *Reflector,* which the editors intended as a kind of final vindication. For the next few months Livingston sought unsuccessfully to secure a printer in Philadelphia and Boston. Finally, he induced Henry De Foreest, the publisher of the defunct *New-York Evening Post* to come out of retirement for the purpose. De Foreest did not enjoy a good reputation for craftsmanship, and Livingston was not happy about the choice, but he had no alternative.

The vindication took the form of a thirty-one page *Preface,* which appeared in February, 1754. Since neither Parker nor Gaine would permit it to be advertised in their newspapers, Livingston was compelled to announce its appearance in a broadside.[105] He promised buyers a full exposé of the arbitrary and wicked craft by which "some *Episcopal Bigots*" had silenced him, and a full refutation of all the "vile Calumnies" of his adversaries. When the *Preface* appeared, however, it proved to be a disappointment. Written in haste, it contained none of Livingston's characteristic vigor and eloquence; its contents were merely a rehash of ideas already expressed in the *Reflector.* The only novelties were the account of Parker's treachery in suspending the journal so precipitously and Livingston's charge that "insidious and indirect practices" had been employed by the Anglicans to secure that end. The title page of the *Preface* bore the ominous inscription: "The Independent Reflector . . . Printed (until tryannically

---

even more unusual. See Harold L. Nelson, "Seditious Libel in Colonial America," *American Journal of Legal History,* III (1959), 160–172.

[105] Dated February 29, 1754, the broadside is bound with the New York Public l ibrary set of the *Reflector.* There is another copy in the Peters Papers, III, Historical Society of Pennsylvania, and a reproduction in I. N. P. Stokes, *The Iconography of Manhattan Island,* 6 vols. (New York, 1915–1928), IV, 647. Livingston was also under the necessity of selling the *Preface* through a local bookbinder, Robert McAlpine, since De Foreest no longer had a shop of his own.

suppressed) in MDCCLIII." The publication assailed priestcraft in general and the "scurrilous scribblers" of the *Mercury* in particular; defended Livingston's peculiar brand of "unadulterated" Christianity, free of the "voluminous rubbish and pious villainy of ecclesiastics"; disavowed any hostility to religion as such; disclaimed any intention of promoting Presbyterianism at the expense of either the Episcopal or Dutch Reformed faiths; and reiterated the *Reflector's* opposition to the "unreasonable encroachments" of the Church of England and not to its religious tenets.

The college came in for extended discussion. Livingston reviewed the entire affair, renewing his demand for a "public academy" and charging the Anglicans with responsibility for slowing progress on the project. Anglican pretensions had aroused his opposition, and Anglican obstinacy would assure a continued fight for a "free" college, where children of all Protestant persuasions would possess a "perfect parity of privileges" and where superstition would not make its "gloomy abode" nor persecution "unfurl his bloody standard." [106]

Anglican clergymen were neither impressed nor disturbed by the appearance of Livingston's latest diatribe, and none considered it worth a reply. They decided, in fact, to terminate their paper warfare. For the next ten months, the columns of both the *New-York Mercury* and the *New-York Gazette* were silent on the college affair. The Anglicans were confident that the battle was won and that Lieutenant Governor James De Lancey would grant the desired charter on the terms outlined by spokesmen of the Church.

Livingston confessed in private that the first round had been lost. The lottery trustees had invited the Episcopal cleric, Dr. Johnson, to accept the presidency of the college, and Trinity Church had added an offer of an assistancy at £150 per annum more. Only the *Reflector's* "gallant Opposition" had prevented churchmen from monopolizing the governance of the academy. There were some grounds for optimism, however. The Dissenters were beginning to rouse themselves; the Church's "unreasonable Encroachments" had been exposed; the residents of Queen's

[106] *Independent Reflector, Preface,* pp. 2–3, 14–22, 24–25, 30–31.

County were preparing a legal challenge to the local Episcopal parson's right to a salary from public funds. To yield in the face of apparent defeat was not even remotely in Livingston's thoughts. The battle for a "free generous and Catholic" academy would go on; and if the conflict required weapons more sturdy than a quill, they would be found. "If a Man must be knocked down," Livingston wrote his brother, "at all rates he may as well fall fighting, as running away." [107]

8

The contest over the founding of King's College was even more protracted and more exciting than the controversy over the *Reflector*, but it is a tale worth telling independently, and there is no space here to detail the events.[108] For the next two years the battle was waged in the chambers of the lottery trustees, the Assembly, the Council, and "out of doors" — in the taverns, the streets, and "the fields." Nor were the printing presses silent for very long. In addition to broadsides and pamphlets, two new essay series were set off by the controversy. The first was a serialized column in the *New-York Mercury* titled "The Watch-Tower." Its authors were, like those of the *Reflector*, shrouded in the familiar anonymity of obscure signatures — "F," "W," "M," "B," "Common Sense," "Joseph Plain-Truth," and "Publicola"; but the camouflage fooled no one. Episcopal penmen had no doubt that "whatever new Names they have since been pleased to take, whether Philo-Reflector, Reverberator, Watch-Tower, or Querist, still you may read the Reflector in all." [109] The Anglicans re-

[107] Livingston to Welles, February 1, 1754, JFP, Yale; to Robert Livingston, February 4, 1754, Livingston-Redmond Collection, Franklin D. Roosevelt Library, Hyde Park, N. Y.

[108] There is no full account of the college controversy in print. Histories of Columbia University are rather thin on the events surrounding its inception. The most comprehensive treatment of the literature of the controversy is in McAnear, "American Imprints Concerning King's College," *Papers of the Bibliographic Society*, XLIV (1950), 301–339.

[109] *New-York Mercury*, December 30, 1754. *The Querist* was the title of one of the pamphlets born out of this later phase of the controversy. Written by Livingston and Smith, it appeared late in 1754 and raised forty-eight questions concerning the Anglican-proposed charter. The "Watch-Tower" series itself ran from November

sponded with a shorter-lived paper, titled *John Englishman, In Defence of the English Constitution*; and what they could not crowd into its two-page issues, they included in separate communications to the *Mercury*.[110] That newspaper became so filled with contentious articles by both disputants that Gaine, its publisher, was frequently compelled to print a supplement to carry the regular news and advertising!

The Anglicans ultimately received their charter, but Livingston's political strength in the Assembly was sufficient to deny them the lottery funds or legislative approval. The Episcopalians opened the college in July, 1754, but as a "child of bitterness," it remained weak and insecure in the face of the triumvirate's continuing assault. Lieutenant Governor De Lancey expected that his grant of the charter would increase his political influence with churchmen both at home and abroad, but his action only harvested him a bitter crop of political animosity. Anglicans criticized him for failing to silence the *Reflector* coterie or to secure the lottery funds for the charter college. The Livingstons were able to employ the college issue as the rallying point around which to unite dissident Dutch, Presbyterian, and anti-gubernatorial elements into a new political party, the most formidable the De Lanceys had ever faced. There was good reason why De Lancey, with considerable asperity, refused to attend meetings of the King's College Trustees. He had already contributed enough to their cause, he remarked sharply, in the loss of his reputation and "the breaches upon his popularity without doors." [111]

The official end of the controversy came in December, 1756, when a political deal resulted in a division of the lottery funds between King's College and the Corporation of the City of New York. The latter would use its half of the money for erecting a new jail and house of detention for the crews of infected ships. William Smith, Sr., could not miss the wry humor of the situation: the financial compromise rid the province of its bone of contention by dividing the money "between the two pest

---

25, 1754 to November 17, 1755. A fifty-third number was published separately on January 16, 1756.

[110] *John Englishman* ran from April [9?] to July 5, 1755.

[111] Smith, *History*, II, 238–239.

houses." [112] Dr. Samuel Johnson was sanguine that the compromise would permit the college to flourish free of political factionalism; De Lancey expected the settlement to reunite his party in the Assembly; the legislators were eager to eliminate an issue that had "kindled such a flame" in the province.[113] Honors were about even. The Anglicans secured their charter college but without public support. The Livingstons failed to secure their free college but denied the Episcopalians legislative sanction for their own.

Only William Livingston remained unreconciled and unsatisfied. He viewed the compromise as a defeat, and he found its memory too odious to recall a year later. To Welles he wrote:

Relative to the affair of the Coledge; we stood as long as our legs would support us, and, I may add, even fought for some time, on our Stumps; but to recount, at present, the particular manner in which we were vanquished, *Animus meminisse Horret Luctuque refugit.*[114]

A decade later, Livingston could remember the affair with less rancor, but the passage of time did nothing to moderate the intensity of his earlier convictions. Writing to his son, he observed:

You are very severe on our famous New York College, but I believe not more sarcastical than it deserves. It makes indeed a most contemptible Figure, and I rejoice that I have been so greatly instrumental in giving it the *betale vulnus* in its first origination. The partial bigotted and iniquitous plan upon which it was constructed deserved the opposition of every Friend of civil and religious Liberty; and the clamour I raised against it in conjunction with two or three friends when it was first founded on its present narrow principles, it has not yet and probably never will totally silence.[115]

Livingston's suspicions of the college were not shared by other members of his family. Some served on the college Board of Trustees, and others sent their sons to it; but until the Revolution, the

[112] *Colonial Laws of New York*, IV, 104–105, 160–162; *Assembly Journal*, II, 512–513, 520; Smith, *History*, II, 238.

[113] *Samuel Johnson Writings*, I, 35–36, 268, IV, 44.

[114] Livingston to Welles, August 8, 1757, JFP, Yale. The quotation is from *Aeneid*, II, 12: "My mind at the remembrance shudders, and from the grief recoils."

[115] Livingston to William Livingston, Jr., July 15, [1768?], Livingston Papers, Box 12, MHS.

public at large viewed the institution as the ill-begotten offspring of the De Lancey — Church "interest." It did not receive popular support, and it did not exert much influence. Yet in many respects King's College was more liberal than Yale. Dr. Johnson at the outset assured New Yorkers that students would not be compelled to attend Episcopal services on the Sabbath nor would the faculty impose on the scholars "the peculiar Tenets of any particular Sect of Christians." The same could not be said of the New Haven institution, where students were required to attend Congregational services and received heavy doses of its theology in the classroom.[116] Nevertheless, the New York college continued to carry the stigma of illiberality and narrow sectarianism which the *Independent Reflector* first affixed to it in 1753. When a writer in a journal of 1790 remarked that the college did not flourish before the Revolution because of the "contracted" plan upon which it was first founded, he was paying high tribute to Livingston's skill as a propagandist.[117]

The *Reflector's* contemporary popularity is more readily inferred than demonstrated. No subscription list has been located, but if the names inscribed in sets that survive are any measure, the journal's audience was wide. Franklin, among other Philadelphians, received both the *Reflector* and the *Reverberator*.[118] Bostonians read the paper, and its printers found some of the essays attractive enough to reprint in their own magazines.[119] John Adams knew of the triumvirate as the authors of the *Reflector* long before he met them in 1774, and Princeton students, on the eve of the Revolution, were using the paper's essays as models for their undergraduate declamations, finding them admirable for "energy and eloquence." The *Reflector's* popularity survived the

[116] *New-York Mercury,* June 3, 1754, December 7, 1772; Louis L. Tucker, "The Church of England and Religious Liberty at Pre-Revolutionary Yale," *William and Mary Quarterly,* XVII (1960), 314–328.

[117] *The New-York Magazine,* I (May, 1790), 256. The Reverend Andrew Burnaby, on his travels through New York in 1760, found the college to be "far from . . . flourishing." Rufus R. Wilson, ed., *Andrew Burnaby's Travels Through North America* (New York, 1904), p. 117.

[118] Franklin's sets of both journals are in the Princeton Library. The Library of Congress has a set of the *Reflector* owned by another Pennsylvanian.

[119] *The New-England Magazine* (Boston, 1758) reprinted No. XL in its first issue (August, pp. 33–38) and part of No. XLVI in its second (October, pp. 19–22).

Revolution, even though Episcopal clergymen dismissed the essays as the "fleeting foibles of their day." When Mathew Carey launched the *American Museum* at the end of the war, essays from the *Reflector* found a ready place among its contents.[120] Even in the twentieth century, the editor of a small Minnesota paper could find in the "honest old type" of the *Reflector* cause for admiration; and when a reader compared the modern periodical to its colonial forebear, the Minnesota editor accepted the compliment, observing; "However successful The Bellman may be in emulating the high principles, the courage, the truth and fidelity of the Independent Reflector, it can never hope to equal it in the use of elegantly polite language." [121]

The *Reflector's* importance stemmed from its substance far more than from its style. Its essays on education helped to plant the seed of revolt against the traditional system of church-controlled schooling which bore final fruit in 1787 with the establishment of the University of the State of New York. The plan of a Board of Regents, nonsectarian in character, appointed by the legislature, and charged with the civic responsibility of supervising the education of all of the state's youth bears a striking similarity to Livingston's proposals.[122] In the essays on religion and government the colonists found a textbook in Whig political theory especially adaptable to American use. New Yorkers employed the principles two decades later to good advantage; and if they voiced these principles with particular ease, it was because their schooling in "popular" theories had begun early.[123] Livingston was no democrat, but his political philosophy was broad enough to appeal to both future Sons of Liberty and landholding

[120] *The Works of John Adams*, II, 349; Sedgwick, *A Memoir*, p. 96; James Madison to Theodore Sedgwick, Jr., February 12, 1831, in *The Writings of James Madison*, Gaillard Hunt, ed. (New York, 1900–1910), IX, 441. No. XIII appeared in the *American Museum*, VIII (October, 1790), 176–178, and No. IX in VIII (November, 1790), 233–235.

[121] William C. Edgar to William H. Dunwoody, January 31, 1907; *The Bellman* (Minneapolis, Minn.), February 9, 1907, both bound with William L. Clements Library (Ann Arbor, Michigan) copy of the *Independent Reflector*.

[122] Sidney Sherwood, *The University of the State of New York: History of Higher Education in the State of New York* (U. S. Bureau of Education, Circular of Information No. 3, Washington, D.C., 1900), pp. 49–88, 92–99.

[123] Rossiter, *Seedtime of the Republic*, p. 108.

aristocrats. He could not, of course, foresee the dilemma his radical Whiggism would pose two decades later for many of these "dilettante democrats" of the 1750's. Ultimately they would have to decide whether the bold principles and the high-flown rhetoric of the *Reflector* were worth the price of treason. William Smith, Jr., for one, decided they were not; and when the Revolution came, he remained loyal to the Crown. Livingston chose otherwise. He not only joined the patriot cause but helped to lead it. As a member of the Continental Congress, commander of New Jersey's militia, governor of that state throughout the Revolution, and one of the ablest and most effective propagandists on the American side, he gave convincing proof that the fervid language of the *Independent Reflector* and its "independent" theories of government were not those of a "sunshine soldier" or a "summer patriot."

———————————

When the Reverend Samuel Miller, pastor of New York City's First Presbyterian Church, published his curious and interesting *Brief Retrospect of the Eighteenth Century* in 1803, be observed that

When the future historian shall desire to obtain a correct view of the state of literature and of manners, during this period, he will probably resort to the periodical publications of the day, as presenting the richest sources of information, and forming the most enlightened and infallible guides in his course.

The good doctor did not capitalize on his own perception. His two volumes contain not a word on one of the most revealing periodicals of the century. The reason for his neglect is as baffling as that of his twentieth-century successors. The *Cambridge History of American Literature* dismissed the journal as one of that "strange assortment" of colonial literary creations that was neither magazine nor newspaper, and Frank Luther Mott's standard *History of American Magazines, 1741–1780*, gave it only four lines in 848 pages.

The most charitable explanation of this inattention to one of the most lively and pungent of colonial periodicals is the failure of these literary historians to read it. Political historians have even less excuse for ignoring the *Reflector*. For those who seek to understand what Jefferson meant when he admitted to Richard Henry Lee in 1825 that the sentiments in the Declaration of Independence were no more than the "common sense of the subject" and "an expression of the American mind," the *Independent Reflector* is an indispensable source. It would be fatuous to claim for this publication or for William Livingston, its editor, originality in formulating the natural rights philosophy incorporated into the Declaration. Jefferson acknowledged only Aristotle, Cicero, Locke, and Sidney as his sources; but the political theory of the American Revolution was not transmitted directly from these men to the Revolutionary generation. Nor was it transmitted in precisely its original form. Colonial America had its own spokesmen of the rights of man, and they communicated the European principles in a distinctively American idiom and to a distinctively American audience. Livingston was just such a spokesman, and the *Reflector* was his medium.

Few publications contain so comprehensive a statement of the Whig liberalism of the Revolutionary leadership at so early a date. Over twenty years before Lexington and Concord, this little journal schooled New Yorkers in the belief that Americans were "Subjects of the same King, with the People of England; . . . and therefore entitled to equal Privileges with them"; that "Government . . . is an human Establishment, depending upon the free Consent of Mankind, whereby one or more Individuals are . . . cloathed by them with their united Power, which is to be exercised in an invariable Pursuit of the Welfare of the Community"; and that if princes violate their oath, "the People have a Right to resist them, because . . . they . . . are considered, as in a State of Nature, to have broke the original Compact." A new generation of Americans, again confronted with a challenge to its philosophy of freedom and the rights of man, may do well to go to school once more with the *Independent Reflector* under its arm. Shorn of its eighteenth-century references, it still provides inspiration for all who seek, like William Livingston, to contrast "the amiable Charms of *Liberty*, with the detestable Nature of *Slavery* and *Oppression*."

49

INTRODUCTION

In the preparation of this first republication of the *Independent Reflector* since its original appearance in 1752–53, I have received assistance from numerous colleagues but more particularly from innumerable reference librarians. Without their knowledge of specialized works of reference, always cheerfully shared, the editing of the text would have been almost impossible. At Long Island University, Professor Elliott S. M. Gatner, Reference Librarian, and Miss Marcia Schwab, graduate assistant in the Department of History, submitted graciously to my endless requests for reference materials. Professor Howard Adelson of the Department of History at The City College, New York City, lent his expert knowledge of the Classics in making the many translations from the Latin which the editing required. Mr. Roger Berry of the Department of History at Kent State University, Ohio, directed me to useful sources of information on James Parker and colonial printing. I am particularly indebted to the Lilly Foundation for a summer fellowship in 1961 which permitted me to spend a month at the William L. Clements Library and to use its magnificent resources, along with those of the University of Michigan Library, in collecting material for the Introduction. My wife, Margaret Klein, assisted me in every stage of the editorial task.

Long Island University   Milton M. Klein
June, 1962

NOTE ON THE TEXT

No attempt has been made in this edition to modernize consistently the original orthography of the *Independent Reflector* or to impair the flavor of its eighteenth-century idiom. Inconsistencies in spelling within the text have been retained, such as the varying use of "public" and "publick," "ballance" and "balance." However, where the original spelling seemed so awkward as to interfere with easy reading, modern orthography has been substituted. Thus "intire" has been changed to "entire," "inconnected" to "unconnected," "OEconomy" to "Economy," etc. Errors that seemed to be obviously typographical have also been corrected. No alterations have been made in the original capitalization or in the often excessive punctuation except, again, where the latter seemed to impair the sense of the language for the modern reader. Superfluous quotation marks which, in the original, appear at the beginning of each line of an extended quotation have been eliminated, and unusually long quotations have been indented and the quotation marks eliminated entirely.

The numbered notes at the end of each paper are those of the present editor. All other notes appear as in the original.

As indicated in the Introduction, except for a single reprinting of the first six issues, the *Independent Reflector* was published only once, as separate issues of the weekly journal, though a number of complete sets may have been bound for sale by the printer. The present edition reproduces the bound volume in the New York Public Library.

THE INDEPENDENT REFLECTOR

THE

INDENPENDENT REFLECTOR:

O R,

Weekly Essays

O N

Sundry Important S U B J E C T S.

More particularly adapted to the PROVINCE *of* NEW-YORK.

Ne quid falfi dicere audeat, ne quid veri non audeat.
CICERO.

N E W - Y O R K:

Printed (until tyrannically fuppreffed) in MDCCLIII.

[The title page for the *Independent Reflector*, printed in 1753–54 for binding with the collected issues]

Number I

The INTRODUCTION, *or Design of this Paper* [1]

W<small>HOEVER</small> sets up for a Reformer of public Abuses, must expect to encounter innumerable Difficulties. It seems to carry with it an Air of Superiority, to which Mankind submit with the greatest Reluctance. The Office of giving Advice, is naturally obnoxious to Ill-Will, as it implies either some Fault, or a less Degree of Understanding, in the Person who is to take it; for which Reason it is seldom taken. Nor is any Thing more difficult than to eradicate popular Prejudice. Errors, like Families, demand Respect on Account of their Antiquity. Opinions long entertained, and embraced by the Majority, plead both Prescription and Precedent, for their Continuance. The most ridiculous Notions are rendered venerable by Time, and acquire a Kind of Sanction by being diffused thro' Numbers: Nay, it is looked upon as disrespectful, to controvert the Sentiments of our Ancestors, to oppose an ancient and prevailing Opinion. But such Over-Nicety and Excess of Complaisance, is the Source of innumerable Mischiefs, by tending to the Perpetuation, and (if I may be allowed the Expression) the Immortality of Error.

Some Persons owe their Prosperity to the Violation of their Trust; and to the Concealment of such Violation from the Public Eye. The Interrupting those in their iniquitous Obscurity, by dragging them into open Day-light, is much-what as agreeable as letting in the Light of the Sun upon a Nest of Owls, to whom it is painful and offensive.

The Ignorance of others is their distinguishing Characteristic: From whence spring Pride and Self-Conceit; which germinate and flourish with peculiar Vigour in a Soil so congenial to their Natures. Light poured in upon such Minds, is always disgustful: It is like holding a Candle to a Lady celebrated for the Opposite of Beauty: They hate it, because it discovers their Imperfections,

55

mortifies their Pride, and exposes them to the Contempt of the World.

Others there are of a supine and slothful Temper: These in Society, are like Drones in a Hive. Does their Country flourish; they partake of the Fruit of its Prosperity: But Indolence so enervates their Powers, that they will neither bestir themselves to promote its Interests; nor make a Stand when Oppression, like Poverty, *invades as an armed Man.* They wish it well, and a Wish is the boldest Exertion of their Activity: They swim with the Current; believe as others, and act, if at all, with the prevailing Majority. As such Men are never for Redress; so those who labour to effect it, are, in their Opinion, Enemies to the publick Tranquility and Repose.

But whether their Opposition springs from Corruption, Ignorance, or Indolence; or however different their Motive, they generally agree in giving an invidious Turn to the Design of the Writer. If he discants with Spirit, on the Rights of the Subject; he is an Enemy to Monarchy, and a latent Promoter of republican Principles. Does he insist on the due Extent of Prerogative; he is a Tool to the Administration, and an Advocate for lawless Dominion. If he combats the Libertinism of the Age; he is an enthusiastic Zealot, or a knavish Impostor. Does he plead for the free Exercise of Conscience, and disclaim the Unreasonableness of Persecution; he is dissafected to the Church, and a Foe to Religion.

None of these Discouragements shall, however, deter me from vindicating the *civil and religious RIGHTS* of my Fellow-Creatures: From exposing the peculiar Deformity of publick *Vice*, and *Corruption*; and displaying the amiable Charms of *Liberty*, with the detestable Nature of *Slavery* and *Oppression.* — I have the Magnanimity to attack the Enemies of [the] human Race, in whatever dignified Shape they appear, and to burst the Chains they cast over their Species: To assert the native inherent Rights of Mankind: To stigmatize the public Robber; and inculcate that Devotion to the Public, from whence so many ROMAN Names, immortaliz'd in Story, drew their Lustre. I shall prosecute my Undertaking, with a firm Assurance, that it is not Quality, but Innocence, that ought to exempt Men from Reproof: And that Vice and Folly ought to be attacked where-ever they are met with; and especially when placed in high and conspicuous Stations. In a Word, I shall dare to attempt the Reforming the *Abuses of my Country*, and to point out whatever may tend to its Prosperity and Emolument. Nor will, 'tis to be hoped, a Design so generous and humane, tho' not executed with that Skill and Dexterity wherewith it might be carried on by an abler Genius, prove altogether unacceptable to the Public: Nay, I flatter myself, that whoever may be displeased with me, I shall be approved by all whose Praises do Honour to the Person on whom they are bestowed: And if I have the Happiness to obtain *their* Approbation, I shall not trouble myself about the Sentiments of those whose Censure is Applause, and their Commendation dishonourable. From my own Countrymen especially, to whose more immediate Service a considerable Number of these *Weekly* Speculations will be dedicated, it will be less Presumption to expect a suitable Encouragement.

The Author being under no Attachment to any Party, thinks himself the better qualified to make impartial Remarks on the Conduct of every Party, so far as it proves injurious to the Public, and farther he is determined not to interfere with the political Controversies of his Country.

The Espousing any polemic Debate between different Sects of Christians, shall be the last Charge against him; tho' he shall be ever ready to deliver his Sentiments on the Abuses and Encroachments of any, with the Freedom and Unconcernedness becoming Truth and Independency.

The Imputation of Indecency, and the Use of rude and virulent Expressions, he will take particular Care not to deserve: Nor shall personal Reflections ever blemish his Writings. But Corruption in Office shall be boldly reprehended; and if it cannot be exposed without pointing out the Person, he shall hold himself inculpable: For there, not the *Man*, but the *Officer*, is attacked; and public Villainy ought to be rendered publickly infamous, whatever private Detriment it may occasion to the corrupt Individual.

When I protest against Ill-Manners and scurrilous Language, I mean not to debar myself the Privilege of lashing Guilt and Corruption in the strongest Terms. It would not, for Instance, be Slander or Virulence, to call a *Chartres*,[2] or a *Wild*,[3] Rogue and Robber. On the contrary, tho' these Appellatives might not be within the Intent of the Statute, that requires the Description of Persons by their proper Additions; yet would they be within the original Design of Names, which Antiquarians tell us, were either agreeable to Men's Persons, or descriptive of their natural or moral Qualities.

Neither Hope nor Fear shall influence the Author to suppress his Zeal for the Service of his Country, however offensive it may prove to Men whose Conduct or Pretensions cannot abide the Test of an impartial Examination. He shall not sit unconcerned amidst publick Mismanagement; nor be a silent Spectator of the general Calamity. Where the Rights of the Community are infringed, or violated, no Titles however august, no Persons however exalted, shall find a Shelter from the Treatment they deserve; but he "will exert his Endeavours, at whatever Hazard, to repel the Aggressor, to drag the Thief to Justice, whoever may protect them in their Villainy, and whoever may partake of their Plunder."

Public Abuses are, in their own Nature, progressive; and tho' easily removed in their Origin, acquire Strength by their Duration, and at last become too potent to be subdued. The Cockatrice is easily crushed in the Egg, but in full Growth, a formidable Enemy. A perfect Supineness under the least Invasion of civil or religious Liberty, is an Encouragement to greater, and presages mightier Evils to come; while a seasonable Opposition might not only have vanquished the present, but discouraged all future Abuses of the like Nature.

When I have no Opportunity of serving my Country, by pointing out public Grievances, or proposing beneficial Regulations, I shall take the Liberty to make Excursions into the World of SCIENCE; confining myself however to the most important Speculations, and such as most nearly coincide with my principal Design of opposing Oppression, and vindicating the *Liberty of Man*:

THE DESIGN OF THIS PAPER

But in Subjects meerly literary, I shall rarely indulge myself.

The Author will ever be open to Truth and Conviction; nor will any Person be more ready to detect his Errors, than he to correct them. But on the Slander and Scurrility of his Enemies, if such it should be his Misfortune to create, he will look down with a Sovereign Contempt.

If after All, he should fail of Success, he will be sure of the Testimony of a good Conscience. Should his Speculations prove beneficial to his Country, sufficient will be his Reward. But if he finds himself obliged to drop his Design, for Want of Encouragement; he will enjoy the inward Satisfaction of having, at least, attempted to promote the public Welfare.

Z.

ADVERTISEMENT

It being unimaginable, that the Author can prosecute his Design, as explained in the preceeding Paper, at his private Expence, he flatters himself, that all Persons disposed to encourage so laudable an Undertaking, and which is the first Attempt of this Nature that ever was made in this Part of the World, will readily contribute towards its Continuation, while he continues to deserve the Encouragement of the Public: To which End, he will at all Times be glad of the Correspondence and Assistance of any Person, inclining to convey his Thoughts on any Subject within the Scope of his Design, thro' the Channel of this Paper, who is desired to transmit his Compositions directed, To the INDEPENDENT REFLECTOR, *to the Care of Mr. Parker; which the Author, when ever he thinks it expedient, will publish, and if necessary with his own Corrections. Such Gentlemen, also, who can serve their Country, by suggesting good Thoughts, and a true Account of Facts, but have either no Leisure for, or are not used to Composition, or such as are fearful of appearing in print, may depend on having a due Regard paid to their Collections; and that no ungentleman-like, ungenerous, or ill Use, shall be made of their Manuscripts. — The Author also declares, that he is influenced in his Design, by a sincere Love of Mankind, and actuated by no private Views whatever: His Circumstances, thanks to Heaven! put him above the Aids of this Paper for Subsistence; for which Reason, he has so calculated the Price of it, as barely to pay the Printer, without any Compensation for his own Time and Labour.*

59

1. The manuscript draft of this first issue is preserved among the William Smith Papers, New York Public Library (No. 212). It bears the title originally selected for the series, "The New-York Guardian."

2. Philippe II, duc de Chartres (1674–1723), regent of France during the minority of Louis XV, and noted for his cynicism and immorality.

3. Jonathan Wild (1683–1725), a notorious English criminal who headed a well-organized and profitable gang of thieves.

Number II

THURSDAY, DECEMBER 7, 1752

Remarks on the EXCISE; and the Farming it, shewn to be injurious to the Province

Calm thinking Villains, whom no Faith can fix,
Of crooked Councils, and dark Politics. POPE [1]

O F all public Robberies, none are so atrocious in their Natures, or mischievous in their Consequences, as those perpetrated under the *Sanction of LAW*. For this Reason, it may justly be wondered, that the civil Ruler, whose Office it is to punish illegal Invasions of the Rights of the Subject, should suffer a Prostitution of his Authority, in Support of the most flagitious Encroachments. This Defect in public Administration arises chiefly from a partial Consideration of those Evils which any particular Law is designed to remedy. The *smallest* Injuries are often very apparent, while the most *flagrant* Enormities, by being less exposed to View, affect us not so nearly. Errors of this kind have formerly been very frequent in this Province; the Consequences of which, Time and Experience have, in many Instances, sufficiently evinced. Among others, the EXCISE, or Duty laid upon the Retailing of Strong Liquors, as the Manner of it is hurtful to the Subject, falls properly under the Consideration of the *Independent Reflector*.[2]

It must be confessed, that no Method can be more effectual, to restrain Luxury and Intemperance, than subjecting them to Duties or Penalties: Hence an Excise upon Retailers of Strong Liquors, may be both useful and necessary. Besides, when the Public has Occasion for a Sum of Money, it is raised by a Tax; and it is far more reasonable to tax the *Luxury*, than the *Industry* of a People: For which Reason, every Retailer of Strong Liquors, is loaded with a supernumerary Tax, to which Men of other Occupations are not *immediately* liable: Yet as the Retailer, by Reason of the

Tax, is obliged, in Justice to himself, to sell his Liquors at a more advanced Price, than otherwise he would, the Community in general must *eventually* feel the Weight of an EXCISE. And tho' the Justice of this Imposition cannot be denied; the Method used to raise the Monies for which it was laid, ought to be carefully attended to.

It is a standing Maxim of *English Liberty*, "that no Man shall be taxed, but with his own Consent." When the Legislature decree a Tax, as they represent the Community, such Tax ought to be considered as the voluntary Gift of the People, to be applied to such Uses, as they, by their Representatives shall think expedient: It follows, therefore, that the Legislature is bound to raise and dispose of the public Monies, in the Manner intended by the Community. Nor can any Government be supposed faithfully to discharge their Trust, in the Disposition of the Sums arising from Taxes, contrary to the Design with which the Subject submitted himself to them. But I appeal to the Judgment of my Readers, whether the Excise has been managed, in the Manner they would have chosen, had it been left to their Choice and Direction. — During the Administration of Governor *Hunter*, in the Year 1713, an Act was passed for laying an Excise, on all Strong Liquors retailed in this Colony. The Monies arising by Virtue of that Act, were to be applied "to and for the paying and discharging, the public Debts of this Colony, such and in such Manner, as should be directed and ascertained, in an Act thereafter for that Purpose to be made." This Act the Legislators themselves must have thought defective: For tho' it was, the same Year, continued by another Act, it is certain, that a few Days after, they passed a Third, entitled *An* Act *for taking away Doubts and Scruples relating to letting the Excise.*[3] But notwithstanding any Thing, that might therein have been advanced, as explanatory of the first Act, it is certainly very faulty and defective. By an Act passed in the Year 1739, this Excise Act was again continued till the Year 1757, and particularly applied to sinking two Emissions of Bills of Credit, the first amounting to the Sum of £27,680, raised by an Act commonly called the *first Long Bill*, passed in the Year 1714, for paying off the provincial Debts; the Second, to the Value of

41,517½ Ounces of Plate, equal, to £16,607 Currency, raised by another Act for the same Purpose.[4] And indeed this Application was extremely proper: For whenever an Emission of Money is made upon the Public Credit, to answer any particular Emergencies, the Government ought to provide proper Means to sink it; otherwise that Credit must of Course diminish, and its Bills depreciate in Value, in Proportion to the Time they remain current. But whether those Emissions are entirely sunk, is not in my Power to determine. By annual Acts, which our Assemblies, have of late Years, thought expedient to pass, the Excise is applied to sink the Emissions of Bills of Credit issued upon that Duty, pursuant to the Directions of an Act for that Purpose, passed in the twenty first Year of his present Majesty's Reign. Through the Defects of the first Act, and of the general Tenor of the yearly Acts, the Subject has already suffered many Grievances, and may hereafter sustain fresh Impositions, by Exactions of the Farmer, on legal Pretensions, but in direct Contradiction to the Spirit of the *British Constitution.*

One of the greatest Defects of those Acts, is, that the Farmers are not thereby requir'd, to grant the Excise to the Retailers, even tho' the latter should be willing to pay them the whole Amount of the Duties, imposed upon their Liquors, by the first Clause of the first Act. This will appear to any One, who will give himself the Trouble of perusing the Acts. And altho' our Excise Law, grants the Farmer nothing more, than the Duties laid by Act of Assembly, upon retailed Strong Liquors; yet, as he is not prohibited, from demanding of the Retailers, more than the Duties of their Liquors amount to, nor obliged by Law to grant the Excise to any One; instead of being content, with what the Law particularly grants him, he may take Advantage of our defective Acts of Assembly, by preventing Persons from retailing, unless they chuse to pay whatever extortionate Sums, he, in his great Mercy, shall think proper to demand. A terrible Alternative this, for a Free-born Subject to be reduced to! He must even be denied the Privilege of retailing his Commodities for home Consumption, or purchase that Privilege at too dear a Rate, for a bare Subsistence: Should he attempt to assert his native Freedom, and retail without a License, nothing less than his total Ruin would compensate for so daring a Presumption. His Liquors would become a Prey, to the Avarice and Extortion of a Fellow-Subject; and those Means of Life, for which he had pawned his Credit or Estate, fall a Sacrifice to the insatiable Vengeance of the *Farmer*. But that the Legislators, ever intended to grant, so unlimited a Power to those rapacious Monopolists, cannot by any Means be supposed: Why then, should those petty Tyrants be licensed, to depredate the Fortunes and Liberties of the Subject, while the same enacting Power, that gave them a civil Existence, can, at any Time annihilate them, and rid the honest Retailer, of so unjust an Impediment to his Industry and Happiness? How vain are all our Pretensions to Liberty, while we expose our civil Privileges to be thus trampled upon, by the most *unworthy, insignificant Members of the Community!*

The Excise is, indeed, exposed to yearly Sale; by which Means there is a bare Possibility, of our being annually freed, from a Subjection to the Farmers. — But as long as there are Men amongst us, whose Consciences will suffer them to live by Extortion, I fear, we shall never want Chapmen for so alluring a Bargain: And therefore, the Provision made by the first Act, that the Justices of the respective Counties, upon Default of Farmers, shall dispose of the Excise to the Retailers, will seldom, if ever, produce a Jubilee to the latter.

Another disadvantage, flowing from the Imperfection of our Excise Law, is, that by enabling the Farmers, to exert so unlimitted a Power over the Retailers; the Freedom of Elections, that greatest Badge of *British* Liberty, is in imminent Danger of being wrested from us, when ever it suits the Farmer's Interest, to busy himself in Matters of that Kind.

If we look into the Parliamentary Proceedings of our Mother-Country, we shall find, that the main Objection against the famous Excise Bill, was, that an Increase of the Number of Officers, dependent upon the Crown, would tend to the Advancement of regal Prerogative; and expose the Liberty of the Subject, to be trampled upon by mercenary Placemen: And tho' the Circumstances of the Province, refuse a Similitude in this Article; yet our *Excise Scheme*, should it be suffered to continue, as it does inevitably abridge our Constitutional Privileges, so must it perpetuate to the latest Posterity, a most despicable Opinion, of the civil Principles of their Ancestors. It is not to the Invasions of the Crown, that our Liberty is exposed, but to the daring Encroachments of every designing Fellow, of some Credit, and no Conscience; to him, who can give Sureties, for Payment of the purchase Money into the Treasury, on Condition of exacting from his Fellow-Subjects, without Mercy or Restraint. Should it be urged, that the Number of Farmers in the Province, is too small to have any considerable Influence in Elections; this I must positively deny. The Interest of a Set or Party of Men, is not only to be measured by their own Number, but must also be estimated, from the Number of Votes at their Command. It is easy then, to conceive, that a Farmer of the Excise, having many who hold the Liberty, of maintaining themselves and their Families at his Election, and during his Sovereign Will and Pleasure, may oblige those, who dare not forfeit his Favour, to vote as he pleases. But should it even be supposed, that such an Interest as this, could have no great Prevalence in an Election, one single Vote obtained by coercive Means, is an Infringment and Abuse of our Constitution; and deprives the Elector of that Liberty, which not even the Crown, much less an iniquitous Subject, should be suffered to ravish from him.

But further to inforce this Reasoning, I beg Leave to produce an Example, which, from its Parity to the present Case, may be more convincing to many, than the most elaborate Arguments. In the Debates of the House of Commons, upon the above mentioned Excise Bill, Sir *Thomas Aston*, declares, "That it was his Misfortune to know too much of the Influence, that the Officers of the Custom and *Excise*, had at Elections: For at his own *Election*, there were many of the Voters so free and open, as to come to him, and tell him, that they would vote for him, rather than any other; but that those Officers had threat[e]ned to ruin them if they did." [5] May we not justly be supposed, to run the same Hazard with our Farmers of the Excise? It is in their Power, to sway the Voices of the Retailers; and should the latter refuse to submit, the *Farmers* may, for the same Reason, *threaten to ruin them*. They are able to carry the Matter still farther: — For should they incline to be CANDIDATES, by their Power in Elections, they would, perhaps, procure themselves, to be chosen into the Assembly. So that one Day they might be seen hurrying to the House, to give their Votes, for enhancing the Severities of our Excise Laws; and soon after, industriously reaping the Fruits of their Labours, by plundering their Fellow-Subjects, under so venerable a Sanction. Nor (shocking as it may seem) do we want Proofs, in the Behaviour of many of the Representatives in our *former* Assemblies, that this has actually been the Case. It was their common Practice yearly to purchase the Excise. It is difficult for any Man to distinguish the public, from his own private Interest; nor were they, so much possessed of the Virtue of Self-denial, as to prefer the former to the latter: In short, they were not ashamed of being less governed, in the Exercise of their legislative Capacities, by a laudable Ambition to serve their Country, than by a boundless Desire, of augmenting their private Fortunes.

These are Considerations sufficiently important to merit the Attention of the Legislature: Nor would their Interposition, in a Matter of such high Concern, to the Welfare of the Province, be an inconsiderable Accession, to the Glory of their Administration. They are exalted above the common Level, not as Objects to be gazed at by the Vulgar, but that by their Elevation, they may be enabled to look down on the Actions of Men, and discriminate the honest Subject, from the designing Villain. The illustrious Orb of the Sun, is not placed on high, to strike us with his magnificent Appearance, but to dispense his genial Influence to the whole System. They are cloathed with Power, not to sport with the Interests of Human Nature, but to be faithful Guardians of the Liberties of their Country. One may therefore modestly hope, they will no longer suffer, so unjustifiable an Encroachment, to shelter itself under the awful Sanction of Law. And glad should I be, to have it in my Power to congratulate my Countrymen, on so memorable a Deliverance; whilst I left the Enemies of Truth and Liberty to humble themselves in Sackcloth and Ashes. But this being too extensive a Subject, to be fully discussed at present,

REMARKS ON THE EXCISE

the Reader may expect to see it resumed, in some future Paper.

B.

The Author acknowledges the Receipt of the Letter subscribed Politicus; *but begs the Gentleman's Excuse for suppressing it, as containing a strong Tincture of Party-Spirit, which, he thanks Heaven, is of late so happily subsided, that he should think himself ill entitled to the Character of a* Lover of his Country, *was he in the least instrumental in its Renovation, or the kindling it up a-fresh. But on any unexceptionable Subject, he will be proud of the Correspondence of so ingenious a Writer.*

The Gentleman who is so pressing, for the Remedy of the Grievances he mentions, and who discovers such an animated Zeal for the public Welfare, as renders his Sincerity altogether unquestionable; is hereby desired to accept the Author's most grateful Acknowledgment for the Letter signed Shadrech Plebianus,[6] *and the many valuable Hints wherewith he has furnished him; several of which had already engaged his Attention, and the rest he may depend upon seeing wrought up in some future Numbers of the* Independent Reflector.

The Letter signed Atticus, *is also come to Hand, and would not fail of instantly meeting with proper Regard, had not the elegant Writer bestowed such Encomiums on the Author, as might occasion an ill-natur'd Construction on his Modesty, was it published before he is convinced by the general Voice, that they do not exceed his Merit; for which Reason, he hopes it will give no Offence to defer its Publication to a more seasonable Opportunity. He cannot, however, sufficiently admire the Wit and Humour it contains, and ardently wishes for more Examples of the flowing Vein, and ornamental Style, of so masterly a Writer.*

1. From "The Temple of Fame," lines 410–411.

2. The practice of farming out the excise tax on liquor to the highest bidder, initiated by the Dutch in 1656, by 1752 was highly lucrative. The privilege of dealing in liquors was sold to retailers on exorbitant terms, and New York City abounded in taverns and drinking clubs. Dr. Alexander Hamilton, briefly visiting the city from Maryland in 1744, concluded that "the readiest way for a stranger to recommend himself" to New Yorkers was to "drink stoutly" and "pour down seas of liquor." Arthur E. Peterson and George W. Edwards, *New York as an Eighteenth Century Municipality* (New York, 1917), I, 48, II, 68–69; Carl Bridenbaugh, ed., *Gentleman's Progress: The Itinerarium of Dr. Alexander Hamilton* (Chapel Hill, 1948), pp. 43, 88.

3. A law dated October 23, 1713, deals with the liquor excise, but no text is published. *The Colonial Laws of New York from the Year 1664 to the Revolution*, 5 vols. (Albany, 1894), I, 789.

4. October 25, 1739. *Ibid.*, III, 21–31.

5. The "famous Excise Bill," Walpole's proposal of 1733 to impose duties on wine and tobacco to permit a lower land tax, aroused violent opposition because of the army of officers it would sire. The remarks quoted were by Sir Thomas Aston, member from Liverpool, March 16, 1733. Walpole was compelled to withdraw the bill, and the word "excise" continued to be regarded, in Dr. Samuel Johnson's words, as "a hateful tax levied upon commodities, and adjudged . . . by . . . wretches hired by those to whom excise is paid."

6. For the identification of Shadrach Plebianus, see Appendix II.

Number III

THURSDAY, DECEMBER 14, 1752

The Abuses of the ROAD, and CITY-WATCH

The following Letter, came to my Hands a few Days ago, and well deserves a Place in this Paper.

To the INDEPENDENT REFLECTOR

SIR,

A GENTLEMAN in my Neighbourhood, whose Charity has often kept me from perishing, calling the other Day at my House, and finding me in Tears (which alas is no new Thing with me!) he enquired, with a compassionate Tone of Voice, the Reason of my Sorrow. I frankly unbosom'd my Affliction, by relating my mournful Story. In particular, I told him the Hardship I lay under, in being obliged to pay, towards the Expences of the Road, and City Watch, as much as the richest Man in the Town. This I was enabled to represent in the most lively Colours, as the Impression of my last Payment to the Road, was, by Reason of the peculiar Circumstances which attended it, still fresh in my Mind: These, Sir, I shall disclose to you presently. My Benefactor sympathized in my Sorrow, and recommended to me, to transmit my Complaint to the REFLECTOR, who, says he, I am confident will not desire a more grateful Employment, than to relieve the Miserable, and lash the Oppressor. Accordingly I take the Liberty to unfold to you my doleful History, entirely submitting this Letter to your Correction, not being myself acquainted with the Beauties of a good Stile, tho' I am sure the Subject is equally important and rueful.

I was once, Mr. *Reflector*, alas, could I recall those happy Days! I was once in easy, if not in affluent Circumstances. But my Husband, in other Respects, a valuable Man, too fond of making a Shew beyond his Substance, soon ran thro' the Fortune which I brought him; and then, was himself remov'd by Death, leaving me with two helpless Orphans, in the greatest Poverty. My eldest Child is a Boy of twelve, and my chief Support by selling Oysters, the opening of which is our only Profit upon them. Miserable Degradation, from the Rank I once sustained, in my Youth and Prosperity! To those who have lived well, Poverty has a double Sting. May you, Sir, never experience the fatal Truth! My youngest is a little Girl, just turn'd of Eight. Poor little *Nancy!* she stands now at my Elbow, and cries for a Piece of Bread and Butter, which I have not to give her. My *Tommy* just now entered the Room, all sad and dejected, because he had spent the whole Morning, in selling but fifty Oysters. Alas, my dear little Darlings, had we now but the thousandth Part, of what your unhappy Father has profusely squandered! — Almighty GOD, who is the Father of the Widow and the Orphan, relieve your and my Necessities! If I write broken and unconnected, you Sir, will not be at a Loss to guess the Reason. Just now my Tears, interrupted my Story; but I will endeavour to resume it, or rather, to relate the Occasion that introduc'd it. Know then, that instead of having my Sorrows alleviated, by the Provision of the Public, they are aggravated under Colour of Law. But, as I remember, my Husband used to say, the Law was never contrary to Reason. Some Time ago, in came a Fellow (he look'd like a Thief) and demanded Half-a-Crown, for working on the Road, and said he must have the Money instantly. As I found him to be a low-liv'd Fellow, I was determin'd to give him no Reason to insult me. But, if you'll believe me, it was the last Farthing I had in the House. For Heaven's sake, Mr. *Reflector,* exert your Endeavours for my Relief; and if the Public does not lighten, let it not increase my Burthen. Let, at least, poor Widows be exempted from the Tax. I have not seen the Road these ten Years; and, as for the Watch, alas, where is our Property to guard? Yet I annually pay Twenty Shillings, towards these two Charges, which is a grievous Tax to one in my Condition. If you represent my Case in your Paper, and remove this heavy Burden, I will give you — all I have to give, my earnest Prayers for your present Prosperity, and everlasting Happiness; and remain with the profoundest Gratitude,

Your Most Humble Servant,

M. K.

Methinks this venerable Widow, may be fitly compar'd to a Pyramid plac'd in a Valley, which is still a Pyramid, notwithstanding its humble Situation. There is a certain elegant Simplicity in her Letter, that discovers the Politeness of her Education, and shews her to be a Lady, tho' a Lady in Ruin. Doubtless she deserves a better Fortune, than she is Mistress of. But I hope her present Calamity, instead of subduing her Patience, or throwing her into Despair, will raise her Hopes of being, e'er long, exalted to that nobler State of Existence, where all the seeming Irregularities of Providence will be rectifyed, and the Ways of

God to Man compleatly vindicated. In the mean Time, I should think myself happy, could I contribute to the Suppression of the Grievances that overwhelm her. I am obliged to her, for the good Opinion she seems to entertain of me, and which I am sensible my Capacity doth not deserve, tho' my Inclinations induce me to covet. It cannot be denied, that the Subject of her Letter, is, as she herself expresses it, *equally important and rueful*; and I can assure her, it has often been the Topick of my Meditation, and never without a Mixture of Compassion and Horror.

In every well policed State, the Legislature has been greatly attentive, to the Regulation of the public Roads. The *Romans* were extremely expensive in their High-Ways; and their *Via Attica* and *Flaminia*, were Works of incredible Magnificence, and are still sufficient, tho' greatly decayed, to give us a just Idea of the *Roman* Grandeur. Nor hath our Mother Country, been indolent in an Article, of so great Importance, to the Common Wealth. On the Contrary, the public Ways have often employed, the Consideration of the British Parliament, and given rise to sundry Statutes in their Favour. We too, in this Province, have several Acts of Assembly for the Regulation of Roads; but unhappily, in one Respect, they are all miserably deficient. They have provided no Security, against the Frauds and Embezzlements of the Overseers, nor made them accountable for the Overplus of Fines. — A great Opportunity to rob the Public; and it is well if none have embrac'd it!

But the Act for the Amendment of the Road, from *New-York* to *Kings-Bridge*, is introductive of greater Mischiefs than any of the rest.[1] The Overseers in the Counties can, at most, be only insignificant Pilferers; but it is in the Power of our Surveyor, to be a mighty Robber. They may finger the public Money by Shillings, but he can defraud his Country by Pounds, nay by Hundreds.

The Act enacts, That the Road, as far as to the House of *Joachim Anderson*, shall be repaired and amended by the Inhabitants, of all the several Wards of this City, except the Out-Ward, and empowers a Surveyor, appointed by the Justices, to summon such, and so many, of the said Inhabitants, at such Times and

Places, and with such Tools and Carriages, as the Surveyor shall think necessary and proper.

Now, this Act naturally occasions these two obvious Remarks. In the *first* Place, it equally subjects the Poor and the Rich, to defray the Expence of the Road; and *Secondly,* puts it in the Power of the Surveyor, to defraud both of such Sums, as he, in his great Wisdom, shall think proper. A very unequal Distribution of Taxes, and a Prerogative not inferior to that of an absolute Monarch!

With Respect to the first Point, nothing appears more unjust, than for the Poor to contribute as much as the Rich, either to that or any other public Expence. What! shall the penurious Widow, surrounded with a plaintive Circle of Orphans uncloathed, unfed, and almost unhous'd, pay for the Reparation of a Road she never uses, as much as the Man of Wealth and Affluence, who daily deepens its Ruts with his gilded Chariot! Whatever may be the Sentiments of others, concerning so unequal, I had almost said, so barbarous a Tax; I could never think of it without the greatest Surprize, that it has so long escaped the Attention of the Legislature. The Subject pays Taxes for the Support of the Government, by the Laws of which, he acquires a Property in his Acquisitions; and by the Laws of which, he is supported in the Enjoyment of such Property. Without Government, he could have no Property; and without Taxes there could be no Government. This is the grand Reason of the Equity, as well as Necessity of public Taxations. Whence the Absurdity, of making the Man of little or no Property, contribute equally to the public Charge with the most opulent Possessor. And, indeed, this is our own Rule, or pretended Rule, in levying all other Taxes, except that of the Road, and the City-Watch; and to what Fatality it is to be ascribed, that in those two only, we should blaspheme common Sense, and subvert the Order of Things, is humbly submitted to those at the Helm.

The other Defect I mentioned, was, the Legislature's submitting it to the Discretion of the Surveyor, to pocket the public Cash. Nay, what is worse, he may repeat his Depredations annually, and defraud the People of immense Sums. This is the more astonishing, as our Assemblies have in other Respects, been justly applauded for their prudent Economy, and parsimonious Disposition of the public Monies. The Occasion, therefore, of their enabling an Overseer of the Roads, to despoil the City of Hundreds, must to us, petty Mortals, remain an inscrutable Mystery.

What has been done by former Surveyors, I will not take upon me to determine; but I am told, that every Family in this City, of which there are about Two Thousand, are called upon at least twice a Year, to bestow a Day's Labour on the Road, or pay their Two and Six-Pence. I believe no Man that ever blush'd, will pretend a Necessity, for four thousand Days Work annually, to keep that Spot of a Road in Repair. It would be an Affront to common Sense, and an impudent Insult on the Public. Four Thousand Men in a Day, might almost cut a Road thro' Mount *Athos*; at least they might make our Road vie with those of antient *Rome*, and like some of them, pave it with Pebbles. I am confident, it might be kept in good Repair, for less than One Hundred Pounds per Annum; and yet four thousand Days Work, at Two Shillings and Six-Pence per Day, amounts to Five Hundred Pounds. What becomes of the remaining Four Hundred Pounds, is no difficult Matter to guess, it being notorious, that the greatest Part of the Inhabitants of this City, instead of going themselves, or sending a Person in their Room, constantly pay their Half-a-Crown on every Summons.

This may be one Way of making a Fortune; but it is making it out of the Blood and Vitals, of the Poor and Wretched!

The City-Watch is another Grievance of the first Magnitude.[2] The Citizens are summoned, at least four Times a Year to watch, or pay their Two and Six-Pence to a Parcel of idle, drunken, vigilant Snorers, who never quelled any nocturnal Tumult in their Lives; but would, perhaps, be as ready to join in a Burglary, as any Thief in Christendom. A hopeful Set indeed, to defend this rich and populous City, against the Terrors of the Night! *Quis custodes ipsos custodiet?*[3] And yet this is a Charge on the Inhabitants, of a Thousand Pounds per Annum; tho' a good Watch might be maintained, for less than Five Hundred Pounds a Year. Whence it follows, that in these two Articles,

Nine Hundred Pounds might be annually saved to the City; which of itself, is an ample Fund for a College, and more by Six Hundred Pounds, than the yearly Interest, of the Money, raised for erecting the College.   *Sic vos non vobis mellificatis apes.*[4]

If, therefore, it be impartial Equity, to proportion a Tax, to the Circumstances of the People: If it be great and glorious, to relieve the Poor, and allay the Calamity, of the Widow and the Orphan: If the Prevention of public Robbery and Oppression, be the Duty of the Legislature; and the diffusing Joy and Gladness, through a thousand Breasts, generous and God-like: If removing a general and well-grounded Complaint, be an Act of Benevolence, and the pleasing Talk of Patriot-Statesmen; it is to be presumed, that the Legislature will speedily remove these crying Grievances, nor suffer it to remain in the Power of any Man alive, to accumulate a Fortune, by plundering his Country.

X. & Z.

The Author desires all those wrathful Gentlemen, who, with the Devils in the Gospel, fearing to be tormented before their Time, make it their Business to vilify his Paper, by insinuating, that he intends to write contemptuously of Government, to forbear their Scurrilities; assuring them, that as their Apprehensions, can only proceed, from their own Guilt, and the Terror of their Consciences: Such Insinuations, will prove so far from deterring him out of his Design, that they will rather accelerate their Doom, and provoke him, the sooner to make them the Marks of the public Resentment, as they have been the Authors of public Roguery. — He flatters himself, he has, at least, as high a Regard for Authority, *for Authority unabus'd and unprostituted, as those who notoriously debase and pervert it; and hope, notwithstanding, to screen themselves from Censure, by blending the Detection of their Iniquities, with a Contempt of their Offices. But he begs Leave to inform them, that "it is the Shrine he venerates, and not the Beast that bears it on his Back." Accordingly he shall ever treat* Government, *which is sacred and venerable, with the Honour and Reverence it deserves; saving nevertheless, and always reserving to himself, the Privilege of a free* Briton, *to expose the Abuses of Government; and, when Occasion offers, to animadvert on the lawless Conduct of his Superiors, (by such Conduct infinitely his Inferiors) with the Decency becoming a* Gentleman, *and the Spirit peculiar to an* Englishman — N. B. *I shall, in my next Paper, give these Wretches, the Idea of a Government, suitable to their slavish Dispositions.*   Z.

ABUSES OF THE ROAD

1. This act, passed in 1741 and amended in 1751, made the city's inhabitants responsible for maintaining the Kingsbridge (or Boston Post) Road, which ran from lower Manhattan to the Harlem River at Spuyten Duyvil. Three surveyors chosen by the justices of the peace to supervise the work had broad powers to requisition manpower, horses, wagons, and tools. Persons summoned for road service could escape by sending a substitute or paying a charge of six shillings for each day's absence. Peterson and Edwards, *New York* . . . II, 163; *Colonial Laws of New York*, III, 162–166, 844–847.

2. A citizens' watch had been instituted as early as 1731, and despite experiments with paid constables and regular troops, it was still in existence in 1752. Inhabitants of the various wards were expected to serve or to pay for a substitute. Peterson and Edwards, *New York*, II, 119–124.

3. *Quis custodiet ipsos custodes?* "Who will guard the guardians themselves?" Juvenal, *Satires*, VI, 347.

4. "Thus do you bees make honey, but not for yourselves." Attributed to Virgil. Livingston had used the same aphorism several years earlier in a slashing attack on the legal apprenticeship system he met as a clerk in James Alexander's office (*New-York Weekly Post-Boy*, August 19, 1745).

Number IV

THURSDAY, DECEMBER 21, 1752

The different Effects of an absolute *and a* limited
*Monarchy: The Glory of a Prince ruling
according to Law, superior to that of
an arbitrary Sovereign; with the
peculiar Happiness of the*
BRITISH *Nation*

WHEN one considers the Difference between an absolute, and a
limited Monarchy, it seems unaccountable, that any Person in his
Senses, should prefer the former to the latter. For, notwithstanding the pretended Advantages under an unlimited Prince,
Despotism is a Task above the Capacity of human Nature. Power
of all Kinds is intoxicating; but boundless Power, is insupportable
by the giddy and arrogant Mind of MAN. So exalted an Elevation,
hath seldom fail'd to turn the Head of its Possessor. The frail and
delicate Structure of the human Eye, is not more incapable of
enduring the dazzling Lustre of the Sun, than the Heart of Man,
the bewitching Charms of despotic Sovereignty. Hence most absolute Monarchs have acted more like imperial Wolves, or rather
Beasts in human Shape, than rational and intelligent Beings. 'Tis
true, that a Prince, who would never abuse his uncontroulable
Authority, might, in some Instances, promote the public Welfare,
beyond a Ruler whose Hands are tied by the Law: But such a
Prince is rather a Creature of the Imagination, than a real Existence; and so unequal are the Chances against it, that it is the
Height of Phrensy, to make the Experiment.

In *limited* Monarchies, the Pride and Ambition of Princes, and
their natural Lust for Dominion, are check'd and restrained. If
they violate their Oath, and sap the fundamental Constitution of

the State, the People have a Right to resist them; because by that Means they put themselves in the Condition of private Persons, and act with unauthoritative Power: For such is all the Power they can have, inconsistent with, or in Opposition to the Laws. Hence they are to be considered, as in a State of Nature, to have broke the original Compact, abdicated their Thrones, and introduced a Necessity of repelling Force by Force.

But where the People have voluntarily resigned their natural Liberty, without any Restriction, as in *absolute* Monarchies; they must be content to fall a Prey to the brutal Passions of their Sovereign, whenever he thinks fit to resemble Satan, under the Character of the Lord's Anointed. Thanks be to GOD, this is not our Case. Our sage and provident Ancestors, were inspired with too great a Love for *Liberty*, and too tender a Concern for the Happiness of their Posterity, to make such an unconditional Submission, and entail upon them so fatal a Calamity: For, such is the Nature of our excellent Constitution, that amidst all the Prerogatives of the Crown, which are great and splendid, the *Liberty of the Subject*, is secure and inviolable. How must it swell the Breast of every BRITON, with Transport! while he surveys the despicable Slaves of *unlimited* Princes, to reflect, that his Person and Property are guarded by Laws, which the Sovereign himself cannot infringe: Nay, that in a Trial between his King and himself, his Majesty is obliged to put himself upon the Country, and submit the Controversy to the Decision of the Peers of his Subject.

Happy for us, were we duly thankful for those inestimable Blessings, and endeavoured to excel other Nations, as much in Virtue and Piety, as we do in our civil and religious Privileges! For my Part, I can never think of the late horrid and impious Attempt on our happy Constitution, without the warmest Gratitude, for that gracious Interposition of Providence, which averted the impending Ruin, and preserved our auspicious Government. Had our unrelenting Enemies succeeded in their detestable Designs; instead of enjoying our invaluable Liberties, we had long e'er now, beheld *Persecution* brandish her Sword, and felt the insulting Victor loading us with Chains: In a Word, we had seen *Tyranny*, like a ravenous Harpy, devouring the Fruits of our Industry;

and *Popery,* with her malignant Spirit, plunging us into the Depths of Misery.

Liberty gives an inexpressible Charm to all our Enjoyments. It imparts a Relish to the most indifferent Pleasure, and renders the highest Gratification the more consummately delightful. It is the Refinement of Life; it sooths and alleviates our Toils; smooths the rugged Brow of Adversity, and endears and enhances every Acquisition. The Subjects of a free State, have something open and generous in their Carriage; something of Grandeur and Sublimity in their Appearance, resulting from their Freedom and Independence, that is never to be met with in those dreary Abodes, where the embittering Circumstance of a precarious Property, mars the Relish of every Gratification, and damps the most magnanimous Spirits. They can think for themselves; publish their Sentiments, and animadvert on Religion and Government, secure and unmolested.

> *O happy Men, born under good Stars,*
> *Where, what is honest, you may freely think;*
> *Speak what you think, and write what you do speak;*
> *Not bound to servile Soothings!*   MARSTON's *Fawn.*[1]

But in *absolute* Monarchies, the whole Country is overspread with a dismal Gloom. *Slavery* is stamp'd on the Looks of the Inhabitants; and *Penury* engraved on their Visages, in strong and legible Characters. To prevent Complaints, the PRESS is prohibited; and a Vindication of the natural Rights of Mankind, is Treason. Every generous Spirit is broke and depressed: Human Nature is degraded, insulted, spurn'd, and outrag'd: The lovely Image of GOD, is defaced and disfigur'd, and the Lord of the Creation treated like the bestial Herd. The liberal Sciences languish: The politer Arts droop their Heads: Merit is banished to Cells and Deserts; and Virtue frowned into Dungeons, or dispatched to the Gallies: Iniquity is exalted: Goodness trod under Foot: Truth perverted; and the barbarous Outrages of Tyranny, sanctified and adored. The Fields lie waste and uncultivate: Commerce is incumbered with supernumerary Duties: The Tyrant riots in the Spoils of his People; and drains their Purses, to replenish his insatiate Treasury. He wages War against his own Subjects: Rapine and Plunder are his royal Amusements: His Sword is Reason and Law. *Stet pro Ratione voluntas.*[2] For the Extent of Territory, and to flatter his boundless Ambition, the Blood of the Subject is inhumanly squander'd; and a whole Nation devoted to Indigence and Ruin. Or if he spares the Wretches a miserable Morsel; ecclesiastic Tyranny snatches it up like a rapacious Vulture. Persecuting Zeal slashes the devouring Torch, and bathes the Sword in unbelieving Blood. Let but a Priest long for a Man's Fortune, or his Wife, and he pronounces him an Heretic; which renders his Death inevitable: Without further Ceremony, his Body is burnt for the Good of his Soul; and the Father of Mercies glorified by the cruel Slaughter of his rational Creatures. Visionary Monks turn plain Devotion into a solemn Farce, and make the ignorant Multitude proud of their Bondage, and exulting in their Infamy.

Does any one think the above Representation, the Result of a roving Fancy, or figur'd beyond the Life; let him take a Survey of *Rome*; e'er-while the Nurse of Heroes, and the Terror of the World; but now the obscene Haunt of sequestred Bigots, and effeminate Slaves. Where are now her *Scipios*, and *Tullys*, her *Brutuses,* and her *Catos*, with other Names of equal Lustre, who plann'd her Laws, and fought her Battles, during her Freedom and Independence? Alas! they are succeeded by cloistered Monks and castrated Musicians, in Subjection to a filthy old Harlot, that pretends to a Power of devouring her Mediator, and claims a Right to eat up her People. Let him survey all *Italy*, once the Seat of Arts and Arms, and every Thing great and valuable; now the joyless Theatre of Oppression and Tyranny, Superstition and Ignorance. Let him behold all this; and when he has finished his Survey, then let him *believe and tremble.*

But far otherwise, is the Condition of a free People. Under the mild and gentle Administration of a *limited* Prince, every Thing looks chearful and happy, smiling and serene. Agriculture is encouraged, and proves the annual Source of immense Riches to the Kingdom: The Earth opens her fertile Bosom to the Ploughshare, and luxuriant Harvests diffuse Wealth and Plenty thro' the Land: The Fields stand thick with Corn: The Pastures smile with Herbage: The Hills and Vallies are cover'd with Flocks and Herds: Manufactures flourish; and unprecarious Plenty recompenses the Artificer's Toil: In a Word, Nothing is seen but universal Joy and Festivity. Such is the Happiness of the People, under the blissful Reign of a good King. But do they get a Prince, whose Heart is poison'd with Regard to regal Authority, and who vainly imagines; that the Grandeur of Princes consists in making themselves feared; and accordingly plays the Devil in the Name of the Lord: They boldly assert their Rights, and call aloud for Justice; They cannot, they will not be enslaved. Sooner shall the royal Sinner have the Honour of Martyrdom, and the *Lord's Anointed* perish for his Iniquity, than the whole Frame of the Government be unhinged and dissolved.

At the same Time, that the Happiness of a *limited* Monarchy, exceeds that of a *despotic* Government, the Person of their King is much safer, as well as his Glory far superior, to the specious Glare, the tinsel Lustre, of an arbitrary Prince: He is beloved by a nation of Freemen and Heroes; while the other is fear'd and flattered by a Crowd of fawning Slaves and abject Dependents: He reigns in the Breasts of his People; and while he preserves their Affection, his Throne is founded on a Rock: Their Lives and Fortunes are at his Service. Where Inclination prompts, there needs no Force to compel, and where that is wanting, all Force is ineffectual. It may overpower, but it cannot conquer. The first Opportunity that offers, their Vengeance will break out; and break out like a smother'd Flame, with redoubled Fury: But the King, who has the Love of his People, is safe and happy: They revere him as their Father, their Benefactor; and consider their Prosperity inseparably connected with his. How miserably deluded, therefore, are such Princes, who place their Felicity in arbitrary Power? For without the Love of their Subjects, vain is Force, or rather the Exertion of it, their Ruin. Force will be resisted with Force; and a War once commenced, the Relation of King and Subject is forgotten, and both consider each other as Enemies, and the Worst of Enemies.

It is not standing Armies, numerous Guards, or a rich Exchequer, that constitute the Safety and Glory of a Monarch. These can only inspire Terror; and that no longer than the People are in a Capacity to defy them. The Prince, who hath Nothing else to maintain himself in the Possession of his Throne, holds it by a precarious Tenure: The Impotence of his People is his only Strength; and when they acquire sufficient Power, he is undone: But a King, who pursues true Glory and real Greatness, will never aim at absolute Dominion. Lawless Power, is a Power over Slaves, and void of every Thing sublime and generous. Obedience by Compulsion, is the Obedience of Vassals, who without Compulsion would disobey. The Affection of the People is the only Source of a chearful and rational Obedience; and such Obedience is the brightest Jewel in the Royal Diadem.

How signal is our Happiness, in being blessed with a Prince, form'd for the Friend of the Nation, and the Defender of the Liberties of *Europe!* A Prince, who despises the Thought of placing his Grandeur in the Violation of the Laws; but is nobly ambitious of reigning in the Hearts of his People: A Prince, who invariably exerts his native Greatness of Soul, and all his inherent and hereditary Virtues, in the Support of Truth, Religion and Liberty: A Prince, in fine, unemulous of arbitrary Sway; but ardently aspiring after those brighter Trophies, that are earn'd in the Paths of Virtue and heroic Deeds; in relieving the Injured, protecting the Oppressed, and by a diffusive Benevolence, promoting the Happiness of Mankind. Long, oh long may he still adorn the Throne of his Ancestors! and when the Sovereign Disposer of Events, shall at last, to the keen and universal Affliction of his People, translate him to the Possession of a Crown, eternal and incorruptible; we may presage, (which will be the only Consideration capable of alleviating our Sorrow,) the greatest Glory, and the brightest Triumphs, from his Royal Highness's eminent Virtues; whose future Reign promises the most distinguished Prosperity to the Nation; and will exhibit to *Britain,* a Monarch, from his benevolent Disposition, and princely Education, the Father of his People, as well as a shining Ornament to that illustrious Family, of which we have already seen two Heroes on the *British Throne;* the Scourges of Tyrants, and the Assertors of Liberty.

Z.

---

1. *Parasitaster, Or The Fawne,* a play (1606) by John Marston (1576–1634), English satirist and dramatist.

2. *Sit pro ratione voluntas.* "Let will replace reason." Juvenal, *Satires,* VI, 223.

Number V

THURSDAY, DECEMBER 28, 1752

On the Importation of MENDICANT Foreigners

To mortal Men great Loads allotted be;
But of all Packs, no Pack like Poverty.   HERRICK [1]

The Ingenuity and Importance of the following Letter, justly entitle it to a Place in this Paper.

To the INDEPENDENT REFLECTOR.

SIR,

I AM one of those, who, from their natural Disposition, and a Sense
of Duty, are strongly urged to pity and alleviate the Wants of human
Nature: Nor is there one, in the whole Catalogue of Christian Virtues,
that so much commands my Esteem, as *Charity*. — I behold, with Eyes
of Sorrow and Commiseration, the afflictive Condition of the Poor of
this City; who, at length, are become so vast a Burden to its Inhabitants, as, in a great Measure, to restrict the Exercise of that amiable
Virtue, in favour of its most worthy Objects. But, besides those abject
Sufferers, who, by the Frowns of Providence, have been cast into the
Hands of their more happy Fellow-Citizens, we are throng'd with
Foreigners, who are also the Subjects of still greater Mourning and
Desolation. Our Streets are daily crowded with *Germans*, whose thin
and ghastly Forms, more resembling Spectres than Men, are deeply
impressed with the dismal Traces of Famine, Sickness, Penury, and
Nakedness. These unhappy Wretches, allured by delusive Promises,
and visionary Prospects, of a comfortable Subsistence, have forsaken
their native Climes, to linger out their Lives amongst us, in the most
miserable inactive State of Poverty and Indigence. Hopeful Means to
settle this Infant Colony! — To what excessive Calamities must these
forlorn Creatures, unassisted by the Charitable and Benevolent, be
reduced! and to a generous Mind, how painful the Prevention of
distributing the Blessings of Prosperity, to the Needy and Distressed!
For what avails the most deep and affecting Sense of their Misery;
while the Regard we owe our own Country, denies us the Liberty of
easing the Weight of their Misfortunes, by a compassionate contribu-

tion to their Support! It is our Duty to feed the Hungry; to cloath the Naked, and to comfort the Sick: Yet amongst the most fervent Exercises of Charity, we are to remember, that the Interest of the Publick claims our continual Aid: Nor should we dispense our Bounties, with an unlimited Profusion, to the Poor, while they are some of the greatest Evils to which civil Society is exposed. — Thus we must often shut the Bowels of our Mercy, or injure the Community, of which we are Members. — Thus that which is virtuous in Theory, becomes vicious in Practice; — and while the mercenary Individual oppresses the Public, by perpetrating the most inhuman Actions, the honest Man is restrained by the Love of his Country, even from exercising the Offices of Humanity and Generosity. Reflections of this Sort must, naturally, enkindle our Resentment, against those who think it venial to enrich themselves, by crowding this City with so many unhappy Objects of Charity. Would they import none whose Indigence would render them burthensome to the Public, their Pretences to supply us with Servants, improve us in Handycrafts, and settle our Lands, might be sufficiently justifiable: But an Increase of the Number of our Poor, occasioned by the Importation of sickly, helpless and mendicant Foreigners, can evidently answer neither of those valuable Purposes.

In short, Mr. *Reflector*, as the Redress of Injuries of this Kind, is properly within your Design; and you have already given manifest Proofs, both of your Capacity, and the Honesty of your Intentions; it would rejoice me much, should this Matter be thought worthy of your Notice. I doubt not, that e'er long, you will have the Satisfaction to reflect, that your *weekly Labours* pass not unreguarded, by those to whose Care, the Welfare of this City and Province is entrusted: For which you may always depend upon the hearty Prayers, and sincere Wishes, of

Your constant Reader, and humble Servant,

T. D.

Di Patrii, servate domum, servati nepotem,
Vestrum hoc augurium, vestroque in numine Tropa est.[2]

VIRG.

CHARITY and PATRIOTISM are in their Natures, Virtues distinguishingly excellent, and merit the profoundest Reverence, in whatever Circumstances they recommend themselves to our View: To pay, therefore, no greater Respect to my worthy Correspondent, who so eminently possesses both, than a private Perusal of his Letter, would essentially derogate from the Character of the *Independent Reflector*. For which Reason, I beg Leave, to trouble the Public, with a brief Consideration of the Subject of his Complaint.

The Importation of indigent Foreigners, into this Infant Country, either for *supplying us with domestic Servants, or our Improvement in Handycrafts and Husbandry*, is a Matter, which, in my Opinion, should always meet with due Encouragement: But as they cannot possibly answer any other laudable Ends; it is undeniably true, that those who are not fit for some or other of those Occupations, must necessarily become a Burden to the Public. The Grievance complained of, consists not in the Importation of able, and industrious *Germans*, unincumbered with the Load of numerous Families; for they, be their Number ever so large, could all find Employments, in which they might be useful both to themselves and Society. But it is absurd, — it is criminal, to stock the Province with such, as, from their natural Indolence, their Ignorance of even the meanest Arts of Life, their bodily Infirmities, or the unhappy Circumstances of their Families, are absolutely incapable of advancing the Interest of the Countries into which they are imported; with such as stroll about our Streets in Idleness, loitering in the most pressing Difficulties; These are not only useless and insignificant Drones in Society; their Beggary and Indigence prove a most grievous Tax, upon the Industry, and other social Qualifications of our Inhabitants. To this calamitous Condition are they reduced, by the Inhumanity of those, who can, without the least Reluctance, sacrifice the Happiness of their Fellow-Creatures, and the Interest of the Public, to the mean, tho' self-delighting Prospects, of an unjust Accession to their Affluence.

A Country, such as was ours in its original Settlement, containing within its Boundaries, the most extensive Tracts unpeopled and unimproved, was naturally exposed to an Inundation of Foreigners. Sensible of this were our *primitive Rulers,** who thought it necessary to guard us with a Law, and set their Authority, as a Wall, around us. They *enacted*, that every *Foreigner*, who should come to inhabit this Province, not having a visible Estate, or manual Occupation, should give sufficient Security, against his

* *The first Assembly after the Revolution: See* Laws of New-York, *Chap.* 6.

falling a Burden upon the *Parish* in which he should reside. *They* also made it penal to Masters of Vessels, neglecting to inform the *Mayor of the City of New-York*, of the Number, Qualities and Conditions of their Passengers, within twenty-four Hours after their Arrival; and laid them under an Obligation, to re-transport those who could not find Security.[3] About thirty Years after,† *our Legislature*, jealous of the Provincial Interest, and fearful of the foreign Invasions of Beggary and Idleness, passed another Law to the like Purpose; by which, Masters of Vessels were required to carry their Passengers back to the Places from whence they came, under the Penalty of *Fifty Pounds*, or give Security, in the like Sum, to indemnify the Parish.[4] Thus armed with legal Authority, we might be effectually guarded against any but *home-bred Poverty and Indolence*, would *all* our Magistrates exert an *equal* Activity, in the Execution of their public Duties. But, alas! far from feeling the happy Effects of the Influence of those Laws, one would naturally imagine, that either thro' Antiquity, or Neglect, they are grown despicable in our Eyes, and have entirely lost their original Authority; and yet, never was their Execution so immediately necessary to the Welfare of this Province, as at present.

The *Small-Pox*, by its dismal Contagion, has spoiled the Habitations of our Poor, aggravated the Sufferings of those *Derelicts of Fortune*, to the highest Degree of Misery, and cruelly roughened the grim Countenance of a hoary and threatening *Winter*.[5] The Support of their Lives is become intollerably expensive; has exhausted the public Fund raised for that Purpose, and reduced our *Church-Wardens*, to the Necessity of borrowing *One Hundred and Fifty Pounds*, upon the Credit of the future Year. Moreover, a great Number of lately-imported *Germans*, of which *our Chief Magistrate, and Father of the City*, has, perhaps, never had an Account, tho' the above Acts ordain it under very severe Penalties, must be provided for at the private Expence of our Citizens. The Reason of this is very evident: It is because our Laws are not put in Execution, and the Masters of Vessels, by whom these Foreigners were imported, have not been required by the *Mayor*, (who has always claimed it as his Right,) to give Security to indemnify

† *See* Laws of New-York, *Chap.* 410.

the Parish: For it would be the highest Absurdity, to suppose that those Masters would voluntarily forfeit *Fifty Pounds* for each, by suffering their Passengers to beg for their Subsistence, had they actually given Security: Besides which, I am informed, that they have been indulged (who dare say for what Reason) in deferring a Submission to the Laws, till by the Death, or Sale of most of their Passengers, they may be reduced to so small a Number, as will render it less hazardous to the *Masters of Vessels,* to comply with the Prescriptions of the Acts. But whether the Ease and Gain of a few Individuals, is a justifiable Reason for oppressing the whole Community, I submit to the Determination of the honest and intelligent Reader. B.

The Author, according to his Promise, now takes the Opportunity to insert such Part of the Letter signed ATTICUS, *as in his Opinion, falls within the Design of his Paper*

To the INDEPENDENT REFLECTOR

SIR,

WHEN a base and servile Adherence to the private Schemes of a Party, has obliterated that Harmony and Union, which constitutes the Glory of a State, it not only erases from the Breast, the godlike Passions of Generosity and Benevolence; but oftentimes imperceptibly warps the Judgment, and throws a wrong Biass upon its calmest Determinations. Hence we find, an Opinion will be formed of a Writer and his Designs, from a pre-conceived Notion, that a Person of this selfish contracted Turn, has imbibed of his civil or religious Principles. Let an Author profess the utmost Neutrality to Party-Animosities, and write with all the Candor and Impartiality he professes; yet the Man who beholds every Object thro' the delusive Medium of his darling Passion, having made a shrewd Guess at the Author, can very readily spy out a political Licentiousness, in the justest Freedom of Enquiry; or infer an unscriptural Heresy, from the most rational Discourse on Religion. When he sets himself to expose the Corruption and Venality of the civil Officer, and the pious Arts of the orthodox Ecclesiastic, Bigotry and Tyranny will always raise a hideous Clamour of Atheism and Faction.

You, *Sir,* cannot expect any Share of the *Aura Popularis,* or Gale of Favour, to blow from this Quarter. A Writer who would employ his Genius in the Service of the Public, must have Constancy enough to bear the severest Reproaches; and a Resolution even to suffer the *Martyrdom* of his Reputation.

But, I am so much prejudiced in Favour of my Countrymen, that I question not there are many Readers among them, unshackled with the Fetters of Prejudice,— Friends to a just Freedom of Thought, and Independency of Reflection. Tho' these may be few in Number; yet I doubt not, as an INDEPENDENT REFLECTOR, you will esteem the Applause of One such, preferable to the Shouts of a Million of abject Slaves and contracted Bigots. In an Age of general Depravity of Manners, the Influence of Probity and Good-Sense is always slow, and gains Ground by imperceptible Degrees: But tho' the still Voice of Reason be not constantly attended to; yet she will force a Passage at last, and triumph over popular Prejudices and private Passions.

As your professed Intention is, to point out the Abuses that have crept into our little State; and to offer such Proposals to your Fellow-Citizens, as you think will have the best Tendency to correct or remove them, — every Friend to the Interest of his Country, must approve and applaud the Design. As your declared Motive is, to oppose the Encroachments of Corruption, and the illegal Domination of Men in Power, — the disinterested Patriot will animate and encourage you. As Prophaneness on the one Hand, and Superstition on the other, are equally to feel the Strokes of your Displeasure, — the rational Religionist will rejoice at the Discovery of an Advocate.

The Life of a periodical Author, like that of a Christian, is a continued Warfare upon Earth. While there are such Passions as Malice, Hatred, and Envy, he can no more hope to escape the Censure and Ill-Will of those whose professed Principles he combats, or whose concealed Practices he detects and exposes, than a celebrated Beauty, can expect to avoid the Obloquy and Detraction, of the less comely Part of her Sex.

But if you, *Sir,* (as you have declared) are exerting your Talents in the real Service of your Country, in Vindication of the civil and sacred Rights of Mankind, and in the Promotion of Virtue and Good-Manners among your Fellow-Citizens; no innocent Person will have Reason to complain, that he has been injured by you, in his Estate, in his Office, or in his Reputation. This Reflection will afford you a solid and well-grounded Satisfaction, amidst the unreasonable Censures of your Enemies: And you will have the Happiness, to retire at last from the public View, conscious of having acted from a benevolent Regard to the Good of the Society, of which you are a Member; and becoming the Character you have assumed of an *INDEPENDENT REFLEC-TOR.*   ATTICUS.

The Gentleman who has so strong a Sense of the Value of Liberty, and so just an Abhorrence of Slavery, may be assured, that the Fact he has suggested, shall be made a proper Use of in some future Paper: —Nor is the Author indifferent, to the Continuation of the Correspondence of a Writer, so ardently enflamed with the Love of his Country.

I also acknowledge the Receipt of a second Letter from my copious Correspondent, Shadreck Plebianus *(who I hope well not forget his Promise of* filling a Ream) *which shall be inserted the first Opportunity.*

1. "Poverty the Greatest Pack," *Hesperides*, 716.

2. "Gods of my fathers: Save this house, save my grandson, Yours is this omen, and under your protection stands Troy." *Aeneid*, II, 703.

3. These restrictions were contained in the provincial statute of May 13, 1691, and the municipal ordinance of April 22, 1691. *Colonial Laws of New York*, I, 237–238; *Minutes of the Common Council of the City of New York, 1675–1776*, 8 vols. (New York, 1905), I, 220.

4. July 27, 1721. *Colonial Laws of New York*, II, 56–61.

5. A smallpox epidemic raged in New York during 1752, so severe that the Assembly was prorogued in March to permit the members to escape to the country. By October almost every family in the city had been infected. Even as this issue of the *Reflector* was appearing, Livingston's infant son succumbed to the disease. Poignantly he announced the tragic event to a friend: "I lost him three weeks ago in the smallpox after my heart was knit to him by a thousand of his little Endearing Tricks and Blandishments." Livingston to Noah Welles, January 17, 1753, Johnson Family Papers, Yale (hereafter cited as JFP, Yale). On the epidemic, see John Duffy, *Epidemics in Colonial America* (Baton Rouge, 1953), p. 86.

Number VI

THURSDAY, JANUARY 4, 1753

A *Vindication of the* MORAVIANS, *against the Aspersions of their Enemies* [1]

Lex Nova non se vindicat ultore gladio.   TERTUL.
Nova et inaudita est ista prædicatio, quæ verberibus exigit fidem.
                                           GROTIUS [2]

To engage in controversial Points of Divinity, and commence a flaming Zealot in religious Debates, is beneath the Character of a Writer, animated with a Love to Mankind, and entertaining a nobler Idea of Religion, than to confine it, to the speculative Opinion of a particular Set of Christians. Besides, it is invading the Province of a certain Profession, who plead a Commission, to wage the wordy War, about the Externals of Religion, and to demonstrate their Devotion to the PRINCE OF PEACE, by virulent Rage, and open Hostilities, against their Brethren. To them, therefore, I resign those unenvied Laurels, those disgraceful Trophies. In such Disputations, I am not ambitious of carrying the Prize. But to defend every Sect, of whatever Denomination, in the undisturbed Enjoyment of their civil and religious Liberties, and to repress every persecuting Spirit that offers them Violence; — to expose that barbarous Zeal, which would even injure their Persons, was it not restrained by the milder Law of the Land; — to promote universal Benevolence amongst Christians of different Professions; — and to beat down all savage Wrath about Opinions, where the Conduct is irreproachable with Immorality: All this falls within my Jurisdiction; and here I claim a Right, by Virtue of the *Reflectorial Authority*, wherewith I am invested, to command the Peace, and humble the Criminal. I consider such ecclesiastical Inquisitors, not only as the Blemish of Christianity, but as frantic Incendiaries, and Disturbers of the publick Tranquility.

Defamation uttered from the Pulpit, is still Defamation; and so much more insufferable, as the Offender prostitutes the Place dedicated to the God of Peace and Love, to discharge his Rage, Invective, and Malevolence.

The Pulpit-Scold is the most despicable Scold in the World. He is a cowardly Scold, that gives his Antagonist no Opportunity of scolding back. From this Paper, therefore, will I preach against every such Preacher, and make the PRESS reverberate the Calumnies of the PULPIT.

Never did any Sect spring up in the Christian World, void of superstitious Rites, and holy Gimcracks, but it gave great Offence to *High Church.** A People who worship God, as he requires to be worshipped, that is, in Spirit and in Truth, are a living Reproach to those, who compliment him with Bows and Capers, and other bodily Adoration, which he never required: Nor can it be otherwise from the very Reason and Nature of Things: For a Religion made by human Contrivance for the Sake of Power and Wealth, must necessarily be at perpetual Variance, with a Religion revealed by God, and consisting in inward Purity, and Holiness of Life. The honest Simplicity and Spirituality of the One, is an eternal Satire upon the antic Mimickry, and idolatrous Trumpery of the Other. Hence such Priests, *as teach for Doctrines the Commandments of Men,* and convert Religion into a Divinity Shop, will ever be misrepresenting and vilifying those pestilent Hereticks, who lower the Price of their Commodities, by acknowledging no other Rule than the Scriptures, and wickedly preferring the Word of God, to the establish'd Orthodoxy. They will load them with all the Infamy and Slander, that impotent Malice and priestly Rhetoric can suggest.

What is the particular Frame and Constitution of the Church of *Moravia,* I never had the Curiosity to enquire; tho' I dare say, if it be replete with idle and ridiculous Gewgaws, it hath the good Graces of not a few Gentlemen in Black.

But the Sect distinguished by that Appellation amongst us, I

* *By* High Church *in this Place, I do not mean any Church in particular; but the Popes and Persecutors of all Churches, whether they be Popes of* Rome, England, Holland *or* Geneva.

have had the Opportunity to be a little acquainted with. Of these I form my Judgment by their Actions, the only Touchstone of a Man's Heart. *By their Fruit ye shall know them.* They are such a People as that no Man can get any Thing by their Religion, but internal Tranquility, and Peace of Conscience, arising from an inviolable Attachment to the Principles and Precepts of it. They are a plain, open, honest, inoffensive People: They profess universal Benevolence to all Men, and are irreprehensible in their Lives and Conversations: In a Word, their whole Conduct evidences their Belief, that *the Kingdom of Christ is not of this World.* Hence it is no Wonder, that they give Umbrage to those of the Clergy, who beg to be excused, from believing that Part of the Gospel, as do but too many of the Priests of all Denominations whatever.

In Regard to their religious Principles, it must be own'd, they have their peculiar Sentiments, which distinguish them from others. But that is saying no more, than that they think for themselves, or at least, that they think not like others; and *Rome* is just as far from *Geneva*, as *Geneva* from *Rome*. For ORTHODOXY, as it is commonly used, is a meer levitical Engine, that has done more Mischief to Mankind, than all the Tyrants that ever ravag'd the Globe. Every Man is *orthodox* to himself, and *heretical* to all the World besides; but that he should therefore be calumniated or butcher'd, the Scripture saith not: Nay, I cannot find, by the Bible-Account of the last Day, that one Interrogatory will be proposed concerning a Man's Opinion; but that every One will be judged *according to the Deeds done in the Body.*

> *For Modes of Faith, let flaming Zealots fight;*
> *He can't be wrong, whose Life is in the Right.*   POPE.[3]

But pray wherein consists the dreadful Heterodoxy of the *Moravians?* They believe that JESUS CHRIST was commissioned by GOD, to teach the Religion contain'd in the *New Testament:* That he prov'd his Mission by Miracles; died on the Cross to expiate Sin; rose from the Dead, and ascended to Heaven. So that it is impossible, they should maintain any Tenets, inconsistent with the Fundamentals of Christianity. For whoever believes, that

Jesus Christ was the promised MESSIAH, sent of GOD, to instruct Mankind, and *practises* the Morality he taught; is to all Intents and Purposes, a compleat Christian; tho' he be as incredulous about the Divine Right of Episcopacy, as the Divine Right of Geography; nor ever heard of the Synod of *Dort* [4] in his Life.

As to their Notion about the Unlawfulness of bearing Arms; it is well known, that the Fathers, upon whose Authority the Clergy so much rely, when it makes for their Interest, were almost universally, as some contend, of the same Opinion; and had all the World been so, Mankind would not have been plagued with those holy Wars, and priestly Massacres, that have so often delug'd the Earth with human Blood.

Great Offence is taken at their Simplicity and Moderation. "This is all Craft and Artifice, to inveigle the Unwary, and make Proselytes, by their courteous Carriage." Be it so. I hope Affability and Condescention, are at least, as Christian, as those *flaming* Expressions of our Love to God, and *burning* Proofs of our Love to our Brethren, that have generally terminated in *material Fire*, or a *real Dungeon*.

But what gives still greater Provocation to ill-natured Ecclesiastics, is that heretical *Moravian* Practice, of washing each other's Feet. No wonder if our Sovereign Lords the Clergy, should libel and defame a Sect, whose exemplary Humility is a perfect Burlesque, upon all spiritual Pride and Precedence. And yet, as the Case happens, this very Practice, in the Judgment of many Learned Men, is as much instituted by the divine Author of Christianity, as *Baptism* or the *Lord's Supper*, and more peremptorily commanded than either; as any One, say they, that will be pleased to consult the 13th Chapter of St. *John's* Gospel, without a priestly Comment, may be convinced of.

It is indeed astonishing, that Dissenters, who *so much*, and *so justly*, magnify the Reasonableness of *Toleration*, when themselves are concerned, should at the same Time treat as Hereticks, a People whom the Parliament hath acknowledged as *good Christians*; which, perhaps, is more than can be said for any Church in the Province.

The Religion of the *Moravians*, is as orthodox as any Religion in the Realm, except only with this Difference, that it promises Nothing but Peace of Mind; while some others are decorated with Places and Preferments, greater Revenues, and better Wages.

Nothing can be more unmannerly, as well as unchristian, than for any Protestant Minister, within his Majesty's Dominions, to stigmatize and vilify, a numerous Body of People, protected by the same Laws, and incorporated under the same Constitution with himself: Nay, the very Thing that ought to inspire these little Popes, with Benevolence and Friendship for this Sect, *to wit,* its having a particular Law in its Favour, seems only to exasperate their Malice, and add fresh Vengeance to their Anathemas. The *Drum ecclesiastic,* has been beat louder than ever, and the Pulpit resounded with the Moravian Heresy.

Ut littus Hyla, Hyla, omne resonaret.　　　VIRG.[5]

Instead of giving them the *Right Hand of Fellowship,* nothing is more common than to see a Parson mount the Pulpit, and like a Dragoon, worry and hector the most peaceable People in the World, for believing in Christ, without worshipping the Clergy.

For my Part, I conceive it would be much more for the Cause of Virtue and Religion, were these fulminating Levites, rather to distinguish their Zeal, by inculcating universal Charity, and the indispensable Duty of a holy Life; than by Mob-Reproaches and Billingsgate Defamation, against a People to all Appearance as good as themselves. Let them calculate their Sermons for the Destruction of the Empire of Darkness, and I am sure, it will tend more to the Happiness and Repose of their Flocks, than a Cart-Load of Libels devised for the Extirpation of *Moravianism.* Nothing can account for this unchristianlike Behaviour, but an inordinate Degree of Pride and Self-Applause, whereby those religious Censors are blindly elevated into a divine Infallibility. For could they imagine themselves liable to err, as well as others; it would naturally affect them with a Diffidence of their own Opinions, and induce them to cast a charitable Aspect, upon the supposed Errors of their Brethren. A proper Consideration of the Frailty of human Nature, might convince them, that their most darling Tenets, founded only upon probable Evidence, may possibly be false; and that in opposing the inoffensive Doctrines of *Moravianism*, they may become *Persecutors of the Truth.* Can they be said to answer the Ends of their Mission, who, instead of pointing out the Road to Virtue and Happiness, denounce the Terrors of the Law, against those whose *Conversation is void of Offence towards God and Man?* Or, can they possibly recommend a *Gospel-Simplicity,* who Execute their Vengeance upon its best Examples?

Without Offence to the Understandings of those enlightened Preachers of the Word, I would recommend to them, as a Pattern, the Sermon of JESUS upon the Mount. This contains a summary Account of the Christian Virtues, and the Happiness attending their Practice. There they may learn, that if they expect to inherit a celestial Kingdom, they must be *Peace-Makers,* and not *Persecutors* of the Consciences of Men; and notwithstanding any Attempt, to oppress the *Lowly in Spirit,* they shall, in the End, *be exalted.*

If in any Case I could recommend it to the Civil Magistrate, to interfere in Matters of Religion, it would be in this; for he should not only avoid persecuting his Subjects, for differing from him in their Opinions; he should also prevent their persecuting each other. Besides, can any Thing argue a greater Contempt of Law, than the Lessons we often receive from the Pulpit, against maintaining any Correspondence with the *Moravians,* when the Wisdom of our Nation, has declared them to be proper Members of Society? In short, our ecclesiastical Dictators should be taught, that they offend their great Master, while

> —— *Their* weak unknowing Hand
> Presume *His* Bolts to throw;
> And deal Damnation round the Land,
> On each *they* judge *His* Foe.[6]

Z. & B.

The Letter and Resolves of the Widows, relating to the Paper on the Road *and* City-Watch, *is come to Hand, and shall have a Place in my next.*

I have also received sundry other Letters; but as the Variety of Business, which multiplies upon me, renders it impossible to insert them at present: I doubt not my kind Correspondents will excuse my deferring their Publication till I am more at Leisure.

1. The Moravians, or United Brethren, were a German pietist sect centered largely in Pennsylvania but with offshoots in Georgia, North Carolina, and New York. At Bethlehem, Pennsylvania, they established a music center famous for its performances of Bach. They aroused hostility, however, by their opposition to military service, denunciation of slavery, and refusal to take oaths in legal proceedings. In New York there were small groups of the Brethren in Dutchess County, Staten Island, and New York City. Livingston defended them in the face of widespread suspicion, even among his own Presbyterian coreligionists, who regarded them as antinomian. The New Jersey Presbyterian preacher, Gilbert Tennent, had publicly warned New Yorkers of their heresies and "detestable Opinions": "I think their Principles are as strange a Medley of Confusion as ever I saw." (*New-York Weekly Post-Boy*, February 1, 1743.) William Smith, Jr., had also charged them with drawing their strength largely from "female proselytes from other societies." (*The History of the Late Province of New-York . . .* , 2 vols. [New York, 1830], I, 261.) Livingston continued to display the same charity toward the Moravians throughout his life.

2. The quotation from Tertullian is translated: "The New Testament does not vindicate itself with an avenging sword." The one from Grotius reads: "This is a new and unheard of prophecy which enforces faith by floggings."

3. *Essay on Man*, Epistle iii, slightly misquoted.

4. The Synod of Dort (or Dordrecht) was the assembly of the Dutch Reformed Church convened in 1618 to settle the bitter controversy between Arminians and Calvinists within the church. The assembly sat for over six months and adopted canons which were generally accepted as the doctrine of the Reformed churches in Holland.

5. "Till all the shore rang 'Hylas! Hylas!'," *Eclogues*, VI, 44. Hylas was Hercules' young companion who, during the voyage of the Argonauts, was lured into a well by the Naiads and disappeared. The Argonauts called to him in vain.

6. Pope, "The Universal Prayer."

Number VII

THURSDAY, JANUARY 11, 1753

A Proposal of some farther Regulations, for the speedier and more effectual Extinguishing of FIRES, that may happen in this City

— Vaga per veterem dilapso flamma culinam
Vulcano, summum properabat lambere Tectum.   Hor.[1]

IT is a common Observation, that the Inhabitants of this City are remarkable for their Agility in extinguishing Fires: And since so judicious a Poet as *Virgil*, hath compared the Industry of the *Tyrians*, to the Labours of the Bee; I think the amazing Celerity, with which my Fellow-Citizens cluster together, at the Ringing of the FIRE-BELL, may fitly be resembled, to the Swarming of those curious Insects, at the Sound of the Instrument used for that Purpose. To pursue the Simile, there is not a Drone amongst them; but the Rich and the Poor, are alike indefatigable in preserving their Neighbour's Property, from the devouring Flames. It is one universal Hurry, and incessant Activity: Nay, they have often exposed themselves to the Peril of their Lives, and performed Feats almost surpassing Comprehension or Belief. They toil with unwearied Diligence, and seem insensible of the Danger which threatens them. In a Word, they stand in the Midst of the Flames, as unconcerned as Salamanders, mocking at Fear, and striving to out-vie each other, in suppressing the general Calamity. A noble Emulation, and worthy the highest Eulogium!

Nor ought the Companies, lately formed for the Preservation of Goods at Fires, be passed over, without that Share of Applause, which is due to so laudable an Undertaking.[2] An Undertaking, that deserves to be commemorated with Gratitude and Honour; as it exhibits a glaring Attestation of their public Spirit, and exemplary Devotion to their Country. They have been at a considerable Expence, in furnishing themselves with a proper Apparatus; and given undeniable Proofs, of the extensive Utility, of their respective Societies. Animated by their Example, many others project Expedients, equally tending to the public Benefit; and reap for their Reward, an equal Share of public Gratitude!

For my own Part, as my future Speculations will, on the one Hand, evince my Reluctance, at sparing the Rod, where Correction is necessary; so they will, on the other, shew my Readiness, to bestow all due Honour, upon whatever deserves the Approbation of the Public. Would to Heaven, I never had an Opportunity but to praise, with an absolute Privation of the least Necessity, for the Exercise of my Chastisements! From this disinterested Impartiality, I cannot refrain from paying to Merit, its just Tribute of Commendation and Renown. I shall therefore, take the Liberty, still a Moment to detain the Reader, in order to express my own, and my Countrymen's grateful Sense of the Corporation's Liberality, in making such ample Provision for the Extinguishing of Fires, that we are in Want of but few Things requisite to that End. As most Inventions, however, arrive at Perfection, by gradual Improvements, there is, I conceive, a Possibility of super-adding sundry Regulations, for the speedier controuling the Rage, of that terrible Element.

It hath more than once been observed, that our Engines are incapable of throwing Water, to such a Height as is sometimes necessary. Of this we had a dreadful Instance, when the Steeple of *Trinity Church* took Fire. On that Occasion, we observed, with universal Terror, that the Engines could scarce deliver the Water, to the Top of the Roof. The Spire, however, was far beyond its Reach; and had not Providence smiled upon the astonishing Dexterity and Resolution of a few Men, who ascended the Steeple within, that splendid and superb Edifice, had, in all Probability, been reduced to Ashes.

We are, therefore, in Want of at least one Engine of the largest Size, which throws Water about One Hundred and Seventy Feet high, discharges two Hundred Gallons in a Minute, and costs about Sixty Five Pounds Sterling. Such an Engine would have another Advantage, besides carrying the Water to so great a Height. The prodigious Quantity it deliver'd, would be of unspeakable Service at all Fires.

Another Thing, in which our present Method of extinguishing Fires, is capable of farther Improvement, is this: It is usual for People, in Cases of Fire, to form themselves into two Lines, the One to convey the full Buckets to the Engine, and the Other to return the empty Ones. Now it frequently happens, that when the Engine is full, Word is given, to *stop Water*. This occasions a total Cessation in the Conveyance of more Water to the Engine, as well as the greatest Confusion in the Ranks; the Consequence of which is, that the Engine is empty, before the Ranks regain their former Regularity, which creates a considerable Intermission in its playing. The mischievous Effects of this are apparent, on the least Reflection; for these Interruptions, be they ever so small, give the Fire Time to resume its Fury, and which, if often repeated, requires a much greater Quantity of Water for its total Suppression, than would be necessary, was the Engine continued in one regular and uninterrupted Exercise. This Inconvenience might, I conceive, be easily remedied, by supplying each Engine with a large Tub, of at least the Size of an Hogshead; which being made of Cedar, might be sufficiently strong, and at the same Time light enough, to be portable by two Men: This Vessel ought to be placed near the Engine, and all the full Buckets to be emptied into it. From this capacious Tub, three or four Men might constantly and equally keep the Engine replenished; which would enable it to play an equable and uniform Stream. The happy Effects resulting from such an Expedient, would, I am persuaded, be immediately visible: And indeed, the Truth of the Proposition is evident, and constantly exemplified in Life: For a Pail of Water, sprinkled by Degrees on a common Fire, will very little affect it: In reality, all the Water may be wasted without extinguishing it; which nevertheless, thrown on it together, would be sufficient entirely to quench it.

Again, Fires often happen so remote from Water, as to occasion a Want of People, and in Places where the Passage is too narrow, to admit of a sufficient Number of double Lines, to supply the Engines. In such Cases, I would propose, that People should form themselves into three single Lines, instead of two double Ones; the two exterior Ones for the full Buckets; which, as they are emptied into the great Tub, should be laid at the Feet of the first Man of the inner Line, to be reconveyed to the Water. This Line would be sufficient, to return the empty Buckets of the other two. And by that Method, three Men might do the usual Business of four, and in three Quarters of the Space of Ground.

This Economy is well worthy our Consideration; nor can we, on these Occasions, be too well supplied with Water. With respect to the Tubs before-mentioned, I must take the Liberty, to entreat our Magistrates, that we remain no longer without them. For could they be applied to no other Use, than what I have already pointed out, that alone would render them extremely serviceable: But they will also, be of signal Advantage in other Respects: They will, in a great Measure, secure the Engines against being clogged and choaked with the Sand and Pebbles scoop'd into the Buckets at the River Side: For the Buckets being emptied into them, the Sand and Pebbles will sink to the Bottom, and the Water only be thrown into the Engines.

Another Advantage that would arise from the Use of such Tubs, is, that no Movement or Change of Situation in the Engine, nor any other Accident that might impede its playing, need occasion any Interruption to the Ranks, in conveying Water; to which, they are at present greatly subject, on every such Emergency: For there being no Reservoir to receive the Water, when the Engine is full, or changing Place, the Lines must, during that Interval, either cease conveying it, or set the full Buckets on the Ground, where they are generally overset, and the Water lost.

It is further to be remarked, that many Parts of the City, too remote from the River, to be supplied with Water from thence, are very deficient in public Wells. I am sensible, that when this has been mentioned, it hath often been esteemed a full Reply, that the People have Wells enough in their Yards. But the Inconveniences generally attending the bringing Water from thence, are sufficient Reasons, for making more public Wells in the Streets: For, without assigning any other, the Opportunity it affords for robbing the Houses, thro' which the Water is brought, is an Evil almost as bad as the Fire itself.

To what hath already been proposed, the Reader will give me Leave to add, that some of my Countrymen, whom Nature hath blessed with better Lungs, than Understandings, are often, on these melancholy Occasions, very loud and vociferous; and others as fond of being Directors, and exercising a kind of Superintendency over the Rest. Thro' this Confusion and Vociferation, the Instructions given by the proper Directors, are often neglected, and generally incapable of being heard. It would therefore, be of great Use, if People would make it a Rule not to speak, but when it is absolutely necessary. In a Word, let them reserve their Loquacity, till they Return to their Spouses, when probably they will be relieved from the Pain, of so long a Silence, by sundry pertinent and momentous Queries.

Add to all this, that it ought invariably to be observed, at great Fires, that all the large Engines play nearly on the same Part of the Fire. The Advantage of this may not, perhaps, appear at first Sight; but on the least Consideration, it will easily be observed, that the Heat of a great Fire, will drink up a single Stream of Water, without any perceptible Diminution; and in like Manner, the several different Parts of it, will bear several different Streams of Water, without being sensibly affected; but let them all be directed to the same Part of the Fire, and they will effectually extinguish it there; which done, the Streams may be directed to some other Part, till the Whole be suppressed. The small Engines may, in the mean Time, be kept employed, in preventing the Communication of the Fire, to the neighbouring Buildings.

The preceeding Proposals are only intended as rude Suggestions, so far to engage the Attention of the Curious, as either to improve these imperfect Hints, or to substitute in their Room, more effectual Expedients, for the readier Extinguishing of Fire: For I am not so attached to my own Notions, as to prefer them, to what may appear more likely to answer the Purpose; but should chearfully insert in this Paper, any more plausible Project, with proper Respect to the ingenious Correspondent.

X.

THO' the following Resolves contain a greater Encomium on the Author, than he thinks himself intitled to; yet as they were drawn up by a venerable Club of Widow'd-Matrons, he thinks himself obliged, in Complaisance to such respectable Correspondents, to publish so precious a Memorial of their well-meant Gratitude: A Memorial which, to a Person of his independent Principles, will be a sufficient Recompence for a Thousand Obloquies of the commission'd Malefactor, or dignified Criminal, who calumniates him, only because he dreads to have his Conduct, scrutiniz'd and expos'd.

To the INDEPENDENT REFLECTOR

SIR,

LAST Monday Night, we, the Subscribers met at the Room of the Widow *M.K.* according to Summons respectively received in the Morning, in order to join with her, in a Letter of Thanks to the *Reflector,* for publishing her Letter concerning the Road and City-Watch, with so much Honour. As soon as we were seated, the Company desired *Mrs. Threadneedle* to read your Paper, with an audible Voice (during all which Time there actually was, however incredible it may seem, a profound Silence,) after which we came to the following Resolves.

Resolved,

That the Thanks of this Club, be presented to the *Independent Reflector,* for engaging so heartily, in the Defence of poor Widows, and pointing out the Defects of a Law, which, in our feminine Opinion, hath neither Rhime nor Reason, but opens a Door for enormous Roguery, and Oppression triumphant.

Resolved,

That he be presented with our humble Petition, to resume the same Subject, by the First of *May* next; unless in the mean Time, there appears convincing Evidence, of the Contrition and Amendment, of our common Oppressor.

Resolved,

That for the Future, *Mrs. Threadneedle* and *M. K.* be a Committee of the whole Club, to consider of Grievances, to be laid before the *Reflector.*

Resolved,

That the said *Mrs. Threadneedle*, do present the Author of the *Reflector*, with a Pair of fringed party-colour'd Mittens, at our joint Expence, as soon as he is discovered, in Memorial of our Gratitude, for his pathetic Representation of our Calamity. In Witness whereof, wishing him a *Happy New-Year*, we have hereunto set our Hands, the First Day of *January*, 1753.

M. K.

Z.

Alice Threadneedle.
Rebecca Nettletop.
Biddy Loveless.
Martha Frost.
Sarah Ridinghood.
Deborah Wrinkle.

The Author takes this Opportunity, for returning his Thanks, to the Reverend Gentleman, who did him such signal Honour, last Sunday, as to make him the Subject of his Sermon; and greatly admires his Ingenuity in proving him to be the Gog *and* Magog [3] *of the* Apocalypse, *who have, hitherto, puzzled all the Divines in the World. Nor doth he despair of the further Honour, to supply this ardent Preacher, in the Course of his Papers, with fresh Materials, to display his Talents, in unravelling Prophecies; in discovering the Accomplishment of many of the Old Testament Types, in the* Independent Reflector, *and exerting his Zeal, against all Sects but his own.*

The Author has the highest Detestation of that Perfidy to the young Lady, mentioned in the Letter signed Philogamus, *from* Newark; *and tho' the Villain that abused her, justly deserves to be stigmatized, yet she, and our Correspondent, must excuse him from any Reflections on a Subject that is not within the Design of this Paper.*

The Letter signed Amicus, *relating to a Light-House, shall not escape my Attention.*

---

1. ". . . as Vulcan slipped out through the old kitchen, the vagrant flame hastened to lick the roof." Horace, *Satires*, I, 5, 54.

2. New York's fire companies, like Boston's, consisted of citizens appointed to fire duty by the common council and organized into companies of seven for each of the city's six wards. They were unpaid but relieved of other civic obligations. Peterson and Edwards, *New York*, II, 135–137; Carl Bridenbaugh, *Cities in Revolt* (New York, 1955), pp. 100–104.

3. The two false prophets sent out by Satan to deceive mankind immediately before the final resurrection, Rev. 20:7–8.

Number VIII

THURSDAY, JANUARY 18, 1753

A brief Consideration of NEW-YORK, with respect to its natural Advantages: Its Superiority in several Instances, over some of the neighbouring Colonies

O fortunatos nimium Bona si sua norint EBORACOS.   *Virg.*[1]

Awake the Muse, bid Industry rejoice,
And the rough Sons of lowest Labour smile.
THOM[SON] *Brit.*[2]

WITH Respect to what Nature has done for us, there is not a happier People in the World, than the Inhabitants of this Province. I hope the assigning a few Instances from whence this Happiness is derived, will not be displeasing to them, as it tends to inflame them with a Love of their Country, and at the same Time excite their Gratitude for the Happiness they enjoy.

The Necessaries of Life, which for that Reason, are its most substantial Blessings, we possess with the richest Affluence. The natural Strength and Fertility of the Soil we live upon, will, by Grazing and Tillage, always continue to us, the inexhaustible Source of a profuse Abundance. There is nothing we possess, that Mankind can well be without, and scarce any Thing they really want, but we either enjoy, or may easily procure, in luxuriant Plenty.

Provisions, in short, are our Staple, and whatever Country sufficiently abounds with so necessary a Commodity, can never fail of Wealth, a sure Magazine! which will always be attended with Power and Plenty, and many other Springs of social Happiness, as its natural Concomitants. The Want of such an unfailing Staple, is a Fountain of Misery, to a Province on the East, of more Shew than Substance, Pomp than Riches. By constant Supplies from our Exuberance, we hold them in Debt, and annually increase it; while we are so happy, as to taste the Sweets of the Truth of what they have remarked, that there are fewer poor Men in this, than in any one of the Plantations on the Continent.[3] I have, myself, spent a Month in their Metropolis, the most splendid Town in *North-America,* not without some Pleasure, in reflecting, that I had not a Morsel of Bread, even at their common Tables, that was not the Produce of this Colony: Nor has the prettiest Beau in the Town, so easy an Access to their Ladies, as a certain Baker of ours, universally celebrated there, for the Goodness of his Biskets.

But this Opulence is not our only Advantage, for raising the Trade of this Province, and enlarging its Extent: Every Thing in it conspires to make *New-York* the best Mart on the Continent.[4] Our Coasts are regular, and the Navigation up to the City, from the Sea, short and bold, and by a good *Light-house,* might be render'd safe and easy.

High-Roads, which in most trading Countries, are extremely expensive, and awake a continual Attention for their Reparation, demand from us, comparatively speaking, scarce any *public* Notice at all. The whole Province is contained in two narrow Oblongs, extending from the City East and North, having Water Carriage from the Extremity of One, and from the Distance of One Hundred and Sixty Miles of the Other; and by the most accurate Calculation, has not, at a Medium, above Twelve Miles of Land Carriage throughout its whole Extent. This is one of the strongest Motives to the Settlement of a new Country, as it affords the easiest and most speedy Conveyance from the remotest Distances, and at the lowest Expence. The Effects of this Advantage are greater than we usually observe, and are, therefore, not sufficiently admired.

The Province of *Pennsylvania,* has a fine Soil, and, thro' the Importation of *Germans,* abounds with Inhabitants; but being a vast inland Country, its Produce must, of Consequence, be brought to a Market over a great Extent of Ground, and all by Land-Carriage. Hence it is, that *Philadelphia* is crowded with Waggons,

Carts, Horses, and their Drivers: A Stranger, at his first Entrance, would imagine it to be a Place of Traffic, beyond any one Town in the Colonies; while at *New-York* in particular, to which the Produce of the Country is all brought by Water, there is more Business, at least Business of Profit, tho' with less Shew and Appearance: Not a Boat in our Rivers is navigated with more than two or three Men at most; and these are perpetually coming in from, and returning to, all Parts of the adjacent Country, in the same Employments, that fill the City of *Philadelphia* with some Hundreds of Men, who, in respect to the public Advantage, may justly be said, to be laboriously idle: For, let any one nicely compute the Expence of a Waggon, with its Tackling; the Time of two Men in attending it; their Maintenance; four Horses, and the Charge of their Provender, on a Journey of One, tho' they often come, Two Hundred Miles; and he will find, these several Particulars accumulate a Sum far from being inconsiderable. All this Time, the *New-York* Farmer is in the Course of his proper Business, and the unincumbered Acquisitions of his Calling; for, at a Medium, there is scarce a Farmer in the Province, that cannot transport the Fruits of a Year's Labour, from the best Farm, in three Days, at a proper Season, to some convenient Landing, where the Market will be to his Satisfaction, and all his Wants from the Merchant, cheaply supplied: Besides which, one Boat shall steal into the Harbour of *New-York*, with a Lading of more Burden and Value, than *forty* Waggons, *One Hundred and Sixty* Horses, and *Eighty* Men, into *Philadelphia*; and perhaps with less Noise, Bluster or Shew, than One.

Prodigious is the Advantage we have in this Article alone; I shall not enter into an abstruse Calculation, to evince the exact Value of it, in all the Lights in which it may be considered; this much is certain, that barely on Account of our easy Carriage, the Profits of Farming with us, exceed those in *Pennsylvania*, at least by *Thirty per Cent.* and that Difference, in Favour of our Farmers, is of itself sufficient to enrich them; while the others find the Disadvantage they are exposed to, so heavy, (especially the remote Inhabitants of their Country) that a bare Subsistence is all they can reasonably hope to obtain. Take this Province throughout, the Expence of transporting a Bushel of Wheat, is but *Two pence*, for the Distance of One Hundred Miles; but the same Quantity, at the like Distance in *Pennsylvania*, will always exceed us *One Shilling* at least. The Proportion between us, in the Conveyance of every Thing else, is nearly the same. How great, then, are the Incumbrances to which they are exposed! What an immense Charge is saved to us! How sensible must the Embarrassments they are subject to, be to a trading People!

There is Nothing more common, in *Connecticut* and the *Massachusetts-Bay* Colonies, in discoursing of their Provinces, than for Gentlemen to urge the great Number of their Towns, as a Proof of the Prosperity of their Country; whereas Nothing can be of more mischievous Consequence to all new Settlements. Sound Policy will teach them, that Husbandry calls for their first Attention; erecting Townships being never adviseable, till the Number of Planters can supply their Necessities; nor even then, are they to be encouraged, unless the Rise of Arts and useful Manufactures, render the reciprocal Aids of the Inhabitants indispensibly necessary. Every Town unemployed in these, is a dead Weight upon the Public; for when Families collect themselves into Townships, many Tracts of Land, must, of Consequence, lie unimproved: Besides, such Persons will always endeavour to support themselves by Barter and Exchange; which can by no Means augment the Riches of the Public. The same Commodity passing thro' never so many different Hands in one Community, tho' it may enrich an Individual, others must be poorer, in an exact proportion to his Gains; but the collective Body of the People not at all: Now, suppose, what really is true, that not a Town in those Provinces, of which there are not less than three Hundred, is, in the least Degree, supported by any kind of Manufacture whatsoever; how vast must be their Consumption! how incredible their Expence! how ruinous the Loss of their Time! and how difficult the Remedy! This Subject puts me in Mind of the Story a Gentleman in this Province told me, of his Tenant. *James* had to his Wife's Portion, a Barrel of Rum, upon the Strength of which he set up for a Tavern-keeper; he purchased a Licence, and the married Couple settled it as an inviolable Rule, that not a Dram should

be drawn, but for Cash upon the Nail: — A Dram was sold, and
James had a Groat for it: The Day after, with that Groat, *James*
purchased a Dram of *Betty*: It was not long, before *Betty*'s Qualms
extorted the Groat for a Dram to relieve her; then *James* took the
Money. The Cash kept a constant Circulation, till the Barrel was
emptied. The Application of this Story to the Provinces I have
mentioned, is as easy, as to determine, whether *James* had increased his Wife's Portion, or not.

Another Consequence of their clustering into Towns, is Luxury; — a great and mighty Evil, carrying all before it, and crum-
bling States and Empires, into slow, but inevitable Ruin. — Like
sweetened Poison, it is soft but strong, enervates the Constitution,
and triumphs at last, in the Weakness and Rotteness of the Patient.
It is almost impossible for a Number of People, and absolutely so,
if they are idle, to live together, but they will very soon attempt
to outvie each other, in Dress, Tables, and the like. This is the
Case in the *Massachusetts-Bay*: Let a Man enter one of their
Country Churches, and he will be struck with the Gaiety of
Ladies, in Silks and Lawn; while, perhaps, the Houses they came
out of, shall scarce afford a clean Chair to sit on. — *Boston* is their
Pattern, and too, too closely imitated! I knew a Gentleman, that
could tell his Distance from it, by the Length of the Ruffles of a
Belle of the Town he was in; and perhaps it may deserve the
serious Consideration, of their *Society for the Promotion of Industry, and Employment of the Poor*, whether the first Step they
took, should not be, to dissipate their Towns, and multiply the
Number of their Farms. I am sure, it would turn out in the End,
a Scheme more to their Advantage, than peopling their *Eastern
Frontiers*; tho' it had no other Effect, than to sink the Ballance we
have against them in Trade; which, as some of their own Merchants, of Truth and Intelligence, have informed me, is not less
than *Forty Thousand Pounds per Annum*, lawful Money of this
Province.

Of the Inconveniencies of too many Towns, we have, as yet,
no Cause of Complaint. The Lands near *New-York*, and at a considerable Distance from it, were, in the Infancy of this Colony,
taken up by a few Gentlemen in large Tracts; which, tho' it has

been some Discouragement, to the Improvement of the Lands within those Grants, has nevertheless had its Use; as, in Consequence thereof, our Settlements have been carried up *Hudson's River*, to the Extremes of the Province; and thereby made that, the Heart of the Colony, and the securest Retreat, which, at every Indian War, would otherwise have been, what our *Northern Frontiers* were the last, derelict and abandoned, or a miserable Aceldama [5] and Field of Blood; but contains now, many Thousands of flourishing Farms; which are daily improving and increasing, as well to the Advancement of private Estates, as the publick Emolument.

A.

Copious as this Subject is, I shall beg Leave to resume it but once, in some future Paper,[6] and in the mean Time, take this Opportunity to fulfil my Promise, by giving Place to a Letter from one of my most industrious Correspondents.

To the INDEPENDENT REFLECTOR

SIR,   *New-York, Dec.* 16. 1752.

Tho' you have, in your two last Papers, given us your Thoughts, on Subjects of sufficient Moment, to merit the sage Deliberation of our Superiors; yet I presume, you are not unwilling, sometimes to quit your more elevated Speculations, and for a While, condescend to take Cognizance of inferior Grievances. The true Sportsman does not confine his Diversion to the Pursuit of a Deer, or the Chase of a Fox; but will often stoop to the meaner Game of the timorous Hare, or the humble Covey. In Confidence of this, I shall lay before you the following Reflections, without troubling my Head about an introductory Apology, convinced as I am, that immediately proceeding to the Subject of my Complaint, will be more acceptable to you, than any Compliment I can make.

It appears, *Sir*, from the most accurate Calculation, that we have in this City, at least a Thousand Dogs: I do not mean of the human Kind; for the Extirpation of those, would prove such an *Augean Stable*, as to require a Labour perfectly *Herculean*. The Dogs I intend, are that real canine Species, which, with their dismal Howlings, disturb the Repose of the Healthy, break the interrupted Slumbers of the Sick, add fresh Horrors to the Night, and render it perillous to traverse our Streets after the Sun is sunk beneath our Horizon. These

Creatures are a perfect Nuisance to the Inhabitants, and, with respect to Forty-nine in Fifty, answer not one valuable Purpose in Life: Nay, should any of them run mad, as have lately sundry of their Species, in many Parts of the Country, how inexpressibly dreadful would be the Consequence to so populous a City!

I may venture to take it for granted, that our Dogs daily consume as much eatable Provision, as would suffice Five Hundred Men: A monstrous Extravagance, and a Piece of Luxury, that would almost redden the Cheek of a *Lucullus!* The Expence of a Thousand Dogs at *a Penny* a Day, amounts to £1,520.16.8 *per Annum.* Or, allow only 500 Dogs, to eat to the Value of *a Penny* a Day, that will amount to £760.8.4, a Year. What Clamour should we hear, was such a Sum to be annually raised by a Tax on the Inhabitants, for the Maintenance of our Poor! We should even be stunn'd with Murmurs, was such a Sum to be levied for the Support of the Clergy: Yet so preposterous are we, as to lavish our Superfluities, on the brutal Creation, while our Ears are sealed against the plaintive Voice of our own Species; and to caress the groveling Quadrupede, when we turn aloof from the *human Face divine.*

There is Nothing more common, than daily to behold at our Doors, the shivering pale-visag'd home-born Poor, and the penurious half-clad Stranger, banished by the Rage of Persecution, from his native Soil, imploring with the persuasive Eloquence of flowing Tears, and silent Sorrow, the cold Morsel, and the scanty Boon, which he is inhumanly refused, while *Towser, Tray* and *Mopsy,* are pampered with Dainties, and gorged with the Fat of the Land!

It may, indeed, be objected, that to Gentlemen they are useful Animals, in guarding their Yards, and proclaiming the Approach of Robbers: But not One in Fifty, to speak within Compass, is kept for that Purpose; and where it really is the Case, let such Persons be compelled to confine them to their Yards, and prevent them from being a Terror and Disturbance to their Neighbours.

I am so great a Lover of Fidelity and Gratitude, in which those Animals often surpass our own perfidious Race; that Impartiality obliges me, not to apply for their Banishment, without doing Justice to their Virtues: I must also allow, that to the Husbandman they are a valuable Part of his Possession. But in a City, they are generally worse than useless: They are noxious, and a meer Burden to the People.

As you, *Mr. Reflector,* seem both able and willing, to contribute to the Redress of our Grievances, I beseech you, to roar like a Lion against those useless Curs; that by a Law of the Corporation, we may speedily be Witnesses of their perpetual Exile.

Z.   *Yours, &c.   Shadrech Plebianus.*

THE INDEPENDENT REFLECTOR

The Letter sign'd Eropaides, *came to Hand last Week, and shall be taken Notice of speedily.*

1. A paraphrase of Virgil, *Georgics*, II, 458: *O fortunatos nimium sua si bona norint Agricolas*, "How excessively fortunate the husbandmen, did they but know their own good fortune." Livingston has substituted "the English" for the husbandmen.

2. "Britannia," a patriotic poem (1729) by James Thomson (1700–1748). In the last edition (1744) the quotation read:
> "Blow the fresh bay, bid Industry rejoice,
> And the rough sons of lowest labour smile."

3. William Smith, Jr., the author of this number, repeated this claim in even stronger language in his *History* (I, 277): "With respect to riches, there is not so great an inequality amongst us as is common in Boston and some other places. Every man of industry and integrity has it in his power to live well, and many are the instances of persons who came here distressed by their poverty, who now enjoy easy and plentiful fortunes."

4. If Smith meant that New York outranked other cities in the colonies as a port, he was writing as a promoter rather than as a chronicler. The city had made enormous commercial progress by 1753 but probably did not yet rank Philadelphia and Boston, or perhaps even Charleston. (A. C. Flick, ed., *History of the State of New York*, 10 vols. [New York, 1933–1937], II, 266, 334; Virginia Harrington, *The New York Merchant on the Eve of the Revolution* [New York, 1935] pp. 204–205; U.S. Bureau of the Census, *Historical Statistics of the United States: Colonial Times to 1957* [Wash., D.C., 1960], pp. 759–760; Emory R. Johnson, *et al.*, *History of the Domestic and Foreign Commerce of the United States*, 2 vols. [Wash., D.C., 1915], I, 120–121.)

5. In Scripture the place purchased by Judas with the betrayal money and where he expired (Acts 1:18–19); or the potter's field purchased by the priests with the betrayal money which Judas discarded (Matt. 27:5–8); hence, figuratively, any field of bloodshed.

6. No. LII of the *Reflector*.

Number IX

THURSDAY, JANUARY 25, 1753

Public Virtue to be distinguished by public Honours: The Selling of Offices, which require Skill and Confidence, a dismal Omen of the Declension of a State

Omnia venalia Romæ.   SAL.

O cives, cives, querenda Pecunia primum est,
Virtus post nummos, —   HOR.[1]

No State or Government can long continue in a flourishing Condition, without observing a proper Discrimination between the Blameable and Praise-worthy of its Subjects. Nor is the Punishment of the Flagitious, a sufficient Encouragement to Virtue, without, moreover, rewarding the eminently deserving. As the licentious Criminal ought to be crush'd by the violated Laws of the Common-Wealth, so also should her dutious Children, who devote their Studies, and consecrate their Talents to her Service, be crowned with her distinguishing Honours. A meer Exemption from Punishment, is too feeble a Spur to great and arduous Undertakings: It only supposes a Man innocent, or negatively virtuous, but is no Recompence to superior Desert, and conspicuous Merit. It is but a small Satisfaction, that we are exempted from the Gallows or Pillory, because we are not Rogues and Villains, while we reap no Benefit by being signally good and meritorious. 'Tis true, every Man ought to promote the Prosperity of his Country, from a sublimer Motive than his private Advantage: But it is extremely difficult, for the best of Men, to divest themselves of Self-Interest: Nor is it rational, to expect great Geniuses, accomplished Heroes, or any other illustrious Characters, in a Government that overlooks Merit; and, like the

Grave, buries the Best and the Worst in one promiscuous and undistinguished Oblivion. Such is the Degeneracy of human Nature, that Punishments to deter, without Rewards to allure, are not sufficient to fix the roving Mind of Man, in the uninterrupted Practice of public Virtue. Hence the Government which inflicts the One, without any Provision for the Other, is partial, and fundamentally defective; but that, on the Contrary, which makes the Service of the Public, the most efficacious Means of promoting the true Interest of every Individual, affords the strongest Proofs of its political Wisdom. GOD himself, hath annexed *Rewards and Punishments,* as the Conditions of the Obedience or Disloyalty of his free and intelligent Creatures. He, whose Omniscience pervades the Heart of Man, hath not denounc'd his Vengeance, to deter him from Evil, without super-adding his Promises, as Inducements to Virtue. In his moral Government of the World, he deals with his Creatures, as with degraded Intelligences, who have lost their primitive Relish for Religion, and want the Allurement of Happiness, to enable them to admire her otherwise uninfluencing tho' amiable Charms. The same holds good, with Respect to political Virtue. The groveling mercenary Soul, is wholly wrapt up in its own Interest; and the most generous Patriot, cannot entirely abstract the Prospect of his Happiness, from the Consideration of his public Services: He is, indeed, not so venal, as to make it the sole Spring of his Actions; but considers it, as the Concomitant of Virtue, and would probably have remain'd inactive, had he been sure of being disappointed: He thinks himself at least, intitled to the Thanks and Applause of his Country, and would, with Reluctance have quitted his Repose, and plunged into Disquietude, could he have foreseen its Ingratitude. The Ambition natural to the Mind of Man, wants, at least, the Prospect of Fame and Honour, to keep him in the Pursuit of Glory. He is soon weary of travelling a Road, that will never carry him to his Journey's End; or if it does, will only introduce him into the Company of Scoundrels and Pick-pockets: But the pleasing and animating View of being distinguished by his Country, from the common Run of his Species, in proportion to his Merit, is a perpetual Stimulation to Virtue: It is a kind of intellectual Gale, that fans the Fire of Ambition, and preserves him from Lassitude in his Pursuit of Glory. Not that he will really obtain the Satisfaction he has in View: All our Hopes of Happiness, from any Thing beneath the Sun, must, by Necessity of Nature, be delusive. No sooner do we arrive to the Point proposed, but the Object on which we had placed our Felicity, eludes our Embrace like a Fantom: Instead of a JUNO, we are deceived with a Cloud. This, however, is considering the Matter in the calm Light of Philosophy: But we must take Men as they are, and if we consult the Motives that generally influence their Conduct, we shall find, that *Rewards and Punishments* are the Hinges upon which all Government ought to turn. For this Reason, I was greatly delighted with the emblematical Representation of JUS-TICE, which I have met with, in the Travels of an Author, whom I cannot recollect: "The Image of JUSTICE," says he, "in their Courts of Judicature, is formed with six Eyes, two before, as many behind, and on each Side one, to signify *Circumspection*; with a Bag of Gold open in her Right-Hand, and a Sword sheathed in her Left, to shew she is more disposed to *reward*, than to *punish*."

The Wisdom of our Ancestors, in rewarding Merit, is never enough to be admired. The ancient *Britons* carried the Matter so far, as sometimes to pass by the right Line, in the Election of their Kings, if any other, for his martial Achievements, and royal Virtues, was more deserving of the Throne.

The Republic of *Holland,* is extremely munificent to her Servants. She presented her Admirals DE RUYTER, DE WITT, and GHENT, each with a golden Cup, on which was engraved their gallant Progress to *Chatham,* to perpetuate the Remembrance of it in their Families: Medals were also struck on that Occasion, on which DE RUYTER is called *Immensi Tremor Oceani, & Archithalassus, Dux & Eques.*[2] Nor was her Liberality confined within the narrow Compass of their Lives: She lavished upon them posthumous Honours, and erected to their Memory, magnificent Tombs.

The *Romans* also, during the Eclat and Splendor of the Common-Wealth, gave the highest Encouragement to Merit; and wisely preferred public Virtue, to Rank and Fortune: Illustrious

Deeds were the direct Road to public Honours; and the impartial Republic seem'd assiduous to aggrandize those, who distinguished themselves by the Prudence of their Councils, or their Bravery in Battle. The Toil of her Warriors was rewarded by Triumphs, and their Renown transmitted to Posterity, by Statues and Monuments. On CICERO, for his indefatigable Care in confounding the *Catalinarian Conspiracy,* they bestowed the glorious Appellation of FATHER OF HIS COUNTRY. But during the pestilent Reign of the Emperors, when Virtue was rather proscribed than honoured, and to be public-spirited became ruinous and capital, this unrival'd Nation gradually sunk into Destruction; and became at last an easy Prey to the barbarous Nations; who, like a desolating Torrent, poured in upon it, from all Quarters, and laid in Ruin that august Empire, which had so long given Law to Mankind, and triumphed over the whole World.

The *Athenians* and *Lacedæmonians* conferred the Honours of the State, according to the real Worth of the Candidates. In those celebrated Common-Wealths, Men rose to the first Rank, by the Strength of their Genius, and their personal Valour. This naturally gave Rise to a numerous Race of Heroes, and produced a Multitude of Philosophers, Statesmen, Poets and Orators: And yet so great was the public Frugality, as to enable them to leave no Merit unrewarded. A Twig of Laurel was as illustrious a Distinction as a splendid Pension. All the Honour conferred on MILTIADES, who delivered *Athens*, from the Invasion of *Persia*, was the placing his Picture at the Head of the Commanders in the *Piazza*, where the Battle of *Marathon* was painted. This Parsimony in the Distribution of Rewards, made them the more glorious: But when the State became corrupted by the Extravagance of their Magistrates, and decreed Three Hundred Statues to DEMETRIUS PHALEREUS, their Favours became multiplied and threadbare, and consequently useless and contemptible.

Justly celebrated for this essential Article of sound Politicks, is a neighbouring Nation, equally famous for their good Cookery, and political Subtlety. The *French* are not more remarkable for the Slaughter of Frogs, the cutting of Capers, or the Consumption of Fricassees, than for their Wisdom, in preferring Persons in proportion to their Deserts. Hence it is, that their Officers, both civil and military, are, perhaps, inferior to none in *Europe*.

With Pleasure I write it, and with Pleasure will it be read, that we rather surpass than rival them in this important Point of political Wisdom. How happy the Nation among whom public Venality and the Sale of Offices, is prohibited by Law! It is impossible for a Man devoid of Merit, to be elevated to an eminent Post; or, for superior Worth to languish in Obscurity and Indigence. SALLUST mentions the Sale of Offices, as a deadly Symptom of the approaching Dissolution of *Rome*. And indeed, I cannot conceive, how a State can long escape its final Period, after the Introduction of an universal Venality: But our Laws have wisely provided against this ruinous Mischief. By our excellent Constitution, an Office, either of the Grant of the King or the Subject, which concerns the Administration or the Proceeding of Justice, the King's Revenue, the Common-Wealth, the Interest and Safety of the Subject, or the like, granted to a Man unexpert, and of insufficient Skill for the Exercise or Execution of it, is meerly void; and the Party disabled by Law to take it, *pro commodo regis & populi* [3]: And no Man, tho' never so skillful and expert, is capable of a judicial Office, in Reversion. Again, where any *bargaining*, or *giving of Money*, or any *Matter of Reward*, etc. for Offices, is mentioned, it shall render the Purchaser incapable. Such being the Law, it affects me with singular Pleasure, to reflect, by Way of Illation, that all our Officers are Men of Skill and Capacity; and that none of them have been guilty of this political Simony, of purchasing their Posts; because that would be supposing our Superiors to have acted contrary to Law; which would be the Height of Absurdity, and a most ill-mannerly Reflection. It would indeed infer little less than Perjury, and be an injurious Calumny on their Reputations. It must, therefore, be taken for granted; that they were preferred for their personal Merit, and that no sinister Consideration entered into the Thoughts of the Grantor.

I have indeed, heard it insinuated, that there have been, even among us, such illegal Practices; but I always considered those Suggestions, as the groundless Aspersions of impotent disappointed

Malice. Can it be presumed, that Persons sworn to execute the Laws, should openly counteract and violate them? Would Offices be put up to Sale, if the Purchase was void, and illegal? Can Men be supposed, to run the Hazard of parting with their Money, on so precarious a Bottom? Behold the calumnious Representations of Envy! the penetrating Invention of Spleen and Malevolence!

Agreable to this glorious Constitution, no unlettered Fop, no wealthy Blunderbuss, can expect to be lifted into a Post of Consequence: His proffered Treasure will be unavailing, and rejected with Disdain. On the Contrary, Ability and Merit need no farther Recommendation: Obscure and sequestred Virtue, and Genius cloathed in Rags, will be compelled out of their awful Retirement, and conspicuously advanced: Calumny must be suffocated in the Midst of her malicious Whispers, nor will there be left the least Pretence to complain, with JUVENAL, of a confused Distribution of Favours and Frowns, Honour and Infamy, without any Regard to personal Qualifications, and intrinsic Worth.

Ille crucem, pretium sceleris tulit, hic diadema.[4]

Z.

To the INDEPENDENT REFLECTOR

SIR,

PROFESSING myself a great Admirer of your Paper, and consequently very anxious about its Success, I am determined to advertise you of every Thing that may derogate from its Character, or have the remotest Tendency to occasion its Discontinuance. With this View, I beg Leave to acquaint you, that the Latin Mottos prefixed to several of your late *Reflectors*, have given great Offence to some of your Superiors: Not that the Meaning of those harmless Sentences, which are placed there for Ornament, and as containing some bright Remark, applicable to the Subject, have excited the Displeasure that alarms me. No, *Sir*, there is not a Person I have met with so fanciful, as to suppose the Authors, from whom you borrow those beautiful Extracts, intended them as descriptive of any Grievance peculiar to us. It is, in short, the Language in which they are delivered, and not the Sense of the Mottos, which has given the Umbrage; and that for no less substantial a Reason, than because many of your Betters are unprovided with Dictionaries.[5]

RALPH SYNTAX.

THE SELLING OF OFFICES

The Letter signed Eboracus, *on the Petition depending before the Corporation, for a Grant of sundry Water-Lots, is come to Hand, and, for its great Importance, shall have a Place in my next.*

Advertisement from the Printer

The great and unexpected Demand for the Reflector, *having taken off all the first Six Numbers, a greater Quantity of the three last have been printed; and the Printer proposes, God willing, to reprint the first Six in the Spring; when those who are still inclined to become Subscribers, may have whole Sets.*

1. The first quotation should read: *Omnia Romae venalia esse,* "At Rome everything can be bought." Sallust, *Jugurtha,* XX, 1. Livingston's own translation of the second, in another publication, was:
> "O Romans, Romans, Gold must first be sought,
> Then Virtue, that's worth but a second Thought."

Horace, *Epistles,* I, 1, 53.

2. De Ruyter commanded the Dutch fleet which, in 1667, successfully attacked the great English naval station at Chatham on the Medway, near the mouth of the Thames. Livingston's reference is not entirely accurate. The medal's longer inscription in part reads *Archithalassus, Dux & Eques* ("Admiral, General, and Knight"). The other motto does not appear, but is that of the knightly Order of St. Michael. De Ruyter is shown wearing the collar and badge of the order. The Dutch used the motto, here and elsewhere, to mean: "the terror of the immense ocean."

3. "On behalf of the interest of the king and the people."

4. Translated freely: "Some are crucified and others are crowned for the same deed." Juvenal, *Satires,* XIII, 105.

5. While Livingston could appreciate the reaction to his Latinisms, he did not let up immediately. The first nine issues had contained some sixteen; the next ten included twenty, but thereafter the number tapered off.

Number X

Remarks on a Petition, preferred to the Corporation in the Year 1748; lately revived, and now under Consultation

Accipe nunc Danaum insidias. Virg.[1]

Howevʀ plain and easy are the Notions of Right and Wrong, there is such a bewitching Charm in Self-Interest, that the Mind, intoxicated by this delusive Syren, is generally impervious to Truth and Reason. It cannot strip the Case under its Consideration of that fallacious Circumstance, which is the sole Cause of its erroneous Judgment. A Man's personal Advantage gives so strange a Biass to his Reason, that he perceives not his own Injustice, where he would condemn the like Action in another, with high Disdain.

Rufus was an able Casuist, and universally celebrated for the Righteousness of his Decisions, in all Controversies relating to *meum & tuum*: He was a great Proficient in the *civil Law*, and of Probity unspotted: For Solidity of Judgment, and the Skill of nicely ballancing the several Degrees of Evidence and Probability, on both Sides, and giving to each their due Weight, he had no Competitor: His independent Fortune, derived from the ample Provision of his Ancestors, enabled him to rival, by his sage Advice, the most eminent Council, without claiming the Title, or expecting the Fees of a Lawyer. Hence, as may well be supposed, he was frequently solicited for his Opinions; which he gave with equal Disinterestedness and Alacrity. Nor do I remember an Instance of any Person's appealing from his Sentence. But it happened on a Time, a Time by Rufus ever remembered with Regret! that himself had a Dispute with Aurelius, in which he fell into a Mistake, without being able to discover it. Aurelius satisfied of the Integrity of his Antagonist, notwithstanding the Error of his Judgment, left him, with a Scheme in his Head, which he soon after executed. He sent Rufus the State of a Case, similar to his own, between fictitious Persons, on which he prayed his Opinion. Rufus decided it without Hesitation; and by the Decision, gave a Verdict for Aurelius against himself, in the first Controversy.

That beautiful allegorical Fable, delivered in holy Writ, by which the Prophet Nathan convinced the *Hebrew* Monarch of his Guilt towards Uriah, is a Confirmation of my Doctrine.[2] David, with all his Royal Virtues, could commit Murder and Adultery, without Contrition; but pronounced Judgment with Justice, against the Transgressor, who took away the poor Man's Lamb by Violence.

Ever since a certain Petition, preferred to the Corporation by Persons who would roar aloud against others, for what they are vindicating in themselves, hath awaken'd the Attention of the Town, I have had a strong Inclination, to make it the Subject of a *Reflector*; but as I could not before, procure such ample Materials, as I was last Week furnished with, in the following Letter, I shall now lay my Thoughts before the Reader, without farther Preface.

To the Independent REFLECTOR

SIR,

THE Matters contained in a certain Petition, preferred to the Common-Council of the City of *New-York*, in the Year 1748, together with the Proceedings from time to time had thereupon, and the astonishing Propositions made by the Petitioners, to a Committee of the Common-Council, are now become a common Coffee-House Topic, and the Subject of almost every Conversation: But equally extensive with their Notoriety, are the Contempt and Indignation wherewith they are heard and uttered, by all Ranks and Conditions of Men, disinterested in the Project: Nor need we wonder at this universal Detestation and Abhorrence, as they contain a manifest Insult on the whole Common-Council, by supposing them, either the most abandoned of Knaves, or the grossest of Fools. But the true State of those Facts not being generally known; nor the laudable Practice of former Corporations, in Matters of the like Nature, within the Sphere of every Man's Enquiry; I shall beg Leave, in the most succinct Manner, to convey them to the Public, thro' the Channel of your Paper, wholly submitting my Observations to your judicious Improvements, Additions or Retrenchments. I shall render it evident, that in Consequence of the Petitioners Proposals, the Value of what they humbly ask of the Common-Council, will, at the Expiration of Twenty Years, such is their Modesty! amount to not much less than *Six Thousand Pounds.* The Facts are as follow.

On the Twenty-eighth of *June,* 1748, a Petition was preferred by five Persons,* praying, *a Grant of the Land from High to Low Water Mark; and also, the Soil under the Water, the whole Breadth of their Lands,* (as they were pleased to term them) *to extend from Low-Water Mark into the East River, two hundred Feet.* Upon reading this Petition, it was, *Ordered, That the Members of the Common-Council, or the major Part of them, be a Committee, to enquire and examine into the subject Matter of the Petition; and that they go to, and view the Lands claimed by the Petitioners, and make Report to the Common-Council, with all convenient Speed.*[3]

That any Obedience was paid to this Order, doth not appear: But the next Notice taken of the Petition, was on the Seventh of *March* 1750, when it was revived, read, and *Ordered, That five Gentlemen of the Common-Council, or the major Part of them, be a Committee to examine into the Allegations of the said Petition, and take to their Assistance one of the Surveyors of this City, and run out the Lots of the Petitioners, hear their Proposals, and make Report thereof to this Board.* 'Tis here to be remarked, that one of this Committee was a Son of one, and Brother-in-Law to another, of the Petitioners, and that another of the Committee claim'd an Interest in the Lands, to which the Water-Lots are contiguous, in Right of his Wife, who was a Daughter of another of the Petitioners; Which I humbly conceive, was a Proceedure not a little beneath the Dignity of the Corporation, and liable to Animadversions greatly injurious to their Sagacity and Honour: For how the Common-Council could, consistent with their Duty, refer a Matter of so great Importance, to Persons concerned in Interest, or related to those who were; or how the latter could have the Modesty, to accept a Commission in an Affair wherein themselves were Parties, I must submit to their own Sense of Honour, and the impartial Verdict of the World; but as an Apology in their Favour, it must fairly be confessed, they did not proceed in the Affair: So that on the sixth of *March* 1752, upon another Reading of the Petition, it was *Ordered, That* a Number of Gentlemen of the Corporation,

* *Here my Correspondent inserts the Petitioners Names, which I pray his Pardon for omitting, to avoid giving Offence.*

whose Names I shall omit, two of whom were, however, nearly related to the Petitioners, *or the major Part of them, be a Committee to receive Proposals from the Proprietors of the Water Lots,†* and *other's Lots, from* James Desbrosse*'s, to* Hughson's-Point, *upon what Quit they shall pay for the same per Foot per Annum; and that they lay out the said Water Lots; and take to their Assistance one of the sworn Surveyors of this City; and make Report thereof to this Board with all convenient Speed.* In Consequence of this Order, the Committee had a Meeting with some of the Petitioners; at which the latter proposed, to *accept of a Grant agreable to the Prayer of their Petition, but to have it gratis* (Posterity will disbelieve the Insult) *for twenty Years, and at the Expiration of that Term, they would most generously vouchsafe to pay* (invaluable Consideration!) *the full Sum of Nine Pence a Foot, per Annum, thereafter.* If it be for Want of knowing their Duty, that the Corporation do so much as hearken to such insolent Offers, (and surely that is the most favourable Construction we can put upon their Conduct) I shall beg Leave to lay before them a few Precedents of former Corporations, in similar Cases, their Imitation of which, I conceive, would greatly redound to their Honour.

The Corporation in the Year 1690 odd, appointed a Committee of some of their Members, to expose at public Auction or Vendue, all the Water Lots, from one Mr. SACKET's, now Mr. DESBROSSE's, to the Water Lots of the late Mr. WILLIAM SHARPAS, now Mr. JOHN BOGERT's, jun. and others; having previous to this Sale at Vendue, given Mr. SHARPAS four Lots, in Return for his uncommon Vigilance, and unblemished Integrity, in the Execution of his Office; which, to his Honour be it spoken, he invariably retain'd to his dying Day. Some Time after this, the Corporation sold their Water-Lots for considerable Sums of Money, to Mr. ELLISON, (now Mr. CROMMELIN's) Mr. GILBERT LIVINGSTON, (now ROBERT LIVINGSTON's, Esq;) Mr. JOHN CANNON, and Col. BEEKMAN. Nor can a single Instance be assigned, that our former Corporations have not made the most of their Water-Lots in the East River, from High to Low Water Mark. The following Instance, is a recent Proof of the Contrary, consistent with the Knowledge of every one in the least acquainted with Corporation Affairs. The Seven Lots to the Westward of the Weigh-House, I mean where Messrs. WALTON and CLARKSON now live, were sold at public Vendue, as also those at the Rear of them, lately possessed by Col. MOORE, etc. all which were Lots between High and Low-Water Mark: The two hundred Feet below Low-Water Mark, were some Years after, purchased by Col. MOORE, and others: For all of which the Purchasers

† *I again omit the Names of the Petitioners mentioned in this Order, which probably by Inaccuracy of the Clerk, supposes the Petitioners to be Proprietors of the very Soil under Water prayed for in the Petition.*

immediately paid *Eighteen Pence* a Foot. These Gentlemen, it seems, were no Adepts in the Art of cajoling Corporations out of their Lands, without a Consideration: Nor did they expect or desire to possess them Twenty Years for Nothing, and then to pay only an annual Quit-Rent of *Nine Pence* a Foot: Nay, they were so totally ignorant of the modern Refinement of claiming without Title, and buying without paying, as chearfully to become the highest Bidders at Vendue, and actually to pay for their seven Lots, near *Fourteen Hundred Pounds*, besides and exclusive of *Eighteen Pence* a Foot, for their Extent of *Two Hundred* Feet into the River.

But the Petitioners in Question do not even propose to give any Consideration at all for the Lots from High to Low-Water Mark; the *Nine pence* a Foot being only for the *Two hundred* Feet below Low-Water Mark; nor that, till *twenty* Years hence; whereas none who have purchased from Low-Water Mark, into the East River, pay less than *Eighteen Pence*, and some even *One Shilling and Nine Pence*, a Foot, *to wit*, from CRUGER's to COENTIE's Corner.

It now follows, according to the Method I proposed, to prove, that these modest Petitioners, in Consequence of their Proposals, ask near *Six Thousand Pounds*. In order to evince this, it will suffice to observe, that the Lots from High to Low-Water Mark, will sell at public Vendue, at least for *One Thousand Pounds*, ready Money, tho' many are of Opinion, for some Hundreds more, and probably with the Reservation of an annual Rent: But suppose only the former; the Interest of that Sum for *Twenty* Years, from the first of *May* next, with Compound Interest, will amount to very near *Four Thousand Pounds*. Now this, the Petitioners, according to their Proposals, would have for Nothing, together with a Fee-simple in the Ground from High to Low-Water Mark. Hence it appears, that should they be gratified in their most unjust and unreasonable Request, that whole Sum of *Four Thousand Pounds*, would be foolishly squandered, to the Prejudice of the City. For the second Proof, to illustrate the Loss above-mentioned, it is highly rational, to suppose, that the Corporation may sell *Six Hundred* Feet in Breadth, along the East River, and extending into it from Low-Water Mark *Two hundred* Feet, which at *Twenty five* Feet in Breadth, will make *Twenty four* Lots: These Lots being granted to the several Purchasers of the Ground between High and Low-Water Mark, at *Eighteen Pence* a Foot; and on Supposition, that the annual Rent should not take Place till the Year 1763, which will be ten Years after the Grants; then the succeeding ten Years will annually bring into the Corporation-Treasury, *Forty-five* Pounds a Year; Which, together with the Compound Interest thereon added to the above-mentioned *Four Thousand Pounds*, will fall little short of *Six Thousand Pounds*. But the present Petitioners, after the Expiration of *twenty* Years, propose to pay only *Nine pence* a Foot; whereas vast Numbers of the Inhabitants of this City, are ready and willing to pay *Eighteen pence* a Foot, *per Annum*, from the Date of their Deeds, for ever.

And now, what Reason can be assigned by the most Sanguine of the Petitioners, or any of their Friends (if any they have, in so exorbitant a Demand) why these Lots should not also be sold at Vendue, to the highest Bidders: But I can urge a good Reason for the Corporation's selling them at Vendue, *to wit*, the large Sums they owe, necessarily occasioned by building that superb † Structure at the Ferry, the Pier at *Coentie*'s Dock, the New Exchange, *etc.*   I am,

Your most humble Servant,

Eboracus.

If the Proposals to the Committee are truly represented in the preceeding Letter, vast indeed, and unreasonable, would be the Donation solicited for by the Petitioners, as evidently appears by the above Calculations; but if, as 'tis pretended by the Petitioners, they proposed to the Committee, to take less than they prayed for by the Petition, the Gift, 'tis true, will be proportionally less, but the Principles they act upon equally absurd: Because whatever be the Quantity they desire, it ought to be exposed to Sale at Vendue.

My intelligent Correspondent hath interspersed so many judicious Reflections, throughout his Narrative, that he hath in a Manner anticipated every Argument that can be urged, against the Corporation's giving into a Scheme so wild, so romantic, and so utterly injurious to their Constituents, as is proposed by the Petitioners. For my Part, I cannot persuade myself, that a single Member of that worshipful Body, will be so infatuated, as to grant such an absurd and irrational Request: A Request, if the Facts in the preceeding Letter are true, wholly destitute even of the Colour of Equity; and an Instance of Modesty, perhaps, unexampled in the Memory of Man! Are they not intrusted with the

---

† *I am sorry my Correspondent has made Use of the Word* superb, *after the Offence it hath given, in my Paper on the* better Extinguishing of Fires: *But as I have not been able hitherto, to discover any Heresy in so harmless an Expression, I suffered it to stand, and, after great Deliberation, determined once more, to send my Adversaries to their Dictionaries, for the Signification of that Term, when applied to Buildings.*

Rights of the Citizens, for the Benefit of those they represent? Are they not to consult the Advantage and Emolument of that Body politic, of which they are the Head? The Aldermen in particular, who are bound by solemn Oath, in express Terms to that Purpose? And shall they profusely lavish, in manifest Violation of their Trust, the Property of the City, to enrich and gratify a few Individuals? especially when by so doing, they may, perhaps, subject their private Estates to a Chancery Decree? I would fain know what Claim the Petitioners can pretend, that every Freeman of the City cannot pretend as well. Does Contiguity of Land infer a Right? If it doth, whence the Necessity of Petitioning at all? But if, in Reality, they have no better Title than others, how astonishing, to desire that *gratis*, for which others are ready to pay Sums so considerable!

I have known Men precipitated by their Passions, into the most flagitious Actions, and betray the Public for the Gratification of private Resentment, or private Affection: But that a Majority, of so conspicuous a Body, as is the Corporation of this City, should join in so iniquitous a Concession, is utterly incredible. Nor ought the Man, who gives his Voice in Favour of the Petition, be ever after intrusted with any Share of the Magistracy. On the Contrary, let him be considered as the Enemy of his Country, and branded with eternal Reproach.   *Hic Niger est, hunc tu Romane caveto.*[4]

In a Word, instead of being re-elected into a Station which he has so notoriously abused, let him be look'd upon as incapable of any Office of Trust, and receive, for the Violation of his Duty, that ignominious Applause, which the Poet, perhaps unjustly, ascribes to the Protector.   *See* Cromwell *damn'd to everlasting Fame.*[5]

There is one Thing, I must embrace this Opportunity to mention, which has escaped, as well the Remark of my Correspondent, as the Notice of our Corporation: — I am informed, that the Quit-Rents reserved in their Deeds, are always in current Money of the Colony: Against which, I have this Exception, that the Value of the Quits is not thereby secured.

It has always been observed, that there is a perpetual Decrease of the Value of Gold and Silver. Dr. Swift, who has taken much Pains to elucidate this Point, insists, that the Truth of it *will plainly appear, from the Course of the Roman History, above Two Thousand Years before those inexhaustible Mines of* Potosi *were known. The Value of an* Obolus, *and of every other Coin, between the Time of* Romulus, *and that of* Augustus, *gradually sunk above five Parts in six; as appears by several Passages out of the best Authors. I have been* (continues the same Gentleman,) *at the Trouble of computing the different Values of Money, for about four Hundred Years past.* Henry *Duke of* Lancaster, *who lived about that Period, founded an Hospital in* Leicester, *for a certain Number of old Men, charging his Lands with a Groat a Week, to each, for their Maintenance; which is to this Day duly paid them. In those Times, a Penny was equal to Ten pence half-penny, and somewhat more than half a farthing, in ours; which makes about Eight Ninths Difference.* The Dean adds, *Several Colleges in* Oxford, *were aware of this growing Evil, about a Hundred Years ago; and instead of limiting their Rents, to a certain Sum of Money, prevail'd with their Tenants, to pay the Price of so many Barrels of Corn, to be valued as the Market went, at two Seasons (as I remember) in the Year. For a Barrel of Corn, is of a real intrinsic Value; which Gold and Silver are not. And by this Invention, these Colleges have preserved a tolerable Subsistence, for their Fellows and Students, to this Day.*[6]

I know of no Reason that can be urged, why the Value of our Paper-Money, should not depreciate, as well as the Coin of *Italy* and *Great Britain;* but could, if it were necessary, easily prove it more liable to Fluctuation, than the Gold and Silver of either of those Countries.— I must therefore, earnestly entreat our Corporation, for the future, to follow the Example of the *Colleges* above mentioned, by the Reservation of Rents, in something more stable than either Silver or Gold, or especially the Currency of the Province; lest the Quit-Rent of *Eighteen Pence* a Foot, lose its present Value, and sink down but to *Two Pence;* and thereby the large Income, expected to arise from that Fund, amount only to an inconsiderable Trifle; to the Prejudice of our Posterity, and the Dishonour of their Ancestors.[7]   Z. & A.

THE INDEPENDENT REFLECTOR

To the Independent REFLECTOR

SIR,

GOVERNMENT is an Institution so sacred in its Nature, and arduous in its Administration, that it is not every Slip or Inadvertence of our Superiors, that should occasion an invidious Representation, or a passionate Arraignment of their Conduct. For my Part, where I am convinced of the Integrity of the Magistrate, I can make great Allowances for human Frailties, and inevitable Errors. An honest Heart, and an upright Intention, ought to atone for many political Blunders, and cover a Multitude of unintentional Peccadilloes. Those who are set over us, are, however, advanced to that Eminence for our Benefit, and to be a *Terror to Evil-Doers:* We have not invested them with their Authority, to be insignificant Idlers, and to *bear the Sword in vain*: No, they are advanced to superior Dignity, to move in an ampler Sphere of public Utility, and to be unto us *Ministers for Good*. When therefore, their Negligence in the Discharge of their Duty, and in the Removal of Grievances in their Power to redress, is clearly pointed out, and they still remain supine and inactive; they ought not to blame a frank Remonstrance against their mischievous Indolence; For in such a Situation of Affairs, the Sufferer has more than a bare Proverb, to intitle him to complain: 'Tis his legal and indubitable Right, to expostulate the Matter with becoming Animation and Freedom.

This, *Sir,* I take to be our Case, in Relation to the *Road*; a Subject you have lately handled with great Spirit, and to the general Satisfaction: For, besides the Defects of the Act, in furnishing the Surveyor with an Opportunity to pick our Pockets, or, as a Poet more emphatically expresses it,

To feed and thrive on public Miseries;

it is in the Power of the Corporation, to prevent such villainous Robbery, by appointing an Overseer, at their very next Sessions, who is willing to give sufficient Security, to account for all the Fines that come to his Hands, and not to abuse his high and mighty Prerogative. Such Provision may at least be made, till the Legislature think proper to remove the Objections, to which the Act is at present liable: Nor can it be effected at any other Season of the Year, than at the Sessions in *February*. And what Reason can there be assigned for leaving it at his Discretion, to depredate our Fortunes, when we may so speedily be delivered from the Fears which justly alarm us? Until therefore, our Justices guard us against all Possibility of such horrid Plunderings, by their salutary Interposition; I shall beg Leave, to think they fail in consulting the public Welfare, and making a proper Use of the Authority wherewith they are intrusted.

REMARKS ON A PETITION

I cannot conclude these Lines, without acquainting you, that I am informed, our Surveyor has vented much Rage and Spittle, against the Author of the *Independent Reflector*, for endangering his great DIANA.[8] I am the more surprized at the Gentleman's Wrath, as you have neither exposed a personal Fault, nor private Foible; no, nor even charg'd him (which I assure you I greatly wondered at) with any Mismanagement in his public Station. You have only display'd the Opportunity he has of being a Rogue, whenever he pleases, with such Advantages of puzzling the Detection of his Iniquity, as renders it extremely improper to leave it at his Option. Hence I doubt not, his Noise and Vociferation will have much the same Influence upon you, as hath the Barking of a Dog upon the Moon; which was never known either to stop her Progress, or eclipse her Lustre.   *Yours,* &c.

Z.   PUBLICOLUS.

1. "Hear now the treachery of the Greeks." *Aeneid* II, 65.
2. II Sam. 12:1–9.
3. By the Montgomerie Charter of 1731 the jurisdiction of New York City was extended to include riparian rights around Manhattan for a distance of 400 feet under the rivers, hence, the "water lots" at issue in this number. They comprised the shore property extending outward beyond the low water mark. As the city grew, they were eagerly sought as dock and ferry-landing sites. (Peterson and Edwards, *New York*, II, 149–151.) The petition was presented on June 28, 1748, by Cornelia Rutgers, Leonard Lispenard, John and Jacobus Roosevelt, and Christopher Banker. That of March 7, 1750, mentioned by the correspondent, cannot be documented. The Common Council appointed a committee of five to look into the matter on March 6, 1752. (*Minutes of the Common Council*, V, 224, 359.)
4. "This man is black [i.e., black-hearted], beware of him, thou Roman." Horace, *Satires*, I, 4, 85.
5. Pope, *Essay on Man*, Epistle iv.
6. From *Some Arguments against Enlarging the Power of Bishops, in Letting of Leases.*
7. The subject of the water lots was continued in No. XIV.
8. I.e., his goddess or shrine; in this case the system of road repair attacked in No. III for permitting unscrupulous surveyors to line their pockets at the expense of the poorer citizenry.

Number XI

THURSDAY, FEBRUARY 8, 1753

The Author's Vindication of himself: The Treatment he has met with, scurrilous and unreasonable; with his Resolution to proceed; and the Disinterestedness of his Labours

Sunt quibus in Satyra videar nimis acer, & ultra
Legem tendere opus; —   HOR.[1]

MALICE and Obloquy have been the never-failing Portion of all Writers engaged in combating Bigotry and Oppression, and vindicating the inestimable Privileges of Mankind. *Censure*, says a great Author, *is a kind of Tribute which all Men of Merit must expect to pay to the Public.*[2] The most unconscionable Rogue upon Earth, cannot bear the Detection of his Iniquities. Nay, the obdurate Criminal, who fears not GOD himself, is seized with a Panic, at the Apprehensions of having his Actions publickly exposed by a Writer of Genius and Magnanimity. Hence infinite Opposition and Clamour, whenever a dignified Offender hath his Conduct dissected.

The Author of this Paper never claimed sufficient Merit, to be treated with Indignity by Men of high Station and Eminence. In proportion, however, to his Services to his Country, he was confident of Opposition: For this Reason, the Noise and Uproar about the *Independent Reflector*, are to him no Matter of Astonishment: He always expected it; and to the Mortification of his Enemies, esteems it his Exultation and Triumph. This Expectation he declares in the very Introduction to his Work: But then he hoped to have been opposed with Decency and Good-Manners. Sensible of his Weakness and Fallibility, he entreated his Readers to point out his Errors, with his Promise to correct them.

And was any Man to rectify his Mistakes with Candor and Impartiality, he shou'd with the highest Gratitude, accept the friendly Office. But he hath been treated with Rudeness and Aspersion, with Billingsgate and Scurrility; he hath been branded with the opprobrious Language of Rascal, Scoundrel, Atheist, Deist, Mocker of Things sacred, and vile Reflector.

From the Clergy, Men of awful Function, and venerable Name, he expected gentler Usage: Yet neither the Holiness of their Character, nor the Place devoted to GOD, hath protected him from devout Rage, and monkish Indignation. But whence all this fiery Zeal and superstitious Ardor? He is neither for curtailing their Salaries, nor assaulting their DIANA. And if the *Moravian Spire* ministers such high Offence, who is to blame for it, but the King and Parliament? The *Reflector* has said Nothing, which any Priest ought to resent, but a Popish Priest. For the sacred Order, he entertains the profoundest Reverence: But unreasonable Pretensions, unreasonable Respect, persecuting Fury, and holy Grimace, he will expose and ridicule. Their very Zeal against him (a Zeal void of Knowledge, void of Christian Humility) is a sufficient Attestation of that ecclesiastical Wrath and Arrogance, which he has endeavoured to repress. It illustrates the Truth of his Opinion, about their persecuting Spirit, and irrefrænable Bigotry.

I never doubted, that the Generality of Priests in all Ages and Countries, were actuated by the same spiritual Pride, the same tempestuous Zeal for Baubles and Conundrums, and the same Impatience under Correction. 'Tis Nothing but the Difference of Government, that restrains the Rapacity of some, and leaves that of others rampant and unbridled. For my Part, I bless my Stars, that I live in a Country, where their utmost Efforts cannot exceed hard Names, and orthodox Cursing. In these rare Times of Felicity, I am at Liberty to entertain what Sentiments I please, and to declare what Sentiments I entertain. But was our Constitution as much calculated for the Advancement of ecclesiastical Domination (and I conceive it is but too much so already) as that of *Spain* or *Portugal*, instead of being traduced and maligned, I had long e'er now been *gag'd* and *flog'd*, if not *burnt* or *butcher'd*. Nor am I even now out of Danger: For, as soon as I am discover'd, the Surveyor of the Roads is to shoot me with his Fowling-Piece; then Mr. *M——* is to run me through the Body; and after that the Clergy are to pronounce *the greater Excommunication*. But might a Criminal be indulged, in appointing the Process of his own Trial and Punishment, I should think it more regular, for his Worship to pass Sentence of Death, in the Capacity of a Judge, then the Surveyor to be nominated my Executioner, and some of the Clergy to favour me with their Prayers at my Exit.

But whatever becomes of me, I claim a Right, (notwithstanding a Thousand Anathemas) to defend every Sect of Christians, in the peaceable Enjoyment of their civil and religious Liberties. For this I want no Dispensation from any Pope: And if a Clergyman insists on an equal Right, to warn his Congregation against Hereticks, (which is a Word that means just every Thing, and just Nothing) there let his Exhortations terminate: But to charge a People, to all Appearance, of Lives unblemish'd, and exalted Morals, with enormous Vices, that have no Existence, but in his own crazed Imagination, is to the last Degree licentious and criminal.

The Author of this Paper is as far from believing the Generality of the *Moravian* Principles, as any Man. All he insists upon, is, that if their external Conduct be moral and unexceptional, they have a Right to enjoy their Principles, be they what they will. But the Passages which, he is informed, have given the greatest Offence to Bigots, are the following.

1. That *Rome* is as far from *Geneva*, as *Geneva* from *Rome*.

2. That every Man is *orthodox* to himself, and *heretical* to all the World besides.

3. That whoever believes that CHRIST was the MESSIAH, and practices the Morality he taught, is to all Intents and Purposes, a complete Christian, tho' he be as incredulous about the divine Right of *Episcopacy*, as the divine Right of *Geography*. [Part of this Proposition I retract, and humbly ask Pardon of the World, for committing so great a Blunder; for that instead of *to all Intents and Purposes*, it should have been, to all Intents and Purposes, except the Purposes of the Clergy.]

4. That any Person so believing and practising, is a Christian to all Intents and Purposes, (except as before is excepted) tho' he never heard of the Synod of *Dort* in his Life.

5. That in the Judgment of many learned Men, the Washing of Feet, is as much instituted by the divine Author of Christianity, as Baptism or the Lord's Supper, and more peremptorily commanded than either.

6. That the Parliament hath acknowledged the *Moravians* for good Christians; which perhaps is more than can be said of any Church in the Province.

These are the Passages which have so greatly disgusted our spiritual Overseers, and their blind Adorers: And as they are not like to be decided by their old Practice of Defamation and Scolding, the *Reflector* is ready to maintain each and every of them, against all the Clergy in the Province. But as he cannot consent to carry on such a Controversy in this Paper (the Design of which is a little superior to that of refuting priestly Nonsense) they may chuse which of the public Papers they please, and he will reply in the same:[3] Moreover, in Complaisance to those of the Cloth, who do not understand *English*, (for verily, gentle Reader, he hath been curs'd by those who cannot read him) they may write either in *Dutch, Latin* or *French*, and he will answer in the Language they write. 'Till they are pleased to accept this Challenge, he humbly conceives, they ought to refrain from their unchristian Slanders, such, as that he is an Atheist, and hath no Religion at all; and that for no better Reason, but because he will neither be Priest-ridden himself, nor suffer his Countrymen to be so, while it is in his Power to prevent it. Even their monkish Trick, of what the Apostle calls, *creeping into Houses, and leading Captive silly Women,*[4] with false Alarms and Suggestions, will not terrify him. If by Religion, they mean an implicit Faith in the Clergy, a silly Fondness for fanciful Observances, and the fostering and enriching Hypocrites and Bigots, he frankly confesses he has no Religion: But if it consists, in believing the Scripture, and practising its Morality, he hopes he has more of it, than those who recommend to others what they neither believe nor practice themselves, and whose whole Religion, notwithstanding their grim Aspects, and reverential Habits, may be summ'd up in one single Line of *Shakespeare*'s, as consisting,

In fair round Belly with good Capon lin'd.[5]

For the Magistracy, as the Institution of the State, and the Ordinance of GOD, he entertains high Regard: But lawless Encroachments, or Neglect of Duty, shall be treated with the utmost Freedom. These are Offences *against* the State, and *against* the Divine Ordinance. In vain, therefore, do they demand Protection under those venerable Names. While he reverences the Institution, he will despise the Persons who profane and debase it. More than once has he seen an Ass loaded with Preferment, and more than once contemn'd him notwithstanding his Preferment. If Monks and Barbers, Buffoons and Fiddlers, have before now been the Favourites of Princes; why shou'd it appear wonderful, that at certain Seasons, Pimps and Panders, Tools and Minions, should be cloathed with the splendid Robe of Magistracy. But if such challenge the same Respect as Men of distinguish'd Sense, and renown'd for Integrity, he must beg Leave to be excused. He reverences no Man for his Insignia and Titles, but for the Talents he possesses, and the Good he does in his Office. Publick Ministers are invested with great Trusts for the Benefit of the People, and are bound by all Ties divine and human, to discharge them faithfully: Why else are they Magistrates; and what else is their Duty, but to watch for the public Good? They become bad by their Idleness, as well as by their Actions. If they do no Good, they do Evil by not doing Good; and ought to be told of their criminal Indolence. "In a Country of Freedom and Law," says an eminent Writer, "all Men claim a Right to judge and censure for themselves; and better it is, that all Men say what they please, than one Man do what he will." The best Way to avoid Reproof, is to avoid ministring Occasion for Reproof: But while they offend, he will stigmatize. While he has misrepresented Facts (which he has never done willfully) let the Error be shewn, and it shall be corrected; a Letter to the Printer will be carefully deliver'd, and attentively consider'd. But unmannerly Insults, and furious Preachments, will be perfectly fruitless and unavailable. To in-

THE AUTHOR'S VINDICATION

timidate him, is not in the Power of Man. He is defended by the impregnable Bulwark of Truth and Righteousness. He exposes none but such as ought to be exposed, nor reprehends any Vice but public Vice. With him the Characters of Men are sacred: Not so the Actions of Rogues, especially dignified Rogues. No honest Man shall ever be injured by him; but Prostitution in Office, shall be the Mark of keen and everlasting Resentment. The Letters which he has received about private Faults, have by him been doom'd to the Flames: But public Mismanagement he will attack at all Hazards; and in this he hopes for the Patronage and Encouragement of every Man of Worth, Truth and Innocence.

> What? arm'd for Virtue, when I point the Pen,
> Brand the bold Front of shameless guilty Men;
> Dash the proud Gamester in his gilded Car;
> Bare the mean Heart that lurks beneath a Star;
> Can there be wanting to defend her Cause,
> Lights of the Church, and Guardians of the Laws?
> Could pension'd BOILEAU lash in honest Strain,
> Flatt'rers and Bigots ev'n in LOUIS' Reign?
> Could Laureat DRYDEN Pimp and Fry'r engage;
> Yet neither CHARLES nor JAMES be in a Rage?
> And I not strip the Gilding off a Knave,
> Unplac'd, unpension'd, no Man's Heir or Slave?
> I will, or perish in the generous Cause;
> Hear this, and tremble! you, who 'scape the Laws.   POPE [6]

The Reflector is determin'd to proceed unaw'd, and alike fearless of the humble Scoundrel, and the eminent Villain. The Cause he is engaged in, is a glorious Cause. 'Tis the Cause of Truth and Liberty. What he intends to oppose, is Superstition, Bigotry, Priestcraft, Tyranny, Servitude, public Mismanagement, and Dishonesty in Office. The Things he proposes to teach, are the Nature and Excellency of our Constitution.— The inestimable Value of Liberty: — The disastrous Effects of Bigotry, and the Shame and Horror of Bondage: — The Importance of Religion unpolluted, and unadulterate with superstitious Additions, and the Inventions of Priests. He should also rejoice to be instrumental in the Improvement of Commerce and Husbandry. In short, any Thing that may be of Advantage to the Inhabitants of this Province in particular, and Mankind in general, may freely demand a Place in his Paper. The Motives which inspire him, are noble and disinterested. They are, the Welfare of Society, and the Felicity of his Country. He aims at no Honour, no Applause, no personal Advantage, or public Promotion. He disclaims even that Portion of Fame (whatever it be) which the Candid and Impartial might pay to his disinterested Labours, because he intends never to be known. He has no other View than the Happiness of the Community, to which he belongs; and the Chastisement of such as abuse and disturb it. To instil into the Minds of his Fellow-Subjects, the amiable Sentiments of Liberty, and to shew them, that our Government is the most eligible and complete, that the good Fortune of Man has hitherto produced, or their Wit been capable of contriving. In doing this, he will neither flatter, nor traduce, idolize or calumniate: But proceed, without Trepidation, and in Defiance of all Tyrants civil or ecclesiastic.   Z.

The Letter in Vindication of the Petition which was the Subject of the Remarks of my Correspondent Eboracus, *is received, and shall be inserted as soon as possible.*

1. "There are some who think that I am too savage in my satire, and carry the work beyond lawful bounds." Horace, *Satires*, II, 1–2.

2. Swift, "Thoughts on Various Subjects."

3. Livingston's critics wasted little time in taking up the challenge. Four days later (February 12) the *New-York Mercury* carried a caustic article signed "Layman," which attacked the *Reflector* for aspersing the clergy "without Provocation." Anglican clergymen like Thomas Bradbury Chandler of Elizabethtown, New Jersey, praised it as "much to the purpose," but Livingston condemned the author as "of a down right slavish Disposition with respect to civil Power, and a furious Bigot in Religion, both of which I hate as the Sin of Witchcraft." (Herbert and Carol Schneider, eds., *Samuel Johnson, President of King's College: His Career and Writings*, 4 vols. [New York, 1929], I, 166; Livingston to Noah Welles, February [19?], 1753, JFP, Yale.) William Smith, Jr.'s reply (*New-York Gazette, or Weekly Post-Boy*, February 19, 1753), signed "Philo-Reflector," was even more vitriolic than Livingston's original essay.

4. II Tim. 3:6.

5. *As You Like It*, Act II, scene 7, line 139.

6. *Imitations of Horace. The First Satire of the Second Book.* Nicolas Boileau-Despreaux was the French poet and critic who parodied well-established older poets during the reign of Louis XIV. The "Pimp and Fry'r" was Friar Dominick in Dryden's *The Spanish Friar* (1680). Although Charles II was not disturbed by this satire, James II was and banned the play in 1686.

Number XII

THURSDAY, FEBRUARY 15, 1753

The Use and Importance of the Practice of PHYSIC; together with the Difficulty of the Science, and the dismal Havock made by Quacks and Pretenders

Honour a Physician with the Honour due unto him, for the Uses which you may have of him; for the Lord hath created him.
He that sinneth before his Maker, let him fall into the Hand of the Physician. King SOLOMON [1]

No Man is of greater Service or Detriment to Society, than a Physician. If he is skilful, industrious and honest, he is of unspeakable Benefit to Mankind: But if Incapacity, Idleness and Roguery are his Characteristics, he is a Curse to the Community, and more to be dreaded, than *the Arrow that flieth by Night, or the Pestilence that walketh at Noon-Day*. A good Physician, from the Nature of his Profession, has, above all others, the best Opportunities for being extensively useful. The Patient considers him as his Friend, his Father, and his Neighbour; and were it not for the Light of Religion, could scarce refrain from adoring him as a Deity. He appears, in short, in the most amiable and endearing Light. 'Tis his Office to relieve the Sick, assuage our Pain, and distribute Health, Felicity and Joy: He even combats for us the greatest of all Evils, and, for a While, retards the mortal Attacks of the *King of Terrors*. This is his proper Duty; but he may at the same Time be instead of a Priest, support our Patience, banish our Fears, or improve them to our best Interests, by raising our Hopes, exercising all our Virtues, and, to speak in the Language of a certain eminent Physician, "if he cannot give a new Lease for our Lives, and Death must come, he can soften us into a Compliance with, and Resignation to, the Will of our common Creator; and thereby reconcile us to the solitary Mansions of the Grave, and prepare us for a State of Exemption from Sickness and Pain, and the Enjoyment of endless and unspeakable Happiness." Methinks there is not a more beautiful Parable in the inspired Writings, than that wherein our Saviour represents a Neighbour under the Character of the *good Samaritan*, who performed the Function of a Physician, upon the unhappy Traveller, who had been wounded by Robbers.*

The Reader may, perhaps, be ready to think, that a Character adorned with such a Constellation of Virtues, is beyond the Reach of human Nature: But there have been Instances, in which all these Endowments have been fully exemplified. They are indeed but rare, and such a Physician is a kind of Phoenix, *rara Avis in Terris:* So much, however, of the preceeding Character, as relates to Morals, is in the Power of every Man to obtain: But to arrive at an equal Knowledge in Physic, requires an uncommon and elevated Genius. It is impossible from the Constitution of Things to be otherwise. Let us consider the Nature of the Science; the Pre-Requisites to the Study of it; the Difficulties attending its Practice; and the Assertion will appear sufficiently elucidated.

Of all Professions, none is so extensive as Physic. There are scarce any of the liberal Arts or Sciences, that are not necessarily to be studied, by him who would attain to any considerable Pitch of Eminency in it. *Latin* and *Greek*, among the learned Languages, he must be intimately acquainted with; as the ancient Physicians, whose Writings are to this Day held in Esteem, were either *Greeks* or *Romans*. Besides, many of the Moderns, now in highest Reputation, have wrote only in the Latin Tongue. Nor would it be an useless Acquisition, if, for the same Reason,

---

* *It is very remarkable, that in this excellent Parable, our Saviour could not more livelily describe the Inhumanity of the Persons who abandoned the wounded Traveller, wallowing in his Blood, than by representing them under the Character of Priests, (as if the Clergy afforded the most expressive Emblems of Barbarity) nor depicture the Commiseration and Succour we owe our Neighbour, in brighter Colours, than by ascribing the friendly Office to a Layman.* See the whole 10th Chap. of St. LUKE's Gospel, [the parable of the good Samaritan], *which contains a most instructive Lesson, not like to be handled in the Pulpit with the Reflections it naturally affords.*

he was furnished with the Knowledge of most of the living Languages of *Europe*.

Natural Philosophy, called in the Schools *Physics*, is a Science, without which the Candidate for this Profession will never be eminent. It teaches us the Qualities and Affections of Matter; whereby we acquire the Knowledge of their different and manifold Influences. The Human Body, is of itself, a World of Wonders; a Subject of endless Curiosities. Its Constitution and Mechanism, must be the grand Subject of his Attention and Study. He must know all its Diversities, Qualities, Motions, Parts, their particular Relations, and those which every Part singly, and the Whole, stand in to all the Bodies that surround it. To that End the Qualities of Air, Fire, Water and Earth, in all their Quantities and Modifications, must be sagaciously investigated. The History of Diseases, and their Symptoms, singly and complexly considered, must be the Subject of his Thought and Study. The Virtues of the Animal, Vegetable and Mineral Kingdoms, are to be explored, and then applied to the Disease of the Patient. For this Purpose they are often to be compounded, and the Momenta of their respective Powers, weighed, added and subtracted, not only by a Ballance, but the nice and cool Judgments of a thoughtful Mind; a Mistake here, instantly issuing in the Death of the Patient. The Investigation of Medicines, is called the *Materia Medica*; and that of itself opens a most extensive Field of Knowledge, thro' which the Student must make an ample Range. Nature must be pried into in her darkest Cells, her most secret and hidden Recesses; to which End, Chemistry must lend her Aid, and employ all her torturing Arts. Further, so much of Metaphysics as teaches the Nature of the Soul, in its various Operations upon the human Economy, must pass under Consideration, since many are the Diseases on which the Passions have a critical Influence. How just therefore, that *Latin* Adage,

Ubi desinit Philosophus ibi incipit Medicus.[2]

In Logic and the Mathematics, if the Physician would think clearly and write methodically, it will be necessary to make some considerable Progress; and several other Branches of Knowledge that might be mentioned, will well deserve his Study, as preparatory to his particular Profession. How vast then, and extensive the Science! There is scarce a Power of the Body, or a single Faculty of the Soul, that must not be entirely engaged in a Preparation for a successful Practice, and be continually exercised in it. How tenacious must be the Memory to retain! how quick the Sagacity to discover! how clear the Judgment to distinguish, and how strong the Powers to reason, where the Objects of the Understanding are so manifold and diversified; and the Matter about which it is conversant, so important, and yet precarious to Mankind! How numerous then the Pre-requisites, to be attended to by him, who would qualify himself for so boundless a Field of Thought, so extensive a Sphere of Action?

First, *A Genius adapted to the Profession.* There is scarce a Calling in Life, but what requires a particular distinguished Cast of Mind, in him who would excel in it. There is no Truth more certain than this; and if we have recourse to History, or make even the most superficial Observation upon Mankind, we shall find it verified beyond Contradiction. The Difficulty lies only in determining, for what a Youth is more especially capacitated. And that indeed is a Task of which but very few are capable. The Fault lies here. The Father or Guardian, puts the Child or Pupil, upon an Employment, without consulting his Genius. And if they happen not to coincide, in vain are his Attempts. He fights against the invincible Law of his Nature, and must finally be disappointed. This has been the Fountain from whence the Ruin of Thousands hath been derived. It is a Rock upon which many have been Ship-wrecked. Infamy and Poverty are the eternal Consequences of a Genius misapplied, unless the Force of Nature, as it sometimes happens, carries off the Person from the Employment he first entered into, to another adapted to his Turn and Capacity. It may not be improper, among a Thousand that offer, to assign a few Instances of this. Sir BARTHOLOMEW SHOWER in *England,* and BOORHAAVE in *Holland,* were designed by their Fathers for the Pulpit: And tho' the Powers of their Minds were naturally strong, there was as little Prospect that either of them would succeed in *Divinity,* as if they had been naturally incapable of any Thing at all. *Naturam expellas furca licet usque recurret,*[3] said an Author, who in the Knowledge of Mankind, was inferior to none. Sir BARTHOLOMEW SHOWER struck into the Study and Practice of the Law, and there gave Play to those Abilities, which otherwise would have been lost to himself and the World. The same may be said of BOORHAAVE, who entered upon the Profession of *Physic.*[4] The first was scarce inferior to any Lawyer of his Day: The other, in the Healing-Art, surpassed all that preceeded him, and, by his most valuable Writings, made larger Accessions to that Science, than any Man: While both amassed to themselves very considerable Fortunes, and acquired a Reputation,

> *Quod nec imber edax, aut aquilo impotens*
> *Possit diruere, aut innumerabilis*
> *Annorum series & fuga temporum.*   HOR.[5]

'Twould supplant the Design of this Paper, should I proceed to expatiate on every Thing, preparatory to the Attainment of a considerable Skill in Physic: Let it suffice to mention, that much Study and great Industry are absolutely necessary. The Candidate must, besides, have the Advantages of Observation and Instruction, in a great Variety of Cases, and a tolerable Fortune, to bear up the Expences that will necessarily accrue, before he is able to practise with Safety; for till then he cannot honestly earn a single Farthing in his Profession. And where all these Things have been wanting in any considerable Degree, we may safely pronounce him a Quack and Pretender; a Wretch of all others, the most despicable in himself; and the most mischievous to Mankind.

I believe there is no City in the World, not larger than ours, that abounds with so many Doctors: We can, at least, boast the Honour of above Forty Gentlemen of the Faculty; and if the Principles before laid down, are true, we may argue *a Priori*, that far the greatest Part of them are meer Pretenders to a Profession, of which they are entirely ignorant. Nor do we want the more convincing Proofs of their known Incapacity, in the daily Examples of their iniquitous Practices: The very Advertisements they publish of themselves, prove them to be ignorant of the very Names of their Drugs; ignorant as Boys of the lowest Class in a Reading-

School, of even the little Art of Spelling. Besides, one needs no other Proof of their being low-liv'd Empyrics, than their infeasible Promises; and the boasting Air, in which they are expressed. How few of the Profession, can even support a Conversation upon the most common Subjects in Physic, without betraying their natural Stupidity and Ignorance! And yet so strangely absurd is our Conduct, that the meanest Quack among them, insinuates himself into a Subsistence: But, good God! what Carnage, what Destruction, must they perpetually occasion! How many of the Lives of the good People of this City, must annually fall a Sacrifice to those Pests of Society, those merciless Butchers of Human Kind! While we are tenacious of our *Property*, and justly glory in Laws wisely calculated for the Preservation of our Possessions, how preposterous is our Conduct, in trusting our *Persons* to murderous Quacks, and licens'd Assassins! By the Law of the Land, a Person is guilty of Murder, for killing a Man, by throwing a Stone from a House into the Street, where People usually pass, tho' there be no Evidence of Malice prepense: And shall an illiterate Mountebank, who deals about the Instruments of Destruction, escape with Impunity, when 'tis as demonstrable, that he has often deprived his Patients of Life, as if he had stabb'd them to the Heart? [6]

The Reader will pardon my Warmth, as the Blood of my Countrymen calls for Vengeance upon the Wretches that lavish it like Water, and afterwards fall upon the bereaved Widow and Orphan, with an extortionate Bill of Fees, to deprive them of the only Solace they have left them.

It is high Time the Arm of the Magistrate should interpose for Relief. The Lives of the People is the most valuable Branch of their Property, and surely the highest Object of the legislative Attention. In most of the well-regulated Cities in *Europe*, the Practisers of Physic are under the Regulation of the Law: That Profession, above all others, ought to be under its Direction, as it is more dangerous to Mankind than any. Thousands may be poison'd, and the Doctor pass unpunish'd: and yet there is none but that, which does not give some Security to the Public, for the Management of it, consistent with the Common-Weal. The *Divine* binds himself in the Presence of GOD, and is exposed to the

Animadversions of the whole World: Every One of his Hearers is a perpetual Spy upon his Principles and Conduct: The same is the Case of the Gentlemen of the *Long Robe*, who, besides being regulated by the Law, are under the Obligation of an Oath, to demean themselves uprightly in their Practice: But upon the Physician, there is no Check. If he heals, he has all the Honour due to him, and often receives it, where Nature would have performed the Cure without, and perhaps much sooner than by his Aid: If thro' Ignorance or Wickedness, the Patient dies under his Hands; he has even then Nothing to Fear: His Faults are often buried in the same Grave with the Deceased: They rise not in Judgment against him; and his Death is solely ascribed to Nature and Providence. T'would exceed the Bounds of my Paper, should I urge the Expediency of a Law, to regulate the Practice of Physic any farther at present. The Matter appears to me of the last Importance; and unless our Corporation think it proper, to take to themselves the Honour of giving a Redress; the Public may be assured, that before the next Sessions of Assembly, the Heads of an Act for that Purpose shall be proposed in this Paper; and I doubt not, the Complaints of a distressed People, against Quacks and Mountebanks, Extortion and Oppression, will find proper Relief from the Legislature, as they shall always command the Assistance of their chearful Advocate the *Independent Reflector*.[7]

A.

1. Ecclus. 38:1, 15.

2. "Where the philosopher leaves off, there the doctor begins."

3. *Naturam expelles furca tamen usque recurret.* "You may drive out nature with a fork, yet still she will return." Horace, *Epistles*, I, 10, 24.

4. Bartholomew Shower (1658–1701), English lawyer, member and treasured of Middle Temple, distinguished for his pleadings as defense counsel in important political and criminal cases. Hermann Boerhaave (1668–1738), physician and professor of botany and medicine, University of Leyden. Livingston had experienced a similar contest of wills with his father, challenging the elder Livingston's choice of the law as his career and proposing painting instead.

5. "Which no wasting rain, or furious north wind can destroy, or the countless chain of years and the flight of time." Horace, *Odes*, III, 30, 3.

6. New York City was not exceptional in this respect. Only about five per cent of the 3,500 medical practitioners in the colonies before the Revolution held degrees; and even in the largest towns, many practised who were

"in a pitiful state of ignorance." Richard H. Shryock, *Medicine and Society in Early America, 1660–1860* (New York, 1960), pp. 9, 17; Whitfield J. Bell, Jr., "Medical Practice in Colonial America," *Bulletin of the History of Medicine*, XXXI (1957), 442–453.

7. The *Reflector's* detailed proposals appeared in No. XXIV. Livingston's criticism of unlicensed practitioners was neither the first nor the last to appear in the New York press. Four years earlier the *New-York Evening Post* (April 3, 1749) had carried a proposal for a licensing law modeled after that of the West Indian island of Nevis; and a year after the *Reflector* essay, another correspondent in the public prints assailed the "daily and innumerable Abuses . . . committed on the Bodies of our Fellow Creatures, in the Practice of Physick and Surgery, by the unskillful Pretenders to both." (*New-York Gazette*, May 20, 1754.) Proposals to limit practice by licensing doctors were not uncommon in the eighteenth century, but rarely did the suggestions arise outside of the medical profession itself.

Number XIII

THURSDAY, FEBRUARY 22, 1753

Of PARTY-DIVISIONS

Furor arma ministrat.   Virg.[1]

*Factions amongst great Men, they are like Foxes; when their Heads
are divided, they carry Fire in their Tails; and all the Country
about them goes to Wreck for it.*
Webster's Dutchess of Malfy [2]

From the Moment that Men give themselves wholly up to a
Party, they abandon their *Reason,* and are led Captive by their
Passions. The Cause they espouse, presents such bewitching
Charms, as dazzle the Judgment; and the Side they oppose, such
imaginary Deformity, that no Opposition appears too violent;
nor any Arts to blacken and ruin it, incapable of a specious Varnish. They follow their Leaders with an implicit Faith, and, like
a Company of Dragoons, obey the Word of Command without
Hesitation. Tho' perhaps they originally embark'd in the Cause
with a View to the public Welfare; the calm Deliberations of
Reason are imperceptibly fermented into Passion; and their Zeal
for the common Good, gradually extinguished by the predominat-
ing Fervor of Faction: A disinterested Love for their Country, is
succeeded by an intemperate Ardor; which naturally swells into
a political Enthusiasm; and from that, easy is the Transition to
perfect Frenzy. As the religious Enthusiast fathers the wild Ravings of his heated Imagination, on the Spirit of God; and is ready
to knock down every Man who doubts his divine Inspiration; so
the political Visionary miscalls his Party-Rage the Perfection of
Patriotism; and curses the rational Lover of his Country, for his
unseasonable Tepidity. The former may be reduced to his Senses,
by shaving, purging, and letting of Blood; as the latter is only
to be reclaim'd by Time or Preferment.

Next to the Duty we owe the Supreme Being, we lie under

the most indispensible Obligations, to promote the Welfare of our Country. Nor ought we to be destitute of a becoming Zeal and Fortitude, in so glorious a Cause: We should shew ourselves in earnest, resolute and intrepid. We cannot engage in a nobler Undertaking; and scandalous would be our Languor and Timidity, where the Sacrifice of our Lives, is no extravagant Oblation. Replete with such illustrious Examples, are the Annals of Antiquity, when the great Men of those heroic Ages, with a kind of glorious Emulation, exerted their Talents in the Service of their Country; and were not only contented, but pleas'd to die for the Common-Weal. Hence CURTIUS and CODRUS,[3] with a splendid Catalogue of others, have rendered their Memories eternal, and acquired a Renown never to be obliterated. "In Nothing (says CICERO) do we bear a stronger Resemblance to the Divinity, than by promoting the Happiness of our Species." *Homines ad Deos nulla re proprius accedunt, quam falutem hominibus dando.*[4] But in vain doth Party-Spirit veil itself with the splendid Covering, of disinterested Patriotism: In vain usurp the Robe of Honour, to conceal its latent Motives. The Disguise may fascinate the Multitude; but appears transparent to the Unprejudiced and Judicious. With all the Eulogiums due to the Advocates for Liberty, without Success doth the self-interested Projector attempt to impose on Men of Sense, with that respectable Appellation. A Zeal for our Country is glorious, but a Spirit of Faction infamous. Nor is the incontestable Maxim of the Orator unlimited; but to be regulated by the sage Advice of the Poet,

> *Est modus in rebus: sunt certi denique fines,*
> *Quos ultrec citraque nequit consistere ratum.*   HOR.[5]

In a Word, there's a great Difference between staring and stark-mad.

When I see a Man warm in so important an Affair as the common Interest, I either suspend my Judgment, or pass it in his Favour. But when I find him misrepresenting and vilifying his Adversaries, I take it for a shrewd Sign, that 'tis something more than the laudable Motive he pretends, which impels him with such Impetuosity and Violence.

The great, as well as the little Vulgar, are liable to catch the Spirit of Mobbing; and cluster together to perpetrate a Riot, without knowing the Reason that set them in Motion. The genuine Consequence this, of Party-Rage and Animosity! For when once we suppress the Voice of Reason, by the Clamour of Faction, we are toss'd like a Vessel stripp'd of Sails and Rudder, at the Mercy of Wind and Tide: But 'tis a Solecism in Nature, that the best End in the World is to be attain'd by the worst Means; or that we cannot be Patriots, till we are fit for Bedlam.

A Man of this Turn, is not half so intent upon reforming the Abuses of his own Party, as discerning the Errors of his Enemies. To view the Virtues of the Side he espouses, he uses the magnifying End of the Perspective; but inverts the Tube, when he surveys those of his Adversaries. Instead of an impartial Examination of the Principles he acts upon, or the Regularity of his Progress, he contents himself with exclaiming against the real or suppositious Faults of his Antagonists. In short, 'tis not so much the Goodness of his own Cause, as the exaggerated Badness of the other, that attaches him to his Leaders, and confirms him in his Delirium. Like a Set of Pagans, he makes the Spots in the Sun, a Reason for adoring the Moon.

There are some enterprizing Geniuses, who love to fish in troubled Waters; and will themselves disturb the Fountain, to acquire a Reputation under Pretence of re-clarifying it to its pristine Purity. A Man who would be overlook'd, or despis'd in times of universal Tranquility, may have a Quantum of Lungs and Impudence, to make himself seem necessary when the Publick is agitated with Storms, and thrown into Convulsions. Nay, a Fellow who has deserved to be hang'd by all Laws human and divine, for his Conduct in private Life, will spring up into an important Champion at the Head of a Party.

"There is a particular Maxim among Parties (says a fine Writer) which alone is sufficient to corrupt a whole Nation; which is to countenance, and protect the most infamous Fellows, who happen to herd amongst them. It is something shocking to common Sense, to see the Man of Honour and the Knave, the Man of Parts and the Blockhead put upon an equal Foot, which is often the Case amongst Parties. The Reason is, he that has not Sense enough to distinguish right from wrong, can make a Noise; nay, the less Sense, the more Obstinacy, especially in a bad Cause; and the greater Knave, the more obedient to his Leaders, especially when they are playing the Rogue." Unspeakably calamitous have been the Consequences of Party-Division. It has occasioned Deluges of Blood, and subverted Kingdoms. It always introduces a Decay of publick Spirit, with the Extinction of every noble and generous Sentiment. The very Names of Things are perverted. On Fury and Violence it bestows the Appellation of Magnanimity and Opposition, and stiles Resentment and Rancour, Heroic Ardor, and Patriot-Warmth. Nor is it ever at a Loss for Pretences to bubble the Mob out of their Wits, and give its wildest Ravings a plausible Colour.

CÆSAR, POMPEY, and CRASSUS, were once the popular Party of *Rome*; and their Agent for managing the Rabble, the famous, or rather the infamous CLODIUS. Yet the first enslaved his Country, which but for him would have been enslaved by the Second; and as for CLODIUS he had Villany enough to have set *Rome* on Fire, and enjoyed the Conflagration, could he have done it with the same Impunity as NERO. CRASSUS was slain for his Avarice by the *Parthians*, who pouring down his Throat melted Gold, filled his Belly with what had ever been the Primum Mobile of *his* Party Spirit.

That the Heads of Parties are frequently actuated by private Views, has given great Handle to Court-Writers, who generally embrace every Opportunity to varnish the Conduct of their Employer, and argue sophistically in Proportion to his Wickedness, to triumph on so plausible a Topick, and cast an Odium on the most justifiable Opposition. Nay, they have carried their mercenary Impudence to such a Height, as to throw out sly Insinuations, that Patriotism itself is a meer Phantom, and endeavour to laugh the World out of one of the most illustrious Virtues in it. No sooner doth a Man, in the Integrity of Soul, dispute the illegal Measures of their Patron, than he is branded with the opprobrious Name of a factious Spirit, and his generous Benevolence to his Fellow Subjects, represented as a covert Project to accomplish his own Exaltation. As well might they impeach the sincerest Piety of Imposture and Hypocrisy, or infer the absolute Non-Existence of Virtue, from the World's abounding with Vice and Knavery.

Thus as the designing Party-Man always appears in the Mask of publick Spirit, and conceals the most selfish and riotous Disposition, under the venerable Pretext of asserting Liberty, and defending his Country; so the ministerial Scribbler, taking Advantage of this frequent Prostitution, gives a sinister Turn to the most laudable Views, and stigmatizes every Man who opposes the Encroachments of the Court. Hence the Necessity of our greatest Caution in siding with either Party, till by a watchful Observation in the Conduct of both, we have plainly discovered the true Patriot from the false Pretender.

Almost all the Mischiefs which Mankind groan under, arise from their suffering themselves to be led by the Nose, without a proper Freedom of Thought and Examination. Upon this Priest-craft has erected its stupendous Babel, and Tyranny rear'd her horrible Domination. And indeed, well may we expect, as the righteous Punishment of our Guilt, to be abandon'd by Heaven to Delusion and Error, if instead of obeying the Directions of that sacred Ray of the Divinity, in Virtue of which we claim kindred with the highest Order of Intelligences, we blindly surrender ourselves to the Guidance of any Man, or Set of Men whatever. And yet I have known Persons of good Sense, and Lovers of Liberty, so infatuated with Party, as to put a whole City and Country in Alarm, and struggle, as if it had been *pro uris et focis* [6] to lift a Creature into a Post, who, after all the Bustle made on his Account, was fitter to guide the Tail of a Plough, than to fill an Office of Skill and Confidence: But their Breasts were inflamed with Party-Spirit, and had the Candidate been a Chimney-Sweep, or a Rope-Dancer, they would have exerted an equal Zeal and Activity.

It must after all be allowed, that a long and uninterrupted Calm in a Government divided into separate Branches, for a Check on each other, is often presumptive, that all Things do not go well. Such is the restless and aspiring Nature of the human

Mind, that a Man intrusted with Power, seldom contents himself with his due Proportion. For this Reason, an unremitted Harmony between several Persons created as a Counterpoize to each other, is suspicious. Their Union may be the Consequence of their keeping within their proper Limits, and it may be the Effect of an iniquitous Coalition. To infer, therefore, that the Liberties of the People are safe and unendanger'd, because there are no political Contests, is illogical and fallacious. Such a Tranquility may be the Result of a Confederacy in Guilt, and an Agreement between the Rulers to advance their private Interest, at the Expence of the People. But this can never be our Case. Agreable to the generous Spirit of our Constitution, we have a Right to examine into the Conduct and Proceedings of our Superiors; and upon discovering them in a Combination of Roguery, if we cannot set them together by the Ears, we can form a Party against their united Strength: And such a Party, I hope we may never want the Spirit to form. To conclude, shou'd a future Governor give in to Measures subversive of our Liberties, I hope he will meet with proper Opposition and Controul: But should a Faction be formed against him, without Law or Reason, may the Authors be branded with suitable Infamy.   Z.

Mr. REFLECTOR,

I HOPE you will not think it a Paradox that I am one of your greatest Admirers, and at the same Time infinitely pleased to find you meet with so much Opposition. Was it not for the Uproar made about your Writings, I should think them useless, and that you combated an Apparition of your own raising. But the terrible Clamour about a Paper wrote in the true Spirit of a Protestant, and I may add with the Benevolence of a Christian, convinces me of the Seasonableness and Utility of your Speculations. Those who traduce you, answer your Description: But your Enemies do not consider that by every scurvy Libel they publish, they present you with Laurels that will bloom and flourish, when their Stupidity is buried in Oblivion. Whoever prosecuted so generous a Design, without raising a Swarm of Slanderers? When the Moon bursts from behind an interposing Cloud, it sets all the Dogs in the Country abarking. While there is a Fool, or a Knave, or a Bigot, they will villify whoever exposes Folly, or Roguery, or Bigotry. But as sure as you answer any of their Jargon, you disoblige one of your best Friends. I would at least insist on your entering the Lists, with some of their Leaders: For tho' the worsting those would be no great Matter of Triumph, it would nevertheless be getting the better of Nonsense, at first Hand. But to engage with every superstitious Idiot, who aims at Renown by your Notice of him, wou'd be a disgrace to your Pen, and a Condescention beneath your Character. No, Sir, maintain your elevated Sphere, and do, as you have promised in your Introduction, *look down upon them with a sovereign Contempt.* Sacrifice not an Hour of the Time you can employ in instructing the Publick, to the immortalizing those, who, unless you give them an Air of Importance, by confuting their Absurdities, will only prove the Beings of a Day, and then sink into Oblivion, like all other dirty Scribblers their Predecessors. You ought rather to thank them for their Scurrility. They are only so many Heralds that proclaim your Praise, and propagate the Reputation of your Writings. Nay, they are more. They will furnish you with Matter for future Speculations: Not by honouring them with Replies, but by acquainting you with the Number of Bigots and Blockheads, and thence extorting from you a Remedy for their Distempers. Proceed, therefore, without Hesitation and Fear, nor slack your noble Progress, by running after every little Insect that would obstruct your Journey. In a Word, scorn to imitate the Crow who descends on a filthy Carrion, amidst a Garden of the most odoriferous Flowers.   *Yours,*

Z.   Timothy Freeheart.[7]

I Have received the Letter signed Sebastian; *and another subscribed* James Change; *a Third from the ingenious* Philander; *and a Fourth from a former Correspondent who signs* A Lover of Liberty and Truth; *all which shall be considered in due Season.*

The Letter signed Simei, *is also come to hand; but as I think it not proper to publish it in the* Reflector, *I beg my Correspondent to signify whether I may insert it in one of the weekly News-Papers.*

The Letter in Vindication of the Petition opposed by Eboracus, *shall be published next Week.*

1. "Rage supplies arms." Virgil, *Aeneid*, I, 50.

2. *The Dutchess of Malfi* (c. 1614), a tragedy, by John Webster (1580?–1625?).

3. Legendary classical heroes who sacrificed their own lives to save Rome and Athens from a natural disaster and a military defeat.

4. Cicero, *Pro Ligario*, XII, 38. Livingston's translation is provided in the preceding sentence.

5. "There is a measure in all things. There are fixed limits beyond which and short of which right cannot find a resting place." Horace, *Satires*, I, 1, 106.

6. Correctly, *pro aris et focis*, "on behalf of altars and firesides," i.e., for religion and country. Virgil, *Eclogues*, VI, 44.

7. This may have been Noah Welles (1718–1776), Livingston's Yale classmate and confidant, whom Livingston had entreated to contribute something to the paper. In mid-February Livingston thanked his friend for "complying with my Importunity," adding: "Your Letter to the Reflector is safely delivered." (Livingston to Welles, January 17, February [19?], 1753, JFP, Yale.) Welles's letter, however, may have been the much longer communication in No. XV. The signature "M" is the same as that in an essay in the later series, "The Watch-Tower," which Welles seems to have written. (Livingston to Welles, December 7, 1754, JFP, Yale; *New-York Mercury*, January 27, 1755.)

Number XIV

[Remarks on the Water Lots, continued]

Acccording to my Promise, I now present my Readers with the Letter in Vindication of the Petition opposed by *Eboracus*.

To the INDEPENDENT REFLECTOR

SIR,   *New-York, 3d February, 1753.*

Tho' I do not remember, that you have in any of your Papers, promised to admit Answers or Replies, to the Letters of your Correspondents, I have notwithstanding, taken the Freedom to make some Remarks upon that signed *Eboracus,* which was printed in your last.[1] It is not my Intention, to oppose either the Principles of that Author, or your own. No, Sir, I aim at nothing more than to except the particular Case which makes the Subject of his Letter, from the Influence of those Principles, and to Point out a few Mistakes in it, which will, as I judge, have a Tendency, to vindicate the Petitioners, from any Surmises of Collusion, sinister Schemes, or Assurance, which Mankind are too apt, without sufficient Evidence, to entertain of them. As I will cast no Reflections whatever, nor even press what I write with Animation and Fire, but confine myself to a short simple Narration of Particulars, for the Benefit of the Innocent, but injured Petitioners; I have the utmost Confidence that you will give my Letter, a Pass thro' your Paper; especially when I entirely submit both its Matter and Dress, to your ingenious Corrections.

First: The Petitioners, as I am informed, are enabled, by the most authentic Records, to prove that the Lands which belong to them, and adjoin to the Soil, for which they have prayed a Grant, were originally bounded by a Street, or Road, that ran along the Edge of the River. They can also render it evident by the Testimony of many living Witnesses, that there was a high Bank, Part of the Petitioners Lands, near the River, which, by the gradual Encroachments of the Water for many Years, is at length entirely wash'd away: And also, that in former Times the Distance between the Meadow belonging to the Petitioners, and the utmost Verge of High-Water Mark, was very considerable, they being separated by the above mentioned Bank; but that at this

151

Day, the Water rises almost to the Edge of the Meadow, and in Spring-Tides overflows the greatest Part of it. Whence it manifestly appears, that part of the very Land prayed for, between the now High and Low-Water Mark, originally belonged to the Petitioners. So that, altho' the Corporation ought to dispose of their Lands at public Vendue; yet, in this Case, a Sale of that Kind would subject the Petitioners to the Necessity, either of paying an exorbitant Price for, or suffering some other Person, who would be the highest Bidder, to take from them what is equitably theirs. I must, therefore, beg Leave to think, that a private Sale to the Petitioners of the Lands they have prayed for, is extremely just and reasonable.

It is also a Mistake in the Letter-Writer, *That all the Water Lots from Mr.* Desbrosse's *to Mr.* Bogart's, *were exposed to Sale at publick Auction, or Vendue.* In Proof of this, I adduce the following Instances. In the Year 1701, a Grant passed to one *Sacket*, of the Soil contained between the Bounds of his Land, and Low-Water, for the Consideration of £90, Part of which is to the Westward of Mr. *Desbrosse's*; and the Breadth of the whole Lands granted, (including Mr. *Desbrosse's* Lot) was no less than Five Hundred and Sixty Feet. This Sale was not at Vendue; nor was there one Farthing as a Quit Rent reserved. Another Grant was afterwards made about the Year 1737, to Mr. *Peck*, subject to the Reservation of one Shilling per Foot, per Annum: But neither was this a Sale at publick Auction. It must indeed be confessed, that most of the Land from the West Bounds of *Sacket*, to the Slip called *Peck's*, was sold by the Corporation at Vendue: But true it is, that every Part of that Land, was near One Hundred and Fifty Feet above High-Water Mark, and lay between that, and the publick Road, commonly called *Queen-Street*. And as to that other Instance mentioned in the Letter, of a publick Sale of the Lots where Messrs. *Walton* and *Clarkson* now live. It is to be remarked, that they were not Water Lots at the Time of their Sale, as the Author asserts, but either Upland unconveyed by the Corporation, or Water Lots which had, before that Time, been filled up at the public Expence. And an annual Sum was paid, as I am informed, to a certain Person for his Care and Oversight of that Business.

Another Mistake in the Letter, is the Assertion, *That the Petitioners proposed to the Committee, to accept of a Grant of the Lots from High to Low-Water Mark, and thence Two Hundred Feet into the River, subject to a Quit-Rent of* Nine Pence *a Foot.* Unhappily, Sir, the Proposals to the Committee were verbal: Nor do I find, that any Minute has been made of them. The Truth, however, of the Matter is, that the Petitioners did not ask of the Committee, any more than the Land from High-Water Mark to *Water-Street*, which is near Two Hundred Feet less than *Eboracus* mentions; for which they offered an annual Rent of *Nine-Pence* a Foot, to commence at the Expiration of Twenty Years, from the Date of their Grant. That such only were the Proposals, I appeal to the whole Committee, and to all the Members of the Corporation, who were present when a verbal Report of the Matter was made; and if they do not unanimously confirm my Account, I will acquiesce in any Conclusion whatever, to the Prejudice of the Integrity and Honour of the Petitioners. Hence it also appears, that the Letter is chargeable with another Mistake, *viz.*

That *the Petitioners did not propose to give any Consideration at all for the Lots, from High to Low-Water Mark.* Whereas if the above Proposals are true, as to the Extent of the Land, the Soil between High and Low-Water Mark, is nearly all that is contained, between High-Water Mark and *Water-Street*; and therefore is that upon which alone the annual Rent of *Nine Pence* per Foot, can possibly be fixed. Nor are the Terms upon which they proposed to take the Lands, so astonishingly absurd as the Letter-Writer pretends. As a great Part of the Land they prayed for, was equitably theirs, it is but reasonable, that the Rent reserved upon those Lands, should be smaller than usual. But, besides, it is a common Practice, with the Corporation, to grant Lands free from Rent for a Number of Years, when their Situation is such as necessarily to subject the Purchasers to great Expence, before they can be made profitable. In this View the Lands prayed for by the Petitioners, are in a worse State than any that have been hitherto granted by the Corporation; and therefore, a Grant unincumbered with a Rent for a Number of Years, is not so great and unreasonable a Donation, as *Eboracus* has laboured to prove.

But further, Sir, excepting a few Instances, it has invariably been the Practice of the Corporation, to grant the Water Lots to particular Petitioners, upon Terms agreed on between them, and not at Vendue. In these Grants, the Preference has generally been given to the Proprietors of the Upland, contiguous to the Water Lots. I have besides heard it asserted by the Petitioners, that, considering the Nature and Situation of the Soil opposite to the Water Lots, the Expence of Dockage will be so great, as that *Nine Pence* per Foot for them, is as much as they thought those Lots were worth. And that if their Proposals are further considered, with relation to the common Terms, upon which the Grants of the Corporation have lately been made, it will appear, that the Reservation of *Nine Pence* per Foot, was as advantageous to the City, all Things considered, as most others that have been made.

Upon the whole, if these unornamented Assertions are true, and I aver them to be so, how little Reason is there for the hard Insinuations, that the Letter-Writer has urged against the Petitioners? Their Petition for a private Grant, besides its being equitable in this Case, as

I have shewn, far from being unprecedented, was wholly agreable to the former and latter Practice in such Cases. The Terms upon which they proposed to take the Grant, were reasonable in their Opinion, and such as they could not exceed without prejudicing their own Interest. And by the Length of Time this Matter has been depending, instead of surprizing the Corporation into a Grant that would prove detrimental to this City, they have given them ample Leisure to consider the Nature of those Proposals. Where then is the Absurdity of their Conduct? What Foundation is there for charging them with astonishing Propositions? Or for the injurious Reflection, that they were endeavouring to cajole the Corporation, into a Step prejudicial to the Inhabitants of this City, with whose Rights they are intrusted. I believe every unprejudiced Man will think they are vanished; and by your Assistance, I hope to have the Satisfaction, to hear many, who were imposed upon by the Letter, confess themselves agreably undeceived.

I am, Your Humble Servant,

AGRICOLA.

The preceeding Letter had been printed sooner, but the Subject of it being a Matter of much Conversation in Town, and the Facts it contains variously represented, I cared not to publish it, till I had sufficiently acquainted myself with the whole Affair, and was enabled to represent the Petition, and the Objections to it, in a true Light.

My Correspondent asserts, that a great Part of the Land within the Grant prayed for by the Petitioners, has from Time to Time been washed away, and that most of the Soil equitably belongs to them. If these Facts are true, the Prayer of the Petition, for whatever they can prove originally theirs, ought in Justice to be granted without any Consideration: And Quære, whether they are not entitled to it without a Grant from the Corporation? But I cannot conceive that the Petitioners Right to a Part of what is now beyond Low-Water Mark, should entitle them to any Thing not included in their just Bounds, at a lower Rate than others are willing to give. For be the Commodiousness or Inconveniency of Situation what it will, the Corporation ought not in Justice to their Constituents, to grant it without a valuable Consideration. The Petitioners propose, for aught I know, as much as any others are willing to give; but what that is, cannot well be determined, till they have had an Opportunity of making their offers. And no Way seems to me so proper, as exposing it to Sale at public Vendue. Nor can the Possessors of the Lands adjoining, have any Reason to think themselves, by this Method, aggrieved, there being no more Colour for pretending, that the Contiguity of their Lands, entitles them to what belongs to the City, than to the Lands of any adjoining Neighbours. The Instances assigned, of Grants by former Corporations to the Owners of contiguous Lands, should be no Argument with the present Corporation to do the like: For if their Predecessors have done Wrong, the present ought not to imitate their Example. Besides, the Water Lots are now of greater Value than formerly; and why the Publick should not have the Advantage of the Rise of Lands, as well as private Persons, I cannot conceive.

It must also be confessed, that if such was the Practice of former Corporations, the Petitioners were injured in some of the Charges of *Eboracus*, as well as my own. For if the Corporation has heretofore made so great a Number of similar Grants, as this Gentleman mentions, their Petition ought not to have been represented in so disadvantageous a Light. The Imitation of a common Practice, could not be an unexampled Piece of Immodesty. So far therefore as *Eboracus*'s Observations were founded upon this Mistake, they must be erroneous; and I am obliged to the Writer of this Letter, for enabling me to rectify his Error, and doing the Petitioners all the Justice in my Power. But I cannot at the same Time help remarking, that the Correction of this Article, will not in the least affect the Principles upon which the Arguments against the Grant prayed for, are founded. Those still remain in full Force, and are absolutely incontestible. It will indeed place the Conduct of the Petitioners in a more favourable Light; but render that of the Corporation, should they give into the Scheme, the more inexcusable and unjust. Have former Corporations made a Practice of giving away the Lands of the City, it should be an Inducement to their Successors, to obliterate the Remembrance of those Transgressions, by a more inviolable Attachment to their Duty. And however they may flatter themselves with a kind of Omnipotence and unaccountable Authority, I doubt not they will experience the Resentment of an injur'd People, at a Time when they are most solicitous about the popular Esteem.

O.

For the Letter from PHILALETHES, *I return my most hearty Thanks; it contains so seasonable and judicious a Defence of my Papers, that in Justice to myself, it shall not remain long unpublished. I flatter myself with the Hopes of some further Assistance, from so ingenious a Correspondent, whose easy, flowing Style, is the most inconsiderable Ornament of his Letter.*

To the Gentleman who is so urgent with me to publish the Names of the Persons who have taken Offence at some of my Papers, and returned them; I answer, That tho' I am obliged to him for the Zeal be expresses in my Favour, yet I can by no Means comply with his Request; exposing the Bigotry, Superstition, Weakness and Ignorance of private Characters, being remote from my Inclination and Design. I suppose it will be a Pleasure to him to be informed, that should Fifty of my Subscribers fall off, there are as many ready to subscribe in their Stead; and if One Hundred were struck out of my List, I can still prosecute my Labours without Expence to myself, or any Discouragement to my Printer.[2]

1. Actually in issue No. X.
2. The cancellations were the direct result of the article on the Moravians. It had "made a most prodigious Noise amongst High Church of all kinds," he informed Welles in Connecticut, "several Bigots having refused to take the paper any longer." He insisted, however, that "Curiosity has since procured more Subscribers than Bigotry had drawn off"; and undaunted, he expressed confidence that "the Author will rise in his Spirit." Livingston to Welles, January 17, 1753, JFP, Yale.

Number XV

THURSDAY, MARCH 8, 1753

The Controversy between the Independent Reflector, and his Adversaries, truly stated, and considered

Tu ne cede Malis, sed contra audentior ito.   HOR.[1]

To heed all the defamatory Libels that are weekly published against me, and the more malignant Slanders wherewith I am daily bespatter'd in Company, were a Task equally impracticable and ungrateful. For this Reason I had determined to follow the Advice of my sage Correspondent TIMOTHY FREEHEART, *not to answer any of their Jargon.* I own, was any Thing advanc'd against me, that bore the Marks of Candour and Impartiality, and an unbiassed Love for Truth, I should think myself bound to give the Author the Satisfaction he deserved, and frankly confess and retract whatever appear'd incapable of a rational Defence. But when a Scribbler demonstrates an incurable Zeal for superstitious Trumpery and Nonsense: When Rage stands for Argument, and Priest for Religion: When like the Worshippers of NEBUCHAD-NEZER's Image,[2] he bends the Knee to a stupid Idol, and not content with his own Idolatry, defames every Man who refuses to join in his absurd Adoration: When instead of a candid Detection of my Errors, so often requested, he rails, and blusters, and scolds, and threatens, and misrepresents: When, in fine, he disavows all Regard for Truth and Decency, but appears incorrigible in his Bigotry, and writes rather to vilify than convince: When this, I say, is the Case, Reason dictates and Prudence enjoins an immovable Stability, and a just Abhorrence of all the Scurrility and Malevolence he utters. When on the Contrary, Men of Honour and Principle inadvertently mistake my Meaning, I think myself obliged by the Laws of Humanity and good Manners, to do Justice to them and myself, by a more explicit and determinate Explanation.[3] As this is fully, and (I may add without Flattery to my Correspondent) elegantly done in the following Letter, which I give my Readers without the Alteration of a single Sentiment, I doubt not they will excuse my inserting it; after assuring them, that by the implacable Rancour of my Enemies, my Advocates have been refused a Hearing in the public Papers; and my solemn Promise, not to trouble them with a farther Vindication of the *Reflector*, 'till something appears of greater Solidity than those Loads of Calumny that have hitherto been disgorged against him.[4]

To the INDEPENDENT REFLECTOR.

SIR,

Many Reasons may be given, why a Writer of eminent Abilities, may be so circumstanced, that a Vindication of his own Productions will come better from an inferior Genius, than from himself. I sit down to write convinced of this Distinction. If you should think proper to produce my Sentiments to the Public, I assure them, I know you not. I have read your Speculations with Pleasure, and I hope with Improvement. I esteem you, because I think, whoever endeavours to cultivate the human Mind, deserves Esteem. My Attempt to vindicate your Writings, arises from my Love of Truth and of Mankind; conscious of these Motives, the Exertion of them gives me Pleasure. If my Essay, is by any received with Insensibility, or with Indignation, I shall feel the Pain of disappointed Benevolence, and be forced to say, *Qui vult decepi, decipiatur.*[5]

Your Two Lucubrations, Number VI and Number XI, have stirred up the Passions of *some*, and been the Subjects of Reflection to *many*.

Tho' it be a mortifying Truth, founded on just Observation of Mankind, *That in Religious Attachments, Prejudice and Passion, do more generally take the Lead, than Reason and Judgment*; yet I have that Honour for, and Dependance upon the Rationality of Human Nature, as to hope and believe, a candid Appeal to the Understandings of my Fellow Citizens on your aforesaid Papers, may, in some Measure, tend to compose that Fermentation of Spirits, which hath been worked up, either by their own Misapprehensions or the disgraceful Influence of *such*, whose Interest it is to lead captive their reasonable Powers.

It would be a painful Task to recollect, it would be an unworthy One to repeat, all the vain Babblings which Ignorance hath thrown out, and the Scurrilities which a reproachful Zeal hath sent forth against you. The Bell-weathers began the Cry, and the simple Sheep set up their Bleatings.

The Accusations against you, may be comprized under two general Heads:

First, That you have departed from the Character under which you introduced yourself to the Public, in your first Number.

Secondly, That you have treated the Clergy of this City and Province, indecently and unjustly.

As to the first Article. Your introductory Paper Number I. is before me. I have carefully reviewed it, and the only Declaration I can find as to Religion, is the following Paragraph, "The espousing any Polemic Debate between different Sects of Christians, shall be the last Charge against him; tho' he shall be ever ready to deliver his Sentiments on the Abuses and Encroachments of any, with the Freedom and Unconcernedness becoming Truth and Independency."

That you will not enter yourself a Party, in any of those religious Controversies, which subsist amongst the different Sects of Christians, is a wise and prudent Resolution; and I challenge your Antagonists to prove, that you have; and I hope that you will not deviate from it. But I must beg Leave to offer an Enlargement to the Words of this Part of your Declaration, and I would have them stand thus: — As I firmly believe the undefiled Religion of the ever blessed JESUS, to contain no one Point of Controversy, I do therefore abhor, despise and renounce, all those Impostors, those Scribes and Pharisees of Christianity, who, under the Names of Fathers, Patriarchs, Popes, Bishops, Priests, Deacons, *etc.* have taught for Doctrines of God, the Commandments and Inventions of Men; have compiled immense Volumes of Falsehood, Nonsense, and Blasphemy, in support of their frantic Zeal, their Impiety and infamous Ambition. And I do hold in equal Detestation, all modern Scribes and Pharisees, who, under the Name of a Christian Clergy, endeavour to impose on, and divide the Professors of Christianity, with the aforesaid Rubbish and Villainy of ancient Falsehoods and Disputations, demonizing the Minds of Men towards each other, by maintaining the Religion of JESUS, upon Distinctions without a Meaning, larding it with metaphysical Riddles, and imposing on the Understandings of their Congregations, by pompous Sounds, and Sacerdotal Artifices.

You go on and say, you "shall be ever ready to deliver your Sentiments on the Abuses and Encroachments of any" Sect of Christians.

The Vindication of the *Moravians,* in your Paper Number VI, which hath occasioned so much hallooing against you, falls evidently within the Plan you prescribed to yourself. You assert, they have been vilified and abused from the Pulpit. I have heard the same from others who were Ear-Witnesses of it; and it has not been contradicted by your Antagonists. So far, therefore, Matter of Fact is in your Favour. That the People called *Moravians,* are a virtuous, peaceable, useful Part of the Community, no one hath attempted to disprove. Your defending them, therefore, from the *jealous Rancour* of priestly Intolerance, was highly commendable, and consistent with your declared Undertaking.

But it is alledged, That in Vindication of the *Moravians,* you have thrown out Invectives against the sacred Order of the Clergy, where your Subject did not require it, and inconsistent with that Character you professed, and by which you recommended your Design to the Approbation of the Publick.

This Objection I apprehend, is grounded upon too warm and mistaken a Zeal for the Word *Clergy,* and the Objectors not being sufficiently aware, of that encroaching Disposition upon the religious Rights of Mankind, and that Thirst of Dominion which hath ever animated the Clergy of all Denominations, proved so fatal to past Ages, and ought to be kept under a strict Curb in every Age.

That the Clergy are a necessary Order of Men, no wise Man will, or at least I think ought to dispute. When the Lives of the Clergy are an exemplary Pattern to all Men: When *they* renounce the Pomps and Vanities of this World, in order to apply themselves the more intensely to prepare their Flocks for a Better; When *they* preach only the Commandments of God: When *they* enforce his Precepts by those Motives alone which he hath thought proper to make known: When *their* whole Ambition is to gain Followers of JESUS CHRIST, not Followers of *them* and *their Doctrines*: When Mildness, Humility, universal disinterested Benevolence, are a Seraphick Guard over *their* Hearts, *their* Words, and *their* Actions: When *their* warmest Endeavours are, to bend the Heart to the genuine Impressions of Christianity, not the Passions to Party Distinctions: When *they* honestly and generously disdain, to advance their Influence upon the too prevailing Ignorance and Superstition of Mankind: To conclude, when *they* reject implicit Obedience: When *they* neither seek for, nor encourage a slavish and illiberal Submission: When the Clergy, or to speak more within Bounds, when *a* Clergyman manifests such a Character as this, we can scarce pay him more Veneration than he deserves. Such a One will shine with redoubled Lustre from the Contrast of your Papers now under Consideration.

This forms the Divine, who is worthy of our warmest Affections. To *him* we may be attached with a Godly Jealousy: And I persuade myself, no Man will pay *him* a more unfeigned Esteem and Veneration, than the *Independent Reflector.*

But the Man who acts inconsistently with the Tenor of this Description; in spite of his priestly Accoutrements, or his solemn Air; whether he be puffed up with the insolent Fumes of Clerical Pride, or distended with luxurious Morsels from a bigoted Laity: Or, whether he be shrivelled into the Size of a mortified *Anchoret*: It matters not. *He* may disgorge his Load of *Latin, Greek,* and *Hebrew,* and make Fools stare, and old Women wonder: *He* may dance upon the Point of a metaphysical Needle: *He* may entertain his Congregation with a Flourish of rabbinical Raphsodies: *He* may fight thro' all the Weapons of the Commentators: *He* may turn a Text into Twenty Meanings it will not bear, and shun that which is evident to common Sense. All this *He* may be, and all this *He* may do; and to the Shame of Mankind it must be confessed, *He* may find stupid Zealots to admire him, and some may groan, and some may grunt their Approbation: But every Man who will suffer his unprejudiced Reason to give a Verdict, will put such a Creature down, for a deceiving impudent Mountebank: And that there are such in Divinity as well as Physic, those who want Proofs, want Knowledge.

There are the Clergy the *Reflector* levels his Resentment against; and whoso is angry, subjects his Wrath to Contempt.

To prove that the Clergy of all Denominations, in every Age of the Christian Church, have made War upon the Understandings of Mankind, have imposed on the Ignorance, encouraged the Superstition, inflamed the Passions, raised and abetted the Prejudices of their Followers: That they have done this from Motives of Envy, Ambition and Avarice; That to maintain and extend this iniquitous Domination, they have raised the most dreadful Commotions in Civil Society, have set Men a worrying each other like Savage Beasts, have inspired them with Enthusiastic Madness and Blood-thirsty Zeal, in Matters of meer Opinion, and oftener of false Opinion: And have marked the Reign of *their* tyrannical Usurpations, and their insatiable Thirst of Power, with such impious Devastations, and such a horrible Carnage of the Human Species, that had the infernal Regions been let loose upon Mankind, they would scarce have equalled. To prove, I say, the Truth of these Things, by an Induction of Facts, would be transcribing the greatest Part of Ecclesiastical History from the third Century, almost every Page of which is stained with Human Gore.

This is a true Picture, warranted by Church and other Histories, of a great Part, I wish it might not be justly said, of the greatest Part of the Clergy of past Ages, of very many in the last Age, and of too many in the Beginning of the present.

Is it not therefore justifiable? Is it not therefore commendable in a public Writer, to put the Community, for whose Sake he assumes that Character, upon their Guard, against any Encroachments upon their Religious Liberties: To animate them with a manly and rational Resentment against the Seductions of Priestcraft: To inspire them with a generous Detestation of any Attacks upon Liberty of Conscience, and the Right of private Judgment in religious Opinions: To warn Men against the Ebullitions of Enthusiasm, the degrading Influence of Superstition, and the fatal Consequences of a bigoted and implicit Submission, to the Dictatorship of the Clergy of every Distinction.

The *Independent Reflector* hath done this: And he hath done it, in my humble Opinion, with the laudable Spirit of a Watch-Man for the public Weal: He hath solemnly professed all that Veneration for the unadulterated Religion of JESUS CHRIST, and the upright Ministers of His Gospel, which becomes a Christian. Who hath he exclaimed against? Such as are a Disgrace to the sacred Character: Such as I have described in a foregoing Part of this Letter. What hath he exclaimed against? A Spirit of Intolerance, Bigotry, Superstition and Enthusiasm.

But it is said Secondly, That you have treated the Clergy of this City and Province, indecently and unjustly.

I must beg Leave to think, the Accusation is false and malicious, and may, with much greater Justice, be retorted upon your Adversaries. For the Word *Clergy*, is an aggregate Term, signifying, an Order of Men appointed to conduct the external Worship of Religion: Of great Part of whom, History and Experience will justify all you have said. If your Accusers will bring the Clergy of this City and Province, within the diabolical Circle, and they really deserve it, (which, for my Part, I am so far from even believing, that I am, as to many of them, morally certain of the Contrary), why, let Satan arise and take them to himself. If our Clergy will imprudently throw themselves into the Circle, and, with the stupid Fondness of Indian Wives, be burnt with their unworthy Mates, I sincerely pity their ridiculous Ardor, and do hereby conjure them, if they have "any Remains of sober Reason, and Christianity left, to be advised by a Friend," to turn about, and escape so great Damnation.

I shall presume to take my Leave of you, with one Word of Advice to yourself, and another to your Antagonists. I hope you, Sir, will consider the Clergy, as Men of like Passions with ourselves, and not expect a Perfection of Conduct and Character, which is beyond the Tether of Humanity. And, whilst you watch over the public Welfare of your Country, you will not disturb it, by too refined Animadversions on the Sacred Order.

To your Adversaries, I beg Leave to recommend that Moderation, that Charity, that Mildness of Temper, so eloquently, so energetically described in the Gospel, as the distinguishing Characteristic of true Christianity. And, with these Virtues of the Heart, to aspire after those of the Head, to cultivate their Understandings, to exert their

Judgments, and thereby make their Religion the Object of a rational Choice, and their religious Attachments the Offspring of a manly Deliberation.

By a suitable Observation of these Admonitions, which I respectfully offer, from the unfeigned Dictates of public Good-Will, I flatter myself, every wise and good Person will be, as I am,

Sir, Your Well-Wisher, and constant Reader,

M.   *New-York, Feb.* 24, 1753.   PHILALETHES.

1. "Yield not to misfortune, but press forward the more boldly." The attribution to Horace is incorrect. It is Virgil, *Aeneid*, VI, 95.

2. Nebuchadnezzar, King of Babylon, erected a golden image on the plain of Dura, commanding that it be worshiped on pain of death. Dan. 3:1–6.

3. When Noah Welles expressed reservations about the *Reflector's* undiscriminating attacks on the ministry Livingston admitted that perhaps he had gone "rather too far in his Notions of orthodoxy," and had not been "particular Enough in distinguishing the Clergy he writes against from those who are an Ornament to Mankind." Livingston to Welles, February [19?], 1753, JFP, Yale.

4. The "Philo-Reflector" letter by Smith in the *New-York Gazette*, February 19, 1753, had given such "high offence" to Anglican clergymen that they brought pressure on James Parker, the printer, to discontinue further contributions from that source. Cancellations to the paper led Parker to decline letters supporting the *Reflector* without the churchmen's approval, and as a result only two more letters appeared (April 9, 16, 1753). For Livingston and his friends the paper became "a fountain sealed." The *New-York Mercury*, printed by Hugh Gaine, an Episcopalian, had, as Livingston complained, "long before been inaccessible to me, or my friends." The *Post*, New York's third regular paper, ceased early in 1753, but it had carried one pro-*Reflector* letter, April 9. On Livingston's difficulties with the press, see *Independent Reflector, Preface*, pp. 8–9; *Samuel Johnson Writings*, I, 169; see also No. XL notes 1 and 4.

5. "Whoever wishes to be deluded, let him be deluded." Attributed to Cardinal Caraffa in the sixteenth century, but the idea appears in many languages and other forms much earlier.

Number XVI

THURSDAY, MARCH 15, 1753

Of the Transportation of Felons

It is plain the Author of the following Letter, designed it *verbatim* for the Press; and indeed, the Subject of it, is of such Importance, and so well expressed, that I shall make no Scruple of laying it before the Public, just as it came to Hand, for the Entertainment of this Day. I wish, the Number of such Correspondents was increased; and shall always be ready to thank this Gentleman, for any future Assistance, adapted to my original Design.

To the INDEPENDENT REFLECTOR

SIR,

The Credit of your Paper is so well established, notwithstanding all the Scurrilities which have been vented against you, that no Man can more advantageously propose a Reformation of any public Abuse, or a new Regulation for preventing Evils, than by an Application to you. The Encouragement you have given, to so good an End, is not better suited to the Continuation of your Papers, and their general Usefulness, than of a Piece with the public Spiritedness you have already demonstrated in them. Thus much, as a Lover of my Country, I thought myself in Duty bound to testify. And, such being my Judgment, as well of your Design, as of your Performances in the Execution of it, I shall be proud of becoming your Correspondent, as often as I can write upon Subjects of sufficient Importance, to merit a Place in your Paper. All I have now to communicate, Sir, is occasioned by the Robberies that have of late been so frequent in this City. A Matter well worth the Animadversions of the *Independent Reflector*.

It is too well known that in Pursuance of divers Acts of Parliament, great Numbers of Fellows who have forfeited their Lives to the Public, for the most atrocious Crimes, are annually transported from Home to these Plantations.[1] Very surprizing one would think, that Thieves, Burglars, Pick-Pockets and Cut-Purses, and a Herd of the most flagitious Banditti upon Earth, should be sent as agreeable Companions to us! That the Supreme Legislature did intend a Transportation to *America*, for a Punishment of these Villains, I verily believe: But so great is the Mistake, that confident I am, they are thereby on the Contrary, highly rewarded. For what in God's Name can be more agreeable to a penurious Wretch, driven thro' Necessity, to seek a Livelyhood by breaking of Houses, and robbing upon the King's High-Way, than to be saved from the Halter, redeemed from the Stench of a Gaol, and transported, Passage free, into a Country, where being unknown, no Man can reproach him with his Crimes; where Labour is high, a little of which will maintain him; and where all his Expences will be moderate and low. There is scarce a Thief in *England*, that would not rather be transported than hanged. Life in any Condition, but that of extreme Misery, will be preferred to Death. As long, therefore, as there remains this wide Door of Escape, the Number of Thieves and Robbers at Home, will perpetually multiply, and their Depredations be incessantly reiterated.

But the Acts were intended, *for the better peopling the Colonies.* And will Thieves and Murderers be conducive to that End? What Advantage can we reap from a Colony of unrestrainable Renegadoes? Will they exalt the Glory of the Crown? Or rather, will not the Dignity of the most illustrious Monarch in the World, be sullied by a Province of Subjects so lawless, detestable, and ignominious? Can Agriculture be promoted, when the *wild Boar of the Forest breaks down our Hedges, and pulls up our Vines*? Will Trade flourish, or Manufactures be encouraged, where Property is made the Spoil of such who are too idle to work, and wicked enough to murder and steal?

Besides, are not we Subjects of the same King, with the People of *England*; Members of the same Body Politic, and therefore entitled to equal Privileges with them. If so, how injurious does it seem to free one Part of the Dominions, from the Plagues of Mankind, and cast them upon another? Should a Law be proposed to take the Poor of one Parish, and billet them upon another; would not all the World, but the Parish to be relieved, exclaim against such a Project, as iniquitous and absurd? Should the numberless Villains of *London* and *Westminster*, be suffered to escape from their Prisons, to range at large, and depredate any other Part of the Kingdom, would not every Man join with the Sufferers, and condemn the Measure as hard and unreasonable? And tho' the Hardships upon us, are indeed not equal to those, yet the Miseries that flow from Laws, by no Means intended to prejudice us, are too heavy not to be felt. *But the Colonies must be peopled.* Agreed: And will the Transportation Acts ever have that Tendency? No, they work the contrary Way, and counteract their own Design. We want People 'tis true, but not Villains, ready at any Time, encouraged by Impunity, and habituated upon the slightest Occasions, to cut a Man's

Throat, for a small Part of his Property. The Delights of such Company, is a noble Inducement, indeed, to the honest Poor, to convey themselves into a strange Country. Amidst all our Plenty, they will have enough to exercise their Virtues, and stand in no need of the Association of such, as will prey upon their Property, and gorge themselves, with the Blood of the Adventurers. They came over in Search of Happiness; rather than starve will live any where, and would be glad to be excused from so afflicting an Antepast of the Torments of Hell. In Reality, Sir, these very Laws, tho' otherwise designed, have turned out in the End, the most effectual Expedients, that the Art of Man could have contrived, to prevent the Settlement of these remote Parts of the King's Dominions. They have actually taken away almost every Encouragement to so laudable a Design. I appeal to Facts. The Body of the *English*, are struck with Terror at the Thought of coming over to us; not because they have a vast Ocean to cross, or leave behind them their Friends; or that the Country is new and uncultivated: But from the shocking Ideas, the Mind must necessarily form, of the Company of inhuman Savages, and the more terrible Herd of exiled Malefactors. There are Thousands of honest Men, labouring in *Europe*, at Four Pence a Day, starving in spite of all their Efforts, a dead Weight to the respective Parishes to which they belong; who without any other Qualifications, than common Sense, Health and Strength, might accumulate Estates among us, as many have done already. These, and not the others, are the Men that should be sent over, for the *better peopling the Plantations*. *Great-Britain* and *Ireland*, in their present Circumstances, are overstocked with them, and he who would immortalize himself, for a *Lover of Mankind*; should concert a Scheme for the Transportation of the industriously Honest abroad, and the immediate Punishment of Rogues and Plunderers at Home. The pale-faced half-clad, meagre and starved Skeletons, that are seen in every Village of those Kingdoms, call loudly for the Patriot's generous Aid. The Plantations too would thank him, for his Assistance, in obtaining the Repeal of those Laws which, tho' otherwise intended by the Legislature, have so unhappily proved injurious to his own Country, and ruinous to us. — It is not long since, a Bill passed the Commons, for the Employment of such Criminals in his Majesty's Docks, as should merit the Gallows. The Design was good. It is consistent with sound Policy, that all those, who have forfeited their Liberty and Lives to their Country, should be compelled to labour the Residue of their Days in its Service. But the Scheme was bad, and wisely was the Bill rejected by the Lords, for this only Reason, That it had a *natural Tendency to discredit the King's Yards*: The Consequences of which, must have been vastly prejudicial to the whole Nation. Just so ought we to reason in the present Case, and we should then soon be brought to conclude, that tho' peopling the Colonies, which was the laudable Motive of the Legislature, be expedient to the Public, abrogating the Transportation Laws, must be equally necessary.

It may perhaps, by this Time, be objected to me, that I have been representing a Grievance, beyond our Power to redress. We cannot, it must be confessed, perfectly prevent the Transportation: We may, notwithstanding, vastly discourage it; and, in some Degree, guard against the Evils that may follow from it for the future. Nor can such Endeavours draw upon us the Displeasure of a British Parliament, since it cannot be supposed, that it was ever the Intention of that most august Body by any of their Laws, to prejudice the Colonies.

The first Statute for the Transportation of Felons, passed in the fourth Year of his present Majesty's Reign: And it is thereby enacted, — *"That the Court, before whom Offenders were convicted, shall have Power to convey, transfer and make over, such Offenders by Order of Court, to the Use of any Person or Persons,* who shall contract, *for the Performance of such Transportation, to him or them, and his and their Assigns, for the Term of Seven Years."*

By another Section, it is further enacted, *"That every such Person, to whom any such Court, shall order any such Offenders, to be transferred or conveyed, shall, before such Offenders shall be delivered to them,* contract *with such Person, as shall be appointed by such Court, and shall give sufficient Security, to the Satisfaction of such Court, for the transporting such Offenders, to some Plantation in* America, *to be ordered by such Court; and the procuring an authentick Certificate, from the Governor or Chief Custom-House Officer, of the Place of the Landing such Offenders, etc. and their not returning by the wilful Default of such Contractor."*

The other Statute relating to Transportation, passed two Years after; and is indeed, only an Appendix to it. The first Section of it impowers the Court, *to nominate, two or more Justices of the Peace, to* contract *with the Transporters of Felons.*[2]

Now, it is obvious to any Man, that both these Statutes suppose Contractors will never be wanting, even tho' Security be demanded, against the Return of the Felon. But no Man, by either of them, is obliged to *contract,* — Nor any Man compelled to transport.

What Reason then can be urged, against a Law in the Plantations, that shall make it too expensive, for any Man, to enter into a Contract, so destructive of our Peace and Security. Let the Attempt be made, and the Preamble of the Law strongly suggest the Reasons for passing it. It is not improbable then, that the Grievances we labour under, may be entirely removed, and the Statutes I have mentioned be speedily repealed, especially if our Agents are furnished with Arguments, and particularly instructed, to unite their Interests, and enabled to point out the Expediency of a Step, so advantageous to the Public, and conducive of our Prosperity.

Whether the Plantations in general, have any other Means of avoiding the mischievous Effects, of the Transportation of Felons, I am not sufficiently acquainted with their Laws to determine. But I rejoice, that it is the Happiness of this Province, that we have it in our Power, in a great Measure to prevent them, could our Magistrates be prevailed upon, to execute the Laws we have already made: Which, as they were passed long before the Statutes for Transportation, will exempt us entirely from all Charge of Disloyalty. The Acts I refer to, are Chapters VI, and CCCCX, in the late Edition of our Laws.[3] By the First, passed in the Year 1691, "*All Strangers of no Estate, nor of manual Occupations, are compellable to give Security, against being a Charge to the Publick, within Two Years; and the Master importing such, as cannot give Security for their good Behaviour, shall immediately convey them out of the Province.*" The Second passed in the Year 1721, and is better calculated for the same good Purposes; and particularly obliges, "*the Master, that imports such, as cannot give a* GOOD ACCOUNT *of themselves, to re-transport them, or give Security in £50, to indemnify the Parish.*" And both Acts made it the Duty of the Master, to "*report the Strangers they bring in, under Penalties annexed to their Omission.*" This seems to be made the peculiar Care, of the Mayor in *New-York*; who is enabled, by the last Act, to execute his Office, by an immediate Distress upon the Goods of the Offender. What Regard has been paid to these necessary Laws, by former Mayors, I cannot take upon me to say, but the Execution of them so nearly concerns the Public, I am in hopes we shall never again, have Cause to complain of so injurious a Neglect: Tho' pity it is, that the Act is defective in not imposing a Penalty, that an Omission of this Duty, whenever it shall happen, may be punished *severely.*

Suffer me now, Sir, to conclude this Letter, with a short Address to our Magistrates, and particularly to those of this City.

"GENTLEMEN,

I HAVE endeavoured to shew you, the unintended bad Effects of the Laws, for the Transportation of Felons. You, in the Exercise of your Offices, have had manifold Instances of their mischievous Consequences; and particularly, in the Thefts and Burglaries lately committed. Two of the Villains punished by an ignominious Whipping, at the Cart's-Tail, I am informed, were Convicts; and it is very probable the Rest are so too. Not that our own Country, is incapable of producing the vilest of Wretches: But it is remarked at *Philadelphia,* that of the great Number of Criminals, for several Years past executed there, scarce any of them were Children of *America*, or honestly came over for a Settlement in the Country. Many Thousands of *Germans*, indigent, and to the last Degree necessitous, have been imported; and yet scarce a Villain has been detected among them; while almost every News-Paper we receive from thence, advertises the Tryal or Execution of an *English* or *Irishman*. For God's Sake, Gentlemen, prevent us from being exposed to the dreadful Calamities they have suffered. I have pointed out a Method: It remains only with you to come into it. Should our Laws be strictly put in Execution, with re-spect to imported Convicts, their Importation might be effectually prevented. For no Man would be so imprudent, as to bind himself for the good Behaviour of those, whose legal Conviction affords the highest Evidence of their Villainy. Laws are made to your Hands, sufficient for our Purpose. It is your Business to execute them. A Law unexecuted is a dead Letter, useless as an antiquated Almanack. 'The Execution of the Law,' said a great Lawyer, 'is not only the *End*, but the *Life* of it.' You are Fathers of our City, shew yourselves therefore, indeed, the Guardians of the Lives and Properties of its numerous In-habitants: And, by your tender Care over us, *may we lead quiet and peaceable Lives.*

"I would not be understood, Gentlemen, to insinuate that any of you *bear the Sword of Justice in vain.* All I intend, is to encourage you, in a bold Discharge of the Trust we have committed to you. It is not long since, one of your own Body, in Execution of our Law against Vagrants, made all the Search in his Power, for suspected Persons in his particular District; intending to banish them from us, or secure us in some Measure against them. The Scheme is good, and he has the Thanks of his Ward for his Vigilance. Let the Search be universal, and often repeated, and the whole City purged of all its Delinquents."

I am, Mr. Reflector, *Your Most Humble Servant,*

A   PUBLICUS.

I Beg Pardon for refusing to publish the Letter signed Civicus; *Whether the Up-Land claimed by the Petitioners, for whom* Agricola *has apologized, belongs to them or to the City, is a Question that our Corporation will undoubtedly consider; and I wish my Correspondent would lay his Arguments for the City, before that worshipful Body. A Trial of the Title must be highly improper in this Paper; and perhaps an Aspersion on the Right of the Petitioners, might expose the Printer to answer for it in a Court of Law. The Piece sign'd* W, *is also come to hand; but the Writer will excuse my not publishing it with that Sub-scription, for a Reason I think not proper to communicate to the World. My judicious Correspondent* Obryan Fitz Taffy, *writes on too important a Subject to have his Letter buried in Oblivion. Nor shall the fair* Mariana, *escape the Notice due to so accomplished a Lady.*

1. The transportation of convicts to America was a regular practice in the seventeenth and eighteenth centuries. The most important laws governing the system were those of 1662, 1670, and 1717. See Abbot E. Smith, "The Transportation of Convicts to the American Colonies in the Seventeenth Century," *American Historical Review*, XXXIX (1934), 232–249, and *Colonists in Bondage* (Chapel Hill, 1947), chaps. 5–6.

2. The reference to "his present Majesty's Reign" is in error. The laws in question were 4 Geo. I, c. 11 (1717) and 6 Geo. I, c. 23 (1719).

3. For these laws, see notes 3 and 4 to Number V.

Number XVII

Remarks on Our Intended COLLEGE

Nullum nos posse majus meliusve Reipublicæ afferre munus,
Quam docendo et erudiendo Juventutem.   CICERO [1]

THE Design of erecting a College in this Province, is a Matter of such grand and general Importance, that I have frequently made it the Topic of my serious Meditation.[2] Nor can I better employ my Time than by devoting a Course of Papers to so interesting a Subject. A Subject of universal Concernment, and in a peculiar Manner involving in it, the Happiness and Well-being of our Posterity!

The most convenient Situation for fixing the Fabric, tho' obvious on the least Reflection, has been made [a] Matter of laborious Enquiry, as well as afforded a copious Fund for private Conversation. That the College ought to be plac'd in or near this City, appears evident from numberless Arguments, that naturally occur to the most superficial Thinker. But while we have been amusing ourselves with Disputations concerning the Situation of the Building, we have been strangely indolent about its Constitution and Government, in Comparison of which, the other is a Trifle that scarce deserves Attention. To expatiate on the Advantages of Learning in general, or a liberal Education in particular, would be equally impossible and useless. Impossible from the narrow Limits of my Paper: And useless, because no Arguments that can be urged, are capable of rendering the Assertion more evident, than the irresistible Demonstrations of Experience.

That the College ought therefore to be situated near our Metropolis, and that it will be productive, if properly regulated, of unspeakable Benefit to this Province, I shall lay down as two *postulata* not to be questioned.

Before we engage in any Undertaking, common Prudence requires us maturely to consider the End we propose, and the Means most conducive to its Attainment.

To imagine that our Legislature, by raising the present Fund for the College,[3] intended barely to have our Children instructed in *Greek* and *Latin*, or the Art of making Exercises and Verses, or disputing in Mood and Figure, were a Supposition absurd and defamatory. For these Branches of Literature, however useful as preparatory to real and substantial Knowledge, are in themselves perfectly idle and insignificant. The true Use of Education, is to qualify Men for the different Employments of Life, to which it may please God to call them. 'Tis to improve their Hearts and Understandings, to infuse a public Spirit and Love of their Country; to inspire them with the Principles of Honour and Probity; with a fervent Zeal for Liberty, and a diffusive Benevolence for Mankind; and in a Word, to make them the more extensively serviceable to the Common-Wealth. Hence the Education of Youth hath been the peculiar Care of all the wise Legislators of Antiquity, who thought it impossible to aggrandize the State, without imbuing the Minds of its Members with Virtue and Knowledge. Nay, so sensible of this fundamental Maxim in Policy, were PLATO, ARISTOTLE, and LYCURGUS, and in short all the ancient Politicians who have delivered their Sentiments on Government, that they make the Education of Youth, the principal and most essential Duty of the Magistrate. And, indeed, whatever literary Acquirement cannot be reduced to Practice, or exerted to the Benefit of Mankind, may perhaps procure its Possessor the Name of a Scholar, but is in Reality no more than a specious Kind of Ignorance. This, therefore, I will venture to lay down for a capital Maxim, that unless the Education we propose, be calculated to render our Youth better Members of Society, and useful to the Public in Proportion to its Expence, we had better be without it. As the natural Consequence of this Proposition, it follows, that the Plan of Education the most conducive to that End is to be chosen, and whatever has a Tendency to obstruct or impede it, ought carefully to be avoided.

The Nature, End and Design of such Seminaries, is to teach

the Students particular Arts and Sciences, for the Conduct of Life, and to render them useful Members of the Community. *"Science in Propriety of Language signifies, a clear and certain Knowledge of any Thing, founded on self-evident Principles or Demonstration: Tho' in a more particular and imperfect Sense, it is used for a System of any Branch of Knowledge, comprehending its Doctrine, Reason and Theory, without an immediate Application thereof to any Uses or Offices of Life."* This twofold Definition of the Word *Science*, I may probably have Occasion to make use of hereafter.

The vast Influence of any Education upon the Lives and Actions of Men, and thence by a kind of political Expansion, on the whole Community, is verified by constant Experience. Nay, it discriminates Man from Man, more than by Nature he is differenced from the Brutes: And beyond all doubt much greater was the Disparity between the renowned Mr. LOCKE, and a common Hottentot, than between the latter and some of the most sagacious of the irrational Kingdom. But the Influence of a Collegiate Education, must spread a wider Circle proportionate to the Number of the Students, and their greater Progress in Knowledge.

The Consequences of a liberal Education will soon be visible throughout the whole Province. They will appear on the Bench, at the Bar, in the Pulpit, and in the Senate, and unavoidably affect our civil and religious Principles. Let us adduce, a few Arguments from Reason, Experience and History.

A youthful Mind is susceptible of almost any Impression. Like the ductile Wax, it receives the Image of the Seal without the least Resistance. "What is learned at that tender Age," says QUINTILIAN, "is easily imprinted on the Mind, and leaves deep Marks behind it, which are not easily to be effaced. As in the Case of a new Vessel, which long preserves a Tincture of the first Liquor poured into it: And like Wool which can never recover its primitive Whiteness after it has once been dyed; and the Misfortune is, that bad Habits last longer than good Ones." [4] The Poet HORACE, to whom it must have been very natural to draw Similes from Liquor, makes use of the same Comparison.

THE INDEPENDENT REFLECTOR

Quo semel est imbuta recens, servabit odorem
Testa diu. ———
What season'd first the Vessel, keeps the Taste. CREECH [5]

The Principles or Doctrines implanted in the Minds of Youth, grow up and gather Strength with them. In Time they take deep Root, pass from the Memory and Understanding to the Heart, and at length become a second Nature, which it is almost impossible to change. While the Mind is tender and flexible, it may be moulded and managed at Pleasure: But when once the Impressions are by Practice and Habit, as it were incorporated with the intellectual Substance, they are obliterated with the greatest Difficulty. *Frangas enim citius quam corrigas, quæ in pravum induerunt,*[6] said an Author, alike celebrated for his Skill in Rhetoric, and his Knowledge of Mankind.

From these Premises, the natural Inference is, that we cannot be too cautious in forming the human Mind, so capable of good, and so passive to evil Impressions.

There is no Place where we receive a greater Variety of Impressions, than at Colleges. Nor do any Instructions sink so deep in the Mind as those that are there received. The Reason is, because they are not barely imprinted by the Preceptor, as at inferior Schools; but perpetually confirmed and invigorated by the Suscipients [7] themselves. Tho' Academies * are generally Scenes of Endless Disputations, they are seldom Places of candid Inquiry. The Students not only receive the Dogmata of their Teachers with an implicit Faith, but are also constantly studying how to support them against every Objection. The System of the College is generally taken for true, and the sole Business is to defend it. Freedom of Thought rarely penetrates those contracted Mansions of systematical Learning. But to teach the establish'd Notions, and maintain certain Hypotheses, *hic Labor hoc opus est.*[8] Every Deviation from the beaten Tract, is a kind of literary Heresy; and if the Professor be given to Excommunication, can scarce escape an Anathema. Hence that dogmatical Turn and

* Note, *That for the greater Variety of Languages, I shall use the Words* Academy, College, *and* University, *as synonymous Terms; tho', in strict Propriety, they are far from being equipollent Expressions.*

174

Impatience of Contradiction, so observable in the Generality of Academics. To this also is to be referred, those voluminous Compositions, and that learned Lumber of gloomy Pedants, which hath so long infested and corrupted the World. In a Word, all those visionary Whims, idle Speculations, fairy Dreams, and party Distinctions, which contract and embitter the Mind, and have so often turn'd the World topsy-turvy.

I mention not this to disparage an academical Education, from which I hope I have myself received some Benefit, especially after having worn off some of its rough Corners, by a freer Conversation with Mankind. The Purpose for which I urge it, is to shew the narrow Turn usually prevailing at Colleges, and the absolute Necessity of teaching Nothing that will afterwards require the melancholy Retrogradation of being unlearned.

From this Susceptibility of tender Minds, and the extreme Difficulty of erasing original Impressions, it is easy to conceive, that whatever Principles are imbibed at a College, will run thro' a Man's whole future Conduct, and affect the Society of which he is a Member, in Proportion to his Sphere of Activity; especially if it be considered, that even after we arrive to Years of Maturity, instead of entering upon the difficult and disagreable Work of examining the Principles we have formerly entertained, we rather exert ourselves in searching for Arguments to maintain and support them.

Tho' I have sufficiently shewn the prodigious Influence of a College upon the Community, from the Nature and Reason of the Thing, it may not be improper, for its farther Corroboration, to draw some Proofs from Experience and History.

At *Harvard* College in the *Massachusetts-Bay*, and at *Yale* College in *Connecticut*, the Presbyterian Profession is in some sort established. It is in these Colonies the commendable Practice of all who can afford it, to give their Sons an Education at their respective Seminaries of Learning. While they are in the Course of their Education, they are sure to be instructed in the Arts of maintaining the Religion of the College, which is always that of their immediate Instructors; and of combating the Principles of all other Christians whatever. When the young Gentlemen, have

175

run thro' the Course of their Education, they enter into the Ministry, or some Offices of the Government, and acting in them under the Influence of the Doctrines espoused in the Morning of Life, the Spirit of the College is transfused thro' the Colony, and tinctures the Genius and Policy of the public Administration, from the Governor down to the Constable. Hence the Episcopalians cannot acquire an equal Strength among them, till some new Regulations, in Matters of Religion, prevail in their Colleges, which perpetually produce Adversaries to the hierarchical System. Nor is it to be question'd, that the Universities in *North* and *South-Britain*, greatly support the different Professions that are establish'd in their respective Divisions.

Sensible of the vast Influence which the Positions and Principles of Colleges have upon the Public, was that politic Prince King HENRY the Eighth. No sooner had he determined to repudiate his Queen, thro' his Love for ANNE BOLEYN, than, the better to justify his Divorce, or rather to guard himself against the popular Resentment, by the Advice of CRANMER, the State of his Case was laid before all the Universities, who, agreeable to his Wishes, determined his Marriage with CATHERINE, to be repugnant to the divine Law, and therefore invalid.

In the Reign of King JAMES II. of arbitrary and papistical Memory, a Project jesuitically artful, was concerted to poison the Nation, by filling the Universities with popish and popishly-affected Tutors; and but for our glorious Deliverance, by the immortal WILLIAM, the Scheme had been sufficient, in Process of Time, to have introduc'd and establish'd, the sanguinary and antichristian Church of *Rome*.

Since then, the extensive Influence of a College so manifestly appears, it is of the last Importance, that ours be so constituted, that the Fountain being pure, the Streams (to use the Language of Scripture) may make glad the City of our GOD.   Z.

I hope my Correspondents will not be displeased, at seeing the Publication of their Letters thus long deferred, after assuring them, that tho' they have, contrary to my Inclination, been unavoidably postponed, they will by no means be forgotten; but receive due Honour, as soon as possible, after I have finished my Remarks on the

REMARKS ON OUR INTENDED COLLEGE

College; which, for its great Importance, will probably engross four or five of my succeeding Numbers.

1. A paraphrase of *Quod enim munus rei publicae afferre maius meluisve possumus, quam si docemus atque erudimus inventutem.* "What greater or better gift can we bring to the commonwealth than to teach and instruct the youth." Cicero, *De Divinatione*, II, 2, 4.

2. Livingston had written to Welles, on the subject September 19, 1747 (JFP, Yale). A number of communications to the press appeared between 1747 and 1749 on the organization and location of the proposed college in language that might well have been Livingston's (*New-York Evening Post*, May 18, August 17, 1747; November 28, 1748; January 9, May 29, 1749; *New-York Weekly Journal*, February 13, 1749); but the most extended exposition of his views on the college were published in a rare nine-page pamphlet (March 1749) and acknowledged as his in a letter to Welles (February 18, 1749, JFP, Yale): *Some Serious Thoughts on the Design of erecting a College in the Province of New-York*, signed with one of his more obscure pseudonyms, *Hippocrates Mithridate. Apoth.* It argued mainly the "numberless Advantages" of a "publick Seminary of Learning," among which he included a few humorous by-products: "that refined Politeness of solliciting People to drink Bumpers . . . will vanish at the Dawn of Learning" along with the "infamous" practices of "breaking Windows, and wresting off Knockers," while "our young Ladies" would become "as great Proficients in the *Belles Lettres,* as they now are in the Mysteries of the Toilet."

3. £3443.18 had been raised by public lotteries authorized by the legislature in 1746 and 1748; in 1751 the money was vested in a board of trustees empowered to set out the funds at interest and to receive proposals for locating the college. (*Colonial Laws of New York*, III, 607–616, 679–688, 731–732, 842–844.) The lottery, a familiar fund-raising device in colonial America, was used to found the Philadelphia Academy (later the University of Pennsylvania), the College of New Jersey (Princeton), and Dartmouth, in addition to the New York college. See John S. Ezell, *Fortune's Merry Wheel: The Lottery in America* (Cambridge, Mass., 1960), chap. 3; Beverly McAnear, "The Raising of Funds by the Colonial Colleges," *Mississippi Valley Historical Review*, XXXVIII (1952), 591–612; A. Franklin Ross, "The History of Lotteries in New York," *Magazine of History*, V (1907), 94–100, 143–152.

4. *Institutio oratoria* I, 1, 5.

5. Horace, *Epistles* I, 2, 69; translation by Thomas Creech (1659–1700).

6. "Evil habits, once settled, are more easily broken than mended." Quintilian, *De Institutio oratoria*, I, 3, 12.

7. Recipients.

8. "This is a toil, this is a task." Paraphrased from the *Aeneid*, VI, 129, where it reads: *Hoc opus, hic labor est.*

Number XVIII

THURSDAY, MARCH 29, 1753

A Continuation of the same Subject

Tros Rutulusve fuat, nullo discrimine habebo.   VIRG.[1]

I HAVE in my last Paper shewn, from Reason, Experience and History, the vast Influence of a College, upon the civil and religious Principles of the Community in which it is erected and supported. I shall now proceed to offer a few Arguments, which I submit to the Consideration of my Countrymen, to evince the Necessity and Importance of constituting *our* College upon a Basis the most catholic, generous and free.

It is in the first Place observable, that unless its Constitution and Government, be such as will admit Persons of all protestant Denominations, upon a perfect Parity as to Privileges, it will itself be greatly prejudiced, and prove a Nursery of Animosity, Dissention and Disorder. The sincere Men of all Sects, imagine their own Profession, on the whole, more eligible and scriptural than any other. It is therefore very natural to suppose, they will exert themselves to weaken and diminish all other Divisions, the better to strengthen and enlarge their own. To this Cause must in a great Measure be ascribed, that Heat and Opposition, which animate the Breasts of many Men of religious Distinctions, whose intemperate and misapplied Zeal, is the only Blemish that can be thrown upon their Characters. Should our College, therefore, unhappily thro' our own bad Policy, fall into the Hands of any one religious Sect in the Province: Should that Sect, which is more than probable, establish its religion in the College, shew favour to its votaries, and cast Contempt upon others; 'tis easy to foresee, that Christians of all other Denominations amongst us, instead of encouraging its Prosperity, will, from the same Principles, rather conspire to oppose and oppress it. Besides *English* and

178

Dutch Presbyterians, which perhaps exceed all our other religious Professions put together, we have Episcopalians, Anabaptists, Lutherans, Quakers, and a growing Church of Moravians,[2] all equally zealous for their discriminating Tenets: Which-soever of these has the sole Government of the College, will kindle the Jealousy of the Rest, not only against the Persuasion so preferred, but the College itself. Nor can any Thing less be expected, than a general Discontent and Tumult; which, affecting all Ranks of People, will naturally tend to disturb the Tranquility and Peace of the Province.

In such a State of Things, we must not expect the Children of any, but of that Sect which prevails in the Academy will ever be sent to it: For should they, the established Tenets must either be implicitly received, or a perpetual religious War necessarily maintained. Instead of the liberal Arts and Sciences, and such Attainments as would best qualify the Students to be useful and ornamental to their Country, Party Cavils and Disputes about Trifles, will afford Topics of Argumentation to their incredible Disadvantage, by a fruitless Consumption of Time. Such Gentlemen, therefore, who can afford it, will give their Sons an Education abroad, or at some of the neighbouring Academies, where equally imbibing a Zeal for their own Principles, and furnished with the Arts of defending them, an incessant Opposition to all others, on their Return, will be the unavoidable Consequence. Not to mention, that Youth may become strongly attached to the Places at which they are educated. At this season of Life they receive the deepest Impressions: And, for the Sake of a Wife or a Friend, and a thousand other Reasons that cannot now be enumerated, a Gentleman may turn his Back upon the Place of his Birth, and take up his Residence where the Morning of Life has been agreeably passed. Hence, besides the Expence of such Education prejudicial to us, we may frequently lose the Hopes of our Country, lose perhaps a Man every Way qualified to defend its Interests, and advance its Glory.

Others, and many such there may be, who not able to support the Expence of an Education abroad, but could easily afford it at Home, thro' a Spirit of Opposition to the predominant Party, will rather determine to give their Children no Education at all. From all which it follows, that a College under the sole Influence of a Party, for want of suitable Encouragement, being but indifferently stocked with Pupils, will scarce arrive to the Usefulness of a *Schola illustris,* which being inferior to a College is, I hope, much short of what is intended by Ours.

Another Argument against so pernicious a Scheme is, that it will be dangerous to Society. The extensive Influence of such a Seminary, I have already shewn in my last Paper. And have we not reason to fear the worst Effects of it, where none but the Principles of one Persuasion are taught, and all others depressed and discountenanced? Where, instead of Reason and Argument, of which the Minds of the Youth are not capable, they are early imbued with the Doctrines of a Party, enforced by the Authority of a Professor's Chair, and the combining Aids of the President, and all the other Officers of the College? That religious Worship should be constantly maintained there, I am so far from opposing, that I strongly recommend it, and do not believe any such Kind of Society, can be kept under a regular and due Discipline without it. But instructing the Youth in any particular Systems of Divinity, or recommending and establishing any single Method of Worship or Church Government, I am convinced would be both useless and hurtful. Useless, because not one in a Hundred of the Pupils is capable of making a just Examination, and reasonable Choice. Hurtful, because receiving Impressions blindly on Authority, will corrupt their Understandings, and fetter them with Prejudices which may everlastingly prevent a judicious Freedom of Thought, and infect them all their Lives, with a contracted turn of Mind.

A Party-College, in less than half a Century, will put a new Face upon the Religion, and in Consequence thereof affect the Politics of the Country. Let us suppose what may, if the College should be entirely managed by one Sect, probably be supposed. Would not all possible Care be bestowed in tincturing the Minds of the Students with the Doctrines and Sentiments of that Sect? Would not the Students of the College, after the Course of their Education, exclusive of any others, fill all the Offices of the Government? Is it not highly reasonable to think, that in the Execution of those Offices, the Spirit of the College would have a most prevailing Influence, especially as that Party would perpetually receive new Strength, become more fashionable and numerous? Can it be imagined that all other Christians would continue peaceable under, and unenvious of, the Power of that Church which was rising to so exalted a Pre-eminence above them? Would they not on the Contrary, like all other Parties, reflect upon, reluct at, and vilify such an odious Ascendency? Would not the Church which had that Ascendency be thereby irritated to repeated Acts of Domination, and stretch their ecclesiastical Rule to unwarrantable and unreasonable Lengths? Whatever others may in their Lethargy and Supineness think of the Project of a Party-College, I am convinced, that under the Management of any particular Persuasion, it will necessarily prove destructive to the civil and religious Rights of the People: And should any future House of Representatives become generally infected with the Maxims of the College, nothing less can be expected than an Establishment of one Denomination above all others, who may, perhaps, at the good Pleasure of their Superiors, be most graciously favoured with a bare Liberty of Conscience, while they faithfully continue their annual Contributions, their Tythes and their Peter-Pence.

A Third Argument against suffering the College to fall into the Hands of a Party, may be deduced from the Design of its Erection, and Support by the Public.

The Legislature to whom it owes its Origin, and under whose Care the Affair has hitherto been conducted, could never have intended it as an Engine to be exercised for the Purposes of a Party. Such an Insinuation, would be false and scandalous. It would therefore be the Height of Insolence in any to pervert it to such mean, partial and little Designs. No, it was set on Foot, and I hope will be constituted for general Use, for the public Benefit, for the Education of all who can afford such Education: And to suppose it intended for any other less public-spirited Uses, is ungratefully to reflect upon all who have hitherto, had any Agency in an Undertaking so glorious to the Province, so necessary, so important and beneficial.

At present, it is but in Embryo, yet the Money hitherto collected is public Money; and till it is able to support itself, the Aids given to it will be public Aids. When the Community is taxed, it ought to be for the Defence, or Emolument of the Whole: Can it, therefore, be supposed, that all shall contribute for the Uses, the ignominious Uses of a few? Nay, what is worse to that which will be prejudicial, to a vast Majority! Shall the whole Province be made to support what will raise and spread desperate Feuds, Discontent and ill-Blood thro' the greatest Part of the Province? Shall the Government of the College be delivered out of the Hands of the Public to a Party! They who wish it, are Enemies to their Country: They who ask it, have, besides this *Anti-Patriotism*, a Degree of Impudence, Arrogance, and Assurance unparallel'd. And all such as are active in so iniquitous a Scheme, deserve to be stigmatized with Marks of everlasting Ignominy and Disgrace. Let it, therefore, ever remain where it is, I mean under the Power of the Legislature: The Influence, whether good or bad, we shall all of us feel, and are, therefore, all interested in it. It is, for that Reason, highly fit, that the People should always share in the Power to enlarge or restrain it: That Power they will have by their Representatives in Assembly; and no Man who is a Friend to Liberty, his Country and Religion, will ever rejoice to see it wrested from them.

It is farther to be remarked, that a public Academy is, or ought to be a mere civil Institution, and cannot with any tolerable Propriety be monopolized by any religious Sect. The Design of such Seminaries, hath been sufficiently shewn in my last Paper, to be entirely political, and calculated for the Benefit of Society, as a Society, without any Intention to teach Religion, which is the Province of the Pulpit: Tho' it must, at the same Time, be confessed, that a judicious Choice of our Principles, chiefly depends on a free Education.

Again, the Instruction of our Youth, is not the only Advantage we ought to propose by our College. If it be properly regulated and conducted, we may expect a considerable Number of Students from the neighbouring Colonies, which must, necessarily, prove a great Accession to our Wealth and Emolument. For such is our Capacity of endowing an Academy; that if it be founded on the Plan of a general Toleration, it must, naturally, eclipse any other on the Continent, and draw many Pupils from those Provinces, the Constitution of whose Colleges is partial and contracted: From *New-England*, where the *Presbyterians* are the prevailing Party, we shall, undoubtedly, be furnished with great Numbers, who, averse to the Sect in vogue among them, will, unquestionably, prefer the free Constitution, for which I argue, to that of their Colleges in which they cannot enjoy an equal Latitude, not to mention that such an Increase by foreign Students, will vastly augment the Grandeur of our Academy.

Add to all this, that in a new Country as ours, it is inconsistent with good Policy, to give any religious Profession the Ascendency over others. The rising Prosperity of *Pennsylvania*, is the Admiration of the Continent; and tho' disagreeing from them, I should always, for political Reasons, exclude *Papists* from the common and equal Benefits of Society. Yet, I leave it to the Reflections of my judicious Readers, whether the impartial Aspect of their Laws upon all Professions, has not, in a great Degree, conduced to their vast Importation of religious Refugees, to their Strength and their Riches: And whether a like Liberty among us, to all Protestants whatsoever, without any Marks of Distinction, would not be more commendable, advantageous, and politic. A.

I Thank Aurelius *for his friendly Advice, and assure him, I no more dread the Power of the Persons he mentions, than I doubt their Malice.*

The Letter from Portius, *containing a Scheme for endowing the College, is also come to Hand, and shall not fail of being duly honour'd.*

1. "Let him be Trojan or Rutulian, I make no distinction." Paraphrase of *Aeneid*, I, 574.

2. Livingston estimated that the English and Dutch dissenters made up nine-tenths of the province; Smith estimated the number of Episcopalians in New York as only one out of fifteen. *Independent Reflector, Preface*, p. 21; Smith, *History*, I, 284.

Number XIX

THURSDAY, APRIL 1, 1753

The same Subject continued

— Timeo Danaos dona ferentes. VIRG.[1]

As nothing would be more fruitless than to excite the Apprehensions, or raise the Hopes of my Readers, by a Prospect of remediless Evils, or unattainable Blessings, I consider my former Papers upon this Subject, only as a Prelude to what is yet to come. It would be of little Use to have shewn the fatal Consequences of an Academy founded in Bigotry, and reared by Party-Spirit; or the glorious Advantages of a College, whose Basis is Liberty, and where the Muses flourish with entire Freedom; without investigating the Means by which the one may be crushed in Embryo, and the other raised and supported with Ease and Security. In all Societies, as in the human Frame, inbred Disorders are chiefly incurable, as being Part of the Constitution, and inseparable from it; while, on the Contrary, when the Rage of Infirmities is resisted by a sound Complexion of Body, they are less inherent, and consequently more medicable. For this Reason, it must necessarily be esteemed of the utmost Importance, that the Plan upon which we intend to form our Nursery of Learning, be concerted with the most prudent Deliberation; it being that alone upon which its future Grandeur must evidently depend.

To delineate a compleat Scheme for so great a Work, is beyond the Stretch of my Abilities: And to imagine that these Imperfect Attempts, will be of any other Use than as a Spur to greater Inventions, is a Piece of Vanity with which the *Reflector* scorns to be thought chargeable. But should they prove useful to his Country, either by inspiring others to communicate something more perfect, or inciting our Legislature to a serious Consideration of

this Subject, I shall think the general Design of these Papers sufficiently answered.

In pointing out a Plan for the College, I shall first shew what
it ought not to be, in order that what it should be, may appear
with greater Certainty.

As Corporations and Companies are generally founded on
Royal Grants, it is without Doubt supposed by many, that our
College must be constituted by Charter from his Majesty, to certain Persons, as Trustees, to whose Government and Direction it
will be submitted. Nor does the Impropriety of such a Plan strike
the unattentive Vulgar, tho' to a considerate Mind it appears big
with mighty Evils.

> *Nec quæ circumstant te deinde pericula cernis*
> *Demens.*—— VIRG.[2]

It is necessary to the well-being of every Society, that it be
not only established upon an ample and free Bottom; but also
secured from Invasion, and its Constitution guarded against
Abuses and Perversion. These are Points of which I beg Leave to
think my Readers fully convinced. Nor can they wonder at the
Novelty of my Scheme, when an University, hatched by the Heat
of Sectaries, and cherished in the contracted Bosom of furious
Zeal, shall be shewn to be the natural Consequence of a Charter
Government.

But to consider an Academy founded on a Royal Grant in the
most favourable Light, Prudence will compel our Disapprobation
of so precarious a Plan. The Mutability of its Nature will incline
every reasonable Man, to prefer to it that Kind of Government,
which is both productive of the richest Blessings, and renders its
Advantages the more precious, by their superiour Stability. A
Charter can at best present us with a Prospect of what we are
scarce sure of enjoying a Day. For every Charter of Incorporation,
as it generally includes a Number of Privileges subject to certain
express or implied Conditions, may, in particular, be annulled,
either on a Prosecution in the Court of *Kings-Bench* by *Quo warranto*, or by *Scire Facias* in Chancery,[3] or by *Surrender*. Nor does
it require a great Abuse of Privilege to determine its Fate by the

two first Means, while mere Caprice, or some thing worse, may at any Time work its Dissolution by the latter. I believe my Countrymen, have too high a Sense of the Advantages of Learning, to risk the College upon so unsettled a Basis; and would blast a Project so ineffective of its true End, to make Room for a Scheme by which the Object of public Attention may be fixed on a Bottom more firm and durable. How would it damp the sanguine Prospects, of the fervent Patriot; disappoint the honest Well-wisher of his Country; and blacken the Hopes of every Lover of the Muses into Despair, should an inconsiderable Mistep subvert so noble a Design! Yet to these fatal Evils would a Charter be exposed: Should the Trustees exceed their Authority, however inconsiderably it might affect the Interest of the College, their acting contrary to the express Letter, would *ipso facto* avoid it. Or should they, either thro' Ignorance, Inattention or Surprize, extend their Power in the least beyond those Limits, which the Law would prescribe upon a Construction of the Charter, a Repeal might be obtained by Suit at Common Law, or in Equity. And perhaps such might be the Circumstances of Things, as to render a new Incorporation at that Juncture, utterly impracticable. Besides, upon its Dissolution all the Lands given to it, are absolutely lost. The Law annexes such a Condition to every Grant to a Body politic: They revert to the Donor. Nor is there much Reason to expect a charitable Reconveyance from the Reversioner.

But if this may possibly be the Case, should even the Scheme of the Instruction of our Youth continue unperverted by the Directors of our Academy, what Abuses of Trust might they commit, what Attacks upon the Liberty and Happiness of this Province might they make, without Correction or Controul, should they be influenced by sinister Views? While the Fountain continues pure and unpolluted, the Stream of Justice may flow through its Channels clear and undisturbed. But should arbitrary Power hereafter prevail, and the tyrannical Arts of JAMES return to distress the Nation, the Oppression and Avarice of a future Governor, may countenance the iniquitous Practices of the Trustees, or destroy the Charter by improving the Opportunity of some little Error in their Conduct; and having seized the Franchise, dispose of it by a new Grant to the fittest Instruments of unjust and imperious Rule, and then adieu to all Remedy against them: For were they prosecuted by his Majesty's Attorney General in the *King's-Bench*, a *Noli prosequi* ⁴ would effectually secure them from Danger; while the Authority of a Governor rendered a Suit in Equity entirely useless. Thus would the Cause of Learning, the Rights and Privileges of the College, our public Liberty and Happiness, become a Prey to the base Designs and united Interest of the Governor and Trustees, in Spite of the most vigorous Efforts of the whole Province: Nor could a happy Intervention to the general Calamity, be expected from the other Branches of the Legislature, while his Majesty's Representative would give a hearty Negative to every salutary Bill, the Council and Assembly should think proper to pass. I say, his Majesty's Representative; for tho' our gracious Sovereign can delegate his executive Authority, he cannot transfer his Royal Virtues; and more than once this Province beheld a Vicegerent of the Best of Princes, imitate the Actions of the Worst. Reflections of this Kind will pronounce it a Truth most glaringly evident, that whatever Care may be taken in the Construction of a Charter to give our College an extensive Bottom, to endow it with the richest Privileges, and secure them by the most prudent Methods, it may still become the Spoil of Tyranny and Avarice, the Seat of slavish, bigotted and persecuting Doctrines, the Scourge and Inquisition of the Land. And far better would it be for us to rest contented with the less considerable Blessings we enjoy, without a College, than to aim at greater, by building it upon the sandy Foundation of a Charter-Government.

But after all, it may be urged, that should the College be founded on a Royal Grant, it might still be raised upon as unexceptionable a Basis, and as munificently endowed with Privileges as upon any other Footing. This is not in the least to be doubted. That a specious Charter will be drawn, and exhibited to public View, I sincerely believe: A Trick of that kind will unquestionably be made Use of, to amuse the unattentive Eye, and allure the unwary Mind into an easy Compliance. But it will be only *latet Anguis in Herba*,⁵ and when a copious Fund is once obtained, a Surrender of the Charter may make Way for a new

One, which tho' sufficiently glaring, to detect the Cheat, will only leave us Room to repent of our Credulity. This is beyond Dispute, a sufficient Reason with some, for establishing the College by Charter, tho', in my humble Opinion, it is one of the strongest Arguments that can be urged against it. We should be careful, lest, by furnishing the Trustees with a Fund, to render themselves independent of us, we may be reduced to the Necessity of being dependent upon them. If the Public must furnish the Sums by which the College is to be supported, Prudence declares it necessary, that they should be certain to what Uses the Monies will be applied; lest instead of being burdened with Taxes to advance our Interest, we should absurdly impoverish ourselves, only to precipitate our Ruin. In short, as long as a Charter may be surrendered, we are in Danger of a new One, which perhaps will not be much to our liking: And, as this Kind of Government will be always subject to Innovations, it will be an incontestible Proof of our Wisdom to reject it for a better.

It has in my two last Papers been shewn, what an extensive and commanding Influence the Seat of Learning will have over the whole Province, by diffusing its Dogmata and Principles thro' every Office of Church and State. What Use will be made of such unlimited Advantages, may be easily guessed. The civil and religious Principles of the Trustees, will become universally established, Liberty and Happiness be driven without our Borders, and in their Room erected the Banners of spiritual and temporal Bondage. My Readers may, perhaps, regard such Reflections as the mere Sallies of a roving Fancy; tho', at the same Time, nothing in Nature can be more real. For should the Trustees be prompted by Ambition, to stretch their Authority to unreasonable Lengths, as undoubtedly they would, were they under no Kind of Restraint, the Consequence is very evident. Their principal Care would be to chuse such Persons to instruct our Youth, as would be the fittest Instruments to extend their Power by positive and dogmatical Precepts. Besides which, it would be their mutual Interest to pursue one Scheme. Their Power would become formidable by being united: As on the Contrary, a Dissention would impede its Progress. Blind Obedience and Servility in Church and State, are the only natural Means to establish unlimited Sway. Doctrines of this Cast would be publicly taught and inculcated. Our Youth, inured to Oppression from their Infancy, would afterwards vigorously exert themselves in their several Offices, to poison the whole Community with slavish Opinions, and one universal Establishment become the fatal Portion of this now happy and opulent Province. Thus far the Trustees will be at Liberty to extend their Influence without controul, as long as their Charter subsists: And thus far they would undoubtedly extend it. For whoever, after being conscious of the uncertain Nature and dismal Consequences of a Charter College, still desires to see it thus established, and willingly becomes a Trustee, betrays a strong Passion for Tyranny and Oppression: Did he wish the Welfare of his Country, he would abhor a Scheme that may probably prove so detrimental to it; especially when a better may be concerted. It would therefore be highly imprudent to trust any Set of Men with the Care of the Academy, who were willing to accept it under a Charter.

If it be urged, that the Reasons above advanced, to prove the Danger and Mutability of a Charter Government, militate strongly against the Consequences I have deduced from them, let it be considered, that it will be in the Power of one Person only, to encourage or oppose the Trustees in the Abuse of their Authority. This Point, I think, is sufficiently evinced. Time may, perhaps, furnish the Trustees with an Opportunity of corrupting him with Largesses; or the Change of Affairs, make it his Duty to encourage the most slavish Doctrines and Impositions. Where then will be our Remedy, or how shall we obtain the Repeal of a Charter abused and perverted? Be it ever so uncertain in its Nature, it will still be in the Power of a Governor, to secure it against the Attacks of Law and Justice: Or, to render us more compleatly miserable, he may grant a new One, better guarded against any Danger from that Quarter. In the present Situation of Things, we have, indeed, no Reason to fear it. But as they may possibly assume a different Face hereafter, let us at least be armed in a Matter of so great Consequence, against the Uncertainty of future Events.

But after all it cannot be expected, that a Charter should at once be so compleatly formed, as to answer all the valuable Purposes intended by it. Inventions are never brought to sudden Perfection; but receive their principal Advantages from Time and Experience, by a slow Progression. The human Mind is too contracted to comprehend in one View, all the Emergencies of Futurity; or provide for and guard against, distant Contingencies. To whomsoever, therefore, the Draft of a Charter shall be committed, Experience will prove it defective, and the Vicissitude of Things make continual Alterations necessary. Nor can they be made without a prodigious Expence to the Public, since, as often as they are expedient, a new Charter will be the only Means to effect it.

I hope my Readers are by this Time convinced, that a Charter College will prove inefficacious to answer the true End of the Encouragement of Learning; and that general Utility can never be expected from a Scheme so precarious and liable to abuse. I shall in my next Paper exhibit another Plan for the Erection of our College, which if improved, will answer all the valuable Ends that can be expected from a Charter, and at much less Expence: While it will also effectually secure all those Rights and Privileges which are necessary to render the Increase of true Literature more vigorous and uninterrupted.

B.

The Letter this Week received from my industrious Correspondent Shadrech Plebianus, *is so important in its Nature, and judiciously written, that the Gentleman may be assured, it shall have a Place in this Paper.*

1. "I fear the Greeks even when bringing gifts." *Aeneid,* II, 49.
2. "Don't you see the dangers that henceforth surround you, madman." *Ibid.* IV, 561.
3. *Quo warranto* and *scire facias* were writs by which the government commenced action to secure forfeiture of a charter, patent, or franchise in the possession of an individual or a corporation.
4. *Noli prosequi* or *nolle prosequi.* An agreement by a prosecutor or plaintiff to discontinue an action which he has instituted.
5. "A snake lurking in the grass."

Number XX

A farther Prosecution of the same Subject

*Si vincimus omnia nobis tuta erunt, Commeatus abunde municipia
atque Coloniæ patebunt; sin metu cesserimus, eadem illa adversa fient.*
SAL.[1]

I HAVE in my last Paper endeavoured to explode the Scheme of
erecting our College by Charter, as a Means wholly inadequate
to the End proposed. Many of my Readers are doubtless convinced, how justly it lies open to the Objections I have raised
against it; and therefore expect, that something more effectual be
proposed in its Stead: While others that remain unsatisfied, may,
perhaps, find their Doubts removed, by perusing the Plan I shall
lay before them.

But I would first establish it as a Truth, that Societies have an
indisputable Right to direct the Education of their youthful Members. If we trace the Wisdom of Providence in the Harmony of
the Creation; the mutual Dependence of human Nature, renders
it demonstrably certain, that Man was not designed solely for his
own Happiness, but also to promote the Felicity of his Fellow-
Creatures. To this Bond of Nature, civil Government has joined
an additional Obligation. Every Person born within the Verge of
Society, immediately becomes a Subject of that Community in
which he first breathes the vital Element; and is so far a Part of
the political Whole, that the Rules of Justice inhibit those Actions which, tho' tending to his own Advantage, are injurious to
the public Weal. If therefore, it belongs to any to inspect the
Education of Youth, it is the proper Business of the Public, with
whose Happiness their future Conduct in Life is inseparably connected, and by whose Laws their relative Actions will be governed.

Sensible of this was the *Spartan* Law-giver,[2] who claimed the
Education of the *Lacedemonian* Youth, as the unalienable Right

of the Commonwealth. It was dangerous in his Opinion, to suffer the incautious Minds of those who were born Members of Society, to imbibe any Principles but those of universal Benevolence, and an unextinguishable Love for the Community of which they were Subjects. For this Reason, Children were withdrawn from the Authority of their Parents, who might otherwise warp their immature Judgments in Favour of Prejudices and Errors obtruded on them by the Dint of Authority: But if this was considered as a prudent Step to guard the Liberty and Happiness of that Republic; methinks it will not be unadvisable, for our Legislature, who have it in their Power, to secure us against the Designs of any Sect or Party of Men, that may aim at the sole Government of the College. If there the youthful Soul is to be ingrafted with blind Precepts, contracted Opinions, inexplicable Mysteries, and incurable Prejudices, let it be constituted by Charter: But if from thence we expect to fill our public Posts with Persons of Wisdom and Understanding, worthy of their Offices, and capable of accomplishing the Ends of their Institution, let it not be made the Portion of a Party, or private Set of Men, but let it merit the Protection of the Public. The only true Design of its Erection, is to capacitate the Inhabitants of this Province, for advancing their private and public Happiness; of which the Legislature are the lawful Guardians: To them, therefore, does the Care of our future Seminary of Learning properly and only belong.

Instead of a Charter, I would propose, that the College be founded and incorporated by Act of Assembly, and that not only because it ought to be under the Inspection of the civil Authority; but also, because such a Constitution will be more permanent, better endowed, less liable to Abuse, and more capable of answering its true End.

It is unreasonable to suppose, that an University raised by private Contribution in this Province, should arrive at any considerable Degree of Grandeur or Utility: The Expence attending the first Erection, and continual Support of so great a Work, requires the united Aid of the Public. Should it once be made an Affair of universal Concern, they will, no Doubt, generously contribute by Taxes, and every other Means towards its Endowment, and furnish it by a provincial Charge, with whatever shall be necessary to render it of general Advantage. But altho' our Assembly have already raised a considerable Fund for that Purpose, who can imagine they will ever part with or dispose of it to any other Uses, than such as they shall think proper and direct. If the College be erected at the Charge of the Province, it ought doubtless to be incorporated by Act of Assembly; by which Means the whole Legislature will have, as they ought to have, the Disposition of the Fund raised for this Purpose: The Community will then have it in their Power to call those to an Account into whose Hands the public Monies shall be deposited for that particular Use: And thus the Sums thought necessary for the Improvement of Learning, will be honestly expended in the Service for which they are designed; or should they be embezzled, it might easily be detected, and publicly punished: Besides, no particular Set of Men can claim a Right to dispose of the provincial Taxes, but those impowered by the Community; and therefore, if the Colony must bear the Expence of the College, surely the Legislature will claim the Superintendency of it. But if after all, it should be thought proper to incorporate it by Charter, it is to be hoped, they will reserve the public Money for some other Use, rather than bestow it on a College, the Conduct of whose Trustees would be wholly out of the Reach of their Power.

A further Argument in Favour of its being incorporated by Act of Assembly, may be deduced from the End of its Institution. It is designed to derive continual Blessings to the Community; to improve those public Virtues that never fail to make a People great and happy; to cherish a noble Ardour for Liberty; to stand a perpetual Barrier against Tyranny and Oppression. The Advantages flowing from the Rise and Improvement of Literature, are not to be confined to a Set of Men: They are to extend their chearful Influence thro' Society in general, — thro' the whole Province; and therefore, ought to be the peculiar Care of the united Body of the Legislature. The Assembly have been hitherto wisely jealous of the Liberties of their Constituents: Nor can they, methinks, ever be persuaded, to cede their Authority in a Matter so manifestly important to our universal Welfare, or submit the Guidance of our Academy to the Hands of a few. On the contrary, we are all so greatly interested in its Success, as to render it an Object worthy of their most diligent Attention, — worthy of their immediate Patronage. Should a Number of private Persons have the Impudence to demand of our Legislature, the Right of giving Law to the whole Community; or even should they ask the smaller Privilege, of passing one private Act, would it not be deem'd the Height of Effrontery? In what Light then ought the Conduct of those to be considered, who, in claiming the Government of our University, ask no less considerable a Boon, than absolute universal Dominion.

To a Matter of such general, such momentous Concern, our Rulers can never too particularly apply their Thoughts, since under their Protection alone Learning must flourish, and the Sciences be improved: It may indeed be urged, that the Nature of their Employment forbids them to spend their Time in the Inspection of Schools, or directing the Education of Youth: But are the Rise of Arts, the Improvement of Husbandry, the Increase of Trade, the Advancement of Knowledge in Law, Physic, Morality, Policy, and the Rules of Justice and civil Government, Subjects beneath the Attention of our Legislature? In these are comprehended all our public and private Happiness; these are Consequences of the Education of our Youth, and for the Growth and Perfection of these, is our College designed.

Another Reason that strongly evinces the Necessity of an Act of Assembly, for the Incorporation of our intended Academy, is, that by this Means that Spirit of Freedom, which I have in my former Papers, shewn to be necessary to the Increase of Learning, and its consequential Advantages, may be rendered impregnable to all Attacks. While the Government of the College is in the Hands of the People, or their Guardians, its Design cannot be perverted. As we all value our Liberty and Happiness, we shall all naturally encourage those Means by which our Liberty and Happiness will necessarily be improved: And as we never can be supposed wilfully to barter our Freedom and Felicity, for Slavery and Misery, we shall certainly crush the Growth of those Principles, upon which the latter are built, by cultivating and encouraging their Opposites. Our College therefore, if it be incorporated by Act of Assembly, instead of opening a Door to universal Bigotry and Establishment in Church, and Tyranny and Oppression in the State, will secure us in the Enjoyment of our respective Privileges both civil and religious. For as we are split into so great a Variety of Opinions and Professions; had each Individual his Share in the Government of the Academy, the Jealousy of all Parties combating each other, would inevitably produce a perfect Freedom for each particular Party.[3]

Should the College be founded upon an Act of Assembly, the Legislature would have it in their Power, to inspect the Conduct of its Governors, to divest those of Authority who abused it, and appoint in their Stead, Friends to the Cause of Learning, and the general Welfare of the Province. Against this, no Bribes, no Solicitations would be effectual: No Sect or Denomination plead an Exemption: But as all Parties are subject to their Authority; so would they all feel its equal Influence in this Particular. Hence should the Trustees pursue any Steps but those that lead to public Emolument, their Fate would be certain, their Doom inevitable: Every Officer in the College being under the narrow Aspect and Scrutiny of the civil Authority, would be continually subject to the wholesome Alternative, either of performing his Duty, with the utmost Exactness, or giving up his Post to a Person of superior Integrity. By this Means, the Prevalence of Doctrines destructive of the Privileges of human Nature, would effectually be discouraged, Principles of public Virtue inculcated, and every Thing promoted that bears the Stamp of general Utility.

But what remarkably sets an Act of Assembly in a Light far superior to a Charter, is, that we may thereby effectually counterplot every Scheme that can possibly be concerted, for the Advancement of any particular Sect above the rest. A Charter may, as I have shewn in my last Paper, be so unexceptionably formed, as to incur the Disapprobation of no Denomination whatever; but unexceptionable as it may be, we cannot be sure of its Duration. A Second may succeed, which, perhaps, would be disapproved of by all but one Party. On the contrary, we are certain that an Act of Assembly must be unexceptionable to all; since Nothing can be inserted in it, but what any one may except against; and, as we are represented in the Assembly by Gentlemen of various Persuasions, there is the highest Probability, that every Clause tending to abridge the Liberty of any particular Sect, would by some or other of our Representatives be strongly opposed. And this will still be the Case, however repeatedly Innovations may be attempted by subsequent Acts.

Another Advantage accruing to the College itself, and consequently to the Community in general, is, that larger Donations may be expected, should it be incorporated by Act of Assembly, than by Charter. Every generous Contributor, would undoubtedly be willing to have some Security for the Disposition of his Gratuity, consistent with the Design of his Donative. Nor is it improbable, that the most bounteous Person would refuse to bestow a Largess, without being convinced of the Honesty and Propriety of its Application. Under a Charter no Security to this Purpose can possibly be expected: This is sufficiently evinced by my last Paper. Besides which, if a Charter be obtained, it will without Doubt, be immediately or eventually in favour of one particular Party; the Consequence of which will be plainly this, that the other Sects amongst us, being a vast Majority, instead of contributing to the Support of our Academy by private Donations, will endeavour to discourage each other from it. But should our University be established by Act of Assembly, as every Individual would bear a Part in its Government, so should we all be more strongly induced, by private Gifts, to increase its Endowments.

Add to all this, that should the Persons intrusted with the immediate Care of our Nursery of Learning, commit any Error in their Conduct, the Act of Assembly would not be void, but in as full Force as if the Error had not been committed. And should they designedly transgress the Bounds of their Authority, the Act might be so constructed, as to disqualify them for holding their Offices, and subject them to the severest Penalties; to be recovered by his Majesty, or the Party aggrieved, or by both. It is also to be remarked, that should the Act of Incorporation be at any Time infringed, and the Liberty of the Students invaded, their Redress would be more easily obtained in a Court of Law.

COLLEGE: A FARTHER PROSECUTION

To this Scheme it may be objected, that the Creating a Body-Politic by Act of Legislation, without a previous Charter, is unprecedented, and an Infringement of the Prerogative of the Crown, and may possibly for those Reasons be damned by the King, who cannot repeal a Charter; and farther, that every End that can be proposed by Act only, may be obtained by a Charter-Incorporation; and an Act posterior, confirming it, and enlarging and regulating the Powers of the Body. In Answer to which, let it be considered, that it is not only the King's Prerogative, to grant a Charter, but also to grant it upon certain Terms; a Non-Compliance with which, will cause its Repeal; and from thence arises the Precariousness of a Charter. Should an Act be passed in Consequence of a Charter, it must be either to prevent its Precariousness, or to add new Privileges to those granted by it. If the former should be the Reason for passing an Act, it would militate against the Royal Prerogative, as well as an Act to incorporate the College; and therefore would, in all Probability, meet with the same Fate, and by that Means the Charter would stand alone. If the Act should be only in Aid of the Charter, it would still leave it in as uncertain a State, as without an Act. So that in either Case the College would be exposed to those Inconveniencies, which, in my last Paper I have shewn to be the natural Consequences of a Charter Government: Besides which, should the College be established by a Charter, the Public will lose most of those Advantages, which I shall in my next Paper propose, as some of the substantial Parts of an Act of Assembly.

Many other convincing Arguments might be urged with Success, in favour of an Act of Assembly for the Incorporation of our intended College, would the Bounds of this Paper admit their Insertion. Those I have had Room to enforce, are, I am convinced, sufficiently striking, to engage the Assent of every candid and unprejudiced Thinker. To the Wisdom of our Legislature, these Hints will be perfectly useless: Nor do I aim at any Thing more upon so important a Subject, than barely to open the Eyes of some of my less impartial Readers; and testify, how entirely the true Interest of this Province commands the most ardent and sincere Wishes of the *Independent Reflector*.   B.

THE INDEPENDENT REFLECTOR

To the Gentlemen who favoured me with their Sentiments on the Subject of the College, in two Letters signed B C. *and* A Friend, *I return my profoundest Thanks.*

1. "If we win, complete security will be ours, supplies will abound, free cities and colonies will open their gates; but if we yield to fear, the reverse will be true. Sallust, *Catiline*, LVIII, 9.

2. Lycurgus, the reputed father of the Spartan constitution of the ninth century B.C. Spartan youth were withdrawn from their parents at the age of seven and enrolled in military-like companies for education and training.

3. Richard Hofstadter and Walter P. Metzger (*Development of Academic Freedom in the United States* [New York, 1955], p. 189 note), have called attention to the similarity between Livingston's proposed method for preventing "party" domination of the college and the political theory expressed in No. X of *The Federalist*, where Madison argued that the remedy for the evils of political factionalism was to "take in a greater variety of parties and interests" to "make it less probable that a majority of the whole will have a common motive to invade the rights of other citizens."

Number XXI

THURSDAY, APRIL 19, 1753

Remarks on the COLLEGE continued

—— *Si quid Novisti rectius istis,*
Candidus imperti: si non, his utere mecum. Hor.[1]

THAT a College may be a Blessing or a Curse to the Community, according to its Constitution and Government, I think appears sufficiently evident from my former Papers. That incorporating it by an Act of Assembly, will be the best Means of securing the first, and avoiding the last, is in my Opinion, equally clear and incontestible. On a Subject of such general Importance; a Subject that concerns our Liberty and our Privileges, civil and religious; a Subject that will affect the Prosperity of our Country, and particularly involves in it, the Happiness and Misery of our Posterity, it would have been unpardonable in a Writer, whose Services are entirely devoted to the Public, to have passed it over in Silence, or handled it with Indifference and Langour. No, it deserves my most deliberate Attention, and fervent Activity; and calls for the Assistance of every Man who loves Liberty and the Province. Fully sensible of its unspeakable Importance, I shall now proceed to point out those Things which in my Judgment, are necessary to be inserted in the incorporating Act, for the Advancement of the true Interest of the College, and rendering it really useful to the Province.[2] Such Things as will effectually prevent its being prejudicial to the Public, and guard us against all the Mischiefs we so justly apprehend, should it ever unhappily fall into the Hands of a Party.

First: That all the Trustees be nominated, appointed, and incorporated by the Act, and that whenever an Avoidance among them shall happen, the same be reported by the Corporation to the next Sessions of Assembly, and such Vacancy supplied by

Legislative Act.[3] That they hold their Offices only at the good Pleasure of the Governor, Council and General Assembly: And that no Person of any Protestant Denomination be, on Account of his religious Persuasion, disqualified for sustaining any Office in the College.[4]

In Consequence of this Article we shall have the highest Security, that none will be dignified with that important and honourable Office, but such as are really qualified for executing it, agreeable to the true Design of its Institution. Should either Branch, or any two Branches of the Legislature, propose and elect a Candidate obnoxious to the Third, the Negative of the latter is sufficient to prevent his Admission. The three Branches concurring in every Election, no Party can be disobliged, and when we consider the Characters of the Electors, all Possibility of Bribery and Corruption, seems to be *entirely excluded.*

Secondly: That the President of the College be elected and deprived by a Majority of the Trustees, and all the Inferior Officers by a Majority of the Trustees with the President; and that the Election and Deprivation of the President, be always reported by the Trustees, to the next Session of Assembly, and be absolutely void, unless the Acts of the Trustees in this Matter, be then confirmed by the Legislature.

By this Means the President, who will have the supreme Superintendency of the Education of our Youth, will be kept in a continual and ultimate Dependence upon the Public; and the Wisdom of the Province being his only Support, he will have a much greater Security, in the upright Discharge of his Duty, than if he depended solely on the Trustees, who are likely to oust him of his Office and Livelihood thro' Caprice or Corruption. That Station being therefore more stable, will at the same Time be more valuable; and for this Reason we have the stronger Hopes of filling the President's Chair, with a Man of Worth and Erudition, upon whose good Qualifications and Conduct, the Success and Improvement of the Students, will eminently depend.

Thirdly: That a Majority of the President and Trustees, have Power to make By-Laws not repugnant to the Act of Incorporation, and the Law of the Land: That all such By-Laws be reported to the House of Representatives at their next succeeding Session, *in hæc Verba,*[5] under the seal of the College, and the Hands of the President and five Trustees; and that if they are not reported, or being reported are not confirmed, they shall be absolutely void.

Hence it is easy to conceive, that as on the one Hand there will be a great Security against the arbitrary and illegal Rule of the President and Trustees; so on the other, the immediate Governors of the College will have all proper Authority to make such salutary Rules as shall be necessary to advance the Progress of Literature, and support a Decorum and Police in the Academy, — as well as maintain the Dignity and Weight which the Superiors of it ought undoubtedly to be enabled to preserve over their Pupils.

Fourthly: That the Act of Incorporation contain as many Rules and Directions for the Government of the College as can be foreseen to be necessary.

As all our Danger will arise from the Mis-Rule of the President and Trustees; so all our Safety consists in the Guardianship of the Legislature. Besides, the Advantage herefore, of being by this Article secured from arbitrary Domination in the College; the Business of the Trustees and President will be less, and they with their Subordinates, more at Leisure to concert the Advancement of the College.

The Fifth Article I propose is, that no religious Profession in particular be established in the College; but that both Officers and Scholars be at perfect Liberty to attend any Protestant Church at their Pleasure respectively: And that the Corporation be absolutely inhibited the making of any By-Laws relating to Religion, except such as compel them to attend Divine Service at some Church or other, every Sabbath, as they shall be able, lest so invaluable a Liberty be abused and *made a Cloak for Licenciousness.*[6]

To this most important Head, I should think proper to subjoin,

Sixthly: That the whole College be every Morning and Evening convened to attend public Prayers, to be performed by the President, or in his Absence, by either of the Fellows; and that such Forms be perscribed and adhered to as all Protestants can freely join in.

Besides the Fitness and indisputable Duty of supporting the Worship of God in the College; obliging the Students to attend it twice every Day, will have a strong Tendency to preserve a due Decorum, Good Manners and Virtue amongst them, without which the College will sink into Profaness and Disrepute. They will be thereby forced from the Bed of Sloth, and being brought before their Superiors, may be kept from Scenes of Wickedness and Debauchery, which they might otherwise run into, as hereby their Absence from the College will be better detected.

With Respect to the Prayers, tho' I confess there are excellent Forms composed to our Hands, it would rather conduce to the Interest of our Academy, if, instead of those, new Ones were collected, which might easily be done from a Variety of approved Books of Devotion among all Sects; and perhaps it may be thought better to frame them as near as possible in the Language of Scripture.[7] The general Forms need be but few. Occasional Parts may be made to be inserted when necessary; as in Cases of Sickness, Death, *etc.* in the College, or under general Calamities, as War, Pestilence, Drought, Floods, *etc.* and the like as to Thanksgivings. Many of the Forms of Prayer contained in the English Liturgy, are in themselves unexceptionably good; but as establishing and imposing the Use of those, or of any other Protestant Communion, would be a discriminating Badge, it is liable to Objections, and will occasion a general Dissatisfaction. As the Introduction of them, therefore, will prejudice the College, it is a sufficient Reason against it. It will be a Matter of no small Difficulty to bring the greatest Part of the Province, to the Approbation of praying at any Time by Forms; but since they are in this Case absolutely expedient, our Affection for the Prosperity of this important Undertaking, should incline us, while we give some Offence in one Article, to remove it by a Compensation in another of less Consequence to the College.

Seventhly: That Divinity be no Part of the public Exercises of the College. I mean, that it be not taught as a Science: That the Corporation be inhibited from electing a Divinity Professor; and that the Degrees to be conferred, be only in the Arts, Physic, and the Civil Law.

Youth at a College, as I have remarked in a former Paper, are incapable of making a judicious Choice in this Matter; for this Reason the Office of a theological Professor will be useless: Besides, Principles obtruded upon their tender Minds, by the Authority of a Professor's Chair, may be dangerous.[8] But a main Reason in support of this Clause, is the Disgust which will necessarily be given to all Parties that differ in their Professions from that of the Doctor. The Candidate for the Ministry will hereby in his Divinity Studies, whenever he is fit for them, be left to the Choice and Direction of his Parents or Guardians. Besides, as most of the Students will be designed for other Employments in Life, the Time spent in the Study of Divinity, may be thought useless and unnecessary, and therefore give Umbrage to many. Nor will their whole Course of Time at the College, be more than sufficient for accomplishing themselves in the Arts and Sciences, whether they are designed for the Pulpit, or any other learned Profession. And it may justly be doubted, whether a Youth of good Parts, who has made any particular Proficiency in the Elements, or general Branches of Knowledge (his Instruction in which is the true and proper Business of a collegiate Education) would not be able to qualify himself for the Pulpit, by a Study of the Scriptures, and the best Divinity Books in the College Library, as well without as with the Aid of a Professor; especially if it be enacted,

Eighthly: That the Officers and Collegians have an unrestrained Access to all Books in the Library, and that free Conversation upon polemical and controverted Points in Divinity, be not discountenanced; whilst all public Disputations upon the various Tenets of different Professions of Protestants, be absolutely forbidden.[9]

Ninthly: That the Trustees, President, and all inferior Officers, not only take and subscribe the Oaths and Declaration appointed by Statute, but be also bound by solemn Oath, in their respective Stations, to fulfil their respective Trusts, and preserve inviolate the Rights of the Scholars, according to the fundamental

Rules contained in the Act.[10] And that an Action at Law be given and well secured to every inferior Officer and Student, to be brought by himself, or his *Guardian*, or *prochein Amy*,[11] according to his Age, for every Injury against his legal Right so to be established.

And in as much as artful Intrigues may hereafter be contrived to the Prejudice of the College, and a Junto be inleagued to destroy its free Constitution, it may perhaps be thought highly expedient, that the Act contain a Clause

Tenthly: That all future Laws, contrary to the Liberty and Fundamentals of this Act, shall be construed to be absolutely void, unless it refers to the Part thus to be altered, and expressly repeals it; and that no Act relating to the College, shall hereafter pass the House of Representatives, but with the Consent of the Majority of the whole House; I mean all the Members of Assembly in the Province.

Nor would it be amiss to prescribe,

Eleventhly: That as all Contests among the inferior Officers of the College, should be finally determined by the Majority of the Members of the Corporation, so the latter should be determined in all their Disputes, by a Committee of the whole House of Representatives, or the major Part of them.

These are the Articles which in my Opinion, should be incorporated in the Act for the Establishment of the College; and without which we have the highest Reason to think, the Advantages it will produce, will at best fall short of the Expence it will create, and perhaps prove a perpetual Spring of public Misery. — *A Cage,* as the Scripture speaks, *of every unclean Bird.*[12] — The Nursery of Bigotry and Superstition. — An Engine of Persecution, Slavery and Oppression. — A Fountain whose putrid and infectious Streams will overflow the Land, and poison all our Enjoyments. Far be it from me to imagine I have pointed out every Thing requisite to the Preservation of Liberty, and the Promotion of the Interest of the College; I only suggest such Heads as occur. Beyond all doubt my Scheme is still imperfect. Should our Legislature themselves enter upon this momentous Affair, the Example of a British House of Commons, in Matters of great Importance, might be worthy their Imitation. I mean, that the Bill be printed and published several Months before it passes the House. The Advantage I would propose from this Step is, that while it only exists as a Bill, the Objections against it would be offered with Freedom, because they may be made with Impunity. The general Sense of the People will be the better known, and the Act accommodated to the Judgment and Esteem of all Parties in the Province. A.

1. "If you know anything better than these maxims, reveal them; if not, accept mine." Horace, *Epistles*, 1, 6, 67.

2. Livingston's detailed plan for a "free" college rather than a "party" seminary was outlined in a bill which his brother Robert introduced in the Assembly on November 6, 1754. Its text is in the *Journal of the Votes and Proceedings of the General Assembly of the Colony of New-York*, [*1691–1765*], 2 vols. (New York, 1764-1766), II, 413-419. It was also printed separately as *A Bill, entitled, An Act further to establish and incorporate a College within this Colony, for the Education and Instruction of Youth in the Liberal Arts and Sciences* (New-York, 1754). Livingston subsequently offered an extended analysis of each provision in his new series of essays, the "Watch-Tower," which ran in the *New-York Mercury*, November 1754 to November 1755. See especially Nos. XLVIII–LII, October 20, 27, November 3, 10, 17, 1755.

3. As Livingston later explained it in the "Watch-Tower," "A public Provision . . . having been made by legislative Acts, for erecting an Academy, it was highly reasonable, that the Legislature should have the Nomination of those Persons, who were to be empowered to dispose of the Monies in the Pursuit of those valuable Ends. . . ." No. XLIX, *New-York Mercury*, October 27, 1755.

4. ". . . as every Man in a protestant State, who acknowledges the Force of moral obligations, excepting Papists, is capacitated by his Principles . . . to be a good Member of that State; . . . no Test can be of any Use to qualify Persons for an Office, unless it effectively excludes the Members of the Church of *Rome*, and gives equal Admittance to Persons of every other Denomination. . . . But a Test . . . to incapacitate all those who do not belong to one particular Church, would be the Height of Absurdity and Injustice, as it would absolutely shut the Door of academical Preferments, to a very great Majority of our Inhabitants, who would still be obliged to contribute to the Support of the College." "Watch-Tower," No. L, *New-York Mercury*, November 3, 1755.

5. "In these words."

6. Livingston's free college bill provided that "No System of Divinity whatsoever shall ever be *publickly* taught in the College; that no Professors shall be instituted *publickly* to teach any such System; and that neither the President nor the Tutors shall read *public* Lectures in Divinity; but that

every Scholar or Pupil be left at Liberty to pursue his own Method in the Study of the sacred Scriptures; and to take such Advice and Direction therein, as he shall think proper." Private instruction by ministers of the Anglican and Dutch churches would be permitted "at their Chambers." "Watch-Tower," No. L, *New-York Mercury*, November 3, 1755.

7. Samuel Seabury, the Anglican rector at Hempstead, promptly challenged Livingston to produce a prayer that would be acceptable to all Christians (*New-York Mercury*, April 30, 1753; *Samuel Johnson Writings*, I, 169); Livingston, aided by Smith, promptly composed one. See No. XXVIII.

8. Livingston reiterated these fears in stronger language a year later. "The greatest absurdities acquire by length of time a venerable deference; and the most ridiculous customs assume the semblance of natural reason. . . . Let but a Nurse or a priest implant the seeds of superstition in a tender mind, and 'tis great odds, but they take root beyond the power of the wisest Philosopher to eradicate." *Independent Reflector*, Preface, p. 1.

9. Hofstadter and Metzger (*Development of Academic Freedom*, p. 191), acknowledge Livingston's liberal ideas on education but criticize his proposal to ban the teaching of divinity in the college because it would deny students the intellectual stimulation provided by "the clash of theologies," a privilege which Harvard's undergraduates were already beginning to enjoy. From the text above, however, Livingston apparently desired precisely such a "free Conversation" on theological issues. In his own college bill he went further by providing that every member of the faculty "countenance and encourage a Freedom of Conversation and Enquiry among the Scholars, upon all polemical Points in Divinity." Indeed, what most shocked Reverend Samuel Johnson, the future president of King's College, was the prospect that "the boys were to be encouraged to dispute all points of religion pro and con." "Watch-Tower," No. LII, *New-York Mercury*, November 17, 1755; *Samuel Johnson Writings*, I, 33–34.

10. In the "free" college bill, provision was made for Quakers to substitute an affirmation for the oath.

11. *Prochein Ami*, "next friend," a term used to describe the person who appears on behalf of a minor in a legal action.

12. "Babylon . . . is fallen, and . . . become . . . a cage of every unclean and hateful bird." Rev. 18:2.

Number XXII

THURSDAY, APRIL 26, 1753

The same Subject continued and concluded in An ADDRESS to the Inhabitants of this Province

> *If we retain the Glory of our Ancestors,*
> *Whose Ashes will rise up against our Dulness,*
> *Shake off our Tameness, and give Way to Courage;*
> *We need not doubt, inspir'd with a just Rage,*
> *To break the Neck of those, that would yoke ours.*
> Tatham's *Distracted State*
> *Flectere si nequeo superos, Acheronta movebo.* VIRG.[1]

MY DEAR COUNTRYMEN,

IN a Series of Papers, I have presented to your View the Inconveniences that must necessarily result from making the RULE of the College, the *Monopoly* of any single Denomination. I have considered it in a Variety of Lights, and explor'd its numerous Evils. To prevent them in the most effectual Manner, I have concerted a Plan, the Heads of which have been offered to your serious Consideration. Throughout the whole, I have given my Thoughts with the Freedom and Independence suitable to the Dignity of the Subject, and the Character of an impartial Writer. Upon my Representation of the Matter, nor Awe, nor Hope, hath had any Influence. But urg'd by the Love of Liberty, and a disinterested Concern for your, and your Posterity's Happiness, I have disclos'd the Importance, — the prodigious Importance of the present Question.

Far be it from me, to terrify you with imaginary Dangers, or to wish the Obstruction of any Measure conducive to the public Good. Did I not foresee, — was I not morally certain of the most ruinous Consequences, from a Mismanagement of the Affair, I should not address you with so much Emotion and Fervor: But when I perceive the impending Evil; when every Man of Knowledge and Impartiality entertains the same Apprehension; I cannot, I will not conceal my Sentiments. In such a Case, no Vehemence is excessive, no Zeal too ardent. The Alarm given is not confined to Particulars. No, the Effects I presage are dreaded far and wide as a general Calamity. Would to God our Terror was merely panic! but it is founded on the unerring Testimony of History, of Reason, and universal Experience.

Nor fancy I aim at warping your Judgment by the Illusion of Oratory, or the Fascination of Eloquence. If in the Sequel, I appear rather to declaim than prove, or seem to prefer the Flowers of Rhetoric to the Strength of Argument, it is because, by the clearest Demonstration, I have already evinc'd the Necessity of frustrating so injurious a Step. My Assertions have not been unsupported by Evidence; nor have I levell'd at your Passions, till I had convinc'd your Reason. After this, you will pardon a more animated Address, intended to warm the Imagination, and excite your Activity.

Of Prejudice and Partiality, I renounce the Charge; having alike argued against all Sects whatever, as I am in reality perfectly neutral and indifferent. For the Sincerity of my Intentions, I lay my Hand upon my Heart, and appeal to the enlighten'd Tribunal of Heaven.

Arise, therefore, and baffle the Machinations of your and their Country's Foes. Every Man of Virtue, every Man of Honour, will join you in defeating so iniquitous a Design. To overthrow it, nothing is wanting but your own Resolution. For great is the Authority, exalted the Dignity, and powerful the Majesty of the People. And shall you the avow'd Enemies of Usurpation and Tyranny, — shall you, the Descendants of *Britain*, born in a Land of Light, and rear'd in the Bosom of Liberty, — shall you commence Cowards at a Time when Reason calls so loud for your Magnanimity? I know you scorn such an injurious Aspersion. I know you disdain the Thoughts of so opprobrious a Servility; and what is more, I am confident the Moment you exert a becoming Fortitude, they will be sham'd out of their Insolence. They will blush at a Crime they cannot accomplish, and desist from Measures they find unsuccessful. Some of you, perhaps, imagine all Opposition unavailable. Banish so groundless a Fear. Truth is Omnipotent, and Reason must be finally victorious. Up and try. Be Men, and make the Experiment. This is your Duty, your bounden, your indispensable Duty. Ages remote, and Mortals yet unborn, will bless your generous Efforts; and revere the friendly Hand that diverted the meditated Ruin, as the Saviour of his Country.

The Love of LIBERTY is natural to our Species, and an Affection for POSTERITY, interwoven with the human Frame. Inflamed with this *Love*, and animated by this *Affection*, oppose a Scheme so detrimental to your Privileges, so fatal to your Progeny. Perhaps you conceive the Business is done. What! do you take it for granted that so it must be! Do you not then think yourselves free? Our Laws, our Assemblies, the Guardianship of our Mother Country, the mildest and the best of KINGS, do they not convince you that hitherto you know not what is Servitude? And will you trifle with an inestimable Jewel? Will you dance on a Precipice, and lay your Hand on a Cockatrice's Den? Unresisting will you yield, and resign without a Struggle? Will you not even venture at a Skirmish, to bequeath to your Posterity the priceless Treasure yourselves enjoy? Doubtless you resent the Insinuation. Courage then my Brethren: Reason is for us, that Reason whose awful Empire is spurn'd by your Adversaries; for such are those whoever they be, that aspire to a Superiority above their fellow Subjects. Whence then should proceed your Remissness in a Concern so momentous? Whence so tame a Submission, so ignominious a Compliance? Thou GENIUS of LIBERTY dispensing unnumber'd Blessings! Thou SPIRIT of PATRIOTISM ever watchful for the public Good! Do ye inspire us with Unanimity in so interesting a Cause, and we will assert our Rights against the most powerful Invasion!

You, Gentlemen of the CHURCH of ENGLAND, cannot but condemn the unaccountable Assurance of whatever Persuasion, presumes to rob you of an *equal* Share in the Government of what *equally* belongs to all. With what Indignation and Scorn, must you, the most numerous and richest Congregation in this City, regard so insolent an Attempt! You who have the same Discipline, and the same Worship with the Mother Church of the Nation, and whose fundamental Articles are embrac'd by all protestant Christendom, — what Colour of Reason can be offered to deny you your just Proportion in the Management of the College? Methinks a due Respect for the national Church, nay common Decency and good Manners, are sufficient to check the presumptuous Attempt, and redden the Claimant with a guilty Blush. Resent, therefore, so shameless a Pretence, so audacious an Encroachment.

Nor can you Gentlemen of the DUTCH CHURCH, retrospect the Zeal of your Ancestors in stipulating for the Enjoyment of their religious Privileges, at the Surrender of the Province, without a becoming Ardor for the same Model of public Worship which they were so anxious in preserving to you in its primitive Purity. Or higher still, to trace the Renown of your Progenitors, recollect their Stand, their glorious and ever memorable Stand against the Yoke of Thraldom, and all the Horrors of ecclesiastic Villainy, its inseparable Concomitants. For their inviolable Attachment to pure unadulterated Protestantism, and the inestimable Blessings of Freedom civil and sacred, History will resound their deathless Praises; and adorned with the precious Memorials of their heroic and insuppressible Struggles against Imposition and Despotism, will shine with eternal and undecaying Splendor. Impell'd by their illustrious Example, disdain the Thoughts of a servile Acquiescence in the usurp'd Dominion of others, who will inevitably swallow up and absorb your Churches, and efface even the Memory of your having once formed so considerable a Distinction. Pity methinks it would be and highly to be deplor'd, that you should, by your own Folly, gradually crumble into Ruin, and at length sink into total and irrecoverable Oblivion.

Remember Gentlemen of the English PRESBYTERIAN Church, remember with a sacred Jealousy, the countless Sufferings of your pious Predecessors, for Liberty of Conscience, and the Right of private Judgment. What Afflictions did they not endure, what fiery Trials did they not encounter, before they found in this remote Corner of the Earth, that Sanctuary and Requiem which their native Soil inhumanly deny'd them? And will you endanger that dear-bought Toleration for which they retired into voluntary Banishment, for which they agoniz'd, and for which they bled? What drove your Ancestors to this Country, then a dreary Waste and a barren Desert? What forced them from the Land of their Fathers, the much-lov'd Region where first they drew the vital Air? What compell'd them to open to themselves a Passage into these more fortunate Climes? Was it not the Rage of Persecution and a lawless Intolerance? Did they not seek an Asylum amongst the Huts of Savages more hospitable, more humaniz'd than their merciless Oppressors? Could Oceans stop or Tempests retard their Flight, when Freedom was attack'd and Conscience was the Question? And will you entail on your Posterity that Bondage, to escape which they brav'd the raging Deep, and penetrated the howling Wilderness!

You, my FRIENDS, in Derision called QUAKERS, have always approv'd yourselves Lovers of civil and religious Liberty; and of universal Benevolence to Mankind. And tho' you have been misrepresented as averse to human Learning, I am confident, convinced as you are of the Advantages of useful Literature, by the Writings of your renown'd *Apologist*, and other celebrated Authors of your Persuasion, you would generously contribute to the Support of a College founded on a free and catholic Bottom. But to give your Substance to the rearing of Bigotry, or the tutoring Youth in the *enticing Words of Man's Vanity*, I know to be repugnant to your candid, your rational, your manly Way of thinking. Since the first Appearance of the *Friends*, thro' what Persecutions have they not waded? With what Difficulties have they not conflicted, e'er they could procure the unmolested Enjoyment of their Religion? This I mention not to spur you to revenge the Indignities offered to your Brethren, who being now beyond the Reach of Opposition and Violence, you, I am sure will scorn to remember their Tribulations with an unchristian Resentment. But to make their inhuman Treatment a Watch-Tower against the like Insults on your Descendants, is but wise, prudent and rational. At present, as ever you ought, you enjoy a righteous Toleration. But how long you will be able to boast the same Immunity, when the Fountain of Learning is directed, and all the Offices of the Province engrossed by one Sect, God only knows, and yours it is to stand on your Guard.

Equally tremendous will be the Consequences to you, Gentlemen of the FRENCH, of the MORAVIAN, of the LUTHERAN, and of the ANABAPTIST Congregations, tho' the Limits of my Paper deny me the Honour of a particular Application to your respective Churches.

Having thus, *My Country-Men*, accosted you as distinct Denominations of Christians, I shall again address you as Men, and reasonable Beings.

Consider, *Gentlemen*, the apparent Iniquity, the monstrous Unreasonableness of the Claim I am opposing. Are we not all Members of the same Community? Have we not an equal Right? Are we not alike to contribute to the Support of the College? Whence then the Pretensions of one in Preference to the Rest? Does not every Persuasion produce Men of Worth and Virtue, conspicuous for Sense, and renown'd for Probity? Why then should one be exalted and the other debased? One preferr'd and the rest rejected? Bating the Lust of domineering, no Sect can pretend any Motive for monopolizing the Whole? Let them produce their Title, and we will submit. Or do they think us so pusillanimous that we dare not resist? What! are we to be choak'd without attempting to struggle for Breath? One would, indeed, imagine the *Business was done*, and that with a Witness. One would fancy he already beheld *Slavery* triumphant, and *Bigotry* swaying her enormous, her despotic Sceptre. But you, I trust, will asswage their Malice, and confound their Devices. You, I hope, will consider the least Infraction of your Liberties, as a Prelude to greater Encroachments. Such always was, and such ever will be the Case. Recede, therefore, not an Inch from your indisputable Rights. On the Contrary declare your Thoughts freely, nor loiter a Moment in an Affair of such unspeakable Consequence. You have been told it, — Posterity will feel it. Indolence, Indolence has been the Source of irretrievable Ruin. Langour and Timidity, when the Public is concerned, are the Origin of Evils mighty and innumerable. Why then in the Name of Heaven, should you behold the Infringement, supine and inanimate? Why should you too late deplore your Irresolution, and with fruitless Lamentation bewail your astonishing, your destructive Credulity? No; defeat the Scheme before it is carried into Execution: Countermine it e'er it proves irreversible. Away with so pestilent a Project: Suffer it no longer to haunt the Province, but stigmatize it with the indelible Brands of the most scandalous Infamy. Alas, when shall we see the glorious Flame of PATRIOTISM lighted up, and blazing out with inextinguishable Lustre? When shall we have *One Interest,* and that Interest be the *common Good?*

To assert your Rights, doth your Resolution fail you? To resist the Domination of one Sect over the Rest, are you destitute of Courage? Tamely will you submit, and yield without a Contest? Come then, and by Imagination's Aid, penetrate into Futurity. Behold your Offspring train'd in Superstition, and bred to holy Bondage. Behold the Province over-run with Priest-craft, and every Office usurp'd by the ruling Party!

Pause, therefore, and consider. Revolve the Consequences in a dispassionate Mind: Weigh them in the Scale of Reason, in the Balance of cool deliberate Reflection. By the numberless Blessings of LIBERTY, heavenly-born; — by the uncontroulable Dictates of CONSCIENCE, the Vicegerent of GOD; — by the Horrors of PERSECUTION, conceived in Hell, and nurs'd at *Rome*; — and by the awful Name of REASON, the Glory of the human Race; I conjure you to pluck out this Thorn, which is incessantly stinging and goading the Bosom of every Man of Integrity and Candour!

Next to the most patriot KING that ever grac'd a Throne, and the wisest LAWS that ever bless'd a People, an equal TOLERATION of Conscience, is justly deem'd the Basis of the public Liberty of this Country. And will not this Foundation be undermined? Will it not be threatened with a total Subversion, should one Party obtain the sole Management of the Education of our Youth? Is it not clear as the Sun in his Meridian Splendor, that this Equality, — this precious and never-to-be-surrender'd Equality, will be destroy'd, and the Scale preponderate in Favour of the Strongest? And are we silent and motionless, to behold the Abolition of those invaluable Bulwarks of our Prosperity and Repose? Is not the Man, — the Man do I call him? Is not the Miscreant, who refuses to repel their Destruction, an Accomplice in the Crime? Does he not agree to sacrifice that which, next to the Protection of our Mother Country, constitutes our Security, our Happiness, and our Glory? He is beyond Question chargeable with this aggravated Guilt. — Let us, therefore, strive to have the College founded on an ample, a generous, an universal Plan. Let not the Seat of Literature, the Abode of the Muses, and the Nurse of Science; be transform'd into a Cloister of Bigots, an Habitation of Superstition, a Nursery of ghostly Tyranny, a School of rabbinical Jargon. The Legislature alone should have the Direction of so important an Establishment. In their Hands it is safer, incomparably safer, than in those of a Party, who will instantly discover a Thirst for Dominion, and lord it over the Rest.

Come on then, *My Country-Men*, and awake out of your Lethargy! Start, O start, from your Trance! By the inconquerable Spirit of the ancient BRITONS; — by the Genius of that CONSTITUTION which abhors every Species of Vassalage; — by the unutterable Miseries of PRIEST-CRAFT, reducing Nations and Empires to Beggary and Bondage; — by the august Title of ENGLISH-MEN, ever impatient of lawless tyrannic Rule; — by the grand Prerogatives of HUMAN NATURE, the lovely Image of the infinite DEITY; — and what is more than all, by that LIBERTY *wherewith* CHRIST *has set you free*; — I exhort, I beseech, I obtest, I implore you, to expostulate the Case with your Representatives, and testify your Abhorrence of so perillous, so detestable a Plot. In Imitation of the Practice of your Brethren in *England*, when an Affair of Moment is on the Carpet, petition your respective Members to take it into their serious Consideration. Acquaint them with your Sentiments of the Matter, and I doubt not, they will remove the Cause of your Disquiet, by an Interposition necessary to the public Prosperity, and eventual of their own immortal Honour.

Z.

The Reflector's Sentiments, relating to the religious Worship of the College, having been objected to under pretence, that no Prayer can be calculated to please all Parties, he intends, in some future Paper, to exhibit a Form, against which no Protestant of the most scrupulous Conscience can except.

1. The English quotation is from *The Distracted State* (1651), a tragedy by John Tatham (fl. 1632–1664); the Latin, from *Aeneid*, VII, 312: "If I fail to influence the powers above, I will move Acheron [i.e., Hades]."

Number XXIII

THURSDAY, MAY 3, 1753

Of *PATRIOTISM*

> ――――― *Oh Greeks, respect your Fame,*
> *Let awful Virtue, patriot Warmth inspire,*
> *And catch from Breast to Breast, the noble Fire!*
>   Pope's *Homer*

Patriotism, or public Spirit, is so essentially necessary to the Prosperity of Government, and the Welfare of Civil Society, that without some Portion of the *former*, the *latter*, I was going to say, cannot long exist; I will venture to say, can have no Existence.

All History conspires to establish this political Maxim, *That the true Dignity and Glory, the Stability and internal Tranquility of every State, were always proportionate to the Strength and Diffusiveness of Public Spirit.* The sublime Genius of the wisest Legislator, the refined Arts of the most skilful Politician, would be but *splendidæ Nugæ*,[1] unavailing Efforts towards the Establishment of Order and Harmony, without the Assistance of Patriotism. It is this divine Principle which alone can give Vitality, Beauty, Strength and Duration to any political Body.

When we consider the astonishing Grandeur, the almost incredible Victories, and that resplendent Figure which the *Grecian* and *Roman* Common-Wealths exhibited to the World, if we examine from what Sources they derived that superior Lustre, which has claimed the Admiration of all succeeding Ages, and been equalled by none; there is no Principle from whence we can with so much Justice, deduce their Glory and Renown, as from that patriot Ardor which warmed every Breast, and beamed forth with so illustrious a Blaze from their Legislators, their Heroes and Philosophers. If on the other Hand we trace them to the melancholy Periods of their Declension and Dissolution, we shall find they sunk in Proportion to their Decay of Public Spirit: And that when selfish Principles and sordid Views became predominant, lawless Ambition reared its destructive Head, generous Emulation took its Flight, and that noble disinterested Love of the Public, which had triumphed over every selfish, every partial Tie, was no longer the ruling Principle of Action. Hence they became a Prey to Tyranny, to Vice, and to abject ignominious Slavery.

It would not be difficult to illustrate these Observations by a Deduction of Facts from the *Græcian* and *Roman* Historians, could so ample a Detail fall within the Limits of this Paper, or so fully answer its present Design. I shall therefore proceed. And

In the FIRST Place endeavour to prove, that ever Member of the Community, who is not actuated by a Public Spirit, or a Patriot Disposition, may and ought to be deemed an Enemy to his Country.

Secondly, I shall attempt to discriminate true Patriotism from its specious Appearance.

That we are not born for our selves alone, is the Voice of sound Philosophy, — the Dictate of unerring Nature. Dependence and social Obligation take Place at the first Dawn of Life, and as its Thread lengthens, continually multiply and invigorate: Amongst these the Love of the Public becomes one of the Strongest. Family Affection and private Friendship, if they so engross our Hearts as to render us insensible of the general Welfare, are not only mean and unworthy Passions, but naturally hurry us into the basest, the vilest, and most immoral Conduct. The Good of the Public, includes the Life and Happiness of Thousands: And it is surely not less absurd than wicked, to give the Preference to the blind Dictates of Passion, or the narrow Ties of personal Attachment.

Not to melt for public Calamities, — not to feel the patriot Glow of Soul, when our Country is crowned with Success, and distinguished with Honour, — to be regardless of its Fame, and unambitious in its Behalf, — to coil ourselves up within the dirty Shell of our own private Interest and Conveniency, careless of the common Good; is denying our Title to Humanity, and forfeiting the Character of rational Beings.

He who is secured to his Country, by no Ties but those of partial Passion and private Interest, will, whenever there arises an Opposition between *that* and *those*, give the Preference to the *latter*, and unrestrained by Fear, is ripe for Rebellion, Conspiracies, Rapine and Treachery. Every such Man is a concealed Mine, which only wants to be properly touched; and as far as his Influence reaches, the Fabric of public Peace, Harmony and Order, will shake and totter.

Meerly to love the Public, to wish it well, to feel for it, in all its Vicissitudes, is not sufficient. The Man may perhaps be honest enough to do no Harm, if it should be in his Power, and may possibly be Proof against any Temptations to injure his Country. But this is by no Means fulfilling the whole of his Obligation to the Community of which he is a Member. To exemplify our Love for the Public, as far as our Ability and Sphere of Action will extend, is true Patriotism. This is the indispensable Duty of every Man, and whoever, from Indolence or Lukewarmness, neglects to advance the common Weal, when it is in his Power, is not only a bad Citizen, but a real Enemy to his Country, in Proportion to the Value and Consequence of his neglected Service. Should this Indolence and Lukewarmness universally infect a People, their Government will be unhinged, they will fall a Prey to their Enemies, and cease to be a Nation.

I go still farther. Whoever is unstudious of the public Emolument, who denies it a Share of his thinking Hours, and refuses to exert his Head, his Heart, and his Hands in its Behalf, is a Foe to Society. Mankind have been more indebted to the patriot Zeal of Genius and Knowledge, than to the conquering Arm of Heroism. And whoso neglects to make the common Good an Object of Reflection, and to plan for its Welfare, robs it of all that Advantage which it might reap by a contrary Conduct.

I am now to distinguish between true Patriotism, and its specious Appearance.

To shine in the first Order of Patriots, has been the Portion of few. That ethereal Spark which pervades and illuminates the Breasts of the choicest Favourites of Heaven, is but sparingly shed amongst human Kind. But let us not envy those elder Sons of immortal Fame, nor murmur at our own Allowance; rather let us endeavour to improve the Talents we enjoy, than with a rash

Ambition grasp at those we are not born to possess. To be in some Degree a Patriot, is in every Man's Power, and is every Man's Duty.

He is a Patriot who prefers the Happiness of the Whole, to his own private Advantage; who, when properly called upon, is ready to rise up in its Defence, and with a manly Fortitude, shield it from Danger. He is a Patriot, the ruling Object of whose Ambition, is the public Welfare: Whose Zeal, chastised by Reflection, is calm, steady and undaunted: He whom lucrative Views cannot warp from his Duty: Whom no partial Ties can prevail on to act traitorously to the Community, and sacrifice the Interest of the *Whole* to that of a *Part*: He whom Flattery cannot seduce, nor Frowns dismay, from supporting the public Interest when it is in his Power: Who mourns for their Vices, and exerts his Abilities to work a Reformation: Who compassionates their Ignorance, and endeavours to improve their Understandings: He who aims to cultivate Urbanity and social Harmony. To conclude, he is a true Patriot whose Love for the Public is not extinguished, either by their Insensibility or Ingratitude; but goes on with unwearied Benevolence in every public-spirited Attempt.

Here I am tempted to stop, and pay my Adorations to those exalted *Patriots,* who were the Glory, the Safe-guard, the Ornaments of their Country: — But I will repress my Emotion and keep to Order.

One would be apt to imagine, *Patriotism* carried such evident Marks of its native Purity, that no specious Appearance of *it* could impose upon Mankind. But if we judge of Human Nature by Experience, we shall be almost tempted to think, Men are formed to deceive and be deceived. 'Tis not in Patriotism only, but in various other Characters, that Mankind are in Masquerade, and Falsehood assumes the Air of Reality. Virtue has something so irresistibly charming, that artful Vice steals her Dress, and often mimics her Air so deceitfully, that it requires more than common Penetration to discover the Delusion.

Under the Disguise of Patriotism, that first-rate Virtue, *Faction, Self-Interest,* and private Ambition are frequently concealed. I have found, and I own my self unequal to the Power of developing all the artificial Windings of *false Patriotism.*

OF PATRIOTISM

But I may venture to pronounce, that where a benevolent Temper, does not display itself in the general Tenor of a Man's Conduct; his Pretences to Patriotism and public Spirit, are very much to be questioned. For Benevolence is the Parent of Patriotism, and where the Father has no Property, what Inheritance can the Son claim?

True Patriotism cannot dwell with a mean, narrow, selfish Disposition: As easily will Figs grow upon Thorns, or Grapes upon Thistles.

The Coward, the Flatterer, the Wretch whose sordid Soul pays Obeysance to the splendid Insolence of Power and Fortune, can never feel the generous Warmth of honest Patriotism.

The noisy intemperate Froth of a political Enthusiast, is as far removed from a steady Principle of Patriotism, as the Dignity of solid Understanding from the Fumes of poetical Madness.—

Party-Faction and personal Resentment, have often imposed themselves upon Mankind for the divine Operations of public Spirit. We shall find Hypocrites of this sort, more frequently inveighing against Men, than reasoning upon Facts: Ridicule is their favourite Engine — to mislead the Judgment by warming the Imagination, is their peculiar Art.

The superstitious Zealot, and the religious Bigot, have not so much as an Idea of a Public: When they presume to act the Part of Patriots, there is something so unnatural and absurd in their Manner, that they can scarcely deceive any but their own Herd.

When these Characters lay Claim to Patriotism, we may be sure they are Impostors, and we should treat them as Hypocrites.

I shall close my Animadversions with an Exhortation to my Countrymen, to cultivate and display this God-like Virtue of public Spirit.

We are, my Friends, but just emerged from the rude unpolished Condition of an Infant Colony: There is a large Field for Improvement open to us. We are set down in a Country whose Fertility will generously reward the Labours of the industrious Husbandman. The Bowels of the Earth already yield us their Treasures, and probably have more and better in Reserve. *Commerce* stretches forth its golden Arms to our Merchants; and our Situation is so pre-eminently advantageous for Navigation, that I am persuaded, it will be our own Faults, if we do not extend and increase our Trade beyond our Neighbours and Competitors. And to crown all, we are blessed with civil Liberty, and the inestimable Privilege of unprecarious Property. Without these, all our natural Advantages, would be no more than a beautiful unanimated Picture. Our Security, our Prosperity, our Duration, by a natural and necessary Connection, will be in Proportion to the Strength and Management of our Patriotism and public Spirit. We are accountable to the Supreme Beneficient Governor of the Universe, as the Donor of these Blessings: We are bound as rational active Beings to improve them, and we are answerable to Posterity for our Conduct.

Let us all then, in our respective Stations, and with our several Abilities, exert our selves as Patriots, that so a united Harmony of public Spirit may arise amongst us. Let the general Good take Place of a contracted Selfishness. Let the public Welfare triumph over private Animosity. Let us discountenance Vice, and revere *that Religion* which will make us wiser and better. Let us abhor Superstition and Bigotry, which are the Parents of Sloth and Slavery. Let us make War upon Ignorance and Barbarity of Manners. Let us invite the Arts and Sciences to reside amongst us. Let us encourage every Thing which tends to exalt and embellish our Characters. And in fine, let the Love of our Country be manifested by that which is the only true Manifestation of it, *a patriot Soul and a public Spirit.*

N.

Whereas some of the Clergy in this City, make a Practice of aspersing the Character of the Independent Reflector *in their Pulpits, by charging him obliquely (tho' too intelligibly to be mistaken by their Congregations) with Infidelity and Contempt for Christianity, in order to discredit his Paper, without any Provocation or the least Foundation for such scurrilous Insinuations from any of his Writings. This is therefore to give Notice (having with great Patience waited for their Reformation) that the first Clergyman, guilty of the like infamous Artifice for the future, shall be treated as he deserves for taking such villainous Liberties.*

1. "Splendid nonsense."

Number XXIV

THURSDAY, MAY 10, 1753

Reasons for the farther regulating of Beef and Pork; together with the Necessity of an Act for the Inspection of Butter

Round social Earth, to circle fair Exchange,
And bind the Nations in a golden Chain.

Thom[son], *Liberty* [1]

Tis the Business of every Government to take peculiar Care of their Staple, whether it consists in Provisions or Manufactures; and to be singularly watchful to have it vended in the greatest Perfection, and with due Weight and Measure. Nor is the public Attention to an Affair so momentous and interesting, more conducive to the common Weal, than to the private Benefit of the Seller himself. It is from an erroneous Notion of his Interest, that the Manufacturer endeavours to put off his Wares in a Condition slight or counterfeit: For when once the Cheat is discovered (and it cannot long escape Detection) the Commodity loses its Character, and will not afterwards sell for even its real Value. As in all other Cases, so in this will it be found, that Honesty is the best Policy, and that the most expeditious Way of acquiring a Fortune, is for every Man to excel in his Branch of Traffic. In short, whoever proposes to become rich by the Commodities he deals in, and has not Virtue enough to restrain him from Knavery, should (as Dr. *Tillotson* [2] observes) be honest from the meer Principles of Roguery.

Pennsylvania (a Province renown'd for its public Spirit, and the Wisdom of its Laws) was the first Colony on this Continent, which put the Exportation of Flour under proper Regulations. At this prudential Step it has ever since had ample Reason to rejoice. Nor was it long before the Effects of their Providence, were felt by the other Colonies. *Philadelphia* Flour rose into Reputation, while ours was continually losing what it had. The former was not only sold at a much greater Price, but while there was a Barrel of it in the *West-Indies*, the latter would frequently not sell at all. Loud and universal was the Complaint against us, which we long endur'd without even essaying a Deliverance.

These were the Considerations which induc'd our Legislature, near three Years ago, to pass an Act for the Inspection of Flour; the happy Consequences of which we have already very sensibly experienc'd.[3] The Flour of this Province, boasts now not only as high a Character as that of *Philadelphia*; but, as I am told, actually commands the Preference where ever we send it. 'Tis this enables the Merchant to purchase it at so great a Price as it bears at present, and may, 'tis to be hop'd, be the Means of recovering some of those Branches of Trade, which we had lost by the Badness of our Flour and other Produce.

The same Reasons that gave Rise to the above salutary Law, are equally cogent for the Regulation of every other Branch of Commerce, which merits the Name of *Staple*. Hence Beef, Pork, and Butter, require an Act for their Regulation and Inspection, upon the same Principles which influenced our Superiors, to interpose (if I may be allowed the Expression) for our Redemption from the Ruins of Trade, when, by the Fraud and Carelessness of our Manufacturers, we were plung'd into a Kind of mercantile Perdition. We have, indeed, an Act *to prevent the Abuses in the repacking of Beef and Pork*, passed the third Day of *November* 1740, enacting among other Things, "That every Barrel shall contain Thirty One Gallons, and that in the repacking, each Barrel shall be twice trodden down at least." [4] But as no Man pretends to be infallible, except the Pope, and some of the Clergy, our Legislators have exhibited in this Clause, a strong Proof of the Fallibility incident to the Rest of the Laity. For as no particular Quantity of Meat, (which is only determinable by Weight) is to be put into a Barrel, it remains at the Discretion of the Packer, to put into the same Barrel fifty Pounds more or less, and yet strictly comply with the Act. This Opportunity for Fraud, arises from the Laws not directing by whom the Beef is to be trodden down; and whether that Operation be performed by a heavy Man or a light Boy, will, I conceive, with Submission to deeper Understandings, make very considerable odds. Nay, was even that ascertained, and had it been expressly enjoined to be done by a Man, still the Quantity would not have been determinate, since Men are of different Sizes, and the same Man tread heavy or light. Add to this, that the Weather at the different Seasons of the Year, must greatly affect the Packing; for when Meat is frozen and hard, 'tis impossible to tread as much into a Barrel, as when it is moist, yielding and soft. Neither is this Opportunity for Fraud, respecting the Quantity, the only Inconvenience. A Barrel of Beef scarcely full, and loosely packed, is much more liable to spoil, than one firmly and well pack'd. The only Way to pack it justly, is to weigh out the Quantity a Barrel is to contain, and then to press it in with Hand-Screws.

Burlington is fam'd for the Goodness of her Pork, which she vends in the *West-Indies* at a higher Price than is given for any other. This I take to be wholly owing to their Care in curing and packing it; and with the like Attention, our Pork would rival, probably excel theirs, since we produce that Commodity in as great, perhaps greater, Perfection than any Colony in *America*.

Irish Beef is esteemed in the *West-Indies* superior to any other; and I am persuaded its Soundness and Reputation, are chiefly to be ascribed to its skilful and artificial Package, tho' doubtless in no small Degree, to their Method of curing it, and the Age of the Beast when he is killed. 'Twere to be wish'd that the People of this Province, were equally skill'd in the Cure of a Production which might be rendered to us, so extensive a Branch of Trade, and the Source of so immense Lucration and Wealth. For unless it be well cur'd, it must, in the sultry Climates to which we transport it, speedily corrupt and putrify. Those Gentlemen, therefore, amongst us, who are acquainted with the Method used in *Ireland*, would, by communicating it, make no unacceptable Present to the Public.

I cannot learn that the packing of Butter for Exportation, was ever regulated by any Act of this Province, tho' it constitutes a Branch of our Trade so considerable, that ten thousand Firkins [5] have, in one Year, been brought to Market in this City. Nor is there any Reason for supposing it would, under proper Regulations, be inferior to the Butter of *Ireland*. Yet by the frequent Frauds committed, and the little Care generally taken in its packing, it hath so greatly suffer'd in its Character, at almost every Market whither we transmit it, that while there is any *Irish* Butter to be purchased, it will not sell, save at a Price too low for a reasonable Profit. In Proof of those reiterated Frauds and Complaints, I believe I might appeal to every Merchant trading to the *West-Indies*. I have myself seen twenty odd Pounds of Salt taken out of one Firkin; and not only Hogs Lard and Tallow, but even Stones and Brick have been sold for merchantable Butter.

A Commodity, therefore, at present so grossly abused, and yet capable, if duly regulated, to form a vast Branch of our Traffic, seems well worthy the Legislative Attention. It may effectually be inspected in the same Manner as our Flour, by perforating one Head of the Firkin with a Gimblet, and transpiercing the Butter to the other with an Instrument like that used for the Inspection of Flour. By this Method the Officer may see the Quality of the Butter throughout the whole Firkin.

'Tis remarkable that a new Regulation is scarce ever proposed, tho' indisputably useful and necessary, but it meets from many with Opposition and Censure. By some the Proposal is rejected out of Obstinacy, and by others from a mistaken Opinion of its affecting their Interest. It is not even unusual for those who are to reap the greatest Benefit from it, to commence its fiercest and most outrageous Adversaries. This was the Case with the Act for the Inspection of our Flour, tho' the Men who were the Hottest against it, have since been the greatest Gainers, and would now, probably, be as furious in opposing its Repeal.

From this incurable Foible of human Nature, I doubt not my present Proposal will be condemn'd by the Country Gentlemen who breed Cattle, because by the Regulation for which I am arguing, a Barrel will contain more Beef and Pork than formerly. But to infer from thence that they will be proportionable Losers, is a Consequence by no Means deducible from the Premisses. For when once the Barrels are known to hold such additional Quantity, and the Character of the Beef and Pork is established abroad, they will inevitably rise in Demand, and their Price increase in Proportion.[6]   X.

That the Practice of Physic is difficult, precarious and dangerous, and ought to be under some Regulation, I have shewn in a former Paper. I shall now, according to my Promise, propose such Heads, which if enacted into a Law, would prevent the Repetition of those innumerable Evils, to which, thro' the Want of it, we have long been most miserably exposed. They are (as I said) but Heads; and many Things, if they are incorporated into a Law, must be added as Auxiliaries to supply their Elipses.

I. That the four eldest Members of his Majesty's Council, the Judges of the Supreme Court, the Representatives of this City in Assembly, our Mayor and Recorder for the Time being, or any Seven of them, with the Assistance of two Physicians, and two Surgeons, by the Majority of them elected; be empowered to examine, and under their Hands and Seals, License all Physicians, Surgeons, and Apothecaries in the Province.

II. That without such Licence, no Person shall practise as Physician, or Surgeon, or vend Drugs as an Apothecary, under a certain Penalty, excepting Bone-setters practising elsewhere than in the City of *New-York*.

III. That the Examiners, at four fixed Times in a Year, meet at the City-Hall in *New-York*, for the Execution of their Offices: That their Examination of Candidates be public; and that Power be given them, to fine and imprison such as disturb them in the Course of their Business.

IV. That the Majority of Seven Examiners annually nominate and appoint, out of such as shall be licensed, and residing in this City, one Physician and a Surgeon, who shall at least four Times a Year, and oftener, if they think meet, enter into any Shop where Drugs are sold, and inspect them; and of all such as they shall think corrupt or defective, they shall make and sign an Inventory, and leave it with the Proprietor; but the Drugs they shall take away, and produce them at the next quarterly Meeting of the Examiners to be proved: That then the Inspectors shall, on Oath, testify as to the Quality of the Drugs, when seized, and that they have sustained no Damage since, thro' their Default; and if the

Majority of the Examiners, with such Assistance as they shall think proper to call, shall condemn the Drugs, they shall be burnt before them; but if they are found good, they shall be returned to the Owner: That such Inspectors shall be obliged to serve one Year; and at their Appointment, take an Oath for the faithful Discharge of their Trust.

V. That if a licensed Physician, Surgeon or Apothecary, shall be convicted and adjudged guilty of Mal-Practice, by the Majority of the whole Number of Examiners they shall be empowered to revoke his Licence; and if he presumes to practice after such Revocation, he shall be subject to the Penalties of such as Practice without Licence.

VI. That no Physician, Surgeon or Apothecary shall sue for his Fees or Drugs, before his Bill is taxed by an Examiner, and a Copy served on the Party chargeable, or left at his Residence. Except where Oath is made before a Judge of the Court out of which the Process shall issue, that the Party chargeable is about departing the Jurisdiction of such Court: In which Case a Copy of the Bill taxed, shall be annexed to and filed with the Declaration. And upon all Trials the Plaintiff shall be non-suited, unless his Licence, or a true Copy of it, be produced and proved.

VII. That all licensed Physicians, Surgeons, or Apothecaries be exempted from being Constable, Collector, Assessor, and all other inferior troublesome Employments.

VIII. That the Majority of the Examiners have leave to appoint a Treasurer, Clerk and Door-Keeper, who shall all be paid out of their Fines; and if a Deficiency shall happen, that it be supplied by the Public. And that the Examiners have Power to make Rules and Orders, and enforce the Obedience of them upon their own Body, and their Officers: And that all their Proceedings be regularly recorded, and in all Courts admitted as Evidence: And that Suits for the Penalties may be brought in the Name of their Treasurer only; but to be disposed of as the Majority of the Examiners shall think proper.

IX. That any Person sued for executing the Act, have Leave to plead the general Issue, and give it in Evidence; and that it be declared a public Act.

REGULATING BEEF AND PORK

It is not to be doubted but that such a Law would be disgustful to knavish and ignorant Quacks; but it is to be hoped, that its being prejudicial to those whose Lives are a continual Prey upon the Public, will be esteemed an insufficient Objection against it. Let it once pass, tho' its Force be limited only to this City, and suspended for ten Years to come. Extreme Misery, even with a distant Hope of Redress, is preferable to light Afflictions with absolute Despair of Relief.[7]   A

1. From Part IV of James Thomson's *Liberty* (1735–1736).
2. John Tillotson (1630–1694), Archbishop of Canterbury (1691–1694). A three-volume edition of his works was published in 1752.
3. The law, passed November 24, 1750, compelled all bakers and bolters to register their names and brand marks with the clerk of the local court, prohibited the export of any flour not of "due Fineness and honestly and well Packed," required all exported casks of flour and biscuits to bear the brand of the baker and bolter, and appointed inspectors to enforce the law. New York City had sought unsuccessfully to do the same thing earlier by municipal ordinance. *Colonial Laws of New York*, III, 788–793; *Minutes of the Common Council*, IV, 83–84, 169–170, 251–252.
4. *Colonial Laws of New York*, III, 77–79. New York City had passed a comparable ordinance in 1731. See *Minutes of the Common Council*, IV, 95–96.
5. A firkin is a small wooden tub with a capacity of about 1/4 barrel.
6. The *Reflector's* complaint regarding beef packing was quickly echoed in letters to the New York press from Boston merchants relating their difficulty in disposing of New York beef because of the irregularity in the weight of the barrels. (*New-York Gazette*, June 4, 1753; *New-York Mercury*, June 25, 1753.)
7. Livingston's proposal formed the basis for New York's licensing law of June 10, 1760 (*Colonial Laws of New York*, IV, 455–456) requiring physicians and surgeons desiring to practice in New York City to undergo an examination by a committee of public officials and to secure a license. Less stringent than Livingston's proposal, the law is the first in any colony to concern itself with fitness to practice medicine. An early New Amsterdam ordinance had prohibited ships' barbers from dressing wounds or prescribing drugs while on shore; and some colonial legislatures granted licenses to individual physicians as a sort of honorary degree; but most colonial legislation on medicine dealt with the control of contagious diseases or the regulation of fees. See Shryock, *Medicine and Society*, pp. 11–12; Francis R. Packard, *History of Medicine in the United States* (New York, 1931), chap. 3; Brooke J. Hindle, *The Pursuit of Science in Revolutionary America, 1775–1789* (Chapel Hill, 1956), p. 110; Daniel J. Boorstin, *The Americans: The Colonial Experience* (New York, 1958), pp. 229–230.

Number XXV

THURSDAY, MAY 17, 1753

Remarks on the EXCISE, *resumed*

————— *Instead of voted Aid,*
Free, cordial, large, a never-failing Source,
The cumb'rous *Imposition follow'd harsh.*

THOM[SON], *Lib*[*erty*]

IT was often observed of a certain Minister of State, that whenever he intended to carry a Point which he knew would be injurious to the Liberty of the *English* Nation, he never failed to introduce it into the House of Commons, by enumerating the pretended Advantages that would accrue from it to the Subject; either by enlarging his civil Privileges, or increasing the public Revenue without much Burthen to his private Interest. But such paltry Schemes are too thinly veiled to elude the Sight, while Mankind are capable of Reflection, or drawing Consequences from certain Premisses laid down. No Imposts upon the People, can ever increase their Privileges, but only answer the Necessities of the Public. It is one Thing to tax the Community for Payment of Debts, and another to enact the Enlargement of their Rights. Whence it is evident, that no Tax should be levied but upon the most pressing Occasions. Nor should the Increase of the Revenue be the sole Object of the Legislators Concern. In some Cases it is highly imprudent to augment it, especially when the Methods used for that Purpose, unavoidably draw after them the Impoverishment of the People. I am sensible there are many half-sighted Politicians, who imagine, that while the Revenue is large, all is safe; that as long as the Treasury is rich, the Province cannot be poor; that if we have Sums in Hand to answer our provincial Debts, we are in no Danger of new Taxes for that Purpose. How unapplicable is this kind of reasoning, which is far from being just to the State of our Affairs! It is an unalterable Rule of Prudence and good Policy, that the Expences of raising and collecting a Tax, should bear a moderate and just Proportion to the Tax itself. A Transgression of this Rule, must ever be attended with the most fatal Consequences to the Community: For instead of having our public Duties easily complied with, the heavy and extravagant Charges at which they are raised, convert those voluntary Contributions into slavish and insupportable Impositions. But our *Excise Scheme* implies still a greater Absurdity. To sell at public Auction our civil Interests and Property, for a small Consideration paid into the Treasury, while even that Payment is made with our own Monies, is something too ridiculous to be accounted for in any rational Manner. What Tax can be called a just One, that is attended with more Expence in levying it, than the Tax itself amounts to? And yet, that this is the Case with our Excise, the following Considerations will render very apparent. We find by the Excise-Act for the current Year, that the Monies thereby enacted to be paid into the Treasury by the several Farmers of that Duty, throughout the Province, amount to no more that £1,612. By computing the Number of the Retailers of Strong Liquors in this Colony, and the *mean* Price at which they purchase their Licences of the Farmers, it will evidently appear, that the Profits of the latter generally equal, if not exceed, the Sum accruing to the Public by Virtue of the Excise. In some particular Counties the Rate at which that Duty is farmed, is so very inconsiderable, as not even to fall within that Proportion. And it deserves to be remarked, that in one of them for which the Excise was farmed in 1751, at no more than £41, the Number of Licenses fell short but Nine of those granted in the City and County of *New-York*, the Excise of which was the same Year farmed at £920. Whence it is easy to conceive, that the Continuance of that Impost, in its present Circumstances, must of Necessity be injurious to the Community. The Support of his Majesty's Government in this Province, the annual Expences of the Public, the Funds necessary for sinking our Bills of Credit, and the Salaries of our civil Officers, are Calls which cannot be satisfied, but at the Expence of a considerable Portion of our Estates. But how little does the Excise contribute to answer our public Necessities! Are the other provincial Taxes much alleviated by it? Or rather would not a small Addition to their Weight destroy the Necessity of it, and at the same Time ease the Province of that prodigious Charge at which it is raised? Oppressive Duties should ever be exclaimed against, even tho' imposed upon the Subject, solely with Design to increase the Revenue: But when they are perverted, to enrich a Set of corrupt Individuals at the Cost of the Community, they become slavish and intolerable. Impositions of this Kind are too commonly ushered in, under the Pretence of general Utility. But, indeed, this, as it can apparently serve little else than to increase the private Fortunes of a few, is the most extraordinary Contrivance that human Wit or Reason could invent. That we should be burthened with a Tax, the Charges of levying which amount to more than the Tax itself; that the Farmers of that Tax should receive more Profit by it than the Public, for whose Use it was wholly designed; and that they should have it in their Power to extend that Profit to an extravagant Degree, by extorting from his Majesty's good Subjects without controul, are Things entirely inconsistent with English Liberty. Let us suppose that a Community whose Constitution essentially included a Right in the People to tax themselves, should enact, that in Consideration of a Sum of Money, paid into their public Treasury by a few Individuals, they should be empowered to assess the Community in at least double that Sum, to be levied for their own private Use, out of the Estates of their fellow Subjects. Could this be done without destroying the very Nature of their Constitution? Yet this is the Case with the People of this Province: We enjoy an inherent constitutional Power of charging our Estates, with such Sums as we ourselves think necessary for the Preservation and Advancement of our public Interest: But by a solemn and public Act, we, in a great Degree annually resign that Power to the Farmers, who, in Consequence of such Resignation, have, by putting our Laws in Execution, a legal Right to charge us with the Imposition of a Sum vastly exceeding the Consideration paid by them into the Treasury.

This Matter considered in any Light it possibly can be, is

either a Robbery committed on the Public, or an Invasion of the private Property of the Subject, under the Colour of Law. If the Sums actually accruing to the public Revenue by Sale of the Excise, and the Money pocketed by the Farmers, be together called the *Impost*, then they are in this Article suffered to run away with, at least, one half of the public Revenue. If the Monies actually arising from such Sale, be *alone* esteemed the Tax, whatever Sums the Farmers receive, above what may be called reasonable Commissions for their Trouble, are unjustly extorted from the Members of the Community. In either Case the Government of the Subject must certainly be duped by the Farmer. If all the Monies arising from the Excise should be applied to public Use, as they really ought, consistent with its true Intention, would it not be most expedient to appoint Officers to collect those Monies, who should be obliged to pay the same into the Treasury, and to whom a reasonable Allowance might be made, for the Execution of that Office? And if the public Necessities require no more than what is actually paid into the Treasury, might it not be raised at the Price of much less than the Farmer's Profit? By this Means the Residue would remain in the Hands of those to whom it of Right belongs; nor would the avaricious Individuals of Society have an Opportunity of pocketing that to which they cannot urge the least reasonable Pretensions. Of the Truth of these Things there is no Room to doubt.

The Manner of the Excise will appear still more inequitable, when we consider the Farmers' Income in a comparative View with the Commissions of the Collectors of our other Taxes. The Profits of the former exceed One Hundred *per Cent* upon the Monies paid into the Treasury; the Wages of the latter bear the inconsiderable Proportion of Five *per Cent*, to the Sums they collect. Nor is there any Thing peculiar in the Nature of the Excise, that can prevent its being raised at the same moderate Charge as the other provincial Imposts. Should a Person unacquainted with the Affairs of this Colony be told, that a small Tax of about £1,600, is more oppressive to its Inhabitants, than all the other public Contributions to which we are subject, he would scarcely believe it: Still it is undeniably true. For the Charges attending the collecting of all our other Taxes, do not equal the Profits made by the Farmer on the Excise. But were it otherwise, it must be allowed, that a Tax, of which scarcely one Half is applied to the Use for which it was raised, is more grievous to the People of any Community, than a Duty ten Times as large that is levied at little Expence, and honestly employed in that Service for which it was originally intended. It cannot indeed be denied, that the largest Imposts bear most heavily upon the Subject; but still they may not be the most grievous, since no Man would think it so great a Hardship to advance a Sum, be it ever so large, to promote his Interest and Happiness, as to disburse a much smaller without any Prospect of a Compensation for it. Should all our provincial Taxes be subject to the same unreasonable expensive Methods of raising them, we might, without a Spirit of Prophecy, easily foresee our unavoidable Ruin. In a few Years, our Wealth would, in a great Measure, be sunk into the Purses of the Collector, and the oppressed Province become poor and indigent. Then indeed there would be no Occasion of new Taxes, when the unhappy People would have scarce any Thing left them out of which a Tax could be raised.

But it surprizes me much, that the Legislature should have esteemed the Excise the only Tax proper to be let to farm. Or if the others would serve that End as well, why have they not farmed them all? Or is the Excise Officers Task so excessively severe as to deserve such accumulated Rewards for his Labour? No: This Tax, as I have said before, might be levied with as little Trouble, and consequently at as small an Expence as any other.

Should the Reasons I have hitherto advanced against farming the Excise, be thought insufficient, let it at least be remembered, that no free Government can, without counteracting their fundamental Principles, grant to any Subject, a Power of taxing the Community: Nor can they do it without exceeding the Limits of that Authority wherewith they are invested by their Constituents. Should the Supreme Head of a free State attempt to lay Impositions upon them, without their Consent, or in other Words, without the Approbation of those who represent them, would it not be deemed such an Advancement of the Royal Prerogative, as is utterly inconsistent with the Nature of such a Constitution? An Attempt of this Kind, would raise an honest Jealousy in the Breast of every Lover of Liberty: For Proofs of this we need not wander abroad, while the English Annals are crowded with Examples of such Encroachments in former Reigns, and the Reception they met with from our brave Ancestors. But why should the Nation deny their Sovereign a Privilege, we are so ready to grant without Discrimination to any of his Subjects that ask it? Perhaps those who are thus fond of resigning our Rights to the Subject, would be the first to oppose such an Extension of the regal Prerogative: Yet, methinks, it would seem somewhat more comely to be enslaved by a Prince than a Beggar. In short, a People cannot be free when they resign the Right of levying their own Taxes to any one: Nor can their Relish for Liberty be the most refined, even should they refuse a servile Subjection to their King; while they voluntarily submit their Privileges to the Discretion of a fellow Subject.

But it is not sufficient to have placed this Excise Grievance in so many glaring Points of Light. My Duty obliges me also to prescribe a Remedy for it: This will demand a very short Attention of my Readers. It is well known that the Rest of our Taxes are levied by Assessors and Collectors, to the latter of whom a proper Allowance is made for their public Service. The Recompence of a Shilling in the Pound, proves to the Collector an ample Satisfaction for the Time he spends in the Employment of the Province, while the Assessor is rewarded with the Approbation of the Public, and an inward Pleasure arising from a Willingness to serve his Country.[1] It might therefore be wished, that the Legislature would think it expedient to repeal our Excise Laws, and settle that Tax on the same Footing with the others to which this Province is subject. It will be as easy for the Assessors to ascertain a reasonable Impost upon the strong Liquors vended by the Retailers, as to tax their Estates, and this is the shortest and least expensive Method that can be taken: For it is very evident, that should the Duties upon Strong Liquors be settled by Act of Assembly, to be the peculiar Care of a Set of civil Creatures created for that Purpose, a great Number of Persons would be necessary, as Commissioners to enter the Liquors of Retailers, Officers to make Seizure of such Liquors as should be sold without Entry, Collectors to receive those Duties, *etc.* To which Offices sufficient Salaries should be annexed, which would also render the Expences of raising those Duties disproportionate to the Duties themselves. I would therefore propose with Submission to our Legislators, that an Act be passed, whereby the Rate of the Excise may be limited to such Sum per Gallon, as they shall think expedient; and that the Assessors and Collectors of each respective Country, City, Township, Borough, or Precinct, *etc.*, within this Colony, appointed or chosen to levy the other Taxes, should also be empowered to assess the Retailers of Strong Liquors according to such Rate. And that no Person, under proper Penalties, should presume to retail without a Licence from such Magistrates or Persons, in each respective County, *etc.*, as should also be thought fit, and appointed for that Purpose by the Government: And that such Retailers as should procure Licences for Tavern-Keeping, should also be obliged to give Security to such Persons, in Behalf of his Majesty, to keep orderly Houses, prevent Riots, Breaches of the Peace, *etc.*, And a List of such Retailers being entered in the Records of every County, *etc.*, would enable the Assessors and Collectors to levy the Excise with the greatest Ease and Certainty.[2]

B.

1. The assessors, elected by wards, received no compensation; the collectors of taxes received a remuneration of from nine pence to one shilling for each pound they collected.

2. Livingston's suggestion bore early fruit. In December 1753 the Assembly ended the practice of farming out the liquor excise and appointed public officials in each county and in New York City to perform the duty. A year later two excise collectors were named for New York City, to receive a five per cent commission on their collections. *Colonial Laws of New York*, III, 951–957, 1000–1007.

Number XXVI

Remarks on our BILLS OF CREDIT, and COPPER-PENCE

Thy Silver is become Dross.
Prophet JEREMIAH.[1]

THAT whenever a base Currency, or Medium of Trade, be admitted in a mercantile Country, it will in Proportion banish from it every better Currency, is a Truth capable of the clearest Demonstration. The same is the Case whenever such a Country sets a higher Value on any one particular Medium of Trade, than is allowed for it by the trading World in general, I mean a higher Value than is proportionably allowed for other Mediums. It is not so in those inland Countries, whose Commerce is entirely confined within their own Limits: For among themselves they may agree to put what Value they please on what they please. They may make Leather, or what would otherwise be but waste Paper, pass for Money: General Consent will give it that Circulation from Hand to Hand which is so well expressed by our common Term *Currency*. But that will only answer as far as such mutual Agreement reaches; for in a Country that carries on any foreign Trade, this kind of Currency will soon lose its Credit, and become of little or no Value. Experience will teach them that the Estimate set on it arose entirely from their own Consent, and that the Rest of the World will desire to be excused from receiving for their valuable Commodities, what has no intrinsic Value. Indeed, Province Bonds or Bills of Credit, such as we commonly term *Paper-Money*, have, in some few of the Colonies that have made Use of them, retained their Credit pretty well; but this has been more owing to the Smallness of the Quantity made in those Provinces, than to the real Value of them, or the Credit of their Funds; for they have generally been issued for the full Sum at which they were payable after long Periods; and let the Funds on which Paper Money is emitted be ever so good, yet if the Quantity made, be so large as to be nearly equal to what the Currency was before in Gold and Silver, it must inevitably fall; and as more is struck, will gradually sink to its true Value — to that of private Bonds payable at the like Periods. But when once a Country exceeds the Credit of its certain Funds, the more Paper Money they strike, the less real Value will they have current in Trade. This Truth, tho' a seeming Paradox, has been fully exemplified in the Provinces to the Eastward, where, after making £1,200,000 of Paper Money, their Medium of Trade was less in Value than when they had only £100,000 of Paper Money; for, as Silver rose from 5s. to 60s. per Oz. (which happened in the Course of but fifty Years) their £1,200,000 at 60s. per Oz. was worth no more than the £100,000 at 5s. per Oz. Besides, when they had only £100,000 in Paper Money, one third of their Currency by credible Information, was Silver; but when they so enormously augmented their Paper Emissions, Silver became a Stranger to the Land. This Province, thank God, has hitherto kept within tolerable Bounds as to their Paper Emissions, tho' at the latter End of the last War, I believe we went almost as far as we could with Safety, I mean without endangering a Depreciation of its Value.[2] Several meer Accidents at that Time happily conspired to keep up the Credit of our Paper Money. These were, our Success during the late War, which supplied us abundantly with a Variety of Commodities for Remittances to *Europe*, and consequently kept Gold and Silver plenty amongst us: We have since reaped eminent Advantages from the Logwood imported from the Bay of *Honduras*. The Discredit of *New-England* Money, was another Accident which helped to keep up the Credit of ours, great Quantities of which circulated in those Provinces. Their own Money being precarious, they were naturally fond of ours, in which, as they could make their Payments here, served them as well as Gold and Silver. Such fortuitous Advantages we cannot always expect, and therefore ought to be cautious for the future of venturing on large Paper Emissions: Its having hitherto kept its Credit, is no Reason why it should continue it. But, by the large Sums of our Paper now yearly cancelled, we are in a fair Way of being preserved from the ill Consequences that might flow from a large Paper Currency, and of discharging a Debt that would otherwise be entailed on our Posterity.

Another grand Evil resulting from a Paper Currency is, its promoting amongst us a Spirit of Extravagance, and a greater Consumption of *European* Goods than the Province will be able to pay for. With this imaginary Money we go to Market, and buy freely what we might often as well be without; and tho' the Merchant be paid, yet if Gold and Silver, or Bills of Exchange, happen to be scarce, he is obliged to give an extraordinary Price for Remittances, and then down goes the Value of Paper Money, and that of all Specialities regulated by it.

On a little Reflection, it will evidently appear to every thinking Person, that the Inhabitants of a Province must be impoverished as they increase the Quantity of their Bills, or at least prevented from becoming so rich as they otherwise would. It must indeed be allowed, that this Province has of late exceedingly flourished; but that is to be derived not only from our extraordinary Success during the War, by our hostile Acquisitions, and Prosperity in some particular Branches of Trade, but also from the great Price given for our Products since the Cessation of Arms. Equally obvious will it appear, that as our Paper Bills are cancelled, our Exchange of Money with *Europe*, must necessarily fall; and the People of this Province grow more frugal and wealthy.

Thus much with respect to Paper Money. I now proceed to shew, that for whichsoever of the common Mediums of Trade, such as Gold, Silver and Copper, a greater Price, in Proportion to the rest, is allowed by any particular Country than by the trading World in general, that Medium will become the prevailing Currency of that Country, and in a great Measure supplant all other Currencies circulating in it.

For, those Mediums are Commodities as proper for Traffic as any other, and more so from their easy Transportation and Unperishableness. Whenever, therefore, the trading World finds, for Instance, that Silver bears a much higher Price at any particular Place, than the common Proportion between Gold and Silver, they will doubtless send their Silver thither, and bring back Gold, till they have received all the Gold of that Place in Exchange for Silver. And that this will be a Loss in Proportion to that Difference is certain; for when the latter are obliged to part with their Silver again, the World will not give them the extravagant Price at which they had received it. The Truth of this is daily evinced in Commerce. No Person will carry Silver from this Province to *Pennsylvania* or *Antigua,* while he can procure Gold. The Consequence is that Gold is the prevailing Currency of those Places, while Silver is scarce.

The most remarkable Disproportion in the Currencies of this Province, is our Price for Copper-Pence, or English Half-Pence, which is far greater than they bear any where else.[3] The Effect of this in the End must be, that Pence will become the chief Currency of this Province. What a horrible Incumberance will such a Currency prove to our Inhabitants? When all Payments are made in Pence, we shall be under the Necessity of having Wheel-Barrows and Carts continually attending us. The poor Countryman will have almost as much Trouble in carrying home his Money, as he had in bringing his Crop to Market. Happy People, to be bending and staggering under the Weight of their Money! But to be serious. It is a Grievance that loudly calls for Redress. The Incumberance just mentioned is not the only Evil to be apprehended from it; what is of more pernicious Consequence, is, the grand Cheat thereby imposed upon every Individual in the Province, to the enriching of a few who import them. To explain and illustrate this, let the real Value of Copper-Pence, the Price allowed for them in the other Provinces on the Continent, and the Rate at which we take them, be considered. In *England* they pass for Half-pence Sterling; but that is more than they are Worth, as they will at the Mint give five per Cent premium to any Person who will take a large Quantity of them. Thus with £100 Sterling, you may there purchase as many as will at Twelve to the Shilling, pass here for £210 Currency; and as Exchange is at most 80 per cent there is an Encouragement of at least £30 Currency on every £100 Sterl. for importing them from *England*.

To shew the Profit accruing on their Importation from the neighbouring Colonies, it will be best to adjust their Value in Pieces of Eight: A Piece of Eight with us passes at 8*s*. and these Copper-Pence at Twelve to the Shilling, so that a Piece of Eight passes for but Ninety-Six of them; at *Philadelphia* a Piece of Eight passes at 7*s* 6, and Copper Pence at Fifteen to the Shilling, wherefore a Piece of Eight there is equal to 112½ of them; at *Halifax* a Piece of Eight passes at 5*s*. Sterl. and these Coppers at Half-pence, so that a Piece of Eight there is equal to 120 of them; in *Boston* to 108, and in *Rhode Island* and *Connecticut* to 112. Whence the Profit on bringing Pence here in Exchange for our Silver, is as follows: From *Boston* Twelve Pence clear on each Piece of Eight; from *Rhode-Island* and *Connecticut* Sixteen Pence; from *Philadelphia* Sixteen Pence Half-Penny, and from *Halifax* Twenty Four Pence. Whether this be not a sufficient Profit to induce some Merchants to import them, in Spite of the utmost Vigilance, I leave every impartial Person to consider.

Copper-Pence certainly have their Conveniences. While we have them in moderate Quantities, they serve us for small Change beyond any Thing else: But to have them become the whole Currency of the Province, must be attended with the greatest Inconveniences. The Quantity of Pence now in the Province is rather greater than is expedient: But if we could keep what we have, without further increasing them, they might be sufferable. I would not therefore attempt their total Expulsion, but only propose fixing them on such a Footing as would neither increase or diminish their Number. Laws to prohibit their Importation will but little avail: For, while it is attended with so great a Profit, there always will be Persons who, more influenced by lucrative Motives than Affection for their Country, will venture to import them in Defiance of Law. The only sure Way is so to ascertain their Price as will leave no Profit, either by importing or exporting them, but rather occasion the Loss of Freight and Insurance in both Cases. This I think may be fully effected, by fixing their Value at Fourteen to the Shilling: Then they will neither be brought from *England* to this Place, nor carried there from hence; since One Hundred Pounds Sterling of them, with the Premium of 5 per cent at Fourteen to the Shilling, will make £180 Currency, which is just the Exchange, and consequently their Import or Export must be attended with the Loss of the Freight, Insurance, Commissions, *etc*. Again, a Piece of Eight with us at Fourteen Pence to the Shilling, will be worth 112 of them; wherefore the Exchange between us and *Philadelphia, Connecticut* or *Rhode-Island,* will also be attended with the same Loss. In sending them to *Boston* there would be a Profit of Four Pence per Piece of Eight, did not the Charge of exporting them amount to that Advance. There will still remain Eight Pence per Piece of Eight difference in the Price of them between this and *Halifax;* but when the Risque and Charge of importing them is deducted, I believe few will be tempted to violate the Laws of their Country for so inconsiderable an Advantage.

Upon the whole, Fourteen to the Shilling appear to be the real Value of Pence in this Province; all Profit on exporting or importing them, being thereby taken away, and a Loss occasion'd in both Cases. Thus we shall keep what we have, and prevent the Increase of our Burthen.[4]

The Gentleman who stiles himself CLEOBULUS, *may rest assured, that while the Author of this Paper employs his Pen in Defence of the Liberties of protestant Mankind, and particularly in unfolding the Grievances of his Country; he shall give himself very little Uneasiness about any Offence he may happen to give to those who have a peculiar Objection against an Examination into their Conduct or Pretensions; nor chuse to be introduc'd on the Stage for a very singular Reason recorded in the* Third *Chapter of St.* JOHN's *Gospel.*

1. The correct reference is Isa. 1:22.

2. New York began to issue paper money in 1709. By 1753 there had been six emissions, the total value of which is difficult to determine since the issues were sometimes valued in English pounds and at other times in dollars or "ounces of plate."

3. Despite efforts by the Crown to achieve uniformity of coin values in the colonies, competition among merchants for hard currency for paying English creditors resulted in widespread variations. The Spanish milled dollar or "piece of eight," one of the most widely circulated coins in the English colonies, varied in value from 4s. 8d. to 8s. Curtis P. Nettels, *The Roots of American Civilization* (New York, 1938), pp. 269–275.

4. The *Reflector's* suggestion to end the overvaluation of copper pence was adroitly carried out by private rather than public action. On December 22, 1753, a group of seventy-two "gentlemen" agreed among themselves not to accept or pass copper pence except at the rate of fourteen rather than twelve to the shilling. Despite some violent protests and rioting "among the lower class of people . . . the scheme was carried into execution, and established in every part of the province, without the aid of a law." Smith, *History*, I, 283.

Number XXVII

THURSDAY, MAY 31, 1753

A PRAYER[1]

A<small>MONGST</small> numberless other Absurdities, it hath often been asserted by those for a partial College, that no **Prayer** could possibly be formed, but what would be rejected by all other Denominations, on Account of the Party by whom it was composed. I shall therefore lay before the Reader, a Prayer wholly collected from the Scriptures, except the Passages in Italics; against which, I presume, no Christian of any Persuasion can object, without at the same Time manifesting his Irreverence for the sacred Oracles.

Rev. iv. 8.

Holy, Holy, Holy, Lord God Almighty! thou art our God, early will we seek thee; our God, and we will praise thee; our Fathers' God, and we will exalt thee. Thou art very great, cloathed with Honour and Majesty; thou coverest thyself with Light as with a Garment. Thou art the blessed and only Potentate, the King of Kings, and Lord of Lords, who only hast Immortality, dwelling in Light, which no Man can approach, whom no Man hath seen nor can see. The Heavens declare thy Glory, and the Firmament sheweth thy handy Work; and by the Things that are made, are clearly seen and understood, thine eternal Power and Godhead. They are Fools without Excuse who say, there is no God; for verily there is a Reward for the Righteous, verily there is a God who judgeth in the Earth.

Ps. lxiii. 1. Exo. xv. 2.

Ps. civ. 1, 2.

1 Tim. vi. 15, 16. Ps. xix. 1. Rom. i. 20. Ps. xiv. 1. Ps. lviii. 11.

Thou *art incomprehensible.* We cannot by searching find out God: We cannot find out the Almighty unto Perfection. As the Heavens are high above the Earth, so are thy Thoughts above our Thoughts, and thy Ways above our Ways.

Job. xi. 7. Isa. lv. 9.

Eternal *art thou and immutable.* Before the Mountains were brought forth, or ever thou hadst formed the Earth and the World, even from everlasting to everlasting, thou art God, the

242

A PRAYER

same Yesterday, today, and forever. Of old hast thou laid the Ps. xc. 2. Heb. xiii. 8. Foundation of the Earth, and the Heavens are the Work of thy Ps. cii. 25, 26, 27. Hands. They shall perish, but thou shalt endure; yea all of them shall wax old like a Garment, and as a Vesture shalt thou change them, and they shall be changed: but thou art the same and thy Years shall have no End.

Thou *art Omnipresent.* We cannot go from thy Spirit, or flee from thy Presence. If we ascend into Heaven, thou art there: if Ps. cxxxix. 7, 8, 9, 10. we make our Bed in Hell, behold thou art there: If we take the Wings of the Morning, and dwell in the uttermost Parts of the Sea, even there shall thy Hand lead us, and thy Right-Hand shall hold us.

Infinite *is thy Knowledge.* Darkness and Night are both alike to thee. Thou knowest our down-setting, and our up-rising, and Ps. cxxxix. 2, 3, 12. understandest our Thoughts afar off. Thou compassest our Path, and art acquainted with all our Ways. O the Depth of the Riches Rom. xi. 33. both of the Wisdom and Knowledge of God! How unsearchable are his Judgments, and his Ways past finding out!

Thy *Sovereignty is incontestible, and thy Power irresistible.* Ps. cxv. 16. Ps. xxiv. 1. The Heavens, even the Heavens are thine, the Earth and the Fulness thereof, the World, and they that dwell therein. Thou dost according to thy Will in the Armies of Heaven, and among the Inhabitants of the Earth. None can stay thy Hand, or say unto thee, What doest thou? Who has an Arm like God, or who can thunder with a Voice like him! Thou measurest the Waters in Job. xl. 9. the Hollow of thine Hand, and metest out the Heaven with a Isa. lxi. 12. Span. Thou comprehendest the Dust of the Earth in a Measure, Ps. xviii. 7. and weightest the Mountains in Scales, and the Hills in a Balance. Ps. xxxiii. 6. At thy Wrath the Earth trembleth, and the Foundations of the Hills are moved. By the Word of the Lord were the Heavens made, and all the Host of them by the Breath of his Mouth. Thou spakest and it was done, thou commandedst and it stood fast.

Thy *Administration is just.* Far be it from God that he should Dan. iv. 35. do Wickedness, and from the Almighty that he should commit Iniquity; for the Work of a Man shall he render unto him. Thy Job. xxxiv. 10, 11. Righteousness is like the great Mountains. Clouds and Darkness Ps. xxxvi. 6. Ps. xcvii. 2. are round about thee, yet Righteousness and Judgment are the Habitation of thy Throne.

Thy *Goodness is inexhaustible*. Thy Mercy endureth forever. Thy Kindness is great towards us, and thy Truth endureth to all Generations. Thy Name is the Lord, the Lord God, merciful and gracious, long-suffering, abundant in Goodness and Truth, keeping Mercy for Thousands, forgiving Iniquity, Transgression and Sin.

Lo these are but Part of thy Ways! How little a Portion is heard of thee! Touching the Almighty, we cannot find him out: He is excellent in Power and in Judgment, and in Plenty of Justice, and he is exalted far above all Blessing and Praise.

Thou art the Father of our Spirits. The Spirit of God hath made us, and the Breath of the Almighty hath given us Life. We are Clay and thou our Potter, we are the Work of thy Hand. In thy Hand is our Breath, and thine are all our Ways. The Way of Man is not in himself, neither is it in Man that walketh to direct his Steps. In thee, O God, we live, and move, and have our Being, for we are thy Offspring. It is of thy Mercy that we are not consumed, even because thy Compassions fail not. They are new every Morning. Great is thy Faithfulness.

O our God, we are ashamed, and blush to lift up our Faces to thee for our Iniquities are increased over our Heads, and our Trespass is grown up unto the Heavens! Thou puttest no Trust in thy Saints. The Heavens are not clean in thy Sight. How much more abominable and filthy is Man, who drinketh in Iniquity like Water! If we justify ourselves our own Mouths shall condemn us; if we say we are perfect, that also shall prove us perverse: For, if thou contend with us, we are not able to answer thee for one of a Thousand. If thou Lord shouldst mark Iniquities, O Lord who should stand: But there is Forgiveness with thee that thou mayest be feared; yea with our God there is plenteous Redemption, and he shall redeem *Israel* from all his Iniquities. They that cover their Sins shall not prosper, yet those that confess and forsake them shall find Mercy. Thy Sacrifices, O God, are a broken Spirit. A broken and a contrite Heart, O God, thou wilt not despise. If we confess our Sins thou art faithful and just to forgive us our Sins, and to cleanse us from all Unrighteousness. Lord thou madest Man upright, but he hath sought out many

Inventions. All Flesh hath corrupted their Way; we are all gone aside, we are altogether become filthy, there is none that doeth Good, no not one. Our Understandings are darkened, being alienated from the Life of God, thro' the Ignorance that is in us, because of the Blindness of our Hearts. Our Neck hath been an Iron Sinew, and we have made our Heart as an Adamant; we have refused to hearken, have pulled away the Shoulder, and stopped our Ears, like the deaf Adder that will not hearken to the Voice of the Charmer, charm he never so wisely. Of the Rock that begat us we have been unmindful, and have forgotten the God that formed us. We have sinned, Father, against Heaven, and have come short of the Glory of God. The God in whose Hand our Breath is, and whose are all our Ways, have we not glorified. As a Fountain casteth out her Waters, so do our Hearts cast out Wickedness, and this hath been our Manner. We have not obeyed thy Voice. We have grieved the holy Spirit of God, by whom we were sealed to the Day of Redemption. O the Riches of the Patience and Forbearance of God! *How long suffering he is to us-ward!*

We avouch the Lord this Day to be our God, to walk in his Ways, and to keep his Statutes, and his Commandments, and his Judgments, to hearken to his Voice, and to be his peculiar People. We are thine, save us, for we seek thy Precepts.

Thou *hast commanded us* to pray always, with all Prayer and Supplication, with Thanksgiving, and to watch thereunto with all Perseverance and Supplication, for all Saints; to continue in Prayer, and in every Thing by Prayer and Supplication, to make our Requests known to God.

But will God in very Deed dwell with Man upon Earth, *that God* whom the Heaven, and the Heaven of Heavens cannot contain, with Man who is a Worm, and the Son of Man who is a Worm! Who are we, O Lord God, and what is our House, that thou hast brought us hitherto, that we have thro' Christ an Access by one Spirit unto the Father! What is Man that thou art thus mindful of him, and the Son of Man that thou visitest him!

And now, Lord, what wait we for? Truly our Hope is in thee. O let not the Lord be angry, if we who are but Dust and Ashes take upon us to speak unto the Lord of Glory. *For* whom have we

Marginal references:

Eph. iv. 18.
Isa. xlviii. 4.
Zec. vii. 11, 12.
Ps. lviii. 4, 5.

Deut. xxxii. 18.
Luke xv. 18.
Rom. iii. 23.
Dan. v. 23.
Jer. vi. 7, xxii. 21.
Eph. iv. 30.
Rom. ii. 4.

Deut. xxvi. 17, 18, 19.
Ps. cxix. 94.

Eph. vi. 18.
Col. iv. 2.
Phil. iv. 6.

2 Chron. vi. 18.
Job xxv. 6.
2 Sam. vii. 18.
Eph. ii. 18.
Ps. viii. 4.

Ps. xxxix. 7.
Gen. xviii. 27, 30.

Ps. lxxiii. 25, 26.
1 Kings, viii. 28.
Deut. xxvi. 15.
Rom. viii. 26.
Ps. xxxi. 1.
 Ps. xxv. 3.
Ps. cxix. 58.
2 Cor. v. 9.
Ps. cxliii. 1.
Ps. cxli. 2.
Zech. xii. 10.
Rom. viii. 15.
Dan. ix. 18.
Ezra. ix. 15.
Heb. iv. 14, 15,
 16.

in Heaven but thee, and there is none upon Earth that we desire besides thee. When our Flesh and our Heart fail, be Thou the Strength of our Heart, and our Portion for ever. Look down from thy holy Habitation, have Respect unto the Prayer of thy Servants, which they pray before thee this Day. But we know not what to pray for as we ought. Let thy Spirit help our Infirmities, and make Intercession for us, with Groanings which cannot be uttered. In thee, O God, do we put our Trust, let us never be ashamed, yea let none that wait on thee be ashamed. We entreat thy Favour with our whole Heart; in this we labour that we may be accepted of the Lord. Hear our Prayers, O Lord, give Ear to our Supplications; in thy Faithfulness answer us. Let our Prayers be set before thee as Incense, and the lifting up of our Hands as the Evening Sacrifice. O pour upon us the Spirit of Grace and Supplication, the Spirit of Adoption, teaching us to cry Abba, Father. We do not present our Supplication before thee for our Righteousness. For we are before thee in our Trespasses, and cannot stand before thee because of them: but in the Name of the great High Priest, who is passed into the Heavens, Jesus the Son of God, who was touched with the feeling of our Infirmities. Let us therefore come boldly to the Throne of Grace, that we may obtain Mercy, and find Grace to help in Time of Need. Behold, O God, our Shield, and look upon the Face of thine anointed.

Ps. lxxxiv. 9.

Ps. xxxix. 8.

Ps. li. 2, 3, 7, 9.

Deliver us from all our Transgressions. Make us not the Reproach of the Foolish. O wash us thoroughly from our Iniquity, and cleanse us from our Sin, for we acknowledge our Transgressions, and our Sin is ever before us. Purge us with Hyssop, and we shall be clean; wash us and we shall be whiter than Snow. Hide thy Face from our Sins, and blot out all our Iniquities. All our Righteousnesses are as filthy Rags. *But* Jesus Christ is made of God to us Righteousness, being made Sin for us, tho' he knew no Sin, that we might be made the Righteousness of God in him. Let us have Redemption thro' Christ's Blood, even the Forgiveness of Sins, according to the Riches of his Grace: For there is no Salvation in any other, there is no other Name under Heaven given among Men, whereby we may be saved. Fulfil *in us* all the

Isa. lxiv. 6.
1 Cor. i. 30.
2 Cor. v. 21.
Eph. i. 7, 8.
Acts iv. 12.
2 Thes. i. 11.

1 Thes. v. 23.

good Pleasure of thy Goodness, and the Work of Faith with Power. The very God of Peace sanctify us wholly, and we pray God, our whole Spirit, and Soul, and Body, may be preserved blameless, unto the Coming of our Lord Jesus Christ.

Replenish this School of the Prophets, with every good and every perfect Gift from above, — from the Father of Lights. Wisdom is better than Rubies, Length of Days are in her Right Hand, and in her Left Hand Riches and Honour: Her Ways are Ways of Pleasantness, and all her Paths are Peace. Let the Knowledge of Wisdom be sweet unto our Souls, as is the Honey-Comb unto the Taste. Let us perceive the Words of Understanding, and cry after Knowledge. Doth not Wisdom cry, and Understanding put forth her Voice? She crieth at our Gates, at the Entry of *this House*, at the coming in at the Doors unto us doth she call, unto us lifteth she her Voice. Let us therefore hear Instruction, be wise and refuse it not: Watching daily at Wisdom's Gates, and waiting at the Posts of her Door: For whoso loveth Instruction, loveth Knowledge.

Jam. i. 17.
Prov. iii. 15, 16, 17.
Prov. xxiv. 13, 14.
Prov. i. 2, ii. 3.

Prov. viii. 1, 3, 4.

Prov. viii. 33, 34. xii. 1.

Unto thee, O God, do we give Thanks, unto thee do we give Thanks. We will praise the Lord for it is good, it is pleasant, and Praise is comely for the Upright. It is a good Thing to give Thanks unto the Lord, and to sing Praises unto thy Name, O Most High! To shew forth thy loving Kindness in the Morning, and thy Faithfulness every Night. We bless thee, that when the Fulness of Time was come, thou didst send forth thy Son made of a Woman, made under the Law, to redeem them that were under the Law, that we might receive the Adoption of Sons. That we have an Advocate with the Father, even Jesus Christ the Righteous. That he is set on the Right Hand of the Throne of the Majesty in the Heavens, Angels and Authorities, and Powers being made subject to him. *That he hath* sent us another Comforter to abide with us forever, even the Spirit of Truth. The Lord is good, his Mercy is everlasting, and his Truth endureth to all Generations.

Ps. lxxv. 1.
Ps. cxlvii. 1.

Ps. xcii. 1. 2.

Gal. iv. 4, 5.
1 John ii. 1.
Heb. viii. 1.

1 Peter iii. 22.
John xiv. 16, 17.
Ps. c. 5.

Let thy Salvation and thy Righteousness be openly shewed in the Sight of the Heathen, and let all the Ends of the Earth see the Salvation of our God. Let the Word of the Lord have free

Ps. xcviii. 2, 3.
2 Thes. iii. 1.
Ps. xxviii. 9.

Isa. xliii. 5, 6.
Mal. i. 11. Isa.
xi. 9.
Eph. vi. 24.
Ps. lxxii. 1, 4, 14.

Prov. xxv. 5. xx.
28.
Ps. xxi. 6, 7.
Ps. cxxxii 18.
Ps. xxi. 4, 5.
Ps. xxvi. 3.
Prov. xvi. 2, 7.
Ps. cv. 22.
Exod. xviii. 21.

Amos v. 24.

Ps. cxxii. 7.
Isa. lx. 17, 18.

1 Cor. i. 10.

Mal. iii. 3.

2 Tim. ii. 24.
1 Tim. iv. 12.

Course, and let it be glorified. Save thy People, O Lord, and bless thy Heritage: Feed them also, and lift them up forever. Bring thy Seed from the East, and gather them from the West: Say to the North give up, and to the South keep not back. Bring thy Sons from afar, and thy Daughters from the Ends of the Earth. From the rising of the Sun to the going down of the same; let thy Name be great among the Gentiles, and the Earth be full of the Knowledge of the Lord, as the Waters cover the Sea. Grace be with all them that love the Lord Jesus Christ with Sincerity. Give King *George* thy Judgments, O God, and thy Righteousness, that he may judge the Poor of the People, save the Children of the Needy, and break in Pieces the Oppressor. Let him redeem their Souls from Deceit and Violence, and let their Blood be precious in his Sight. Let his Throne be established in Righteousness, and upheld with Mercy. Make him exceeding glad with thy Countenance. Through the tender Mercy of the most High, let him not be moved. Cloath his Enemies with Shame, but upon himself let the Crown flourish. Grant him length of Days, and let his Glory be great in thy Salvation. *Bless his Royal Highness* George *Prince of Wales, the Princess Dowager of Wales, the Duke, the Princesses, and all the Royal Family.* May thy loving Kindness be before their Eyes, and may they walk in thy Truth. Smile *on our Governor.* May he walk in Uprightness: And may his Ways please the Lord. Teach our Senators Wisdom. Let our Rulers be able Men, such as fear God, Men of Truth, hating Covetousness. That Justice may run down as a River, and Righteousness as a mighty Stream. Peace be within our Borders, and Prosperity within our Palaces. Make our Officers Peace, and our Exactors Righteousness. Let Violence never be heard in our Gates; Wasting or Destruction in our Borders: Let our Walls be called Salvation, and our Gates Praise. In the Name of our Lord Jesus Christ, let there be no Divisions among us, but that we may be perfectly joined together in the same Mind and in the same Judgment. Purify the Sons of *Levi*; purge them as Gold and Silver, that they may offer unto the Lord an Offering in Righteousness. Let the Servants of the Lord be gentle to all Men, apt to teach — patient

A PRAYER

—Examples to the Believers, in Word, in Conversation, in Charity, in Spirit, in Truth, in Purity.

Let *us know above all Things*, that the Fear of the Lord is the Beginning of Wisdom, and the Knowledge of the Holy is Understanding. Let us Love our Enemies, bless them that curse us, do good to them that hate us, and pray for them that despitefully use us, and persecute us. Father forgive them, for they know not what they do. Now to the King eternal, immortal, invisible, the only wise God, be Glory and Majesty, Dominion and Power, both now and ever, *Amen. Our Father who art in Heaven, etc.*

Prov. ix. 10.
Mat. v. 44.
Luke xxiii. 34.

1 Tim. 1. 17.
Jud. 25.

In like Manner occasional Parts may be composed, adapted to the Morning, and Evening, Sabbath, Sickness, Death, War, Famine, Fasting, Thanksgiving, *etc.*[2]

A. & Z.

1. "The model of an unexceptionable prayer," Livingston wrote a year later, "was not intended as derogatory of the honour of the Common prayer Book; but designed only to advance the true interest of the Academy." *Independent Reflector, Preface*, p. 21. It was composed in response to the Anglican challenge which had appeared in the *New-York Mercury*, April 30, 1753. See No. XXI, note 7.

2. Livingston's Anglican critics immediately attacked the *Reflector's* immensely detailed handiwork as, at best, a Congregationalist formulary, and, at worst, "a disjointed Rhapsody." *New-York Mercury*, June 18, July 30, 1753.

Number XXVIII

THURSDAY, JUNE 7, 1753

On the Delays in CHANCERY

I went to Law in Anno Quadragesimo secundo; *and I waded out of it*, in Anno Sexagesimo tertio.
TOURNEUR's Revenger's Tragedy [1]

THE following Letter is so expressive of the deep Affliction natural to injured Poverty, and calls so loud for Redress and Assistance, that I shall lay it before the Reader without any farther Apology.

To the INDEPENDENT REFLECTOR

SIR,

You have in your Writings so frequently shewn a Disposition to pity and relieve the Poor and Distressed, that I lay my Case before you with all the Freedom of a Child to his Father. If it is in your Power to redress me, I am confident your generous Assistance will not be wanting; and should I be remediless from this Quarter, yet publishing my Story will be no inconsiderable Alleviation of my Sorrows.

My Wife's Father, Sir, was an honest plain good-natur'd Man, and by his extraordinary Industry and frugal Management, acquired a Fortune far beyond the Rank and Station of a Tradesman; for his Estate at his Death amounted to Six Thousand Pounds: But unhappily for his Children, one of his Executors chanced to be a Fool, the other was an artful designing Knave; and, as it is natural to suppose, had the Ascendency of the former, and embezelled a considerable Part of the Estate while his Fellow-Executor was living, at whose Death, which happened soon after their Testator's, he seized the Whole into his own Hands. The Estate was bequeathed to my Wife and her Sister, equally to be divided between them; but being both in their Childhood at the Decease of their Father, and without so much as the Guardianship of a Mother, (for she poor Woman died several Years before) the Estate is as it were vanished away. Thro' the Fraud of one Executor, and the Folly of the other, I have as yet received but Fifty Pounds of the Part bequeathed to my Wife. The affluent Circumstances of her Father induced us to expect a fair Portion; but (I write it with Tears) we are sunk, Sir, into a State little superior to absolute Indigence: We live, (as the Phrase is) from Hand to Mouth, all our Dependence being upon the daily Labour of our Hands. You appear to me a Man of too much Humanity not to sympathize with me in my Sufferings, and will therefore patiently permit me to vent my Grief. My Wife took me in Marriage when I was in penurious Circumstances, contrary to the Advice of her mercenary Friends, feeding herself with the golden Hopes of what she expected from her Father: But now to submit to the meanest Drudgery, for a bare Sustenance, how cutting the Reflection! And yet Thanks to God, impoverished as we are, we enjoy our Health and Senses, which is more than can be said of her Sister, a miserable Widow, who also consoled herself on the Death of her Father, with the full-blown Prospect of inheriting an elegant Sufficiency. But the Miseries of so great a Disappointment, together with extreme Poverty, and an utter Despair of Relief, rendered her many Years ago a perfect Lunatic. She lives in a Cellar-Kitchen rented at Thirty Shillings per Annum, tended by her Daughter, an only Child: And tho' she receives some Help from the Church to which her Father belong'd, I do not think you can find a more wretched, pitiful Object of Charity. In short, Sir, the Calamities that everwhelm us, are too numerous to relate. Scarce an Hour passes without furnishing some stinging Reflection. The Consideration of what we were once, and what we expected to have been, does but impart an additional Weight to the Load of our Sufferings. And better had it been for the Children of the Deceased to have been entirely disinherited, than committed to the Guardianship of his Executors.

Our inexpressible Misery and Indigence, at length, moved the Compassions of a Friend, who knowing we were injured, enabled us to apply to Council at Law. He talked, as I remember, of Trusts and Frauds, and to our still farther Disappointment told us, we were only relievable in Equity, and refused to be concerned for us in any but a Common-Law Court. Our Friend also for a time denied us his Aid in a Chancery Suit. For two Months we had not a Ray of Hope to chear us with the Prospect of better Times, till by manifold Intreaties he reespoused our Cause, and the Councillor for a Sum above the common Fees, filed us a Bill. Here the Cause rests, nothing more having been done for our Relief these Sixteen Years past. For God's sake, Mr. *Reflector*, let me implore and beseech you to consider our Distresses, and if possible lend us your Help for investigating a Remedy. Our Cause is the Cause of the Poor, the Widow and the Orphan. We have been barbarously cheated, we are driven to Penury and Want. You perhaps can relieve us out of all our Distresses, and infuse Joy and Gladness into us and our Children, who without your Interposition, must be finally remediless.   G. R.

Great, indeed, and numerous are the Miseries which my Correspondent has described, and I am sorry so pitiful a Case is beyond my Power to redress. In so helpless and forlorn a State, the best Consolation is drawn from the Exercises of Piety, in a manly Resignation to the Divine Providence, and the Hopes of a Life of Happiness hereafter. A firm Belief that God governs the World, (to use an imperfect Comparison) is to the good Man what the Anchor is to a Ship, sufficient to enable him safely to ride out all the Storms of this tempestuous Sea of Trouble.

Sixteen Years delay of his Suit, is very surprizing, and must be equally distressing. What might have been the particular Causes of it, I cannot take upon me to determine. The Fault may be the Councillors, perhaps the Delay is owing to a Want of Evidence to support the Bill, and might have been occasion'd by a Variety of other Reasons. But sure I am, the Credit of the Professors of the Law, very much suffers by the general Complaints against their dilatory Proceedings in Chancery, and it nearly concerns them to free themselves from the Odium which is so frequently cast upon them.

The Profession is necessary and honourable. As the Security of Men's Properties was the original Motive for forming Society, Courts of Justice for the righteous Determination of Controversies amongst Individuals, become indispensably necessary as a Means to that End. The common Law of *England* is a System of Rules for the Administration of Justice, which tho' more voluminous than the Laws of any other Country, is still preferable to any Collection whatsoever, even that of *Justinian*, so generally received and highly applauded. Its Prolixity so commonly objected to us by Civilians, is so far from disproving, that it rather illustrates its Excellency, since it arises from its Particularity, which directs the Determination of every Point that occurs. Hence it is impossible for a Judge to decide illegally without manifesting his Ignorance, Partiality or Corruption: Among the Civilians, on the Contrary, almost every Thing exists in generals. They Reason from the Spirit of a Law, and must often deduce a long String of Consequences to reach the Case in Controversy; and as every Point admits of Argumentation, the Judgment, instead of being conformable to a plain Rule, is often a meer Opinion, which in different Men, and even in the same Man at different Times, may be perfectly repugnant. The bare-faced Corruption, and known Partiality exemplified in some Admiralty Courts, where the Civil Law is the Test of Decisions, afford sufficient Proofs of the Advantage of the Common above the *Roman* Law, in securing a righteous Adjudication.

The Common Law being general, could not provide for all Emergencies; and therefore, as it might happen that the strict Execution of the Letter, might resist the Spirit and Genius of the Law, and work a Wrong, *summum jus* becoming *summa injuria*,[2] the Court of Chancery very early took its Rise as remedial of its Rigour, and moderating its Severities. Here Cases are considered with a greater Latitude, under all their Circumstances, Relations and Aspects. It in general provides for the Reparation of Damages springing from Trusts, Frauds and Accidents, and is a Court absolutely necessary to the English. But notwithstanding its great Utility, and the excellent Design of its Institution, it can scarcely be named among us in this Province, but with Sorrow and Regret.[3] It is considered by some as a political Evil. Others esteem it a Gulf, that will in the End swallow up the Estates of its Suitors. All complain of its dilatory Proceedings. Justice is so long procrastinated, that tho' a Decree passes in favour of the Complainant, it is not, as some assert, till the Completion of his Ruin. I am further informed by some Gentlemen of the Profession, that frequently, where the Remedy lay only in Chancery, the Client despairing of Relief, and fearing a vexatious Delay, has contented himself with the first Loss. Others aver, that there are Suits in Equity still undetermined, which have been at Issue these thirty Years past. And such is the Prejudice against prosecuting in Chancery, that when a Gentleman of the Law informed his Client, that his Cause was only cognizable there, and recommended him to a Prosecution in that Court, he was contemptuously answered, "that going to Chancery for Justice, was as if he should descend into Hell for the high Road to Heaven."

Whether there is sufficient Ground for such a general Clamour and Dissatisfaction, I pretend not to determine: But that there are some Instances of Delays, great and destructive Delays, in the Chancery, can easily be proved; and whatever may be the particular Reasons of them, sure I am, that the Want of an Office amongst us, like that of a Master of the Rolls in *England*,[4] together with the present low Ordinance of Fees, do not a little contribute to the disadvantageous Character it at present sustains.

The Governors for the Time being, always act as Chancellors of those Provinces over which they respectively preside.[5] And a very few Instances can be assigned of their having been bred to the Profession, or Study of the Law; without a considerable Knowledge of which, it is impossible any Man can be qualified for the important Office of a Chancellor. But should a Governor even excel in his Capacity for exercising the Duties of that high Station in the Law, yet his necessary and proper Business, in the Administration of his Government, as it engrosses almost his whole Time, will delay and embarrass all his Suitors in Chancery. To this Cause it is in some of the Colonies, that the loud Complaints made against that Court, are to be ascribed. The Business of the Public frequently supplants that of private Persons. A short, a common Motion in Chancery,[6] has, for this Reason, been from time to time adjourned, and the Cause delayed, when but one half Hour's Attendance of his Excellency, was all that the Suitor required. I cannot, therefore, with Submission to deeper Understandings, help thinking, that the Governors of the Plantations ought to be relieved of the Trouble and Care to which a Chancellor must be exposed; and that commissioning a Gentleman of more Leisure to that Office, would be a wise Regulation, and render the Business of that Court expeditious and easy. His Judgments should be subordinate to the Governor and Council, who ought to be the dernier Resort in the Province. A small Salary annually defrayed by the Public, and the Perquisites arising from the Causes litigated before him, both amounting to about seven Hundred Pounds per Annum, would not only afford him a genteel Subsistence, support the Dignity of his Office, and probably put him beyond the Temptations of Bribery and Corruption, but enable him to devote his Time entirely to the proper Business of a Chancellor. Nor would Men of Skill and Probity for that important Station ever be wanting; so plentiful a Provision, and so honourable an Employment, would be the Mark of Ambition, at which every Professor in the Law would direct his Aims.[7]

As for the Chancery Fees, they are so insignificant and trifling, that no Gentleman who can employ himself in the Common-Law Practice, will ever for the Sake of them, take upon himself the Trouble and Management of a Suit in Equity. To this the Refusal of the Council which my Correspondent complains of, was doubtlessly owing. The Gentlemen of the long Robe are generally no less fond of advancing their Fortunes, than accelerating Justice; nay, many of them expedite the latter in Proportion to the Client's augmenting the former. They are a Set of Men that hire out their Words and Anger, *Verba et iras locant*.[8] And, who would put himself in a Passion without a valuable Consideration? To be serious. Three Hundred a Year is, as I have been informed, more than can be legally earned in the fullest and most assiduous Practice in Chancery, and yet it is asserted that the Nature of the Business of that Court is such, that almost every Cause which occurs, requires in the Council, besides a Knowledge of the Law, strong Sense, great Care and Attention. Whereas in the Common-Law Practice, general Rules and Forms are prescribed, and the greatest Part of the Business of an Attorney, may be dispatched by his Clerks. No Person, therefore, of Eminence in the Profession will engage in the Chancery, since his Abilities will always find him sufficient Employment at Common-Law where his Rewards are more equitably proportionate to his Services.[9] In Chancery they are undervalued, he despises the Fees of it, and therefore declines its Practice, as indeed he ought, in Justice to himself, his Labours, Education, Reputation and Family. He who has little else to do may practice there, but the Labours of such are generally worth Nothing. The present Ordinance establishing the Fees of that Court, is in the contrary Extream to the first, as contemptibly too low, as that was exorbitantly high. As the Law is the Security of all our social Interests, redresses the Injuries offered to our Persons, Reputations and Estates, it is inconsistent with sound Policy to bear hard upon its Professors. Of the Truth of which this very Ordinance, as it is a grand Cause of the dilatory Proceedings in Chancery, is an irrefragable Proof.[10]   A.

1. "I went to Law in the forty-second year; and I waded out of it in the sixty-third year." *The Revenger's Tragedy* (1607), a play by Cyril Tourneur (c. 1580–1626), English poet and dramatist.

2. "The greatest justice" becoming "the greatest injustice."

3. Governor William Cosby's attempt in 1732 to give the Supreme Court equity jurisdiction without consent of the Assembly provoked the popular outcry leading to the Zenger Case. Governor Robert Hunter had aroused similar opposition when he tried to create a chancery court in 1712. Livingston Rutherfurd, *John Peter Zenger* (New York, 1904, reprinted 1941), pp. 9–10; Herbert L. Osgood, *The American Colonies in the Eighteenth Century*, 4 vols. (New York, 1924–1925), II, 108.

4. The Master of the Rolls was the officer of the Court of Chancery who kept the rolls and grants and superintended the records of the court. New York appears to have had a person in this office as early as 1684, but if Livingston did not know of his existence, there is good reason: the gentleman either did no work or left no records. The office was not reactivated until 1774, and then the Revolution eliminated the immediate need for the position. Paul M. Hamlin, *Legal Education in Colonial New York* (New York, 1939), pp. 111, 113–114 note.

5. The governor's commission made him *ex officio* chancellor of the province. Leonard W. Labaree, *Royal Government in America* (New York, 1958), p. 379.

6. Presumably a motion (or application) for hearing the case more speedily than it would be heard in its regular order, because the issue could be disposed of quickly without taking up much of the court's time. Such suits were called "short causes" and were placed on a special calendar.

7. Not until 1777 did New York establish the position of chancellor separate from the office of governor. The first chancellor of the state was Livingston's own kinsman, Robert R. Livingston, Jr.

8. From Seneca, *Hercules Furens*, 173: *Iras et verba locat* ("He hires out his anger and words.")

9. Livingston himself was earning about £400 a year from his law practice at this time, and many of his colleagues were making even more. See Milton M. Klein, "The Rise of the New York Bar: The Legal Career of William Livingston," *William and Mary Quarterly*, XV (1958), 353–355.

10. English lawyers were similarly concerned with lessening the delay in chancery proceedings, but their protests were as unavailing as the *Reflector's*. Robert Robson, *The Attorney in Eighteenth-Century England* (Cambridge, 1959), pp. 24–25.

Number XXIX

THURSDAY, JUNE 14, 1753

Of the Extravagance of our FUNERALS

As the Dangers flowing from Luxury are evident from the Reason of Things, so are we assured, by the Voice of History, that all wise Legislators have considered public Prodigality as the Bane of Society, and a Kind of political Cancer which corrodes and demolishes the best regulated Constitution. For this Reason they framed Laws to inhibit this formidable Evil, upon the Introduction of which, they thought it impossible to preserve the State from Ruin and Misery. Upon these Principles LYCURGUS, one of the most celebrated Lawgivers of Antiquity, enacted the severest Penalties against this destructive Vice. From the punctual Execution of the *Roman* Laws, in this respect equally rigorous, is, in a great Measure to be derived, the Splendor and Prowess of antient *Rome*. But when in Process of Time, the ambitious Leaders of Faction introduced the luxurious Modes of living, which they had learn'd from the *Grecians* and *Asiatics*, they accelerated the Fall of that mighty Empire, which had reduced the greatest Part of the then known World, to its Obedience.

By the Luxury of the leading Men of *Athens* was that once illustrious State enslaved by PHILIP, who pav'd the Road to that universal Monarchy which was afterwards completed by his Son ALEXANDER.

The same Causes will invariably produce the same Effects; and that Luxury is the Harbinger of a dying State, is a Truth too obvious to require the Formality of Proof. Hence MACHIAVELLI advises a Prince who would destroy a Country, to introduce Vice and Luxury, as the most effectual Expedients for accomplishing his Designs.

Our extraordinary Success during the late War, has given Rise to a Method of living unknown to our frugal Ancestors. At present our Trade is at a low Ebb, but still our Profusion continues un-retrench'd. Amongst other Instances of Extravagance, the following Letter exhibits to our View, a Piece of Luxury that has long been the Complaint of every wise and virtuous Man amongst us. It is wrote by a sincere Lover of his Country, whose Observations I am proud of conveying to the Public.

To the INDEPENDENT REFLECTOR

New-York, March 17, 1753.

INDEED, Sir, it is with Sorrow and Indignation, that I behold your implacable Adversaries, almost weekly violating both Truth and Decency, to malign your Character, and misrepresent your Design. But let it be your Consolation and Crown of rejoicing, that in general you are only calumniated by those, whose Praise would be the greatest Infamy you could suffer.

It affects me at the same Time with singular Delight, that, supported by the Testimony of a good Conscience, you can appeal to the Tribunal of Heaven for your Sincerity; and, being influenced by no View of personal Promotion, are able to pity and despise the Obloquies of an ungrateful, a traducing Generation. This I mention, not by Way of Compliment, but solely to animate you in your Progress, and to enter my Protest against the Discontinuance of your noble Paper, on Account of the stupid Opposition you have met with. From the Example of your Readiness to serve your Country, already exhibited in several of your Productions, I am emboldened to send you the following indigested Hints, which you will be pleased so to range and methodize as not to derogate from the Character of your Writings.

Tho' we are in many Instances luxurious and extravagant, there is, perhaps, no Article in which we carry our Prodigality to a higher Excess, than that of our Funerals. One would think that the Sorrow we feel at the Death of a Relation, was a sufficient Calamity, without the Aggravation of making ourselves anxious about the Preparation of a pompous Interment. Whoever is not insensible to the tender Emotions of Sorrow and Distress, on so melancholy an Occasion, can but ill relish the additional Load of Solicitude, that the deceased is carried to his Grave with the fashionable Apparatus, and buried Alamode. But this is not the worst Part of the Story. Besides the Loss of, perhaps, him who was the only Support of the Family, and whose Death is to the Survivors the Beginning of Calamity and Indigence, the scanty Remainder, which might afford them a comfortable Subsistence, is expended in the idle Magnificence of committing him to the

Tomb.[1] For the Sake of complying with this ruinous Custom, I have known many a Family dissipate at least a fourth Part of their whole Fortune, and disabled to subsist on the Residue without the greatest Shifts and Assiduity. Nor can they, while such is the Fashion, refrain from following it: For were they to consult the deceased's Circumstances instead of his Rank, they would be obnoxious to the ill-natur'd Censures of a malicious World, who would interpret their commendable Parsimony into Avarice, or something more unnatural. The most favourable Construction would be that their deviating from the general Practice, proceeded from their Inability to afford a more magnificent Funeral.

Again, if we consider the Manner in which this ridiculous Expence is conducted, we shall find it a Loss to the Person upon whom it falls, without being an Advantage to any. The Scarfs and the Rings are generally bestowed on the Rich, to whose Wealth they make, comparatively speaking, no Addition, tho' to the Giver they prove a very considerable Burthen. To the Dead 'tis of no Avail. With the Situation of the Mourner 'tis wholly inconsistent, and a Kind of Burlesque on true and silent Sorrow, which endeavours to avoid Pomp and Noise, and chuses the sequestred Haunts of Solitude and Retirement. The Money squandered in Liquor, is often worse than thrown away; it intoxicates and imbrutes that noble Being who prides himself in the Title of rational, and looks erect on Heaven.

As People in the inferior Stations of Life, are extremely apt to imitate those who move in a more elevated Sphere: It ought to be the Endeavour of the latter to set them the laudable Example of suppressing this fantastical and inconvenient Piece of Luxury. Their Circumstances could not be called in Question, and did they retrench all superfluous Articles, it would meet with universal Approbation; because all would agree it was for the Sake of discountenancing so absurd a Custom; and their Inferiors tho' they imitated, would not pretend to rival them. Thus might there be a proper Subordination in the Charge of Funerals, and at the same Time every Class of Men inter their Dead with suitable Decency and Decorum.

Without entering into nice Calculations about this monstrous Piece of Extravagance, let us only suppose, Mr. *Reflector*, that on the Funerals of those in the higher and middle Stations of Life, there is expended, at least, Fifty Pounds beyond what is really necessary and decent; which I take to be a Computation vastly within the Bounds of Reason and Probability: Yet, at this Rate what immense Sums must the intombing of our Inhabitants, in a few Years, amount to? How many indigent Families might be cherished and supported with what is thus ridiculously lavish'd on the Dead?

Nor have I the least Apprehension of being, on this Occasion, charged with Singularity of Opinion. I am not against shewing that Decency, that Respect and even Reverence for the Dead, which has been practised by all civilized Nations, and seems to be the natural Dictate of Humanity refined and cultivated. What I argue against is the needless and exorbitant Expence of Funerals; and in this I have the general Suffrage of my Fellow Citizens. It is almost universally inveighed against and condemned, and yet no one appears to have sufficient Resolution to attempt a Reformation. Happy would it be was this the only Thing in which no Reformation is attempted! In *Holland*, a Republic famed for the Wisdom of its Laws, and generally celebrated for its public Frugality, this Expence is limited by Law, and the Offences against it punished by a Forfeiture. So in *Boston*, where this romantic Affectation of surpassing each other in the Grandeur of their Funerals, was carried to an enormous Profuseness, the Legislature was obliged to interpose, and render it penal to exceed a Sum limited by an Act enacted for its Retrenchment.

Where a Clergyman or a Physician hath deserved well of a Family, by his Attendance on the Deceased, I should not be against sending a genteel Present in a private Manner, in Lieu of the Scarfs, or Rings usually given at Funerals. Was this the Practice, it would only be followed by those who could afford it, as it would not fall within public Observation, by whom it was done or neglected. But such is at present, the *ridiculous* Fondness, of Persons in the most indifferent Circumstances, for imitating the Fashion, that a Clergyman of undoubted Veracity told me, he remembered several Instances of Funerals made at the usual Expence, by Persons who have afterwards pleaded Poverty to obtain the Remission of the burial Fees.

Whether the above Remarks are so far worthy the Consideration of our Superiors, as to turn their Thoughts to plan a Law for the Regulation of this Extravagance, I shall not take upon me to determine. I rather wish our Gentlemen of Figure and Influence would, by their laudable Example, so discountenance this absurd Custom, as to render the Interposition of the Legislature unnecessary, and enjoy for their Reward, that inward and Heart-felt Satisfaction, arising from making their Superiority in Life, instrumental in banishing from amongst us a Practice so greatly injurious to their Country. I cannot, at the same Time help thinking, that a Tax on Luxury and Extravagance in general, in Imitation of the *Romans*, and several other wise Nations, who frequently made sumptuary Laws, by which they turned private Vices into public Benefits; would be highly reasonable and proper.

To prevent the little Critics from all future snarling against my Proposals, I hope, Mr. *Reflector*, you will not fail to refine and embellish, by your masterly Pen, these undecorated Hints, which I offer up from a Soul devoted, according to the best of my Judgment, to the Public Weal, wherein I may probably be no less singular, than in the Name by which I have before subscribed myself,

Your most Humble Servant,

SHADRECH PLEBIANUS.[2]

To the INDEPENDENT REFLECTOR

SIR,

AMONG the many Objections raised by the Enemies of civil and religious Liberty, against your Sentiments on our future College, there is one which for its peculiar Malignity, deserves, in my Opinion, the severest Animadversions. It has often been advanced by Persons equally unacquainted with your Subject and Design, that instead of delineating a just Plan for so noble a Structure, you have endeavoured, by raising the Heat of Parties, to prevent our having any College at all.[3] This Assertion contains a double Charge, either Part of which were it true, would be sufficient to blast the growing Reputation of your weekly Reflections.

For my Part, I have considered your Papers with the Impartiality becoming a Friend of public Virtue, and cannot discover the least Marks of an Attempt to raise Animosities among your Fellow Creatures. You have indeed animated the various Sects among us, to guard against the Encroachments of each other, which to me appears to be the most natural Means for suppressing the Growth of party Zeal: For the Heat of Sectaries consists not in a mutual Watchfulness, by which they severally keep themselves in a State of Independence; but on the Contrary is the natural Offspring of a persecuting Spirit in the prevailing Persuasion, and the just Resentment of the injured and oppressed. Where all Men enjoy an equal Freedom in Profession and Practice, there can be no Room for the Exertion of so uncharitable a Fervour; and nothing but unwarrantable Encroachments can be productive of Heat and Opposition. In endeavouring, therefore, to support the Freedom of each particular Sect, you have evidently aimed at the Repose and Tranquility of the Whole.

But after all, had you arrouzed the Spirit of Party among the People of this Province, is there not sufficient Reason to warrant such a Conduct, tho' so loudly exclaimed against? Does not one Persuasion openly and avowedly claim the Management of an Affair, with which the Happiness of all Sects is most intimately connected? And will not so daring an Encroachment justify the utmost Rage of the Parties insulted? While any Denomination continues so insolent a Claim, it becomes a public Writer industriously to rake up the Sparks of Party, and fan the Fire of Opposition till it mounts into an universal Blaze.

The second Part of the Charge is, that you aim at having no College. And for this Affertion, whoever candidly reads your Papers, will own there is not the least Foundation. You have convinced the World that you are sensible of the vast Advantages of a Public Academy, and would willingly have it secure against the Attacks of every Denomination, that it might continue an inexhaustible Fund of universal Happiness, to latest Posterity. It is true you have declared, that you would prefer our present illiterate State, to all the Benefits we can possibly purchase by raising a College at the Expence of our Liberty: And this, doubtless, is what they mean by your aiming at having no College at all. Nor can they be persuaded, that rough uncultivated Liberty, is infinitely preferable to the most polished and ornamented Servitude.   *I am your Humble Servant,*

B.   ACADEMICUS.

Rye, 18th *May,* 1753.

1. Dutch-type funerals in colonial New York were elaborate and expensive. Invitations were extended by an *aanspreecker* ("funeral-inviter"), paid from eight to eighteen shillings, depending upon the age of the deceased! Mourners invited to watch over the corpse while it lay in state at home were supplied with tobacco, pipes, food, and drink for the vigil. Pallbearers received gloves, rings, scarves, handkerchiefs, or spoons. After the burial the mourners returned to the house for further refreshments, often so lavish as to turn the funeral into a festival. Lower-class persons also gave relatives a "proper" interment. (Alice Morse Earle, *Colonial Days in Old New York* [New York, 1899], chap. 14.) When Livingston's father died in 1749 two ceremonies and gifts cost some £500, even though linen replaced the usual silk scarves! (Theodore Sedgwick, Jr., *A Memoir of the Life of William Livingston* [New York, 1833], p. 64.)

2. The *Reflector's* plea for economy fell on deaf ears even within Livingston's own family. At his mother's death three years later the rites were as elaborate as his father's. Robert, the eldest son and the new manor lord, ordered, among other things, "a barrel of Cutt Tobacco," long pipes, black cloth for the four hearse-horses, silver tankards, and cinnamon for the burnt wine. Livingston Rutherfurd, *Family Records and Events* (New York, 1894), pp. 54–55.

3. This allegation was made in a letter in the *New-York Mercury,* June 4, 1753, in which Livingston was accused of opposing a New York college in order to insure the success of the College of New Jersey (Princeton), which had been founded under Presbyterian auspices in 1746.

Number X X X

THURSDAY, JUNE 21, 1753

The Multiplicity of OATHS, and the Levity and Indecorum wherewith they are administered and taken, pernicious to Society

Thou shalt not take the Name of the Lord thy God in Vain.
MOSES

An Oath is a religious Asseveration, by which we renounce the Divine Clemency, or imprecate the Divine Vengeance, in Case we speak false. When, therefore, a Being Omniscient and Omnipotent is invoked as a Witness to the Truth of our Testimony, it creates the strongest Presumption in favour of our Evidence; it being utterly improbable that any Man should be so abandoned, and consummately impious, as seriously to defy almighty Vengeance, and deliberately irritate a Being of uncontroulable Power. Hence an Oath is justly esteemed the firmest Bond of Society; without a due Regard to which, in the present degenerate Circumstances of Human Nature, no Government could long well subsist. Accordingly, all the Nations of the Earth have paid the greatest Credit to what was delivered on Oath, and expressed the deepest Horror at the Guilt of Perjury. *Our Ancestors,* says CICERO, *could never find any Thing stronger than an Oath, to bind us to the faithful Discharge of our Engagements.*[1] The Historian DIODORUS SICULUS,[2] reports of the ancient *Egyptians, That by their Laws, Persons who had forsworn themselves, were adjudged to capital Punishments, as guilty of the two greatest Crimes; in violating that Piety which they owed to God; and in destroying Faith from amongst Men, the strongest Pillar of human Society.* PLUTARCH carries the Matter so far, as to insist on the Performance of a Promise on Oath, tho' made to an Enemy. *He who deceives his Enemy,* says he, *by an Oath, confesses that he fears him, but despises God.*[3] Nay, the Ancients had so great a Dread of Perjury, as to imagine it would be punished on the Posterity of the Criminal. Hence VIRGIL observes, that the *Romans* were sufficiently punished for the Perjury of the *Trojans*, from whom they claimed their Origin, by a beautiful Allusion to the fabulous Account of LAOMEDON's Perfidy to APOLLO and NEPTUNE.

> *—— Satis jam pridem sanguine nostro,*
> *Laomedonteæ luimus perjuria Trojæ.*[4]

So sensible were the sage Legislators of Antiquity, of the Importance of Oaths, to the Well-being of the Community, that they never suffered them to be taken, but on very necessary Occasions, nor even then, without the utmost Solemnity. They were convinced, that every Thing tending to abate the Awe which Mankind naturally have for an Oath, ought to be discouraged; and on the contrary, whatever conduced to create or preserve a Veneration for that solemn Act of Religion to be countenanced and promoted. And, indeed, the Use and End of an Oath being to procure an accessional Strength to what was before a Duty, and to lay an additional Obligation on the Person sworn, unless it be taken with awful Reverence, its original Design is, in a great Measure, frustrated. And if Men once break thro' this sacred Inclosure, and burst asunder the strongest of all Ties, what can be expected but an Inundation of Perjury and Delusion? For it cannot be supposed, that he who dare provoke the Wrath of God, whose Omniscience is indeceptible, and his Power irresistible, will stand in Awe of the Punishment of Men, who may both be resisted and deluded. For this Reason, I have often been astonished at the Levity and Indecorum, with which our Oaths are administred, together with the almost endless Multiplicity of them in Practice amongst the *English*. Methinks no Part of the late Judge HALE's [5] Character shines with greater Lustre, or does more Honour to his Memory, than that invariable Practice of his, of interrogating every Witness, (who from his Youth or disadvantageous Appearance, afforded the least Ground for the Question,) on the Nature of an Oath, and insisting on its being administred with the greatest Solemnity. And, indeed, the Invocation of the Name of God, in a careless irreverent Manner, is extremely shocking and offensive. It is offering a public Affront and Indignity to the Supreme Governor of the Universe, who ought never to be spoken of but with the profoundest Veneration. It is, to the last Degree, impious and unnatural, to invoke with Levity and Inadvertence that tremendous Name, which Beings of the highest Order of Intelligence profoundly venerate, and dare not mention, but with the most lowly Adoration.

The Writer of Mr. BOYLE's Life [6] tells us, that he never heard or mentioned the Name of God, but with visible Signs of reverential Fear: This great Philosopher, who had pryed into the most secret Qualities of Things, had from thence most justly drawn such astonishing Proofs of the Wisdom and Power of the Almighty Creator, that the Sound of his Name struck him with religious Awe; nor did he ever speak of him but with trembling Lips and a solemn Pause.

It is a common Observation, that no People on Earth is so much addicted to swearing whether common or political as the *English* — An infamous Distinction, which renders them justly contemptible to Foreigners! For Strangers may well question the Veracity of a Nation, who will not take each others Word in the most trivial Matters, without the Sanction of an Oath. As for the Practice of common Swearing, it is indubitably to the last Degree, impious, savage, and disgraceful, and a Vice to which there is not the least Temptation. It defeats the very Intention for which it is used, since every Man must deserve less Credit in proportion to the Proofs of his Wickedness. It is at least, a senseless, insignificant, blustering expletive in Discourse, which gives it neither Strength, Musick or Ornament.[7]

Whether our Magistrates can, consistent with their Oath of Office, hear such Offences, without calling the Criminal to an Account, meerly because he is not informed against, requires no great Share of Casuistry to determine. I have more Manners than to insinuate, that some of their *Worships* themselves, are guilty of this vulgar Practice.

The repeated and unnecessary Invocations of God's holy

Name, even in a judicial Manner, is a great Affront to the Deity, who ought not to be appealed to as a Witness, but on the most important Occasions: Nor can there be the least Doubt, that our Test Oaths are rather prejudicial than serviceable to the Community. And of this Opinion appears to have been the *Marquis* of HALIFAX, who, in the Debates about the Test Act, urged with equal Truth and Eloquence, That "Oaths are no Security to any State; no Man," says he, "would ever sleep with open Doors, or unlock his Treasure or Plate, should all the Town be sworn not to rob him; so that the Use of multiplying Oaths, had been, most commonly, to exclude or disturb some honest conscientious Men, who would never have prejudiced the Government. The Oath imposed by the Bill, contains these Clauses; the two former assertory, and the last promisory. Is it not worthy of the Consideration of the Bishops, to examine, whether assertory Oaths, which were properly appointed to give Testimony of a Matter of Fact, whereof a Man is capable to be fully assured by the Evidence of his Senses, can lawfully be made use of, to confirm or invalidate *doctrinal* Propositions; and whether that legislative Power, which imposes such an Oath, doth not, necessarily, assume to itself an Infallibility? And as for promisory Oaths, it is hoped, those learned Prelates will consider the Opinion of GROTIUS, who seems to make it clear, that such Oaths are forbidden by our Saviour in the Gospel; and whether it would not become the Fathers of the Church, when they have well weigh'd that and other Places of the New-Testament, to be more tender of multiplying Oaths, than hitherto the great Men of the Church have been."

Affidavits in our Courts of Judicature, are almost innumerable. Not a special Motion can be made without one: Nor can an honest Juror leave his Seat, by Necessity of Nature, without a Constable's swearing that no Person shall speak to him during his Evacuation.

· Of most of the swearing Scenes in the Nation, the *Custom-House* must be own'd to carry the Laurel. Every Master of a Vessel is obliged by Act of Parliament, on his Arrival, to swear to the Quantity and Quality of his Cargo; and it is generally supposed, that there is not one in ten of those Dealers in Oaths, but is perjured on that Occasion. Nay, so flagrant are the Instances of their foreswearing themselves, that a *Custom-House* Oath is grown into a Proverb; the literal Meaning of which is downright Perjury.

The Multiplicity of these Oaths hath rendered them so vastly familiar, that Persons who would tremble at the Apprehensions of taking a false Oath on another Occasion, are, by constant Use, brought to perjure themselves there, with greatest Tranquility and Composure: Which brings to my Mind a Story of Mr. LOCKE's, equally melancholy and apposite. His Words are these, "I was once told, in a trading Town beyond Sea, of a Master of a Vessel there, esteemed a sober and fair Man, who, yet, could not help saying, *God forbid that a Custom-House Oath should be a Sin.*"

But of all the Swearers in the Kingdom, commend me to the Church-Wardens in England, who, by their Oath, are bound to present "all that, being of the Age of sixteen Years, do not receive the Blessed Sacrament three Times in a Year at least; all that do not come to Church on Lord's Days, and that do not come at the Beginning of Prayers; and that do not observe to kneel and stand up, as the Rubrick does direct, during the whole Time of Divine Service." But whether any Person was ever presented for such Omissions, is humbly submitted to those ecclesiastical Deponents.

Can a Nation which connives at so horrible a Practice, expect the Divine Blessing! Will that Being, whom they so often insult, continue the Smiles of his Providence! Or may we not rather fear that he will, for the Punishment of this aggravated Guilt, accelerate our final and universal Overthrow!

Z.

To the INDEPENDENT REFLECTOR

SIR,

You have, ever since your first Appearance in Print, distinguished yourself by a warm and hearty Zeal for your Country's Prosperity: Influenced by the same Principle, I beg Leave to congratulate you, upon the just and pleasing Expectation, that a Seminary of Learning will, e'er long, spring up amongst us, from the cherishing Bosom of Liberty. Nothing could have afforded so incontestible a Proof of the Reasonableness of your Reflections, upon the important Necessity of a *Free*

College, as the laudable Endeavours of our Representatives, to introduce the Sciences into this Province, with a View to public Utility. Nor will your Apprehensions of the fatal Consequences of a *Party College*, remain unsupported by the Authority of that great Body, when the Appointment of, such as are now Candidates for the Guardianship of our Academy is once become certain: Thanks to Heaven, the Muses shall not (tho' it was once justly feared) groan under the oppressing Weight of Party Malevolence, but bask themselves in the Sunshine of Freedom, and flourish under the gentle Nurture of Patriotism!

Your most avowed Enemies are those who malign you barely because they suspect you to be of a particular Party. These, however, will be disappointed in their Expectations; nor will they ever have the Opportunity of rioting in that Excess of Exultation and Triumph, which they have so long promised themselves. How will they be ashamed of their blind and intemperate Zeal? They will soon be convinced, by the Nomination of the Trustees, that our Academy is designed not to be made use of as a Tool, either by *Episcopacy* or *Presbyterianism*; but to be serviceable to the Individuals of every Sect without the least Discrimination. In this indeed, they will say (tho' it is the Height of Absurdity) that you are equally disappointed: But of the Truth of this Assertion, he only can be convinced, who conceives it possible for you to wish both for a *Free* and *Party-College* at the same Time.

There is one Thing more, upon the Accomplishment of which, I hope soon to congratulate not only you, but every Lover of his Country. The Nomination of Trustees is not the sole, important and interesting Part of the Work. The Plan is still to be concerted! A Part unspeakably momentous and important! It is to be wished that, the fair Characters of the present Candidates, may not induce our Legislators to be less cautious in securing the College against Abuses, Usurpations, and Encroachments. Let it be remembered, that the Honesty of the first Trustees, will be no Security against the Roguery of their Successors. Let them, therefore, as they are created by the Legislature, be accountable to them for every Part of their Conduct. In fine, *Sir*, as I heartily wish our future Seminary of Learning may be girded round with a lasting Security; should a Plan, something like that with which you have presented the Public, in your XXI Number, be concerted by our Rulers, it would exceedingly rejoice,

Your constant Reader,
And humble Servant,

PHILELEUTHERUS.

1. *De officiis*, III, 31, 111.
2. *Bibliotheca historica*, I, 77, 2.

3. *Life of Lysander*, VIII, 4.

4. "Long enough have we expiated with our blood Laomedon's perjury at Troy." *Georgics*, I, 502.

5. Sir Matthew Hale (1609–1676), English jurist, successively judge of the Court of Common Pleas, chief baron of the Exchequer, and chief justice of the Court of King's Bench.

6. Robert Boyle (1627–1691), English chemist and natural philosopher. The work is presumably Thomas Birch's *Life of the Right Honourable Robert Boyle* (London, 1744).

7. Livingston's distaste for swearing was not an affectation assumed for literary purposes. During his legal apprenticeship, he confided to his Yale confreres that he had the dubious choice of living "in hermitage" or of consorting with a "ridiculous race of mortals" for whom "oaths pass for politeness and debauchery usurps the name of genteelness," and whose conversation consisted in "putting an Enemy in their mouths to steal away their brains." Livingston to Chauncey Whittelsey, August 23, 1744, Letter Book, 1744–1745, Sedgwick Papers, Massachusetts Historical Society; Livingston to Noah Welles, February 10, 1746, JFP, Yale.

Number XXXI

Primitive CHRISTIANITY *short and intelligible, modern* CHRISTIANITY *voluminous and incomprehensible* [1]

> *But in their Room*
> *Wolves shall succeed for Teachers; grievous Wolves!*
> *Who all the sacred Mysteries of Heav'n*
> *To their own vile Advantages shall turn,*
> *Of Lucre and Ambition; and the Truth*
> *With Superstitions, and Traditions taint,*
> *Left only in those written Records pure.*   Paradise Lost [2]

> *Her Priests have done Violence to the Law.*
> > Prophet Zephaniah [3]

THE lowly Author of Christianity declares of himself, that he had not a Place where to lay his Head. The Persons he commissioned to propagate it, abandon'd every Thing agreable to human Nature, and wandered thro' the World, indigent and persecuted, till a Period was put to their Lives, by Executions painful and igno-minious. The Things it proposes to deliver us from, are the Guilt and Dominion of Sin; and the Blessings it promises, the Favour of God here, and an Immortality of Happiness hereafter. Its positive Precepts (unless the Washing of Feet was intended to be perpetually obligatory upon Christians) are but two, and carry their own Reason with them. It enjoins its Disciples as often as they break Bread, to commemorate the Death and Sufferings of their Master, and to baptize their Proselytes as an Initiation into his Religion. Its grand Secret consists in a Revelation of the Re-establishment of our degraded Nature, by an Atonement of in-finite Value; and that the Father of our Spirits is pleased to carry on a Communication with the human Mind, consistent with the Constitution of intelligent Beings, endued with Freedom of

Choice; and by implanting in it an internal Principle of Grace, create a Kind of ineffable Union between the Soul of Man and the eternal Deity. All the Faith it requires is, that *Christ* was the promised *Messiah*, and its moral Directions may be contained in a Sheet of Paper. The Life of its Author is recorded with the utmost Conciseness and Simplicity, and the whole delivered in a Style so artless and perspicuous, that to use its own emphatic Phrase, *he who runs may read.* And who now would imagine that this should have filled Folios, and been converted into an intricate Science? That there should be a Necessity for countless Systems to explain what could not be misunderstood, and to illustrate with endless Comments, what was wrote in Sun-Beams? And yet, what Creeds! what Systems! what Schemes, utterly incompatible and subversive, of each other! what voluminous Treatises of learned Absurdity, and scholastic Gibberish! what laborious Trifling, and cabalistical Jargon! what an Infinity of Sects and Parties! what Subscriptions! what swearing, unswearing, and forswearing! what damning one another, for not believing one another, and persecuting their Fellow Creatures for not renouncing their Senses, and burning their Bibles! For this Day's Entertainment, I shall, therefore, run over some of the numberless Sects, into which those grievous Wolves, spoken of in the Motto of this Paper, have divided and subdivided Christianity. Such a Survey will teach us to be less attached to any Party, and to seek for true Religion where alone it is to be found, in the pure and genuine Oracles of Truth and Inspiration.

The Followers of LUTHER, or rather the Perverters of his Doctrine. BRENZIUS and ANDREAS, differ from others about Predestination, Grace, our Vocation thro' Christ; the Providence of God respecting Evil, Free-Will, the Ubiquity of Christ's Body, Baptism and Consubstantiation. These are again subdivided into *Flaccians*, from MATTHEW FLACCIUS, and *Osiandrites* from OSIANDRUS, who differed from each other, and both from LUTHER.[4]

The *Armenians* or *Remonstrants*, maintain the Law of *Moses*, and the Prophets, to be equally perfect with the Gospel. They deny Election in any other Sense, than as dependent on Faith for its Cause. 'Tis their Opinion, that the Saints do not persevere, but may relapse, and perish eternally. They affirm, that Saving-Faith consists not in believing the Satisfaction of Christ, but in imitating his Example and obeying his Precepts; and that Justification depends on our own Actions: That original Sin is no Sin, properly so called, but only the Punishment of that Sin; for which Reason we are not to pray for the Remission of original Sin; and that Man is not wholly dead in Sin, nor destitute of all Strength.

The *Swenkfeldians* insist, that Faith is not obtained by the Word of God, but by the internal Revelation of the Spirit; and that the Body of Christ was deifyed by Virtue of the hypostatic Union. They also deride the external Ministry of the Church, and deny the Necessity of public Worship.

The *Romanists* are at mortal Odds with the *Protestants* about the Scripture; the Person and Office of Christ; the Roman Pontiff; Purgatory; Councils; the Civil Magistracy; Antichrist; the Adoration of Saints; Relicts and Images; the Church; Holy Days; the Sacraments; Baptism; Confirmation; the Eucharist; Repentance; the Sacrifice of the Mass; Indulgences; extreme Unction; Ordination; Marriage; the State of Man before the Fall; Sin; Grace; Predestination; Free-Will; Justification; Prayer; Fasting and Alms.

The *Apostolians* condemned Matrimony, declaring it to be a Forfeiture of Heaven, and that the Apostles lived in perpetual Celibacy. They inveigh'd against the private Appropriation of Goods, and argued for an universal Community.

The *Socinians* hold that CHRIST was a meer Man, having no Existence before MARY; and deny the Personality of the Holy Ghost; original Sin; the Sacraments; Predestination; Grace, and the Immensity of God.

The *Pelagians* teach, that ADAM's Sin only affected himself, prejudicing his Posterity no otherwise, than as he set them a bad Example; and that the Lust and Concupiscence natural to Man are blameless: For why should one be reprehended for what he needs not to be ashamed of? They deny original Sin; laugh at Predestination, and assert the human Liberty to do Good or Evil, with our Capacity of Meriting the Favour of God, and promoting his Glory.

The *Anabaptists* formerly maintained the Uselessness of the Old Testament; and that our Saviour received not his Body from Mary, but brought it from Heaven; That the Holy Ghost was not given till after Christ's Glorification; and that Regeneration enables us to fulfil the whole Law: That the Patriarchs were evidently ignorant of Christ; and that those are not to be own'd for true Churches which exhibit any Marks of Sin: That the Gospel may be preach'd by Laics, and that the Clergy ought to have no Salaries: That the Sacraments are only naked Emblems of spiritual Blessings; and that the Baptism of Infants is unscriptural: That God neither approves of War, nor political Institutions; but that Christians ought to enjoy all Things in Common: And that the Law concerning Divorce is as much in Force now, as it was among the Jews, whence it is lawful to repudiate a Wife for Obstinacy, Jangling, *etc.*

The *Cerbonists* held, that there were two Gods, and contrary Principles. They rejected the Law of Moses and all the Prophets, who interpreted it, together with the Resurrection of the Body; and maintained that Christ was not a real, but a fictitious Man.

The *Antinomians* are of Opinion, that the Observation of the Mosaical Law is unprofitable; and that good Works do not promote, nor evil Ones obstruct our Salvation, but that Faith alone is sufficient.

The *Arians* deny, that the Son is consubstantial and co-equal with the Father; asserting that he is a Creature made out of Nothing, and in Time, but supremely excellent, and supassing all others. They teach, moreover, that Christ assumed a Body without a Soul; and that the Holy Ghost is the Creature of a Creature, that is, of the Son, to whom they give that Appellation.

The *Antisabbatarians* deny the Holiness of the Sabbath.

The *Eunomians* conceive that Faith is acceptable without Works, and that God may be perfectly comprehended by the human Intellect: That the Son was in all Things, dissimilar from the Father, and the Holy Ghost created by the Son. They also rebaptize those who have been baptized by others; and insist that Christ assumed a Body without a Soul.

The *Anthropomorphites* maintain, that God has a corporeal

Shape, and that Darkness, Fire and Water, are the first Principles of all Things.

The *Ebionites* denied the Divinity of our Saviour, and rejected all the Gospels but St. MATTHEW's. They taught that the Observance of the Ceremonial Law was not necessary to Salvation, and prohibited the eating of Animals.

The *Florianians* maintained that God created Evil, and that the Jewish Ceremonies ought to be retained in the Church.

The *Carpocratians* taught, that we could not avoid the Rage of Evil Spirits, but by doing Evil, for that was the only Way to please them: Hence they abandon'd themselves to Magic, and a libidinous Life. They taught also that CHRIST was a meer Man, and their Master CARPOCRATES the better Man. They denied the Resurrection, and insisted that the World was not made by GOD, but by Satan.

The *Manichees* held, that MANES their Founder, was the Comforter whom our Saviour had promised to send; and that there were two independent and eternal Principles, the one Good and the other Evil: That the God of the Law was not the true God, whence they rejected the Old Testament, and partly mutilated and partly rejected the New. They denied that CHRIST was God, and insisted that his Death and Crucifixion, were only fictitious and imaginary.

The *Monarchicals* alledge that the Father was crucified.

The *Macedonians* deny the Divinity of the Holy Ghost, and assert that the Son was like to, but not consubstantial with the Father.

The *Nazarites* recognized CHRIST for the true Messiah, but esteemed the Observance of the ceremonial Law necessary to Salvation; and that there were more than four Gospels, especially two, the first of which they called the Gospel of *Perfection*, and the other the Gospel of EVE.

The *Nestorians* held two Persons in Christ, the one the Son of GOD, the other of MARY, and that the Holy Spirit proceeded only from the Father.

The *Eutychians* denied the Flesh of CHRIST to be like ours, affirming that he had a celestial Body, which passed thro' the

Virgin as thro' a Channel; and that there were two Natures in CHRIST before the Hypostatical Union, but that afterwards there was but one compounded of both, and thence they concluded that the Divinity of our Saviour did both suffer and die.

I shall barely mention the *Monothelites*, the *Monophysites*, the *Jacobites*, the *Montanists*, the *Ophites*, the *Marcites*, the *Cainites*, the *Sethites*, the *Heracleonites*, the *Cerdonites*, the *Marcionites*; the *Apellitæ*, the *Ascitæ*, the *Ascothyptæ*, the *Pattalorinchitæ*, the *Abelonitæ*, the *Apollinarians*, the *Catharians*, the *Valentinians*, the *Novatians*, the *Cataphrygians*, the *Sublapsarians*, the *Superlapsarians*, the *Pepuzians*, the *Quintilians*, the *Elcesians*, the *Theodocians*, the *Melchisadecians*, the *Noetians*, the *Velesians*, the *Sabellians*, the *Originians*, the *Samosatenians*, the *Photinians*, the *Maletians*, the *Audians*, the *Colarbasians*, the *Ærians*, the *Ætians*, the *Messalians*, the *Hermians*, the *Patricians*, the *Rethorians*, the *Nativitarians*, the *Luciferians*, the *Cellyridians*, the *Severians*, the *Timotheans*, the *Cocceians*, the *Voetsians*, the *Tatiani*, the *Allogiani*, the *Prodiciani*, the *Aquarii*, the *Coluthiani*, the *Aquei*, the *Melitonii*, the *Ophei*, the *Tertullii*, the *Paterniani*, the *Angelici*, the *Artotyrites*, the *Hyerachites*, the *Antidicomarianites*, the *Metangismonites*, the *Proclianites*, the *Theopassites*, the *Arabicks*, the *Archonticks*, the *Gnosticks*, the *Æternales*, the *Nudipedales*, the *Liberatores*, the *Bordesanists*, the *Priscillianists*, the *Tritheists*, the *Jovinianists*, the *Tortullianists*, the *Origenists*, the *Jansenists*, the *Mollanists*, and the *Quietists*.

I shall also omit the Tenets of the *Quakers* and *Moravians*, because whatever Dogmas they may have published, or others forged for them, 'tis evident from their Conduct, that they are *Christians*, which is the less to be wondered at, as the former are not in Subjection to Priests, nor the latter chain'd to Systems.

The *Calvinists* write very elaborately about Predestination, imputed Righteousness, Election, irresistible Grace, saving Faith, irreversible Decrees, Justification, original Sin, Glory of God, Reprobation, the absolute Inability of Man to co-operate with the Spirit of God, and many other Points full of curious and profound Erudition.

Thus have I enumerated the principal Sects, into which Christianity is divided, and run over the Doctrines of many of them with a Waste of Learning, that in the Hands of some might have filled many Volumes; not to mention several of my own Reverend Acquaintance, who could preach at least an Hundred and Fifty Sermons against every one of the above Tenets, except those which luckily happened to be their own. And now, among which of these Systems shall a candid Inquirer after Truth, look for Christianity? Where shall he find the Religion of CHRIST amidst all this priestly Fustian, and ecclesiastical Trumpery? They all claim to be orthodox, and yet all differ from one another, and each is ready to damn all the Rest. O merciful JESUS! how is thy amiable Religion adulterated by those who pretend to be thy Ambassadors! How is thy benevolent Revelation barbariz'd and perverted, and the lovely Simplicity of thy Gospel encumbered with Absurdities that deface its Beauty, and obscure its native Lustre!

Let us therefore hold fast the *Form of sound Words*, and examine for ourselves. Let us assert and vindicate the Honour of our Nature, and disdain to have our Consciences enslaved by Priests and Bigots. Let it be our ultimate Ambition, to read the Scriptures with our own Eyes, and practise their Meaning without being Hood-wink'd by Jugglers and Visionaries. In a Word, let us never desert *the Law and the Testimony*, for the airy Figments of Dreamers of Dreams, Venders of Jargon, gloomy Impostors, devout System-Mongers, and spiritual Conjurers.[5]

Z.

1. With this issue, the *Reflector* turned increasingly toward doctrinal debate with its Anglican critics, initiated by churchmen unwilling to permit Livingston's virulent anticlericalism to go unchallenged and horrified by his proposal to make the New York college "a sort of free thinking latitudinarian seminary." Even before Livingston had completed his essays on the college, Henry Barclay, rector of New York City's Trinity Church wrote to Samuel Johnson, the Anglican pastor at Stamford, Connecticut, and the New York churchmen's choice for the college presidency: "If you think No. 19 [of the *Reflector*], so senseless a Paper, I know not what you will say to the last No. [XX]. I think you would do well to Expose these Numbers the Sooner the Better." Soon a formidable team of Anglican penmen assembled to write "in the church's defense," including, besides Barclay and Johnson, William Smith, later provost of the Philadelphia College but at this time a private

tutor in New York City awaiting Episcopal ordination; Samuel Seabury, the Anglican rector at Hempstead, L. I.; and James Wetmore, the Episcopal pastor at Rye. Apart from a steady stream of letters in the *New-York Mercury* defending their own college scheme, they published early in June two pamphlets to defend "the externals of Religion, and solemn rites of Christian Worship" against the *Reflector's* "indecencies" and "prophaneness." (*A Scheme for the Revival of Christianity* [New-York, 1753]; and Francis Squire, *An Answer to some late Papers, Entitled, The Independent Whig* [New-York, 1753], the latter a reprint of a 1723 English publication.) Livingston responded quickly with No. XXXI of the *Reflector.* See Barclay to Johnson, April 16, 1753, Hawks-Johnson MSS, New York Historical Society; William Smith to Johnson, [May, 1753?], and Johnson to the Archbishop of Canterbury, June 25, 1753, in *Samuel Johnson Writings*, I, 167–169; IV, 3–4. The Anglican counterassault undoubtedly increased the sharpness of the *Reflector's* attack on organized religion, but Livingston's sentiments were not coined for the occasion in 1753. He had been expressing them, privately and publicly, for the past ten years. And long after the *Reflector's* demise he continued expressing his irritation with the type of "polemical Wrangle" that divided Dutch divines over whether "Father our" meant the same as "our Father." Livingston to Henry Laurens, February 5, 1778, Laurens Papers, South Carolina Historical Society.

2. Book XII.

3. Zeph. 3:4.

4. Johann Brenz (1499–1570), Jacob Andrea (1528–1590), Matthias Flacius (1520–1575), and Andreas Osiander (1498–1552) were among many Lutheran divines involved in fractious disputes about the theological course the Reformation in Germany should take.

5. Of all the essays in the *Reflector* this one most offended its readers. Anglicans found it convincing proof of Livingston's "inborn prejudice against the Religion of the Blessed Jesus." (*New-York Mercury*, July 9, 1753); Livingston denied the "calumnious Accusation" in the *Occasional Reverberator* (No. 11, September 14, 1753), insisting that his "Abhorrence of Priestcraft" stemmed solely from his veneration for Christianity, "so villainously perverted and disfigured" by the clergy. In his vindication a year later he again denied that No. XXXI had been intended to discredit religion, but had rather been "more particularly . . . intended to dissuade men, from an inordinate devotion to any religious hypothesis framed by the passion, the ignorance or craft of Monks and Visionaries, while they have an opportunity of consulting the Bible itself." *Independent Reflector, Preface,* p. 4.

Number XXXII

THURSDAY, JULY 5, 1753

Of Elections, and Election-Jobbers

But write him down a Slave, who humbly proud,
With Presents begs Preferment from the Crowd:
That early Suppliant, who salutes the Tribes,
And sets the Mob to scramble for his Bribes.   Dryden [1]

Some of the greatest and best-policied States have been under-min'd by imperceptible Degrees. Corruptions gradually intro-duced, and in Appearance, too trifling to merit Attention, have, in Process of Time, sapp'd the Basis of the wisest Constitution, and laid the most populous Nations in Ruin. A People tenacious of their Liberty, should therefore be rather more apprehensive of *secret* Machinations, than *open* Attacks upon their Privileges. The Thrust of a *Duellist* may be parried, but who can repel the Stab of an *Assassin*? No Man who has projected the Subversion of his Country, will employ *Force* and *Violence*, till he has, by sow-ing the Seeds of *Corruption*, ripen'd it for Servility and Acquies-cence: He will *conceal* his Design, till he spies an Opportunity of accomplishing his Iniquity by a single Blow. — Our natural Love of Freedom, and Aversion to Restraint, render every *visible* At-tempt upon our Liberty, always precarious, and generally abortive. But tho' we keep a watchful Eye on *flagrant* Oppressions, we are wholly inattentive to *subdolous* [2] and *well-dissembled* Encroach-ments. While we endeavour to escape the *roaring Lion*, who *threatens* immediate Destruction, we receive a mortal Sting from the *wilely Serpent*, that lies *concealed* beneath a Bed of Roses. If we credit the Poets, the *Syrens* destroyed more Lives by their *melodious Enchantments*; than all the Race of *Cyclops* by their *undisguised Hostilities*. Instead of using *Compulsion*, the Devil is represented by *Milton*, as effecting the Seduction of *Eve*, by the soothing Arts of *Adulation* and *Blandishment*.

ELECTIONS AND ELECTION JOBBERS

Every Privilege we part with is an Acceleration of our Ruin: Nor is the seeming Minuteness of the Surrender, a Reason for consenting to the Loss. A good Economist comprizes Pence and Farthings in his Calculations; and a wary Merchant considers a Negligence in Trifles as ominous of a total Bankruptcy.

I have often considered our Practice of making Interest for Elections, and intoxicating the People to influence their Voices, with equal Grief and Indignation.[3] It may claim the Authority of Custom, but it is a perilous Invasion of our constitutional Privileges. The Freedom and Independency of Elections, is one of the chief Bulwarks of *British* Liberty: But without a voluntary and unbiass'd Choice of our Representatives, we are governed by Laws enacted without our Consent. It has a Tendency to render the People venal, vicious, insensible of private Virtue, and of public Glory or Disgrace. It creates Ill-Blood, promotes Dissention, and transmits Hatred and Discord from Generation to Generation. It is attended with innumerable Evils, and may lay the Foundation of the most infamous Thraldom. How groundless soever these Suspicions may appear to the inconsiderate Multitude; the very Reflection is enough to make a thoughtful Man melancholy. Tho' it may seem meer Fashion and Custom to *Election-Jobbers*, who may perhaps quote Prescription in their Vindication; I cannot dissemble my Apprehensions, that probably *hæ nugæ seria ducant in Mala*,[4] and what is Play to them, may, eventually, prove Death to Posterity.

In those free Governments of old, whose History we so much admire, and whose Examples we think it an Honour to imitate; a Man would have suffered Death for such an iniquitous Attempt.

In *Rome* there once happened a great Scarcity of Provision: One Spurius Melius, a Man of vast Opulence, intending to turn the public Distress to his private Advantage, bought up a great Quantity of Corn. This, under Pretence of Charity, he distributed *gratis* among several poor Families in the City: But the Thing reaching the Ears of the Senate, they judged it a Matter of so great Importance, that they appointed a Dictator (which was never done but where the Safety of the State was concerned, before the Time of Julius Cæsar) to enquire into the Reason of this Proceeding. The Dictator summon'd SPURIUS MELIUS to answer; and discovering that he had a Design upon public Offices, and took this Method of insinuating himself into the good Opinion of the People before he would declare himself; he was by the Dictator condemned to die, and executed accordingly. Thus fell that subtle Insinuator, a righteous Sacrifice to those Laws which he endeavoured to enervate, by biassing the Voices of his Country-men!

The Liberties of *Rome*, that original Soil of Freedom, were built upon as sure a Foundation as those of *Britain*: Yet as soon as Bribery predominated in Elections, and the People were seduced by the Intrigues and Largesses of artful Candidates, the Government became arbitrary; and that celebrated People who had been so jealous of their Liberties, and so averse to the very Shadow of Tyranny, continued, for many dreadful Ages, the Slaves of a bloody Succession of Emperors, of their rapacious Favourites, of their Minions, their Pimps and Pandars.

How often has a whole County been turned topsy-turvey, by making Interest against an approaching Election? How often have the Votes of the People been purchased in the Face of the Sun, and without the least Endeavour to conceal the Bribery? And how seldom are the Qualifications of the Candidates considered by the Electors? Sometimes a few leading Men will occasion universal Confusion and Misrule, in order to shew their Influence: And at other Times for the meer Sake of Opposition. To these the People, more like a Herd of Slaves, than a Society of Freemen, submit with the greatest Passivity. Submit in what? In a Matter the most momentous, and of general Concern, — In delegating Legislative Authority, to Men with whose Merit they are wholly unacquaint-ed, and whose Characters they never examined: Nay, often to Men who are a Dishonour to the Species, — human Beings in Shape, and inferior to some of the Brute Creation in the Facul-ties of the Mind. I might here take Occasion to expatiate on that refined Policy practis'd in some Colonies, of sending blank Com-missions previous to Elections, to the respective Court-Sycophants of each County; but that is a Subject which I shall reserve for a future Paper.

ELECTIONS AND ELECTION JOBBERS

'Tis the Opinion of Mr. RAPIN,[5] that there is no forming a true Judgment of the Sense of the People, by the Choice of their Representatives: But tho' this Assertion may be too general, sure I am, that People who are tampered with before an Election, and allured to sell their Voices for Beer and Brandy, are not left to their own voluntary and uncorrupted Determination.

When a People are reduced to such a miserable State of Depravity, it is almost impossible they should long preserve that Love of Liberty, which always was, and I hope ever will be, the distinguishing Characteristic of *Englishmen*. This can only be affected by keeping alive the Spirit of public Liberty in the Body of the People, and inflicting exemplary Punishments upon whomsoever introduces Venality, and paves the Way to Vassalage and Corruption.

'Tis true, we consent to become the supple Tools of Candidates, and agree to be inebriated out of our Senses. But are Shame and Servitude the less opprobrious, because they are of our own procuring? Or will a voluntary Renunciation of our Liberty, atone for its Loss? To a Man of Reflection, it will rather aggravate the Calamity. That ourselves were accessary to our own Undoing, must swell the Anguish of our Bondage, and render the Horror of our Guilt, the more exceeding horrible. Rather than commit Suicide, I would fall by the Hands of the most merciless Robber. What! exchange an inestimable Jewel for a brutal Carouse, and sell my Voice for a Pound of Beef! No, if I must lose my Liberty, let it be *as by Fire*. Let me sell it at the dearest Rate, and struggle while there is a Glimmer of Hope for its Preservation. Then shall I at least, enjoy the Satisfaction of having resisted, while Resistance was available; and that I was at length not so properly conquered as over-powered. But sell my Birth-right for a Song, and barter away my greatest Privilege for a Treat, or a Frolick! This, indeed, is astonishing Madness, and more than brutal Stupidity.

To ask a Man for his Vote, is a Confession in the Candidate, that he is suspicious of his own Merit. 'Tis a Proof of his Apprehensions, that the Sense of the Public is against him. Why else such hawking of Liquor, and purchasing of Interest? Why all that Servility and Abasement, to a Fellow he wou'd not give a Shilling to save from the Gallows, the Moment he has carried his Point? It proceeds from a Man's Ignorance of the Dignity of his Nature, not to resent so outrageous an Insult on his Honour and Conscience. Was he duly sensible of the Affront, he would apply a Handful of Dirt to that impudent Mouth, which, under the specious Pretence of asking a Favour, insinuated his Meaness, and called him a Scoundrel.

To ask a Man's Vote, is a tacit Declaration that he acts from Caprice, and abandons his Reason. But to wheedle him into a Choice against his Inclination, by Treats and Frolicks, is downright Bribery and Corruption. Up then, for Shame, my Countrymen, and vindicate the Dignity of your high-born Natures; exert yourselves and be Men. Dare to follow the honest Dictates of your own Hearts. Dare to think for yourselves, and scorn to be bought and sold. Scorn to give up your Liberty for Scraps and Offals, for Wine and Brandy; and despise the Men, who, by artful Infusions, and insidious Harangues, offer to warp or debilitate your Judgement. Lavish not, with Æsop's Cock, a precious Pearl for a worthless Barley-Corn;[6] but testify a just Abhorrence of so insolent an Attempt, not only in Regard to your own Honour, but to preserve pure and inviolate,

> *The Laws, the Rights,*
> *The generous Plan of Power, deliver'd down,*
> *From Age to Age by your renown'd Forefathers;*
> *(So dearly bought, the Price of so much Blood.)*

In this Article, be not ambitious of rivalling your Mother-Country, but chearfully resign the ignominious Trophy, and glory in an Integrity, immoveable and immaculate. Transmit to your Posterity, your inestimable Privileges. — Privileges little prized while possessed, but fruitlessly to be deplor'd, should they be ravish'd from you; and with aggravated Lamentation, that you lost them by your own ridiculous Collusion. In a Word, let your Choice be free as Air, and scorn to be either brib'd, or dram'd, or frolick'd, or bought, or coax'd, or threaten'd out of your Birthright.

You, especially, my Fellow-Citizens, ought to be above accepting any Consideration for your Voices, not only from a Consciousness of your native and political Dignity; but also from a Sense of Gratitude, one of the most amiable of Virtues. Your Representatives have, generally, serv'd you gratis: That Time which they might have gainfully employed in their private Business, they have generously devoted to you and their Country; in planning your Laws; consulting your Welfare, and advancing your Happiness. 'Twas, therefore, unreasonable, unmanly, ungrateful, to load them with the additional Expence of popular Festivity, and costly Revels.

I wou'd not be understood by any Thing before advanc'd, that I thought it possible for any Part of his Majesty's Dominions to be totally bereft of their Liberty, either by Corruption in Elections, or the Oppression of Governors, since we may resort for Redress to the Fountain of Justice, before whom every such Attempt must be blasted, and the wicked Author meet with the Vengeance due to his Crimes. But the Miseries of this and a neighbouring Province, under the wild and stormy Administration of *Coot* and *Cornbury, Campbell* and *Carteret*,[7] are sufficient Proofs of the Folly of suffering ourselves to be reduced to the Necessity of appealing to our Sovereign, while we can preserve our Privileges without so difficult an Application.

Nor would I be understood to insinuate, that our former Members, who have *treated* the People either before or after an Election, intended to bribe them. I am confident it would be an injurious Reflection on their Characters. As the Practice had obtained the Sanction of Custom, they might incautiously, have slid into it, meerly for the Sake of following the Mode. Nay, they might have done it to avoid the Reputation of avaricious, for not rivalling the Liberality and Expence of their Predecessors: But by whatever Means they were surpriz'd into an Action so pregnant with Mischief, 'tis humbly to be hop'd that none of our future Candidates will imitate so pernicious an Example. On the Contrary, 'tis the Wish of every Lover of his Country, that they adopt the Conduct of a late Member, whose Name, had I the Liberty to mention it, should, on this Occasion, be remembered with suitable Applause. This elevated Spirit, disdaining to owe his Election to the Distribution of his Largesses, or the Solicitations of Interest, but solely to the free and uninfluenc'd Voice of his Country; with a noble Singularity, burst the Fetters of Custom, and instead of squandering his Money in debauching his Fellow-Subjects, charitably delivered it to the Overseers of the Poor for more valuable Purposes. Thus, instead of being stung with uneasy Reflections for corrupting his Countrymen, he advanced into Dignity, with the glorious Satisfaction of relieving the Miserable, of raising the drooping Head of Poverty, and infusing Joy and Transport into the Bosom of the wailing Widow, and the helpless Orphan.   Z.

1. The "Fifth Satire" of Persius.

2. Crafty or cunning.

3. Colonial New York's electorate was relatively broadly based, and popular participation in elections was fairly widespread. Despite "influence" exerted by wealthy landholders, the voters exercised a degree of political independence which candidates recognized by sometimes furious electioneering that included the dispensation of beer, brandy, and beef, door-to-door solicitation, and press broadsides. See Milton M. Klein, "Democracy and Politics in Colonial New York," *New York History*, XL (1959), 221–246; and Nicholas Varga, "Election Procedures and Practices in Colonial New York," *ibid.*, XLI (1960), 249–277.

4. "These trifles will lead to serious mischief." Horace, *Ars Poetica*, 451–452.

5. Paul de Rapin (1661–1725), author of the popular *History of England*, which appeared in French beginning in 1723 and in translation, 1726–1731. "Rapin . . . in my opinion . . . carries the Palm among the writers of our Story, and wants nothing but a reduction of his Enormous Bulk to about half the Present Size, and to have his Language a little enlivened . . . , to render him an inestimable Treasure of knowledge." (Livingston to Welles, August 18, 1759, JFP, Yale.) When Smollett's *History of England* appeared in 1757, Livingston advised his law clerks that it ranked with Rapin "for the English History." ("Some Directions relating to the Study of the Law," in Livingston's *Lawyer's Book of Precedents*, pp. 139–142, New York State Library, Albany.)

6. In the fable, "The Cock and the Jewel," the cock scratches up a jewel which he discards for a grain of more familiar barley, covering his ignorance by remarking contemptuously that his taste runs in quite another direction.

7. Four unpopular governors: Richard Coote, Earl of Bellomont, governed New York from 1698 to 1701; Edward Hyde, Viscount Cornbury, served in the same capacity from 1702 to 1708. Philip Carteret was New Jersey's first chief executive, 1665–1682; Lord Neill Campbell administered the province for a short time between 1686 and 1687.

Number XXXIII

THURSDAY, JULY 12, 1753

A *Discant on the Origin, Nature, Use and Abuse of* Civil Government

Disce ———————
——————*Quem te Deus esse,*
Jussit et humana qua parte locatus es in re.[1] PERS. *Sat.*

NOTHING can be a greater Proof of the Wisdom and Prudence of the Civil Magistrate, than an Exertion of his Authority, consistent with its original Intention. On the Contrary, every improper Step in the Execution of his public Duties, is a strong Indication of his Ignorance of civil Economy: After the many Examples of the natural Effects of good or mal-Administration, with which Antiquity abounded; modern Rulers could find no Room to deviate from the Rulers of true Government, were Examples alone sufficient to direct them. In the Field of Nature, almost every Phenomenon that presents itself to the Philosopher, passes equally under the Observation of any Man that has the Use of his Senses: But with this Difference, the former by the Exercise of his Reason, investigates the Causes, discovers the Natures, and traces the Design and Tendency of those natural Appearances; while the latter contents himself with a bare Sensibility of their having occurred. The Physician, thro' his Acquaintance with the Constitution of the animal Nature of Man, sees every Disorder to which his Patient is subject: His Knowledge of the various and different Properties of the several Parts of the vegetable Creation, furnishes him with proper Remedies for those Disorders, while the Patient, by his own unhappy Feeling, is barely convinced that he is subject to Sickness and Mortality, without being able to dissipate the former, or prolong the Event of the latter. Thus it is in civil Polity. Examples alone can never teach the Magistrate the Rules of true Government, nor lay open to him the Basis upon which a well-regulated Community should be founded. Does he turn his Attention to the Monuments of ancient History, he beholds a thousand exemplary Facts crowding in upon his Mind, attended with Circumstances sufficient to enamour him with their Beauty, or terrify him with their Deformity. He sees that a NERO, a CALIGULA, were Monsters equally formidable to themselves and to their Subjects; while TRAJAN could taste the Sweets of real Felicity, in being the Father of his Country, and a Lover of Mankind. But if we consider those different Springs from which good or bad Actions flow; the different Principles, Prejudices, Passions and Interests, that variously influence every civil Event, it will appear undeniably evident, that the Force of Example can never teach a Ruler the Methods of just Administration. He must carry his Inquiries much higher, view Government in its first Rise, trace Communities back to their Original, and acquaint himself with the formal Reasons of Society. Such Investigations as these, will convince him, that Communities were formed not for the Advantage of one Man, but for the Good of the whole Body: That Government was instituted, not to give the Ruler a Power of reigning despotically over the Subject, but to preserve and promote the true Interest and Happiness of both: Thus he will learn, that while he acts agreable to the true End of his Institution, he justly merits the Love and Obedience of his Subjects, and that he cannot deviate from it, without involving both in Misery; and must consequently, forfeit his Right of Government. Would he grow wise by Example, he must view Facts not only as having happened; he must investigate the Causes whence they sprung, discover the Motives upon which former Rulers have acted, the Passions and Vices to which they were subject, and the Principles of Virtue whereby they were influenced. Furnished with this important Stock of Knowledge, he will be enabled to determine what Qualifications are expedient to form the true Character of a just and wise Ruler, and what Acts are necessary to promote the real Happiness of a People. But should we suppose him to be influenced solely by Observation of the Event of Things, without adverting to their Causes, he must be continually liable to err, even when he most imagines himself right. The Passions and Prejudices of human Nature, represent Objects to our Sight in so deceptive and flattering a View, that the very Means he would employ to procure the Welfare of his Subjects, might, perhaps, inevitably draw after them public Misery and Oppression. The Character of such a Magistrate contains not the least Ingredient of Virtue; the whole Composition is Vice of the blackest Hue.

Ignorance, tho' in many Instances pardonable in the Subject, is absolutely criminal in the Ruler; for no one has a Right to govern but he that is wise. CHARLES I paid his Head as a Tribute to his Ignorance: Had he ruled with Wisdom, and consequently with Moderation, his Reign might have been long and prosperous. His Ignorance of civil Government threw the Nation into such Tumults and Convulsions, that nothing less than the Deprivation of his Royalty could restore it to its Original Peace and Tranquility: He was too weak for a King, too powerful for a Subject, and therefore the Nation, very prudently, put an End to his Administration, which he had forfeited by his Crimes. But how exactly have we copied the Behaviour of the *Romish* Church, by inserting his Name in *red* Letters in our Kalender. *Her* Martyrs and Saints are famous for their Ignorance and Bigotry: *Our* royal Saint and Martyr did, by the same divine Qualities, entitle himself to Canonization. Yet in this Character he may be of some Service to us, which had he liv'd, we should never have experienced. His Anniversary may serve as a continual Warning to future Princes, and teach them, that while our Nation preserves its native Principles of Liberty, a Crown can never rescue its iniquitous Possessor from that Punishment which his Crimes may justly demerit.

This kind of Reasoning, may, perhaps, incur from one Quarter, the Character of civil Libertinism. But I am far from being under any Solicitude or Concern at Reflections of that Sort. Men of true Principles would rather return to a State of primitive Freedom, in which every Man has a Right to be his own Carver,[2] than be the Slaves of the greatest Monarch, or even suffer under the most unlimited Democracy in the Universe. It is true, that Society is the most eligible State in which Man can exist; nor can it also be denied, that Government is absolutely necessary for the

Happiness of Society. But still, it will appear to every one who is not bigoted to the slavish Doctrines of *passive Obedience* and *Non-Resistance,* to be the height of Madness, to purchase the Advantages of Society, by giving up all our Title to Liberty. Government, at best, is a Burden, tho' a necessary one. Had Man been wise from his Creation, he would always have been free. We might have enjoyed the Gifts of liberal Nature, unmolested, unrestrained. It is the Depravity of Mankind, that has necessarily introduced Government; and so great is this Depravity, that without it, we could scarcely subsist: Yet who does not see, that our Nature would teach us to live void of that Restraint, could we receive all the Advantages arising from a Subjection of this Kind, or greater, in a State of absolute Liberty and Independence? Who can deny, that we have ceded a Part of our original Freedom, to secure to us the rest, together with the other Blessings of Life? Without this Prospect, it is plain, no Man would ever subject himself to the Dominion and Rule of another. And therefore, tho' Government is necessary to our Well-being, it must be such as is consistent with it.

My Opinion might, perhaps, be expected, relating to the different Kinds of Government, of which, at present, I shall say no more than that a Compound of Monarchy, Aristocracy and Democracy, such as is the English Constitution, is infinitely the best. But as the most robust and durable Frame of animal Nature, is incapable of withstanding the incessant Shocks of Debauchery and Intemperance, so the best devised civil Constitution, is subject to Corruption and Decay, thro' the Pride, Ambition, and Avarice of those in whose Care it is lodged. While our Rulers make the Happiness of the Subject, the Standard of their public Acts, their Administration must be unavoidably productive of the most abundant Blessings to Mankind. But if Passion and private Interest be the only Principles upon which they act, what can the unhappy People expect, but Oppression, Poverty and Ruin? These different Principles are the two grand Causes of the opposite Effects of public Administration; the former will always be attended with public Profit and Advantage, the latter must end in the Ruin of a Community. A Difference of this Kind arises, not always from the different Forms of Government, but often from the proper Use or Abuse of the same Kind of Government: For tho' that Constitution is best which most securely guards the Rights of the Subject, yet none can be so restrictive upon the Ruler, as to deprive him of all Power of oppressing the People. The very Notion of Government, supposes in some Person or other, a Right to decree and execute Justice; and therefore this Power may be well or ill applied, as such Person may be inclined to act, either upon public Motives, or Views of Self-Interest. Deprive the Ruler of this discretionary Power, you destroy the Government; grant it to him, and your Liberties are at best precarious. The only Conclusion that can be drawn from hence is, that a People should be careful of yielding too much of their original Power, even to the most just Ruler, and always retain the Privilege of degrading him whenever he acts in Contradiction to the Design of his Institution.

That the same Government may be productive of very different and even opposite Effects, will evidently appear to any one who has the slightest Acquaintance with the Roman History. After the Change of Government wrought by the Usurpation of *Julius Cæsar*, the Emperors were, in Fact, vested with absolute Power: And tho' the Commons retained some small Shadow of their pristine Liberty, yet at every Appearance of the Legions, who were entirely under the Command of the Emperor, they were dispersed, like the Shades of Night by the Splendor of the rising Sun. In this Situation, the People were entirely subject to the Will of their *Cæsars*; they had given up to them so much of their original Power, that they had not enough left to secure themselves against Slavery and Oppression. When their Ruler found his Happiness in the Prosperity of his People, they enjoyed the Sweets of Liberty; but no sooner did his Views center in the Pursuit of his own Interest, and the Gratification of his private Passions, than they were reduced to the wretched Condition of Slaves.

It would, indeed, be unreasonable to expect, that by elevating the Magistrate above the common Level of his fellow Creatures, he should be deprived of those Passions which constitute a Part of his Nature. Far from desiring this, as they are necessary in private Life to stimulate Man to Action, they are much more so in public Stations, where the Ruler's Duty requires the utmost Efforts of human Nature. He should neither be dispassionate, nor disinterested, but should make his Passions and Interest center in the Happiness of his People: Let him soar upon the Wings of Ambition, but let the State mount with him the Summit of real Grandeur: Is his Courage matchless and undaunted, it should be exercised with Wisdom in the Defence of his Country: Is he armed with Power, let it be exerted in executing Vengeance against the Enemies of the State: Is his Nature generous and benevolent; it should deluge down Favours and Blessings upon his Subjects: In short, as he is the Vicegerent of Heaven, let his Administration bear all possible Resemblance to the Government of the supreme Ruler of the Universe.

From what has hitherto been advanced, I am evidently far from encouraging a Spirit of unbounded Licentiousness in the People: It is, I hope, a Charge that never will be laid against me. I have already enforced the Necessity of civil Government, and preferred the English Constitution as the most eligible in Nature. Nor do I want Reason to convince me, that a due Obedience of the Subject, is absolutely requisite under a Government like ours, or that Libertinism unrestrained, has a natural Tendency to destroy it. Let us be content with that Portion of our natural Liberty, which we thought proper to retain at the original Formation of the Community, neither encroaching on the Prerogative of the civil Magistrate, nor suffering our indisputable Rights to be invaded. Let us watchfully observe the Actions of the most just and temperate Ruler, and vigilantly guard against the Attacks of lawless and arbitrary Sway: But let us still remember, that as the Magistrate is cloathed with Power for the Security of the Subject, the People cannot strip him of his Authority, without reducing themselves to their original Independency, the most joyless uncomfortable State in which human Nature can possibly exist.[3]   B.

1. "Learn . . . what part God has ordered you to play and at what point on the human [scene] you have been placed." Persius, *Satires*, III, 72.
2. I.e., the maker or carver of his own fortune.
3. Livingston's vigorous pronouncement of the Lockean philosophy of

government in Nos. IV and XXXIII (and later in Nos. XXXVI–XXXIX) was not new on the American scene in 1752–1753. John Wise had expounded the social contract theory of the origin of government in 1717 in his *Vindication of the Government of New-England Churches*, and Jonathan Mayhew had preached a spirited sermon against the doctrine of non-resistance in 1750; but both of these clergymen developed their arguments in a religious context. Of the two, Mayhew had the more fully developed philosophy of government: but he saw the "great end of government" as first, the glory of God, and second, "the good of man"; and he justified resistance to tyrannical monarchs on the ground that they ceased thereby to be "ministers of God" by "enjoin[ing] things that are inconsistent with the commands of God." To Livingston, on the other hand, the end of government was solely the preservation of the liberty and happiness of the subject; and resistance to arbitrary rulers was justified on legal not religious grounds: they had broken their contract, abdicated their thrones, and placed themselves in the position of private persons. Livingston's essay, then, appears to be the first public expression in the colonies of the right of resistance that was rooted exclusively in a natural rights philosophy and expounded within a purely secular and legalistic framework. Certainly it was one of the clearest and most forceful assertions of the Lockean theory of government. On Wise and Mayhew, see Max Savelle, *Seeds of Liberty* (New York, 1948), pp. 309–311; Clinton Rossiter, *Seedtime of the Republic* (New York, 1953), chaps. 8 and 9; Alice M. Baldwin, *The New England Clergy and the American Revolution* (New York, reprinted 1958), pp. 28–30, 44–45.

Number XXXIV

THURSDAY, JULY 19, 1753

Of the Veneration and Contempt of the Clergy [1]

They would request us to endure still the Rustling of their silken Cassocks; and that we would burst our Midriffs, rather than laugh to see them under Sail in all their Lawn and Sarcenet, their Shrouds and Tackle. MILTON [2]

THAT Mankind are extremely apt to place Religion in being ridden by Priests, is attested by the universal Voice of History; and that being priest-ridden, is worse than having no Religion at all, is as evident as that the entertaining dishonourable Thoughts of the Divine Being, is worse than the disbelieving his Existence. It is therefore of the greatest Importance to the Cause of Religion, as well as the Happiness of Society, to place aright that Redundance of Respect which is promiscuously paid to the most worthless, and the most excellent of the ministerial Function.

To contemn the Priesthood itself, for the Wickedness of those who dishonour it, is as unreasonable as to insult a good Man, because his Grand Mother was a Strumpet. The Order is a valuable Institution while it is kept within due Bounds, and confined to instructing instead of riding the Laity. An indiscriminate Contempt of Ecclesiastics, is, therefore, both absurd and immoral.

But if, on the Contrary, instead of regarding them in the Light of Spiritual Teachers, and paying them Reverence in proportion to their Merit, we fall down to every black Petticoat or sweeping Cloak that comes in our Way, we are guilty of Idolatry; and instead of worshiping GOD, run the Hazard of adoring Idols, worse than any golden Calf that ever was deifyed in *Palestine*.

Whether, a general indiscriminate Contempt or Veneration of the Clergy is like to prove most prejudicial to Religion, is a Question not easy to decide: And while it remains doubtful, it must be owned, that too great an Influence from that Quarter, may be as dangerous as no Influence at all. Nay, if we argue from Experience it is evident, that the Clergy, even in Christian Countries, have done more Mischief than Good. For this Assertion I appeal to the Testimony of ecclesiastical History. It follows, therefore, that an inordinate Veneration for Priests, and reposing an implicit Faith in their Documents, may be least, be as destructive of Religion as the most general Contempt. A Man of Sense and Impartiality, will, however, preserve the golden Mean. As he is sensible on the one Hand, that a Disrespect for the Order itself, may be attended, with the pernicious Effect of disregarding their most salubrious Instructions: So is he on the other Hand convinced, that a reverential Awe for every Creature habited in black, and swallowing the greatest Nonsense only because he utters it, is to raise the enormous Fabrick of Priestcraft on the Ruins of Religion. But the Bulk of Mankind are apt to run into the latter Extreme. The World has always paid Homage to one Idol or another. Priests, Monkeys, Dogs, Onions, Crocodiles, Serpents, nor even Devils, have escaped the popular Adoration. Nor is it much to be wondered at, that the unenlightened Pagans, should so naturally slide from the Worship of a Monkey into that of a Priest. Upon the Death of the God *Apis*, the *Egyptians* looked out for a Calf that most resembled him.

A Priest with an odd Dress and demure Countenance, will attract the Regard of a whole Parish, as a Conjurer with his *Hocus Pocus*, sets a Multitude agape. A Number of unintelligible Sounds, pronounc'd with a devout Phiz, and attended with violent Gesture and Distortion of Face, astonishes the Ignorant, and excites the profoundest Admiration of the *holy Man of GOD*.

Above one-half of Mankind, are struck with the exterior Garb. A worthless Fellow may wear a red or a blue Coat to Eternity, without being esteemed more knowing or virtuous; but let him cover his Body with black Crape of a particular Cut, and from a Cheat or Debaucheé, he is transform'd into an Angel. A *romish* Priest equipp'd in his Canonicals, and muttering his Gibberish inspires a whole Audience with Reverence. And yet a well-tutor'd Ape or Baboon accouter'd in the same Habiliments, would both out-mimic and out-mutter the Parson.

No Man on Earth has a greater Regard for the virtuous Clergy than myself.[3] But am I to adore a Man's Impudence out of Complaisance to his Function. Or do I affront the Order, by despising him whose Conduct and Manners, disgrace and vilify it? No greater Honour can be paid to the Priesthood, than by exposing those who are its Reproach and Blemish, nor is there a more successful Method to propagate the benevolent Religion of JESUS, than to divest it of all the Villainy and Fustian with which it has been disgraced and disfigured, by designing and ambitious Ecclesiastics.

There is not a more lovely Character in Nature, than that of a good Clergyman. He is the Glory and Ornament of Society; and forever rever'd be his Name, who goes into Orders for the Reformation of Mankind; and makes the Promotion of Religion, and Christian Morals, the Business of his Life. Scarce too much Respect can be paid to so amiable a Character, and so greatly conducive to the Felicity of Man, considered either in a religious or political View. In a moral Consideration, he smooths and facilitates our Journey to Heaven; assists our pious Researches in the sacred Writings, exalts our Affections above the Gratifications of animal Nature; enlightens our Understandings, and lends his Aid to make us more than Conquerors over our spiritual Adversaries. He, at the same Time represents the Deity as a consuming Fire to the incorrigible Sinner, and reconcilable to a penitent World, by the Mediation of his Son; and unfolds the sublime and luminous Plan of the Redemption of Man. In a political Regard, he is instead of twenty Magistrates, who can only deter from Vice by the Punishment of the Criminal: Whereas he, by inculcating internal Purity of Heart, may prevent the Necessity of Punishment. Accordingly such a Man will never have Reason to complain of the Want of Respect: The World will be ready to idolize him. But when a little airy Coxcomb, too lazy to work, and too proud to beg, without Learning or Virtue, jumps into Commission with a Lye in his Mouth, that he is mov'd by the Holy Ghost, when his highest Aim is a fat Living, nor feels any other Motion than that of an empty Stomach; when such a one, I say, exacts our Obeisance whether we will or not, what can he expect but universal Contempt for his Effrontery? Is Mankind obliged to fall prostrate and worship a black Coat, tho' it covers nothing but Guilt and Deformity? Or is a silly half-witted Fop, or gloomy Pedant, instantaneously inspired with Grace and Knowledge by the Touch of a Bishop, or the Imposition of a Set of Presbyters? And yet what is more common than to see such a raw illiterate Prig, who before he was commissioned to utter his Nonsense for the Word of God, would not have been admitted into Gentlemen's Company, immediately on his Ordination, strut like an Emperor, or demand the Respect due to a Minister of State?

These reverend Gentlemen have a very wicked Trick of confounding the Words *Religion* and *Clergy*: Two Words that have no Manner of Connection, either in Sound or (for the most Part) in Sense. By Virtue of this odd heterogeneous Jumble, a Man can neither examine into their Pretensions, nor expose their Encroachments, but he inclines to Infidelity, and aims obliquely at Religion. Christianity itself is pretended to be affected, and frequently the whole Constitution lugg'd into the Quarrel. But however glib so strange a Position may go down in Popish Countries, it is a very disagreeable Potion to a Protestant Stomach. For my Part I always understood that Religion existed long before the Clergy; and that the Clergy may exist without Religion, I would even venture to leave to a Convocation.

Another Artifice of theirs is the Use of certain Words of a very solemn and pompous Sound, but of dubious and uncertain Signification. If, for Instance, by being the Lord's Ambassadors, and commissioned from Heaven, they mean, that a Number of Men reposing Confidence in their Integrity and Learning, have contracted with them for a valuable Consideration, to deliver weekly Lectures on Religion, and perform other Duties stipulated in the Agreement; their Meaning is very just, tho' not expressed in the properest Manner. For I distinguish between the Office and the Officer; the first is divine, and intended by Christ to be continued in his Church to the End of the World; but that there is any Divinity in the Appointment and Person of the Officer, I absolutely deny. So that, if they intend any Thing farther, every Man has a Right either to demand a Sight of their Commission, or to question their Honesty. Thus, again, if by being our spiritual Overseers, they understand an Authority derived from the People, of laying their Sense of Scripture before their Hearers, and submiting it to their Judgment and Examination, their Overseership is mighty plain and intelligible. But if by this sonorous Phrase they intend a Right of obtruding upon them Absurdity and Jargon, it is very paradoxical and mysterious. Thus also to a Man who takes his Religion from his Bible, the Words *spiritual Dominion* and *ecclesiastical Lordships*, have as odd a Sound as the Terms, *temporal Heaven* and *political Christianity.*

It is impossible for a Clergyman who conducts himself agreeable to his Function, as delivered in holy Writ, to miss of the Reverence due to his Character. But if a Priest, in Defiance of all the Humility and Condescention taught him by his divine Master, will preposterously assume an Air of Arrogance, and aspire to temporal Domination, which his Lord himself utterly disclaimed, he deserves the universal Contempt of all serious and intelligent Beings. But, that Religion must naturally suffer by such Contempt, is much what as intelligible, as that the Law is endangered, and the Constitution shaken, by laying a knavish Attorney by the Heels.

I have the highest Respect for the Function of a Clergyman. But if he is wicked or impudent, how can I help despising him? To challenge my Esteem on Account of his Dress, when himself is a Dunce or a Libertine, (which two Distinctions comprehend above half of the Cloth) is desiring me to commit downright Idolatry. I cannot reverse the Order of Nature, and discern Beauty in Deformity; or call Discord, Harmony. There is no Virtue in a twisted Rose, nor any Grace or Sanctity in a blue Coat with a black Cape. A ministerial Band is no greater Sign of a good Heart, than a secular Cravat; nor hath a black Petticoat more Learning than a scarlet Breeches. How then can I worship such a meer *Priapus,*[4] who, instead of reforming the World, shews no Sign of Reformation in himself? To expect our Homage without a suitable Merit, is either insulting our Understandings, or proclaiming our Bondage.

Another Pretence of these Gentlemen, whenever they are surprized in a Piece of Iniquity, is, that they are Flesh and Blood as well as others. For my Part, I am so far from denying them their full Share of Flesh and Blood, that I know several of them who are nothing else. But their Inference is inconsequent. Their having so great a Proportion of Flesh and Blood, may perhaps be a good Reason for compassionating their Frailties, but not for insisting on the same Respect, with those who have a little reduced their corporeal Redundances, and can boast some spiritual Graces amidst all their Carnality. But while they are totally corrupt, and voluptuous themselves, what Right have they to lord it over others, under Pretence of greater Sanctity? Pray let them shake off their Subjection to Satan, before they attempt to enslave their fellow Creatures. Why should they hector and domineer over the Laity, when themselves are in Bondage to Sin? Or can Mankind conceive it an Honour, to become the Servants of the Servants of the Devil?

The Clergy of all Men in World, stand the best Chance of being respected, and will never be despised unless they deserve it. In pagan Countries they have the making, the unmaking, the irritating, and the placating of their wooden and marble Divinities. In the Romish Church they are possessed of the Keys of Heaven, and can admit or exclude at Pleasure. Amongst Protestants indeed, their Authority is not quite so extensive; but even there some of them claim the Power of Absolution, tho' among Men of Sense, none gain any Credit, except those who, by turning Doctors, can *bind* and *loose*, not by an Interest with Heaven, but by plain Astringents and Laxatives. Their Empire, however, is secured by other Methods. We imbibe a Respect for them in our very Infancy. A good Grand-Mamma, will as soon forget to hear little Master's Prayers or Catechise, as her Injunctions that he must make a very low Bow to the Parson. We naturally conclude they must needs be very wise and holy, who document a thousand Hearers at a Time, without being contradicted by one, for surely the Teacher must be more knowing than the Pupil. Nor do these our infantile Prejudices always wear off with our riper Years. They often become strengthened by Habit, and continue to warp the Judgment to the End of our Lives.[5]   Z.

1. Livingston had given fair warning of his irreverence for the clergy three years earlier: As Englishmen, "We are equally at Liberty to lash the Clergy and Laity; and if we meet with a reverend Rogue, he has nothing but impotent Rage to combat our Reprehensions." *A Letter to the Freemen and Freeholders . . . of New-York* (New York, 1750), p. 3. Though published anonymously, contemporaries recognized the author as "W——L——."

2. *Of Reformation*, Book II.

3. Livingston was not dissembling. His dearest friend, Noah Welles, was minister of the Congregational Church, Stamford, Connecticut; many of his former classmates were also ministers; and as a close friend of the Rev. Aaron Burr, president of the College of New Jersey, he was the family's choice as eulogist at Burr's funeral, at which Livingston paid tribute to clergymen who represented "religion as the offspring of light, and the parent of liberty." *A Funeral E[u]logium on the Reverend Mr. Aaron Burr. . . .* (New York, 1757; Boston ed., 1758), p. 12.

4. The Greek god of procreation, usually represented as very ugly.

5. Despite the anguished retorts from Anglican clergymen which this number provoked, Livingston did not retreat an inch. He repeated the charges the next year: ". . . tho' the order is of divine institution, and therefore to be greatly revered; many of its members are the most abandoned of the species, and therefore to be equally abhorred"; and "the plain and amiable religion of Christ, hath by the voluminous rubbish and pious villainy of ecclesiastics been so mangled, disfigured and contaminated, that it is at present no where to be found pure and genuine, save only in the volume of inspiration itself." (*Independent Reflector, Preface*, pp. 3–4.) At the same time, he continued to pay his respects to "the Clergy of *real Piety*" while reiterating his disdain for "those whose *Religion* is only *external.*" (*Occasional Reverberator*, No. II, September 14, 1753).

Number XXXV

THURSDAY, JULY 26, 1753

Of Abuses in the Practice of the LAW [1]

> —— *Which dark insidious Men,*
> *Have added, cumb'rous, to perplex the Truth,*
> *And lengthen simple Justice into Trade.*   THOMSON [2]

As no civil Society can exist without Laws, nor every Individual be so well acquainted with them, as he who devotes his Life to the Study and Practice, it is evident that the Profession must be necessary and honourable. There is not a more amiable or refulgent Character than that of a Lawyer of Capacity and Honour: He is a kind of Star in the Firmament of the Common Wealth, and his House as it were an Oracle to the whole Country around him. His Office is to support the State by maintaining the Laws upon which it is founded, to advance the Cause of Righteousness, and defend the Innocent; to detect the Villain, *and break in Pieces the Oppressor.* The genuine Tendency of the Science that employs his Thoughts, is to enamour him with Justice, and render him an implacable Enemy to Fraud and Dishonesty. To every such a Lawyer, we may apply what the incomparable Author of the Motto of my Paper does to My Lord TALBOT.[3]

> *In him* Astrea *to this dim Abode,*
> *Of ever-wandering Men, returned again:*
> *To bless them his Delight, to bring them back,*
> *From thorny Error, from unjoyous Wrong,*
> *Into the Paths of kind primeval Faith,*
> *Of Happiness and Justice. All his Parts,*
> *His Virtues all, collected, sought the Good*
> *Of human Kind,* ——

But glorious and praise-worthy as such a Character must be thought, detestable and infamous is the Pettifogger. To him is to be imputed that Prejudice against the Profession which so generally and unjustly prevails. Unjustly, I say: For shall he whose Life is spent in the Service of his Country, be loaded with that Infamy which another deserves? Shall the Profession be condemned, because Rogues have perverted it, whose Conduct in such Perversion, is repugnant to its Precepts, and punishable by its Penalties? With equal Reason might we reject the Purity of Christianity, because Bigotry, Priestcraft, and Superstition have introduced Scenes of unexampled Wickedness, and deluged the World with human Blood. As well might we proscribe the skillful and honest Physician, because the Practice is disgraced by ignorant Quacks and Pretenders. A Pettifogger is one of the most mischievous Pests of Society: His Characteristics are, Ignorance, Artifice and Chicane: He hunts for Employment, and foments Disputes: To encompass his Aims, he stoops to the lowest Offices, and wades thro' the thickest Dirt of Extortion, Injustice and Corruption: Numberless are his Artifices: Hypocrisy and Falsehood his main Instruments; and an insatiable Avarice the grand Spring, the *primum Mobile*[4] of all his Enterprizes. The Author of the following Letter, who I am proud to call one of my most useful Correspondents, points out some Abuses in the Profession of the Law, and chiefly aims at the Character I have inveighed against. I shall lay it before the Reader, and conclude with some Reflections to which it gave Rise.

To the INDEPENDENT REFLECTOR

SIR,

I AM one of those who are not used to Composition, and should therefore never have ventured to appear in Print, had it not been for the inspiriting Encouragement that my Productions were to undergo your impartial Refinements. But however incapable of the Ornaments of Language, or the Flowers of Rhetorick, I boast a Soul inflamed with unextinguishable Ardor for the Service of my Country; and to contribute towards the Reformation of its Abuses, would be my highest Ambition and Glory. That we labour under a lamentable Variety of public Grievances, is equally indisputable and melancholy. But the Customariness of the Thing hath lull'd us into a Kind of mental Lethargy, and we are supine under our Distresses, for no better Reason than because we have long been distressed. 'Tis on you, Mr. *Reflector*, that the public Eye is in a great Measure fixed, as on a Writer, unaw'd and independent, and one who, 'tis presum'd, will neither suffer the Sanction of Time, nor the Reverence claimed by Custom to suppress that intrepid Spirit, nor stifle that patriot Warmth which have hitherto animated your Speculations.

Long have I look'd around me with the utmost Impatience for some dauntless and incorruptible Genius, who would scorn to stoop to a Sect or Party, but ascend aloft on the Wings of public Spirit; and after having taken a wide Survey of the Vices and Follies of his Country, distribute with unsparing Hand, his salutary Reproofs. If you are the Man, I bid you thrice welcome, and will in my humbler Sphere, assist your generous Labours, by inclosing you for the present a few Hints, which if you judge worthy your Notice, you may depend on being hereafter furnished with larger Supplies. For the present, indulge me in a few Animadversions on the Conduct of some of our Attornies. Our Supreme Court, to the universal Joy of the Province, is adorned with Judges of known Integrity, and unquestionable Skill. Many of our Practisers are also Gentlemen of eminent Capacity, and unsullied Reputations. Men who have restored the Profession, formerly by the Baseness of Pettifoggers profan'd and dishonour'd, to its original Dignity and Grandeur. But not a small Number of the lower Class call aloud for the Chastisements of your Pen. Fear not, Mr. *Reflector*, to disturb their wicked Repose, tho' they be like a Nest of Hornets. Let them know as with the Voice of Thunder, that we apply to them in Confidence of their Probity, and are even profuse in our Largesses to attach them to our Interest. How detestable then their dilatory Wiles! How abominable their Arts to procrastinate Business, and obstruct the Recovery of our Rights! What a horrid Perversion of Law, which is framed for our Relief, and to procure us speedy Justice?

By Reason of the quick Rotation of the Terms in the Mayor's Court,[5] most Causes may be decided in three or four Months, and yet how often are they kept depending above a Year? This is the greater Grievance, as that Court was instituted for the Dispatch and Acceleration of Business. The Supreme Court has four Terms annually, and without special Pleadings, a Cause may be brought to issue in less than six Months, and tried the Term following. But far otherwise is the present Practice. An Action is often delayed two Years, and sometimes much longer. How repugnant this to the Spirit of the Law, which delights in expeditious Remedy! Such dilatory Attornies are therefore the Bane of Society, the Pest and Contagion of the Community, and ought to be hunted down like Beasts of Prey, that riot on the Spoils of honest Industry, and unletter'd Confidence. They postpone the Trial by a Thousand evasive Quirks, and indulge each other in their pernicious Delays. When the Client is at last bereft of all Patience, and the Lawyer cannot invent a fresh Excuse (which never happens till all Expedients are exhausted) he prepares for the Trial with regret and reluctance. But when the Day, the great and important Day, arrives, then and not till then, the sagacious Gentleman discovers a Necessity for submitting the Matter to Arbitration; for truly the Jurors are incompetent Judges of so intricate a Business, and Referees will admit as Evidence, what the Court, for want of strict legality, may reject. All this specious Harangue, the credulous Client swallows with an implicit Faith, and perhaps tips his imaginary Benefactor with another Pistole for his friendly Admonition. Not, *Sir*, that I would discourage the referring of Causes. So far from it, that I am convinced it is generally the most equitable Way of deciding the Controversy, and more satisfactory to both Parties.[6] What I am opposing is the Delay of Attornies till the Cause is ripe for Trial, and advising a Submission when they have swell'd the Costs to their *ne plus ultra*.[7] Thus of twenty Causes, in which Notice of Trial was actually given, and *Venires*[8] issued, I have known not above half a Dozen determined in Court. Mean and ungenerous Proceeding, to give it no harsher Epithet. Wou'd they serve their Clients with Fidelity and Honour, they might render their Practice beneficial to themselves, as well as of public Utility, by a quick Circulation of Business, and consulting the Dispatch of their Employers.

Part of these Delays is, nevertheless, to be ascribed to the Conduct of some Deputy Sheriffs. These Fellows frequently return a Writ, with a *non est*,[9] where the Defendant is known to walk the Streets every Day of his Life. To what the Procrastination of these Officers is to be ascribed, I will not pretend to determine. But it certainly gives Room for a very disadvantageous Construction, as it is incredible they should be willing to resign their Fees for serving the Process, without a valuable Consideration. But be the Reason what it will, it is certainly a mischievous Practice, and greatly injurious to the Plaintiff, as well as manifestly perversive of Justice.

I cannot pass by a Practice with which the Attornies in general are chargeable, I mean their Endeavour to puzzle and confound their Adversaries' Witness. Unless a Man rivals them in that Portion of Brass which is so conveniently placed on their Foreheads, it is impossible for him not to be non-plussed. One would indeed think it was their Office to suppress, instead of investigating the Truth, and that they conceived themselves under Obligations to their Clients, to patronize Falsehood and Delusion. Are they hired to defend Fraud and Injustice, or retained to vindicate the Lives and Properties of their fellow Subjects? For my Part, I entertain a more honourable Idea of the Function, than to believe a Lawyer obliged to maintain a desperate Cause at all Events. The Profession itself ought to be held in high

Veneration, and would never fail of meeting with Respect, was it not debased and prostituted by Pretenders and Pettifoggers.

Let them urge the Antiquity of Custom with all the Pomp of Eloquence, I will maintain against the whole Body of the Law, that any Attempt to puzzle an honest Witness with Questions foreign to the Purpose, till he is bewildered into inadvertent Contradictions, discovers more Front than Conscience, and greater Assurance than Love of Justice. But how unparallel'd the Effrontery, to urge to the Jury those very Contradictions into which he has drove the Witness by insidious Questions, as Arguments against his Veracity, and to invalidate his Testimony. Indeed, the aspersing a Man's Character in Court, because it may be done with Impunity, is so mean and ungentlemanlike a Practice, that I should not scruple to supply the Defect of the Law of the Land, by having Recourse to the Law of the Woods, and effect by the Oil of Hickory, what could not be obtained by the Verdict of my Peers.

Yours,

SHADRACH PLEBIANUS.

Nothing can be more reasonable and politic, than that where any Body of Men have so extensive an Influence upon the public Weal, as that of the Profession of the Law, the Community should have the highest Security imaginable, for the due Observance of their Duty. The Gentlemen of the long Robe are under the Obligation of an Oath for their just and upright Demeanour, and for Mal-Practice, obnoxious to the Law, which subjects them in some Cases to the Animadversions of the Court, and in others they are compellable to recompence the Party injured, in Damages. But with Submission to our Superiors, the Public ought, and may easily be still farther secured.

The Power of licensing Attornies is lodged with our Governors, who grant them upon Letters recommendatory from the Judges of those Courts, for the Practice of which the Candidate is to be licensed. As to many of the inferior Judges, I believe no one will say, that their Recommendation, justly considered, ought to have the least Weight, the Judges themselves, (such is the Infancy of our Country) understanding as little of the Law as any Yeoman in their Jurisdiction. I could wish their Ignorance was the only Thing they were chargeable with. But to the Infamy of the Guilty be it spoken, that our former Governors have so far been imposed upon, that in some Counties in particular, not only several of the meanest Wretches in them, appear at their Bar licensed Attornies; but others who do not, nor ever intended it, have been recommended to the Practice, only to free themselves from being elected into the Offices of Constable, Collector, and the like, when they have been incapable of discharging their Duty to the Public, in any superior Employment. Blessed Guardians such Judges of the Rights and Properties of the Subject! His Excellency in the License, makes a pompous Certificate of the Ability, Learning, and Integrity of him, whom every Man in the County knows to be unable, illiterate, and dishonest. A horrible Abuse, and most scandalous Prostitution of so useful an Office! An Office requiring not only eminent Abilities, but the most exemplary Probity! Nay, so extremely inattentive are we, to a Regulation in the Practice of the Law, that several Instances may be assigned of such as have acted, and now act as Attornies in several of our County Courts, without any Licence at all. A Degree of Arrogance and Assurance this, highly deserving the Penalty of the Law against Maintenance; and, considering its great Tendency to move Contentions among the People, encourage LawSuits, and endanger private Property, I cannot think it would redound to the Honour of our Inferior Court Judges, to recommend such Criminals to the Animadversions of a Grand Jury.

Had I the Honour of a Place in the House, I should think it my Duty to move for an Act to redress the Grievance against which I have complained. This might be compleatly effected by commissionating the Judges of the Supreme Court, to examine every Candidate for the Profession and Practice of the Law, in open Court, and without whose Approbation, he should be incapable of a License. It is not to be doubted, but that his present Excellency would heartily concur in such a Law, since he has hitherto granted no Licences to practise in that Court, but upon the Recommendation of its Judges. By this Means, the Honour of the Profession would be retrieved and preserved, and the good of the Public promoted; Without which, the former must sink into greater Contempt, and the latter, in Consequence of it, suffer no inconsiderable Diminution and Prejudice.[10]   A & Z.

ABUSES IN PRACTICE OF LAW

1. The immediate impetus for this essay appears to have been provided by an Anglican challenge for Livingston to dissect "Lawcraft" with the same scalpel already applied to "Priestcraft," warning that if the bar escaped the editor's attention, "People will think thou art a Lawyer thyself." (*New-York Mercury*, June 25, July 23, 1753.) Livingston required little prompting. He had written letters to the press on abuses in the legal apprenticeship system and on the indiscriminate licensing procedures for lawyers, as well as a satiric poem on the "unletter'd Blockheads" who were bringing the profession into public disrepute. *New-York Weekly Post-Boy*, August 19, 1745; *New-York Gazette*, February 18, 1751; *The Art of Pleading, In Imitation of Part of Horace's Art of Poetry* (New-York, 1751). See also Klein, "The Rise of the New York Bar," pp. 335–339.

2. *The Seasons: Winter*, slightly misquoted.

3. Charles Talbot, Baron of Hensol (1685–1737), Lord Chancellor of England (1733–1737), and patron of James Thomson. The extract is from Thomson's "To the Memory of the Right Honourable the Lord Talbot" (1737).

4. "Prime mover [i.e., motivation]."

5. The Mayor's Court was a court of petty civil jurisdiction. There was one in Albany and in New York City.

6. The practice of referring disputes to private arbitration was particularly common in New York, the Dutch having used this procedure extensively. The award of the arbitrators had the effect of a verdict by a jury. See Richard B. Morris, *Studies in the History of American Law* (New York, 1930), pp. 60–61; also Richard B. Morris, ed., *Select Cases of the Mayor's Court of New York City, 1674–1784* (Washington, D. C., 1935), pp. 43–44.

7. "Furthest limit."

8. Writs directing a sheriff to summon a jury.

9. "Not found."

10. Livingston's plea for a stricter licensing system was in vain. The legislature took no action to fix licensing requirements, and the governor continued to grant licenses upon the recommendations of the judges in the various courts. Because the county judges were themselves poorly trained, the men they recommended for admission to the bar were "of the meanest abilities." The caliber of licentiates in New York City remained fairly high because the Supreme Court since 1730 had required a seven-year clerkship for prospective lawyers of that court. Even these requirements seemed too unexacting to Livingston and some of his colleagues, who tried for several years to secure by unofficial measures what the legislature declined to do by statute. Livingston and Smith continued to complain that "the door of admission into the practice is too open" and that, as a consequence, the province was crowded with "Mountebank Lawyers." Livingston to James Stevenson, April 18, 1754, March 28, 1755, Letter Book A, 1754–1770, Livingston Papers, Massachusetts Historical Society; Smith, *History*, I, 316; Hamlin, *op. cit.*, pp. 35–40; Klein, "The Rise of the New York Bar," pp. 338, 356.

Number XXXVI

THURSDAY, AUGUST 2, 1753

The Absurdity of the civil Magistrate's interfering in Matters of Religion
PART I

Jura inventa metu injusti fateare necesse est,
Tempora si fastosque velis evolvere mundi.   Hor.[1]

Mankind being naturally free, and with respect to a Right of Dominion, upon a perfect Equality; it is absurd to suppose, that any Man, or Body of Men, would ever have consented to resign that Freedom, and Equality, by submitting to the Government and Controul of another, but for some Advantages they expected from such Submission. Nor would they have acted rationally in thus subjecting themselves from the Prospect of any Advantages unequivalent to their natural Liberty, voluntarily surrendered; because that would have been parting with a greater for a lesser Good, or an Alienation of an inestimable Jewel, without a valuable Consideration. It is therefore unreasonable to imagine they had less in View, than a Remedy for the Inconveniences that sprang from a State of Nature, in which, for want of a Judge, armed with proper Authority, to decide Controversies, the Weak were a perpetual Prey to the Powerful, who were under no other Restraint from violating the Possessions of their Neighbours, than the Dictates of Reason, which were seldom sufficiently regarded. It was therefore to avoid those Inconveniences that they entered into Society. Now these being only evitable by investing one or more with sufficient Authority, to preserve to every Individual, the undisturbed Enjoyment of his Acquisitions, and the Security of his Person; or, in other Words, to repel every unreasonable Attempt upon his Person or Fortune; Magistrates were appointed, and invested with the total Power of all the Constituents, subject to the Rules and Regulations agreed upon by the original Compact, for the Good of the Community, and the Ease and Tranquility of the People under their Government. This Tranquility and Advantage, consisting in defending every Member in the Possession of his legal Rights, (that is, of those Things which by the original Laws of the Society were to be personally his) against every illegal Invasion, or, which is the same Thing, in Opposition to all Violence contrary to those Laws; it follows, that while the Magistrate defends his Subjects in the peaceable Possession of their Rights, by punishing the Invader, *etc.* he acts in Character, and answers the Design of his Appointment: But when he interferes with Things foreign to that Business; as whether a Man will say his Prayers standing or kneeling, whether a plaited Surplice, or a sweeping Cloak be most Apostolic, or whether Pope *Joan* was a Man or a Woman, with other Points of equal Importance to the Interest of the Common-Wealth; he exceeds the Bounds of his Authority, and takes Cognizance of what was never submitted to his Jurisdiction. Nothing, therefore, but what is injurious to the Society, or some particular Member of it, can be the proper Object of civil Punishment; because, nothing else falls within the Design of forming the Society. For this, and this only, was the Magistrate invested with his Power, over the Persons who submitted themselves to him. But the religious Opinions and Speculations of the Subject, cannot be prejudicial to the Society, as a Society; nor to any particular Member of it; because such Opinions and Speculations are not injurious either to the Person or Possession of another: And all that is necessary to the Welfare of the Society, is, that no such Injury be committed. Matters of Religion relate to another World, and have nothing to do with the Interest of the State. The first resides in the Minds and Consciences of Men; the latter in the outward Peace and Prosperity of the Public. It is the Business of the civil Power, to see that the Common-Wealth suffer no Injury, whether it be attempted on a religious, or any other Pretence. But provided he hurt no Man, every Subject has a Right to be protected in the Exercise of the Liberty of thinking about Religion, as he judges proper, as well as of acting in Conformity thereto. Religious Opinions and Speculations come not therefore within the Design of cloathing the Magistrate with a Superiority over the Subject; nor are they proper Objects for the Exercise of his Authority. Neither did there arise any Inconveniences from such Opinions in a State of Nature, nor consequently could their Regulation or Restraint, be any Part of the Origin or Intention of entering into civil Society. And every Exertion of Power contrary to, or which was no Part of, the Design of creating the Magistrate, must of Necessity be Usurpation and Tyranny. It must be injurious and oppressive, and all his Decisions concerning Matters of Religion, are to be regarded as unauthoritative Adjudications. For surely it could never enter into the Heart of Man to submit his Judgment in Matters of Religion to his Ruler, not only because it is impossible for all his Subjects to concur with him in Opinion, but also because no Man, of any Religion at all, would reduce himself to the Necessity of worshipping God in a Manner he thought disagreable to him; which must often be the Case, if he is obliged to be of the Magistrate's Religion. From all which it clearly follows, that the civil Power hath no Jurisdiction over the Sentiments or Opinions of the Subject, till such Opinions break out into Actions prejudicial to the Community, and then it is not the Opinion, but the Action that is the Object of the Punishment.[2] For tho' a Man entertained such Opinions as would, if reduced to Practice, be dangerous to the Society, yet while they lie dormant in his Breast, they injure no Man: and if no Person is injured, no Crime is committed; and without a Crime, there can be no Room for Punishment. On the Contrary, should a Man's Sentiments be never so rational or (what is a more acceptable Phrase to some never so) orthodox, yet if he damaged others by his Actions, there is no Doubt of his deserving Punishment, with all his Orthodoxy about him.

And of this Opinion appears to have been the famous GALLIO, of whom St. LUKE makes such honourable mention in the Acts of the Apostles. The Jews it seems, not being able to maintain the Field against St. PAUL by Reason and Argument, very orthodoxly had recourse to the secular Arm, and indeed fell to downright Mobbing. The Apostle's dissenting from the established Synagogue was magnified into Sedition, and his preaching the Word of God represented as an atrocious Crime against the State. But GALLIO, a Man of Sense and Discretion, accurately distinguishes between political Offences and religious Opinions. He tells the Complainants, that if the Apostle had been guilty of a *civil* Injury, or Breach of the Law, he would take Cognizance of the Matter, and punish the Offence. But if the Controversy turn'd upon theological Speculations, about *Words* and *Actions*, Forms and Ceremonies, he had no Authority to interfere in the Case. "And when GALLIO (says the sacred Historian) was the Deputy of *Achaia*, the Jews made Insurrection with one accord against *Paul*, and brought him to the Judgment Seat: Saying, this Fellow persuadeth Men to worship God contrary to the Law. And when *Paul* was now about to open his Mouth, GALLIO said unto the Jews, if it were a Matter of Wrong, or wicked Lewdness, O ye Jews, Reason would that I should bear with you; But if it be a Question of Words and Names, and of your Law, look ye to it; FOR I WILL BE NO JUDGE of such Matters. And he drove them from the Judgment Seat." *Acts* xiii. 12, *etc.*[3]

Hence it appears, what little Foundation there is for calling in the secular Arm for the Support of Religion, or forcing the Conscience by *Pains and Penalties*.

Nor are the Advocates for religious Tyranny, greater Enemies to the Liberties of Mankind in general, than to the Repose of Princes in particular. For tho' the Spirits of Men may for some Time be broke and depressed, by an usurped Domination over their Judgments, yet will they sooner or later burst their Fetters, assert their Rights, and shake the Throne of their ruthless Oppressor. This was the Case of that unhappy Monarch, who, intoxicated with the Notion that he might lawfully and innocently do what Mischief and Wickedness he would, and had a Charter from GOD to resemble the *Devil*, usurped such an Authority over the Consciences of his Subjects, as cost him his Throne, and sent him to count his Beads in a Convent. The Truth is, Religion is not to be propagated by Violence: It was not originally established by Persecution, nor will Persecution ever be the proper

Means of defending it. Fully sensible of this was the great De-
liverer of the Nation, the glorious *King* WILLIAM, of *immortal
Memory*, when he declared, that "he would maintain and defend
the Church, but would hurt no Man for dissenting from it." Nor
can I forbear concluding this Paper with those beautiful Verses
which Mr. WALSH has put into the Mouth of that illustrious
Prince, when he introduces him sailing to *England*, on the god-
like Design of delivering us from *Popery and arbitrary Power*.[4]

> Firm on the rolling Deck he stood,
> Unmov'd, beheld the breaking Flood,
>   With black'ning Storms combin'd:
> Virtue, he cry'd, will force its Way,
> The Wind may for a while delay,
>   Not alter our Design.
>
> The Men whom selfish Hopes inflame,
> Or Vanity allures to Fame,
>   May be to Fear betray'd:
> But here a Church for Succour flies,
> Insulted Law expiring lies,
>   And loudly calls for Aid.
>
> Yes, *Britons*, yes, with ardent Zeal,
> I come the wounded Heart to heal,
>   The wounded Hand to bind:
> See Tools of arbitrary Sway,
> And Priests, like Locusts, scout away,
>   Before the western Wind.
>
> Law shall again, her Force resume,
> Religion clear'd from Clouds of *Rome*,
>   With brighter Rays advance.
> The *British* Fleet shall rule the Deep,
> The *British* Youth, as rous'd from Sleep,
>   Strike Terror into *France*.
>
> Nor shall these Promises of Fate,
> Be limited to my short Date,
>   When I from Cares withdraw:
> Still shall the *British* Sceptre stand,
> Still flourish in a female Hand,
>   And to Mankind give Awe.

But know these Promises are given,
These great Rewards imperial Heaven,
   Does on these Terms decree;
That strictly punishing Men's Faults,
You let their Consciences and Thoughts
   Rest absolutely free.

Let no false Polticks confine,
In narrow Bounds, your vast Design,
   To make Mankind unite;
Nor think it a sufficient Cause,
To punish Men by penal Laws,
   For not believing right.

Rome, whose blind Zeal destroys Mankind,
Rome's Sons shall your Compassion find,
   Who ne'er Compassion knew,
By nobler Actions theirs condemn;
For what has been reproach'd in them,
   Can ne'er be prais'd in you.

                      Z.

1. "If you will but turn over the annals and chronicles of the world, it must be acknowledged that justice came from fear of injustice." Horace, *Satires,* I, 3, 112.

2. Not until the Virginia Statute of Religious Freedom (January 16, 1786) did Livingston's trenchant asseveration of the principle of freedom of thought receive official expression, and then in words similar to the *Reflector's*: "it is time enough for the rightful purposes of civil government, for its officers to interfere [in the field of opinion] when principles break out into overt acts against peace and good order." Compare also Mr. Justice Holmes's doctrine of "clear and present danger" (Schenck *v.* United States, 1919).

3. The correct reference is Acts 18:12–16.

4. William Walsh (1683–1708), English critic and poet. The extract is from his imitation of "Horace. Ode III. Book III" (1705).

Number XXXVII

THURSDAY, AUGUST 9, 1753

The Absurdity of the civil Magistrate's interfering in Matters of Religion

PART II

Having in my last Paper shewn, that Government was a Means calculated to secure Mankind in the free and unmolested Enjoyment of their political Rights, every Perversion of such Means must evidently be an Abuse of Government, and an Infringement of that native Power in Man from which all civil Authority by Delegation originally sprang. Power unduly exercised becomes Oppression; and that Liberty, for the Preservation of which civil Power was instituted, degenerates into Slavery. It was wisely observed by one of the greatest Patrons of English Liberty and Learning, *that wheresoever Law ends Tyranny begins;* [1] and it might justly be added, that *whenever the Legislature pervert the true Intention of that Power with which they are invested, by instituting such Laws, as tend to abridge the Liberty of human Nature, it is the Height of Tyranny and Oppression.* Nay, it is so much worse than open Violence, as they screen their Conduct under the specious Appearance of Law and Equity.

But among the many Instances of the Abuse of Government, there is none more immediately destructive of the natural Rights of Mankind, than the Interposition of the secular Arm in Matters purely religious. The Efficacy of human Laws is limited to the exterior Acts of Man, as they affect Society, and consequently can enforce nothing as a Duty, but what springs from the Circumstances of Man, considered as a Member of Society. Hither may we trace the Origin of many moral Obligations which are binding upon us, not as rational Creatures in a distinct, but a collective View.

CIVIL INTERFERENCE CONTINUED

It will, however, be difficult to settle, in a few Words, the just Bounds of civil Power, beyond which the Legislature cannot pass, without infringing the unalienable Privileges of human Nature. The Actions of Men are the proper Objects of civil Power. *Government* (says a great Philosopher) *was instituted for well ordering the relative Actions of Man*; and that, not only as they may immediately, but also consequentially affect our Fellow Creatures. Man, by entering into Society, necessarily inhibits himself the Performance of all Acts tending to the Detriment of that Society, which in a State of Nature he might have prosecuted without contradicting the Rules of Justice: For *every Man might then take to his Use what he pleased, and make Consumption of what he thought good in his own Eyes.* In a social State, as in ours, Property is originally centered in the *supreme Head,* and therefore no Man can assume to himself that Privilege, without breaking in upon the Rights of his Sovereign. In a State of Nature, every Man without Labour might content himself with subsisting upon the common Fruits of the Earth: In a social State, the chief Support of which is the Industry of its Members, no Man should be indolent, as he may consequentially injure the Society in which he lives.

Mankind willing to give up their original Privilege, of ranging at large in the ample Field of Nature, submitted themselves to the Restrictions of Society, the better to defend their Lives and Liberty, and to ascertain their Property, for which alone Government was instituted. But how great is the Absurdity to suppose, that Government was ever designed to *enslave* the *Consciences of Men!* Is it possible for Man to divest himself of Thought, which is essential to our Existence? Equally preposterous is it to suppose, that the inward Exertions of the Soul, should be regulated by any external Laws. The Understanding, upon surveying a Set of Ideas that form a Proposition, must either determine, that it be true or false; or the Judgment must be suspended for want of clearer Light and Information. But in either Case can the Force of civil Authority have any Efficacy? The Mind must, if at all, be determined by the highest apparent Reason, and of that the *Mind itself* is the only *competent Judge.* Exterior Force may compel the

313

Man to act in Opposition to his Judgment, but can never gain the Mind's Assent to the Fitness of an Action, which is contradictory to the Dictates of its own Judgment, be it wrongly or rightly informed. Whence it evidently follows, that if the Legislators interfere in Matters of Opinion, they are guilty of the greatest Tyranny and Oppression, and instead of advancing and protecting the Rights of Mankind, enslave the Consciences of their fellow Creatures.[2]

To apply this Reasoning to *Matters of Religion*, let it be considered in the true Abstract and not under any particular Denomination. The Etymology of the Word, shews that Religion conflicts either in a Choice or Obligation to do certain Acts in Conformity to the Will of our Creator, which the Laws of Reason, or any other Methods of discovering his Will, dictate to us, or rather in both. In this View, there is an immediate Relation subsisting between the Creature and the Creator, from whence the Duties of Religion must necessarily arise. Those Duties, as they are incumbent upon Man, either as they appear reasonable, or have been revealed to him, must infer a Right in him to chuse his own Religion. This Right in Man, cannot be alienated or usurped: It cannot be alienated, without destroying those two Means for the true Discovery of religious Duties wherewith God and Nature have furnished Man; nor usurped, without supposing that Man is capable of adding a greater Obligation, to the Performance of religious Duties, than the divine Being. Besides, it is impossible that any one without Belief, can be subject to the Performance of religious Duties; and he may justly be said not to believe, whose Religion receives all its Force from external Obligation. The Absurdity of a Religion, supported and enforced by the Terrors of the Law, is too apparent to need much farther Display. The Matter in short stands thus: Does a Man act in a conscientious Obedience to the Law of God, without Doubt such Act is religious; but on the contrary, should he only be governed by a Submission to the Law of the Magistrate, such Act can never claim a moral Consideration, even tho' it be really in exact Conformity to the Will of the supreme Legislator of the Universe.

Again, as Government was instituted for the Establishment

and Preservation of our civil Interests, it is an Abuse to suppose the Magistrate can have any Right to interfere in Matters of religious Belief. *Religion* (to speak with a Man of great Learning) *consists in the inward Perswasion of the Mind, and cannot fall within the Province of our civil Rulers, their Power consisting only in outward Force.*

The Restraint of civil Authority, in different Countries and Ages, upon the free Exercise of human Reason, has ever been attended with a Decay of all valuable Knowledge and Literature. It is as impossible for the Sciences to grow and flourish under the Frowns and Terrors of Oppression, as for a People to breath Liberty under the savage Administration of a Tyrant. The Advancement of Learning depends upon the free Exercise of Thought; it is therefore absurd to suppose, that it should thrive under a Government that makes it Treason even for a Man to think. How injurious this is to the Cause of Religion, requires no great Sagacity to conceive. The Enlargement of our reasoning Powers depends entirely upon the Exercise of them, to which nothing can be more conducive than the Encouragement of Learning. Our Duties increase with our Knowledge, and no Man has so much Reason to be religious as he whose Knowledge is most extensive. It has therefore always been the Care of the wisest Administrations, to encourage a Liberty of Thought; and as he who thinks freely is most likely to think aright, that Religion which proceeds from a Man's own free Thoughts, must certainly be the most agreeable to the Deity.[3]

Had our Legislature always thought so, (and I am sure they would have thought justly) our public Annals would never have been stained, nor their august Beauty disfigured with the unforeseen Consequences resulting from the famous and ever memorable Test Act.[4] The English *Constitution* has always been celebrated for its Aptitude to *promote the true Ends of Society*; our *Courts of Justice* admired for their *impartial Methods of trying civil Causes*: But unreasonable it is, and highly to be deplored, that our Rulers should ever have attempted to *arraign and try the Consciences of Men.*

The true Happiness of a People consists in the Wisdom of

their Governors. On the Contrary, when the Legislature set no Bounds to the Extent of their Power, Misery and Oppression are the unhappy Portion of the Subject. Yet it is obvious, that there are many Men who, not content to submit their Persons and Property to Slavery and Oppression, are never satisfied, till they have resigned their Liberty of Conscience, and esteem it a Hardship to be suffered to think for themselves. Persons of this Stamp are entirely ignorant of the true Nature of Religion. They imagine, that a blind Obedience to the arbitrary Dictates of our Superiors, cuts a most splendid Figure in the Catalogue of Christian Virtues; — that the Magistrates have a Right to fashion our religious Principles, and the People are bound by an indispensable Obligation to practise upon them; — that if the Subject will not embrace the Religion of his Prince, he may be compelled to it by Fire and Faggot. But those who are thus obstinately Fond of Opinions so disgraceful to the Dignity of human Nature, should be left to cherish the comfortable Prospect, as well as enjoy the most righteous Experience of having *their Bodies punished for the Good of their Souls.*[5]

I will venture to appeal to all those who are any Ways acquainted with History, and more especially with those voluminous Legends usually stiled *Church History*, that whenever Men have suffered their Consciences to be enslaved by their Superiors, and taken their Religion upon Trust, the World has been overrun with Superstition, and held in Fetters by a tyrannizing Juncto of civil and ecclesiastical Plunderers. As soon as Men are abridg'd in the Liberty of chusing for themselves, and instead of using their own Reason, compliment their temporal and spiritual Directors, by surrendering to them the Right of private Judgment, the State has generally sunk into Barbarism, and every Appearance of real substantial masculine Piety vanished the Nation.

I shall close this Subject with a Quotation from a certain REVEREND DIVINE, now alive, and one of the greatest Ornaments of the Church.[6]

'Tis therefore but too natural to suspect, that the secret Intention of all ghostly and spiritual Directors and Guides in decrying Reason, the noblest Gift of God, and without which even the Being of a God, and the Method of our Redemption by Jesus Christ, would be no more Significancy to us, than to the Brutes that perish, is in Reality the Advancement of their own Power and Authority, over the Faith and Consciences of others, to which sound Reason is, and ever will be an Enemy: For tho' I readily allow the *great Expediency* and Need of divine Revelation, to assist us in our Enquiries into the Nature of Religion, and to give us a full View of the Principles and Practices of it; yet a very small Share of Reason, without any supernatural Help, will suffice, if attended to, to let me know that my Soul is my own, and that I ought *not to put my Conscience out to keeping* to any Person whatsoever, because no Man can be answerable for it to the great God but myself; and that therefore the Claim of Dominion, whoever makes it, either over mine or any others Conscience, is mere Imposture and Cheat, that hath nothing but Impudence or Folly to support it; and as truly visionary and romantick as the imaginary Power of Persons disorder'd in their Senses, and which would be of no more Significancy and Influence amongst Mankind than theirs, did not either the Views of ambitious Princes, or the Superstition and Folly of Bigots, encourage and support it.

On these Accounts, it is highly incumbent on all Nations, who enjoy the Blessings of a limited Government, who would preserve their Constitution, and transmit it safe to Posterity, to be jealous of every Claim of spiritual Power, and not to enlarge the Authority and Jurisdiction of spiritual Men, beyond the Bounds of Reason and Revelation. Let them have the freest Indulgence to do good, and spread the Knowledge and Practice of true Religion, and promote Peace and good Will amongst Mankind. Let them be applauded and encouraged, and even rewarded, when they are Patterns of Virtue, and Examples of real Piety to their Flocks. Such Powers as these God and Man would readily allow them; and as to any other, I apprehend, they have little Right to them, and am sure they have seldom made a wise or rational Use of them. On the Contrary, numberless have been the Confusions and Mischiefs introduced into the World, and occasioned by the Usurpers of spiritual Authority. In the Christian Church they have ever used it with Insolence, and generally abused it to Oppression, and the worst of Cruelties. And though the History of such Transactions can never be a very pleasing and grateful Task, yet, I think, on many Accounts, it may be useful and instructive; especially as it may give Men an Abhorrence, of all the Methods of Persecution, and put them upon their Guard against all those ungodly Pretensions, by which Persecution hath been introduced and supported.[7]   B.

1. John Locke, *Second Treatise of Civil Government* (1690), Par. 202.
2. In more pungent language Livingston quipped two years later that

"A religious Tyrant is, of all the Tyrants in the World, the most unmanageable and sanguinary: He punishes you for your own Good; pains your Body for the Health of your Soul: and breaks your Head, to illuminate your Mind." "Watch-Tower," No. XVIII, *New-York Mercury*, March 24, 1755.

3. Three years earlier Livingston had denominated "Freedom of Inquiry into Matters of Religion" and the "Security of our Persons and Properties" as two of the "most inestimable Blessings that Man can conceive or desire." *A Letter to the Freemen and Freeholders* . . . (1750), p. 3.

4. The English Test Act of 1673 required, among other things, that all civil and military officeholders take communion in the Anglican Church.

5. In similar language Livingston had expressed his satisfaction that "We . . . can thank our Stars, that while an irritated and vindictive Priest is damning our Souls, he is restrained from hurting our Bodies." *A Letter to the Freemen and Freeholders* . . . (1750), p. 3.

6. Possibly Jonathan Mayhew (1720–1766) or Charles Chauncey (1705–1787), Boston Congregationalists who preached the right of private judgment on rationalist grounds.

7. Livingston's two essays on the relationship between church and state brought quick rejoinders from the Anglicans. They derided the "imaginary" compact to which Livingston had attributed the origin of government as a "whimsical Foundation"; insisted that man had never lived in a state of nature without society, since God had created both man and society; claimed that religion had properly been a concern of the civil magistrates beginning with Moses; declared religion to have been coterminous with society and hence subject to community regulation; and blasted Livingston's theories of government as fresh evidence of his contempt for religion itself. (*New-York Mercury*, August 27, September 3, 10, 1753.) Livingston responded in the *Occasional Reverberator*, No. II (September 14, 1753), in whose columns the debate was now carried on.

Number XXXVIII

THURSDAY, AUGUST 16, 1753

Of Passive Obedience and Non-Resistance

As a roaring Lion, or a ranging Bear; so is a wicked Ruler over the poor People.   King Solomon [1]

> *From Heav'n pretending Right to break Heav'n's Law,*
> *Uncheck'd and unresisted —— Doctrines strange*
> *And foul, debasing Man, blaspheming God —*
>   Thom[son], Lib[erty]

Nothing has a happier Tendency to cherish and perpetuate that Spirit of Liberty, whereby we are so honourably distinguished from the Slaves of despotic Princes, than a frequent Review of our excellent Constitution, and a Refutation of those servile Principles, which would rob it of its brightest Glory, by exalting a limited Monarch, into an arbitrary and unaccountable Potentate.

Many of those reverend Dreamers called the *Fathers*, among the rest of their Trumpery, have, as it is said, laid down the Unlawfulness of resisting the Supreme Ruler, for a Position never to be questioned. Not a few of their Successors, more remarkable for imitating their Absurdities, than their Virtues, have adopted the generous Maxim. There's scarce an Instance in the English History, where the Sovereign has attempted to enslave the People, but the Pulpit has rung with *jus divinum* and *hereditary Succession*.

> *Ev'n from that Place, whence healing Peace should flow*
> *And Gospel Truth, inhuman Bigots shed*
> *Their Poison round. ————*   Thom[son], Lib[erty]

The Tyrant used to club with the Clergy, and set them a roaring for the divine Right of royal Roguery. 'Twas a damnable Sin to resist the cutting of Throats, and no Virtue more christian

319

and refulgent, than a passive Submission to Butchery and Slaughter. But the Conduct of those feeble Trumpeters is not to be wondered at: As they exalted the regal Prerogative above the Laws, the Hierarchy in return, was by the Monarch aggrandized, in Defiance of Scripture. Besides, not a few of the Cloth, like the *Swiss* Soldiers, have fought for or against Satan, as they have been paid for doing the one or the other.

But to propagate such reverend Fustian in *America*, and that in the Reign of the best of Princes, tho' it can be of no Use but to the worst, argues a Disposition prone to Servility, without even a valuable Consideration. And yet 'tis not above four Years ago, that in this very Province I heard a dapper young Gentleman, attired in his Canonicals, contend as strenuously for Non-Resistance, as if he had been animated with the very Soul of SACHEVEREL.[2]

In absolute Monarchies let the Prince tyrannize, and like a rabid Lion gorge himself with Blood. He has a political Power to treat his Subjects cruelly, if they have submitted to his arbitrary Will, which however is scarcely supposable. But in limited Governments there are inherent Rights, and fundamental Reserves. The resisting therefore the Person or Will of the Ruler, when he rescinds those Rights and Reservations, is not resisting the Ordinance of God, (which is the Frame and Constitution of the Government, not the Person or Will of the Prince) but plainly defending it, against the powerless, unauthoritative, and illegal Attempts of the Superior. — A very pretty Compliment truly to the Source of universal Good, and unerring Rectitude, to make him the Author of infamous Barbarity and Outrage, and to represent horrible Misrule, the most sanguinary Cruelties, and all the baneful Villainies of rampant Tyranny, as his sacred Institution!

To the Objection, that there can be no Resistance by the Law of the Land, I reply, that indeed the Law hath not clearly pointed out the Time when Resistance shall take Place, nor ascertain'd the particular Acts of the Prince that shall justify an Opposition; the Reason of which I shall shew presently. But 'tis at the same Time observable, that when a Person asserts the absolute Unlawfulness of Resistance, because it is not agreable to Law, he confounds a moral and political Legality, and says little to the Purpose, while he seems to argue unanswerably. The Law hath not, however, been wholly silent on a Subject of such high Moment. In the parliamentary Debates, I find the following Quotation of a Clause in King *Henry*'s Charter, "*If the King invade those Rights, it is lawful for the Kingdom to rise against him, and do him what Injury they can, as tho' they owed him no Allegiance.*" "*Licet omnibus de regno nostro, contra nos insurgere et omnia agere, quæ gravamen nostrum respiciant, ac si nobis in nullo teneretur.*" Much to same Purpose is in King JOHN's Charter, which I find thus quoted, "Et illi barones, cum communitate totius terræ, distringent et gravabunt nos, modis omnibus quibus poterunt; scilicet per captionem castrorum, terrarum, possessionum, talibus modis quibus potuerint, donec fuerit emendatum, secundum arbetrium eorum, salva persona nostra et reginæ nostræ, et liberorum nostrorum." From whence my Author draws this Conclusion, that "true Allegiance does not tie us from resisting illegal Force, and intolerable Encroachments upon our just Rights." Thus by the Act *for abrogating the Oaths of Supremacy and Allegiance, and appointing other Oaths*, passed in the first Year of King WILLIAM and Queen MARY, the Declaration enjoined to be taken by several Acts in the Time of King CHARLES the Second, to this Purpose, *that it is not lawful on any Pretence whatsoever, to take up Arms against the King*, was taken away. And in the Act for *declaring the Rights and Liberties of the Subject*, passed in the second Session of that Parliament, Notice is taken, *That the late King JAMES did endeavour to subvert and extirpate the Protestant Religion, and the Laws and Liberties of the Kingdom; and that it had pleased Almighty God to make the Prince of Orange, the glorious Instrument of delivering the Kingdom from Popery and arbitrary Power.*[3] And if the Instrument who accomplished that never-to-be-forgotten Deliverance, was upon that very Account *glorious*, the Means he used for effecting it must also be glorious, and those being Resistance, the Legality of Resistance is evidently avowed by the supreme Legislature of the Nation. Thus, what was before immutably and eternally righteous, has derived to itself an additional Splendor, from the signal Lustre and Renown of that ever memorable Event, and the Eulogy passed upon it by the most august Assembly in the World.

Nor let me forget the Opinion of that learned Civilian, the incomparable GROTIUS, delivered in a Passage, exactly adapted to the Constitution of *England*, the Sense of which I take to be this, "If the King has one Part of the supreme Power, and the People or Senate the other, Force may be used against the King for invading that Part which doth not belong to him, because his Power doth not extend so far." And which I take to be true, even where the Power of declaring War is lodged solely in the Prince; for that must be understood to relate only to foreign War. But at Home, it is impossible for any to have a Share in the supreme Power, and at the same Time not to have a Right to defend that Share.

It further appears, by several Instances enumerated in the last mentioned Act of Parliament, that at the Time of the Revolution (an Era of Renown unperishing, and to every true *Briton* ineffably precious) there was a total Subversion of the Constitution, which is a Case the Laws of *England*, could never suppose, nor consequently provide for. Neither, indeed, if such Subversion was foreseen, would there be a Necessity for prescribing a Remedy, because the Subversion itself amounts, at least with Respect to the Subverter, to a reducing the Society to its first Principles, and puts it, as to him, in *statu quo*, as if he had never politically existed. Besides, it would be a most palpable Absurdity in any Government, to make a Law which could only take Place when that Government is dissolved, because such a Law supposes an Authority in the Ruler which in Reality is extinct that Moment it becomes necessary to be executed. Whence I argue, that tho' Resistance may, for the Reason before, be, in one Sense, unlawful, or more properly without Law; yet in another Sense, from the particular Exigence of Affairs, and the Necessity of the Thing, (which hath no Law) it becomes both morally and (in the comprehensive View of the Nature and End of civil Society) even politically legal, tho' there be no express Law to warrant it. Nor is the Proposition in the least paradoxical, but the necessary Consequence of human Laws, which cannot be supposed to have in View the Subversion of the Government; it being for that Reason to be considered as extraordinary and unprovided for by Law, requires the Application of an extraordinary Remedy, not contrary to the Spirit and Design of the Law, but allowable on Account of its unavoidable Imperfection and Defectibility. Thus for Instance, in the Time of HENRY VII. there occurred a Difficulty, which according to the above partial Idea, of *unlawful*, must have occasioned a perpetual Chasm in the Constitution, for Want of express Law to remove it: But as the Case was unusual and extraordinary so was the Expedient and Solution. The Case stood thus: HENRY was attainted for High-Treason, which prevented the Descent of the Crown upon him; and the Generality of his Friends were also attainted, and thereby rendered incapable of sitting in Parliament, 'till the Attainders were reversed. HENRY declined calling a Parliament, 'till his Friends were capable to sit there; nor could he create Judges 'till he was King, which appeared a Difficulty insuperable: But the Resolution of the Judges was agreeable to the Exigency of the Case. They declared, that Sir WILLIAM STANLEY's placing the Crown on the Earl of *Richmond's* Head, purged his Attainder, and that he thereby became King of *England*; and so being King, was enabled to constitute Judges, and these Judges to reverse the Attainder of all the King's Friends. Nor do I remember, that his Title to the Crown thus procured, was ever called in Question, tho' he never pretended to hold it in Right of the Heiress of the House of *York*, when he married.[4]

Neither cou'd an express Permission by Law to resist illegal Power, be properly denominated a Gift of a new Right, which the People had not before, or wou'd not have had without such Law: It would only be an explicit Reservation, of what the very Reservation admitted to inhere previously in them, and what without such Reservation must equally have continued to reside in them, till an express Surrender. Such Reservation would only be corroborative of their radical inherent Right of Self-Defence; which is not the Donation of Law, but a primitive Right, prior to all political Institution resulting from the Nature of Man, and inhering in the People till expressly alienated and transferred, if it be not in its Nature unalienable, which may admit of Debate: Thus much however, is evident, that the People retain of it just so much as they have not surrendered to the political Power. Besides, there is no Necessity for the Formality of a judicial Procedure in a Thing so manifest as the Subversion of the Constitution: Nor is the Defence of our Lives and Properties in such Case, an Act of Judgment, or the Object of Law: It is a Privilege of Nature, not an Act of Jurisdiction. Hence these indisputable Maxims, *Vim vi repellere omnia jura permittunt; defendere se est juris Natura; defensio vitæ necessaria est,* and *a jure naturali profluit;* [5] with many others to the like Purpose. It must be owned, that there is no formal legal Tribunal to call the Prince to an Account, because he is irrevocably, except in Case of Tyranny, invested with the formal Sovereignty, executive Authority, and royal Dignity, by the People. And for this Reason, the Trial of King CHARLES I was absolutely illegal and absurd: But yet the People are superior to him, in respect of their Fountain-Power of Sovereignty, which remains virtually in them. Whence it follows, that tho' they give him a political Power for their Security, they retain a natural Right of reassuming that political Power, whenever it is employed in their Destruction. And this is contain'd in the very Idea of all fiducial Authority, which is in its Nature repealable when absurd and perverted; and the Person violating his Trust, must necessarily become accountable to his Constituents. For were it otherwise, I would fain know the Difference between an absolute and a limited Monarchy. What signify the Reservation of certain Rights, and the making only a conditional Submission, if those Rights may notwithstanding be invaded, and those Conditions infringed without Remedy or Redress? All Government upon that Supposition, is equally arbitrary, and all Limitations perfectly useless.

The Arguments urged by the Advocates for Non-Resistance, from the Topic of *Allegiance,* is nothing to the Purpose; because our Allegiance is proportioned to the Nature and Frame of the Constitution. Hence the King being sworn to keep the Laws and Customs of *England;* our Allegiance to him, is the Allegiance due to a King who keeps those Laws and Customs; and must of Consequence cease to be due when he ceases to be King; which I conceive he does when he ceases to keep those Laws and Customs. Our Allegiance therefore being only our legal Duty, has nothing to do with illegal Force. It may indeed be objected, that the Kings of *England* are Kings before their Coronation, because the Crown, by Policy of Law, and to prevent an Interregnum, descends on the Successor *eoinstanti* [6] of his Predecessor's Demise: But this will not help the Matter; because the Crown must devolve, subject to the same Rules and Restrictions by which the Predecessor held it; and that I take to be the Reason why Allegiance is due before the Coronation-Oath.

With unavailing Ostentation do the Doctors of Passive Obedience, urge the Authority of St. PAUL. The Apostle says not a Syllable about the Person of the Magistrate; but treats expressly of the Magistracy itself: He does not say, there is no Prince, but there is no Power except what is of God; and evidently restrains his Precept to a lawful Magistrate: But whatever is discordant and tyrannical, cannot be the Ordinance of infinite Rectitude, and the God of Order. Nay, to prevent all Possibility of Misconstruction, he gives his Reader a Definition of the Magistrate to whom he enjoins the Obedience he inculcates: The Magistrate, says he, *is not a Terror to good Works, but to evil: Wilt thou then not be afraid of the Power? for he is the Minister of God to thee for good.* [7] And to such a Magistrate no honest Man would refuse a chearful Submission: But to a Magistrate who falls not within his Definition, no Obedience is commanded: Whenever therefore the Supreme Ruler acts contrary to what St. PAUL describes as his Duty, and characteristical of the Magistracy, which he terms the Ordinance of God, no Obedience is due from this Injunction, which is plainly limited by the Definition. How then does this inspired Writer prohibit Resistance to the Power of a Robber or a Tyrant, who if he is still to be called a Magistrate because he has Power, tho' instead of being a Minister of God, he introduces keen Distress and diffusive Misery; by the same Reason, may the Devil himself become a Magistrate, because he hath more Power than any Man.

In Reality, it is not the Business of Religion to settle the

Authority of the Prince, nor the Submission of the Subject: Its Province is only to secure the legal Authority of the one, and enforce the due Obedience of the other, from the Consideration of a future Existence. It neither constitutes the Magistracy, nor determines the Bounds of Prerogative or Liberty; but leaving the Constitution as it finds it, corroborates our antecedent Duty, by divine Command, and the Promise and Denunciation of future Rewards and Punishments. And was this Distinction sufficiently adverted to by all those who blow the Trumpet in *Zion*, they might safely bury their politico-theological Jargon in everlasting Oblivion, without any Prejudice to the Edification of their Hearers.

If the Magistrate exercises Force unauthorized by Law, the Violence he offers must be considered as the Violence of a private Person, which the People have an undoubted Right to repel; because such Acts as exceed or are repugnant to an express Limitation or prescribed Duty, have in them no political Power, tho' the Person hath to other Purposes. Whenever the Magistrate acts in Opposition to his political Power, he cannot do such Acts as Magistrate; but must be esteemed a Person exerting Strength without Power, that is, legal Power; which every Man of superior Strength hath, by the Law of Nature, a manifest Right to oppose. To resist in such a Case, is not resisting his Authority, but Force illegal and unauthoritative.

That the Person of the King is sacred, may safely be admitted, without giving our Adversaries any room to triumph: For it is his Authority which he originally derived from the People, as the Head of the Society, and the Fountain of Justice, that constitutes his Sacredness: But when a Monarch violates that Authority, and becomes the dreadful Instrument of universal Evil; Sanctity can only be ascribed to him with the same Propriety that Holiness is imputable to *Beelzebub*; or, in the Words of the Earl of *Rochester*,

> *If such Kings are by God appointed,*
> *The Devil may be the Lord's Anointed.*[8] Z.

1. Prov. 28:15.

2. Henry Sacheverell (1674?–1724), high church Anglican clergyman, impeached by the House of Commons (1710) for his bitter sermons against the principles of the Revolution of 1688.

3. The extract from Magna Carta, Article 61, is: ". . . and they, the twenty-five Barons, with the community of the whole land, shall distress and harass us by all the ways in which they are able; that is to say, by the taking of our castles, lands, and possessions, and by *any* other means in their power, until the excess shall have been redressed, according to their verdict; saving *harmless* our person, and *the persons* of our Queen and children." The clause in King Henry's Charter which Livingston's parliamentary reporter cites cannot be located in the Coronation Charter of Henry I (1100) or in the Great Charters of Henry III of 1216, 1217, and 1224–5. The other acts cited are 1 Wm. and Mary (Sess. 1), c. 10 (1688); and 1 Wm. and Mary (Sess. 2), c. 2 (1688).

4. The hereditary claim to the throne of Henry Tudor, Earl of Richmond, a Lancastrian, was remote. He won the Crown by defeating Richard III of the House of York at Bosworth Field in 1485. By marrying Elizabeth, the daughter of the Yorkist Edward IV, he strengthened his position but did not legitimize it. This was done by parliamentary action in 1485.

5. "All laws permit one to repel force by force; it is the nature of law [for one] to defend oneself; the defense of [one's own] life is necessary, and it arises from natural law."

6. "At the instant."

7. Rom. 13:3–4.

8. John Wilmot, 2nd Earl of Rochester (1647–1680), the profligate author of witty satires and lyrics. Livingston had quoted this same bit of caustic verse in criticizing colonial governors who violated their trust. *A Letter to the Freemen and Freeholders* . . . (1750), p. 7. The quotation is from Rochester's *History of Insipids, A Lampoon of 1676.*

Number XXXIX

THURSDAY, AUGUST 23, 1753

Further Reflections on the Doctrines of PASSIVE OBEDIENCE and NON-RESISTANCE, drawn from a Consideration of the Rights and Privileges of human Nature, and the due End and Extent of Government

As if for one, and often for the worst,
Heav'n had Mankind, in Vengeance only made.
THOM[SON], [*Liberty*]

THERE is no Truth in Nature more strongly verified by Observation than this, that all Governments are subject to continual Vicissitudes, both from the Imperfections of their Constitution, and the Misconduct of those in whose Hands they are entrusted. Most Men being naturally ambitious, and aspiring after illimitable Dominion, are too apt to measure the Extent of justifiable Authority, by their insatiable Appetite for an unbounded Licentiousness. This giddy Pursuit after absolute Rule, has hurried on the Fate of all Governments that have hitherto shone in History, either for their constitutional Excellencies, or acquired Grandeur. Thus, as the Majesty of *Rome* was founded upon that Spirit of Liberty, which reigned in the happy Interlude between her Kings and her Emperors, so must her total Dissolution be attributed to a blind and implicit Obedience, extorted from the People by the lawless Exercise of imperial Tyranny. Such, is the Nature of Society, that while its Individuals are subject to Passion and Prejudice, the Ruler's Task is arduous and difficult to accomplish. But this is too often an Excuse for those lawless Depredations, which alone perpetuate the Memory of some Princes, to whose Fame and Power the Grave would otherwise have put one common Period. For were the Imperfections of the Ruler considered with due Attention, that System of Civil Rule, which is nothing more than the Will of a despotic Tyrant, would quickly be exploded. It is unreasonable to suppose, that Government which is designed chiefly to correct the Exorbitancies of human Nature, should entirely consist in the uncontroulable Dictates, of a Man of equal Imperfections with the Rest of the Community, who being invested with the Authority of the Whole, has an unlimited Power to commit whatever Exorbitancies he shall think fit.

The Doctrines of *Passive Obedience and Non-Resistance,* have in all Ages proved the fittest Engines of arbitrary Sway; nothing being more easy, than to persuade Mankind to submit, to the most unreasonable Impositions, by false Motives of Duty and Interest. And when the Beast is tamed, load him with whatever Burdens you please, he patiently endures the Oppression, without being able to rebuke the Cruelty of his merciless Master.

But altho' the deceitful Charms of absolute Rule have proved an alluring Bait, even to some of the best of Princes, and the deadly Bane of most Nations and Governments, methinks nothing is more absurd and disgraceful than those Maxims upon which it is founded. Is there more Honour, or real Glory, in governing those, who, upon their own Principles, are mere necessary Agents, than in ruling a Nation, warm with the Spirit of Liberty, and blest with the Power of acting freely, which is the most distinguishing Excellency of a rational Existence? Or rather, should not the high Prerogative of governing those, who, by their Conduct really shew themselves Men, be preferred to the Power of commanding a Set of Beings, whose Motives and Actions scarcely discriminate them from the Brute Creation?

Should the Imagination of my Readers take a wide Survey of the British Annals, they would readily discover, that this Nation wears the different Faces of Happiness and Misery, in Proportion to the Prevalence or Neglect of a blind Obedience to the Will of their Sovereigns; and that whenever the Doctrines of *Passive Obedience and Non-Resistance* were in highest Repute, our happy Constitution was in the utmost Danger of tumbling into irrecoverable Ruin.

The Study of human Nature will teach us, that Man in his original Structure and Constitution, was designed to act in a natural and moral Dependence on his Maker alone, and created solely for the Enjoyment of his own Happiness. His being a rational Creature necessarily implies in him a Freedom of Action, determinable by the Dictates of his own Reason, the self-resolving Exertions of his own Volition, and a Reverence to the Laws prescribed to him by his omnipotent Creator. From these three Heads, as from a copious Fountain, flow the whole Variety of moral Obligations. This Liberty of Action, however modified by human Policy, cannot in the Nature of Things be separated from his Existence. For by admitting the Rationality of Man, you necessarily suppose him a free Agent. And as no political Institutions can deprive him of his Reason, they cannot by any Means, destroy his native Privilege of acting freely.[1]

It may perhaps be asked, how Mankind in this View, can possibly be bound by the Laws of Society? This Question will easily admit of a Solution, by the following Reasons. Besides the Power of acting freely, we are imbued with a Propensity to Society as an accessional Means to the Increase of our Felicity. To this State are we impelled, not by a Necessity of Nature, but by an eligible Prospect; the Attainment of which depends upon the self-determining Power of our Will. Whence it plainly results, that every Member of Society, must be supposed voluntarily to have entered into it for the Advancement of his Happiness, as the only rational Motive by which his Will could be determined.

It is further evident, that as the divine Architect has adorned us with the Powers of Reason, it is utterly impossible for Man in a social State, to resign the Conduct of those Actions that result from it, to the absolute Rule of a fellow Creature.[2] The silent Exercise of the Mind is not the only indispensable Duty of his Nature: A Conformity of Action thereto, built upon an inherent unalienable Spontaniety, is also unavoidably necessary. For how little would avail our reasoning Faculties, were it possible for us to resign our native Right to a Freedom of Action. It would be absurd to suppose, Man a rational Creature, and at the same Time subject to be justly reducible, by the natural or acquired Authority of a fellow Mortal, to the State of a necessary Agent. The Liberty of the human Will, and a Power of acting in Conformity thereto, are not only his indisputable Right, but also constitute his very Essence as a rational Creature; and cannot therefore, by any Means whatever, be alienated from him in a social State. Thus, as Government is a Society, tho' of the highest Rank, no Man can submit to it upon the Terms, of entirely resigning his original Freedom and Independency of Action, to the Will of his Ruler, it being an essential Property of his Nature, which he cannot transfer, nor be equitably divested of. But how far he may become bound by civil Obligations, the subsequent Reflections will fully shew.

From what has already been advanced, it is evident, that Man is a Being imbued with an unalienable Right to think and act freely, according to the Dictates of a self-determining Will. Nor can a Subordination to his omnipotent Maker, be supposed in the least to restrain his natural Liberty. For tho' the Laws of his Reason, or the Will of his Creator, which in Effect are the same Things, as they influence his moral Actions, inhibit him the Practice of Evil; yet while he is considered as a rational Agent, his Will must be allowed to have an independent Right of determining itself, upon a Supposition that he will always chuse to do good, as the proper Means to secure his ultimate Happiness. And in this View, our original State of Rectitude must properly be considered.

But when the Depravity of human Nature, had invalidated the Efficacy of moral Obligation, there was a manifest Necessity for establishing some more forcible Motives, to compel and inhibit the Practice of Right and Wrong: Here we may justly fix the Origin of civil Obligations. And therefore all Governments must originally and intentionally be an Erection or Elevation of one or more Men above the Rest, dependent upon the free Exertion of the Will of the latter, for the Good of the Whole. It must further be admitted, that all Men have a Capacity to do good Actions; and consequently upon a Supposition, that they would always act up to the Dignity of rational Existences, there could be no need of Government: For it would be absurd, to institute a Power to compel those, who voluntarily do good Actions. Thus circumscribed within those Bounds, Civil Authority can never infringe the Rights and Privileges of Man; but on the contrary stimulate him to the Performance of those Duties, which as a rational Being, unimpressed by the Force of exterior Law, he would be obliged to perform. By reasoning in this Manner, we obtain the following determinate Idea of Government: It is an human Establishment, depending upon the free Consent of Mankind, whereby one or more Individuals are elevated above the Rest, and cloathed by them with their united Power, which is to be exercised in an invariable Pursuit of the Welfare of the Community, and in compelling the Practice of Justice, and prohibiting the Contrary.[3] From this Definition of Government, the Truth of the subsequent Propositions may be fairly argued.

First, That as the Magistrate is invested with his Authority for certain Purposes only, his Subjects must still retain a Power to disobey and withstand his Commands and Actions, that are not directed to the particular Ends of his Investiture. And therefore,

Secondly, That notwithstanding our Subjection to Government, we may justly claim an absolute Freedom, an undoubted Right of contradicting the Will of those who are entrusted with it, in the Prosecution of our Happiness, by the Practice of those Things which, in a View to Society, are either beneficial, or wholly indifferent: For if, the Authority of the Magistrate extends no farther, than the Welfare of the Community and its Individuals, whatever Determinations or Acts of his, have not a Tendency to that End, cannot be effected by him in Quality of a Magistrate, but are to be considered as the injurious Efforts of a private Trespasser, which every Man, consistent with his Submission to Government, may lawfully repel.

Thirdly, That in the Investiture of every supreme Magistrate, there must be either an express or implied Condition of prosecuting the public Welfare, upon which he is to hold his Office; since it is both impossible and absurd, as I have shewn above, that Mankind should have submitted themselves to Government, but upon the Terms of their Advantage. And also, that a Breach of such Condition, must necessarily be attended with the Loss of his Power; and that those who have cloathed him with Authority, have a Right to strip him of it, whenever he abuses it.

PASSIVE OBEDIENCE CONTINUED

Fourthly, That whatever Actions of the civil Ruler tend to diminish, abridge or destroy, the Happiness of his Subjects, they may not only justly oppose, but also deprive him of all Possibility of exerting any Power that is contrary to the Design of his Institution.[4] For as his Authority is conditional, a Breach of those Terms upon which he holds it, evidently amounts to a Forfeiture of his Rights, and depresses him from his elevated Station, to a Level with the rest of Mankind, who in that Case have a Privilege of judging for themselves, and resenting without Appeal, every Offence he offers them.

Under the Influence of these Rules, are all Governments whatever to be considered. Nor is it necessary to suppose some written or express Compact, between the Ruler and the Subject, in order to evince the Falsity of the Doctrines of Passive Obedience and Non-Resistance. For if all Governments imply the Welfare of the Community, as the Condition upon which the Magistrate's Authority is founded, whenever his Determinations or Acts are contrary to such Condition, the Subject has the clearest Right to disobey and oppose him. Neither can the Administration of the most absolute Monarchs, be excluded from this Construction. Give the despotic Prince a Power of enacting Laws, and putting them in Execution according to his sovereign Will and Pleasure, you allow him all that Man can possibly ask, or you bestow. But this cannot, in the Nature of Things, be supposed to entitle him to commit the most flagitious Outrages, without Contradiction or Controul. His Authority is founded upon the voluntary Gift of his Subjects, and designed not to gratify his Pride, or delight his Vanity. Has the Community invested him with illimitable Dominion, his Investiture was intended to promote the Happiness of his People, and to guard them from Injury and Violence; and therefore, he cannot claim a Privilege of exerting himself, but in the Prosecution of the *public Good*. On the Contrary, every Act of his Prerogative, that does not bear this Stamp, is unauthoritative, the Person at whom it is aimed has an indisputable Right to resist him; and whenever the Oppression is general, the Community, who are the Fountain of Civil Power, may punish their Trustee, and deprive him of those Means which, instead of employing them,

333

in advancing the publick Interest, he has unjustly perverted to injure and oppress his helpless Subjects.

PASSIVE OBEDIENCE and NON-RESISTANCE, are often arrogated as the Right of Princes, and the Duty of Subjects, upon a Supposition that the former are the Vicegerents of Heaven: But the Truth is, they receive not their Authority from God, but from the People, as has been shewn in my last. Let it, however, for the present be supposed, in the first Sense of the Word, that *the Powers that are, are ordained of God.* It will follow that they are bound, in Consequence of their pretended Commission, to do nothing that is inconsistent with, or contrary to the Will of that Being whose Rectitude is infinite and unerring; and therefore, that they are not warranted by such Delegation, in committing Acts of Cruelty, Violence and Oppression. And if they are distinguished from their Subjects, by nothing but a Commission *to do Good,* as the Case must necessarily be upon the Supposition of a Vicegerency, whenever they exceed the Bounds of that Commission, they are to be considered as perpetrating Evil in a private Capacity, and therefore may be resisted as well as any other Individual of the Society.

Upon the whole it is evident, that as the Civil Magistrate, was intentionally set over us for good, he cannot, consistent with his Character, be guilty of such Acts as are injurious to our Persons, Liberty or Property, without justly subjecting himself to the Resentment of his Subjects, who, in that Case, would both have a Right to disobey his Commands, and oppose his Conduct.[5]

B.

1. Livingston's faith in reason was the rock-bed of his religious and political philosophy. At twenty-one he was writing to his Yale cronies: "for as Mankind are conscious that they are reasonable creatures, it is generally more effectual to appeal to [their] reason (from whence there are no demurrers . . .) than to abuse their nature, thunder vengeance in their Ears and treat them like unintelligent Idiots." Livingston to Noah Welles, November 14, 1743, JFP, Yale; to ———, [October, 1744?], Letter Book, 1744–1745, Sedgwick Papers, Massachusetts Historical Society.

2. On similar grounds Livingston had rejected the religious doctrines of the Great Awakening. The revivalists erred, in his view, in insisting that "mankind are purely passive in their reformation from vice to virtue, . . . and that the Conversion of Sinners is *wholly* performed by a superior and

irresistible agency." This reduced men to "mere machines, void of intelligence and free volition." Livingston to Welles, January 13, 1746, JFP, Yale.

3. Cf. the Declaration of Independence: "to secure these rights, governments are instituted among men, deriving their just powers from the consent of the governed."

4. "And if a People can be presumed to have a Right . . . to oppose the undue Measures of an arbitrary Ruler, when they strike at the very Vitals of the Constitution, they are certainly justifiable, in opposing them not only with the Pen, but even with the Sword." "Watch-Tower," No. X, *New-York Mercury*, January 27, 1755.

5. One reflection of the bitterness engendered by Livingston's defense of the compact theory of government was James Parker's effort to dissociate himself from the paper's editorial views. Unlike previous issues, which carried the printer's note that letters to the editor would be "taken in" at the printing office or "carefully delivered" to the editor, this and succeeding numbers bore only the notation: "New-York: Printed by J. Parker, at the New Printing-Office in Beaver-Street." Of the Anglican reaction to his two essays on passive obedience and non-resistance, Livingston remarked tartly: "[When] I engaged in demolishing the horrid and impious doctrines of passive obedience and non-resistance, the public was told that mankind was born with yokes and fetters; and that the original equality and independence of the species, was a chimera in politics, and blasphemy in religion." *Independent Reflector*, *Preface*, pp. 7–8. For the Anglican attacks, see *New-York Mercury*, September 10, 17, 24, October 15, 1753.

Number XL

Of the Use, Abuse, and LIBERTY OF THE PRESS [1]

————————*Arts in my Train,*
And azure-mantled Science, swift we spread
A sounding Pinion.———— THOM[SON], *Lib*[erty]

WHETHER the Art of PRINTING has been of greater Service or Detriment to the World, has frequently been made the Subject of fruitless Controversy. The best Things have been perverted to serve the vilest Purposes, their being therefore subject to Abuse, is an illogical Argument against their Utility. Before the Invention of the Press, the Progress of Knowledge was slow, because the Methods of diffusing it were laborious and expensive. The shortest Production was too costly to its Author; and unless the Writer had an opulent Fortune, or rich Patrons to pay off his *Amanuenses*, he was driven to the Necessity of retailing his Compositions. To arrive at Fame and literary Glory, was not in the Power of every great Genius; and doubtless Posterity has lost the Sentiments of many eminent Men, which might have been equally useful and important, with the Writings of those, who make the brightest Appearance in the Annals of Fame. It is otherwise since the Discovery of the Art of *Printing*. The most inferior Genius, however impoverished, can spread his Thoughts thro' a Kingdom. The Public has the Advantage of the Sentiments of all its Individuals. Thro' the Press, Writers of every Character and Genius, may promulge their Opinions; and all conspire to rear and support the Republic of Letters. The Patriot can by this Means, diffuse his salutary Principles thro' the Breasts of his Countrymen, interpose his friendly Advice unasked, warn them against approaching Danger, unite them against the Arm of despotic Power, and perhaps, at the Expence of but a few Sheets of Paper, save the State from impending Destruction. The Divine is not confined within the narrow Limits of his parochial Duties, but may preach in his Writings to the whole World. Like Powers in Mechanics, he does as it were, multiply himself: For at the Instant he Visits the Sick of his own Parish, he is perhaps consoling Hundreds against the Fears of Death, in foreign Nations and different Languages, and preaching to many Thousands at the same Time. And surely his Pleasure must equal his Labours, when he reflects, that his pastoral Care extends thro' the whole christianiz'd World; that however thin and secluded his particular Parish may be, yet that several Nations are within the Sphere of his Influence; that he shall even live after his Death, and Thousands whom he never saw, be his Crown of rejoicing at the great Day of Judgment. Such also are the Advantages of *Printing*, to the Philosopher, the Moralist, the Lawyer, and Men of every other Profession and Character, whose Sentiments may be diffused with the greatest Ease and Dispatch, and comparatively speaking at a trifling Expence. In short, as the glorious Luminary of the Heavens, darts its Rays with incredible Velocity, to the most distant Confines of our System, so the Press, as from one common Center, diffuses the bright Beams of Knowledge, with prodigious Dispatch, thro' the vast Extent of the civilized World.

Secrecy, is another Advantage, which an Author had not before the Art of *Printing* was discovered. As long as Power may be perverted, from the original Design of its being lodged with the Magistrate, for protecting the Innocent and punishing the Guilty, so long it will be necessary to conceal the Author who remarks it, from the Malice of the Officer guilty of so pernicious a Perversion; and by Means of this Art he may write undiscovered, as it is impossible to detect him by the Types of the Press.

It must indeed be confessed, that this useful Discovery has, like many others, been prostituted to serve the basest Ends. This great Means of Knowledge, this grand Security of civil Liberty, has been the Tool of arbitrary Power, Popery, Bigotry, Superstition, Profaneness, and even of Ignorance itself. The Press groans under the Weight of the most horrid Impieties, the most ruinous and destructive Principles in Religion and Politics, the idlest Romances, the most contemptible Fustian, Slander and Impotence. But to shut up the Press because it has been abused, would be like burning our Bibles and proscribing Religion, because its Doctrines have been disobeyed and misrepresented; or like throwing off all Law and Restraint, and sinking into a State of Nature, because the over-grown Power of the civil Ruler, abusing his Trust, has sacrificed the Lives and Properties of his Subjects, to lawless and tyrannical Sway. The horrid Practices of NERO, would by no Means have been a sufficient Reason for the Destruction of the Roman Polity. Nor had it been less than Madness in the *English* Nation, to have dissolved the Bonds of our Constitution, and sunk into Anarchy and Confusion, even tho' CHARLES I and JAMES II had provoked the just Resentment of an injured and oppressed People. Such a Condition would have been worse than that of SYRACUSE, under the most unlimited Despotism. The Truth is, the Tyrant should in such Case be deposed, but the State should survive him; and rather than live without Law, without Society, and the innumerable Blessings it includes, better would it be, to suffer with only a distant Hope of Redress, the ungoverned Sway of the most arbitrary Monarch the World ever saw.

The wide Influence of the Press is so dangerous to arbitrary Governments, that in some of them it is shut up, and in others greatly restrained. The Liberty of complaining, of carrying that Complaint to the Throne itself, and of breathing the Sighs of an afflicted, oppressed Nation, has too great a Tendency to produce a Revolution to be suffered in despotic Governments. No Press is tolerated in the *Ottoman* Empire. Power supported without Right, cannot bear, and therefore will not submit itself to a public Examination. Knowledge inspires a Love of Liberty, — and Liberty in the People, is incompatable with the Security of an arbitrary Legislator. To the same Causes are to be ascribed, the Restrictions on the Press in Roman Catholic Countries: Notwithstanding which, the Grand Segnior surpasses the Pope in Policy, which is not the only Proof of his Holiness's Fallibility. That Hierarchy which supports itself by keeping the People in Ignorance, and inhibiting its Devotees the Use of the Bible, oppugns its own Principles, by admitting the Use of the Press; which, as it affords the Opportunity of diffusing Knowledge and Truth thro' the World, must, by inevitable Consequence, equally spread abroad a Contempt of his *Holiness*, and the Worship, Discipline and Doctrines of his Church. Neither the Amours of HENRY VIII which to asperse Protestantism, the Papists ascribe as its Origin, nor any other natural Cause, had so happy [a] Tendency to destroy the Power of the See of *Rome*, as the Liberty of the Press. Popery and Slavery could not stand before true Religion and Liberty; and as the Press was the Instrument of both, the Rights of St. PETER's Chair were no sooner publicly contested, than despised and diminished.

No Nation in *Europe*, is more jealous of the *Liberty of the Press* than the *English*, nor is there a People, among whom it is so grossly abused. With us, the most unbounded Licentiousness prevails. We are so besotted with the Love of Liberty, that running into Extreams, we even tolerate those Things which naturally tend to its Subversion. And what is still more surprizing, an Author justly chargeable with Principles destructive of our Constitution, with Doctrines the most abject and slavish, may proceed even with inveterate Malice, to vilify, burlesque and deny our greatest Immunities and Privileges, and shall yet be suffered to justify himself under the unrestrainable Rights of the Press. An Absurdity grossly stupid and mischievous. What! sap the Constitution, disturb the public Tranquility, and ruin the State, and yet plead a Right to such Liberty derived from the Law of that State! The *Liberty of the Press*, like Civil Liberty, is talked of by many, and understood but by few; the latter is taken by Multitudes, for an irrefrainable Licence of acting at Pleasure; an equal Unrestraint in Writing, is often argued from the former, but both are false and equally dangerous to our Constitution. Civil Liberty is built upon a Surrender of so much of our natural Liberty, as is necessary for the good Ends of Government; and the Liberty of the Press, is always to be restricted from becoming a Prejudice to the public Weal. The Design of entering into a State of Society, is to promote and secure the Happiness of its Individuals. Whatever tends to this End, is politically lawful, and no State can permit any Practice detrimental to the public Tranquility, but in direct Opposition to its fundamental Principles. Agreeable to this Doctrine I lay it down as a Rule, that when the Press is prejudicial to the public Weal, it is abused: and that the Prohibition of printing any Thing, not repugnant to the Prosperity of the State, is an unjustifiable and tyrannical Usurpation.

If, on the one Hand, we suppose any broader Foundation for the *Liberty of the Press*, it will become more destructive of public Peace, than if it were wholly shut up: And a Freedom of publishing what is not prejudicial to the general Good, must be allowed; because, what can do no Harm can be no Evil, and there can be no Punishment without a Transgression. Besides, a Promotion of the public Welfare, of which the Press is often an Instrument, should be so far from suffering Discouragements, that as it is a political Virtue, it merits rather the Rewards than the Frowns of the Magistrate. Thus the Press will have all that Liberty which is due to it, and never be checked, but where its being unrestricted will prove an Evil, and therefore only where it ought to be checked. Liberty and Science may then spread their Wings, and take the most unbounded Flights. But should Tyranny erect its formidable Head, and extend its Iron Scepter, the Nation may publish, and any private Person represent the general Calamity with Impunity. Does Corruption or Venality prevail, the Patriot is at Liberty to inveigh and suppress it. The boldest Criminal lies open to Censure and Satire, and any Man may expose and detect him. The Divine may put Vice at a Stand; every Attack upon the publick Welfare may be reprehended, and every destructive Scheme baffled and exposed; for all Men are free in that Way, to defeat every Project that is detrimental to the Public. This Privilege is a great One, and we should all conspire to maintain it. This is the true LIBERTY OF THE PRESS, for which Englishmen ought to contend. Such a Liberty can never be dangerous, either to the Public, or their Ruler; but on the contrary may often be necessary.[2] What a certain great Politician said of the Freedom of Speech, is so applicable to that of the Press, that I cannot omit its Insertion. "The more," says he, "Men express of their Hate and

Resentment, perhaps the less they retain, and sometimes they vent the Whole that Way: But these Passions, where they are smothered, will be apt to fester, to grow venemous, and to discharge themselves by a more dangerous Organ than the Mouth, even by an armed and vindictive Hand. Less dangerous is a railing Mouth, than a Heart filled and inflamed with Bitterness and Curses; and more terrible to a Prince, ought to be the secret Execrations of his People, than their open Revilings, or, than even the Assaults of his Enemies."

All those who oppose the Freedom I have contended for, — a Liberty of promoting the common Good of Society, and of publishing any Thing else not repugnant thereto, — are Enemies to the Common Wealth; and many will fall under this Character, who are as ready to cry out for the *Liberty of the Press* as the warmest Patriot. Of this the various Orders that obtain amongst Men, furnish sufficient Examples: I shall instance but in two.

Never does a Writer of Genius and Spirit appear, unshackled with blind Prejudices and little Attachments to Party. A Writer who exposes the Roguery of Ecclesiastics, and displays the Beauty of genuine unadulterated Christianity, but he gives as it were Birth to a swarm of impotent Scribblers, who arrogate to themselves an Authority from God, to anathemize and deliver him over to the Devil; and the sooner to compleat his Doom, will invoke the secular Arm for Assistance. Strange that they should have a Power from God, to consign a Man over to eternal Torments, and yet be restrained by that very God, from illuminating his Understanding by Fire and Faggot, unless at the good Pleasure of the Magistrate! Such as these I call Enemies, both to the Press and the Public, tho' the former groans under the Burden of their Nonsense, Superstition and Bigotry,

The Press is for ever in the Mouths of Printers, and one would imagine, that as they live by its Liberty, they would understand its true Limits, and endeavour to preserve its rightful Extent. But the Truth is, there is scarce one in Twenty of them; that knows the one or aims at the other.

A Printer ought not to publish every Thing that is offered him; but what is conducive of general Utility, he should not refuse, be the Author a Christian, Jew, Turk or Infidel. Such Refusal is an immediate Abridgement of the Freedom of the Press. When on the other Hand, he prostitutes his Art by the Publication of any Thing injurious to his Country, it is criminal, — It is high Treason against the State. The usual Alarm rung in such Cases, the common Cry of an Attack upon the LIBERTY OF THE PRESS, is groundless and trifling. The Press neither has, nor can have such a Liberty, and whenever it is assumed, the Printer should be punished.[3] Private Interest indeed has, with many of them, such irresistible Charms, and the general Good is so feeble a Motive, that the only Liberty they know and wish for, is of publishing every Thing with Impunity for which they are paid. I could name a Printer, so attached to his private Interest, that for the sake of advancing it, set up a Press, deserted his Religion, made himself the Tool of a Party he despised, privately contemned and vilified his own Correspondents, published the most infamous Falsehoods against others, slandered half the People of his Country, promised afterwards to desist, broke that Promise, continued the Publication of his Lies, Forgeries and Misrepresentations; and to compleat his Malignity, obstinately refused to print the Answers or Vindications of the Persons he had abused; and yet even this Wretch, had the Impudence to talk of the *Liberty of the Press.* God forbid! that every Printer should deserve so infamous a Character.[4] There are among them, Men of Sense, Ingenuity, and rational Lovers of Liberty, for which the greater Part are less solicitous than the Generality of other Men, as a Confinement of the Press to its true Limits, is more frequently opposed to their private Advantage. It would be easy to enumerate a Variety of others, equally Pretenders to a Regard for the *Liberty of the Press,* and as evidently Enemies to the *Press* and the *Public:* But I shall reserve the farther Consideration of this Subject for a following Year, when the Conduct of Bigots and their Adherents, will, probably, supply me with some necessary Remarks.[5]   A.

I Thank Laura *and* Aurelia, *for the Honour of their Letter and Journals; and am sorry the Design of my Papers, prevents a Compliance with the Request of those fair Correspondents.*

1. This essay was the direct outcome of the editors' inability to secure a hearing in the regular newspapers for exchanges with their critics. Parker had already closed the *Gazette* to both sides. Although the *Mercury* was the Anglican mouthpiece, Smith and Scott tried submitting some pro-*Reflector* letters to Hugh Gaine, its printer. When Gaine refused, the triumvirate retaliated in three ways: first with this number of the *Reflector*; shortly thereafter by republishing a 1720 anti-Anglican tract of Thomas Gordon, with a new preface assailing Gaine for using "the vilest Arts . . . for the suppression of the Truth" and accusing him of printing seventy-six lies about the *Reflector* in his paper; and lastly by an attack in the *Occasional Reverberator*, I, September 7, 1753. See *The Craftsmen: A Sermon from the Independent Whig . . . With a Preface . . . by Philo-Reflector* (New-York, 1753); MS of the Preface in William Smith Papers, No. 212, New York Public Library; Paul L. Ford, ed., *The Journals of Hugh Gaine, Printer*, 2 vols. (New York, 1902), I, 9–10, 65; also No. XV, note 4 above and note 4 below.

2. Although this enunciation of the principle of freedom of the press was immediately intended to embarrass Gaine, Livingston's position and convictions were not new. In 1750 he had written: "As to civil Liberty, the English are secured against every Injury to their Persons, and every Invasion of their Property, by the strongest Barrier. . . . They not only speak, but print their Sentiments on Politicks without Fear or Reserve. A wicked Minister can find no Sanctuary against the Animadversions of his Countrymen. His Conduct is dissected, and his Corruption exposed. . . . Neither Wealth nor Power can screen the most independent Rogue from the most pungent Satyr [*sic*]." (*A Letter to the Freemen and Freeholders*, p. 4.) He defended "Freedom of Thought and Enquiry" as indispensable for "the proper Culture and Growth of Learning." Only by permitting scholars "the unrestrained publication of their scientific Discoveries" could a state flourish and "improve in general Stock." ("Watch-Tower," No. XLIX, *New-York Mercury*, October 27, 1755.)

3. Leonard W. Levy has minimized the libertarian character of this plea for press freedom on the ground that it was not broad enough to encompass criticism of elected legislatures. In Levy's view freedom of the press was a useful instrument for leaders of the "popular party" to employ against governors; but colonial advocates of such freedom would not invoke it to justify printed attacks on assemblies. (*Legacy of Suppression* [Cambridge, Mass., 1960], pp. 48–49, 141–142.) Livingston's view of freedom of the press was never so constricted, but the course of New York's political history and his own Whiggish liberalism did, in fact, place him on the side of the legislature more often than in the camp of "the Court." To a sincere "Promoter of the publick Interest," this was not at all surprising. While it was not inconceivable that "a Man may act the true Patriot in joining with the Court," it was not likely to happen too often, since for every "once that an Assembly has embark'd against the Interest of a Province, most Governors have play'd the Devil twice." (*A Letter to the Freemen and Freeholders*, pp. 10–11.) Livingston never exempted legislative bodies from the sting of his pen and publicly criticized the New York Assembly in 1755, 1769, and 1770. The distinction he drew in this issue was not between a legitimate use of the

press against executive prerogative and its abuse when employed against legislatures but rather between a press employed to promote liberty and one used to advance what he regarded as "superstition and thralldom." Livingston relished press warfare too much to squelch expressions of opinion on religious or political topics. "I have an undoubted Right to publish . . . my Sentiments," he wrote one of his Anglican critics, "as you . . . have . . . to oppose them." "In matters of a public Nature, every Man has a Right publicly to communicate his Sentiments; and if he delivers them with good Manners, . . . they ought to have a favourable reception." See *Occasional Reverberator*, Nos. II, III, September 14, 21, 1753.

4. The veiled allusions to Hugh Gaine in this paragraph were made savagely explicit in the *Occasional Reverberator* (September 7, 1753), where Gaine was accused by name of abandoning the interest of the public and the liberty of the press for his own "mean . . . base . . . mercenary" purposes, reproached for deserting the Presbyterian church in favor of the Episcopal, castigated for conducting a "party, partial, mercenary News-Paper," and indicted for his "unpardonable Crime" in refusing contributions to his press from the *Reflector's* supporters.

5. Livingston's violent demand for press liberty had little effect. The *Gazette's* editor announced (September 3, 1753) that he would not make his journal a "party paper." Gaine printed the letter in which Smith and Scott had threatened him with retaliation when he refused their original contribution; charged that the rejected essay was plagiarized from the English journal, *The Spectator*; and then mimicked his critics by listing 163 lies about himself that had appeared in the *Independent Reflector*. (*New-York Mercury*, September 3, 1753; *Journals of Hugh Gaine*, I, 15–16.)

Number XLI

THURSDAY, SEPTEMBER 6, 1753

A *Defence of* RIDICULE

Quid vetat ridentem dicere verum?

HOR. [1]

'T WERE to be wished that naked Truth, or Truth in any Dress was always sure of a welcome Reception. But the intellectual Taste of many Readers, is as incapable of relishing simple Truth, as their corporeal Appetite plain Cookery. They chuse to have it garnished with the Knicknacks of Humour, and rendered more palatable with the Sauce of Wit. Sensible of this were the delicate Authors of the Spectator.[2] They have embellished the gravest Precepts with the Decorations of Gaiety, and discussed the Profundities of Philosophy, in a Stile almost poetic. They *laugh* Folly out of Countenance, and inculcate the sublimest Morals in a satirical Vein. And yet, who are they that have wrought a greater Reformation in the Kingdom? Who has been more successful in refining the Taste, and restoring good Sense and Politeness, which were degenerated into low Quibble, to their original Reputation and Dignity? Who has been more happy in dissecting Human Nature, and exposing its every Foible?

The Independent Whig [3] has gone farther towards shaming Tyranny and Priestcraft (two dismal Fantoms not over-apt to blush) with downright Banter, than could have been effected by austere Dogmas, or formal Deductions. He has often displayed their Deformity with a Sarcasm, and struck Terror into a whole Hierarchy, by raising a single Twitter.

Many rational Discourses have proved disgustful on Account of their Formality. For tho' Mankind are willing to be facetiously taught, they care not to be dogmatically tutor'd.

The pious Mr. LAW [4] has recommended the severest Mortifi-

345

cation and Austerity of Manners, by giving his Works the Air of Novelty, and consulting the Taste in Vogue. He has dropt the rigid Pedant for the familiar Gentleman, a Character which sits upon him with a better Grace than on most of his Order. ISAAC AMBROSE [5] preaches up the same self-denying Doctrine, but it is his Manner of *preaching* that renders him distasteful to a modish Palate. 'Tis true, a pleasant Method of treating Subjects that have been solemniz'd by Priests and Nurses, is deem'd a little heretical. But,

I confess I could never understand the mighty Danger of Wit. It is impossible for Virtue and Merit to be placed in a ludicrous Light. Should a forward Wag clap a Fool's Cap on a Man of Worth, instead of derogating from his Character, or raising a Laugh, he would run the Hazard of being entertain'd with an universal Hiss for his misplaced Drollery. The Spectators could not be ignorant, that the Cap was not there 'till the Buffoon clap'd it on; for which the mistaken Object of his Waggery could not be answerable. If the building Castles in the Air, and then attacking them for Giants, be Humour, it is the Humour of a *Quixote,* and the World will sooner smile at the Knight, than be diverted with his Phantom. I own an ingenious Misrepresentation, may extort a Laugh from the Ignorant; but in that Case their Mirth is grounded upon a Belief of the Fact. Divest it therefore of its Colouring, strip off the Disguise, and the Joke is demolished, or retorted on the Witling. *My Lord* SHAFTESBURY [6] tells us, it was the saying of an ancient Sage, "That Humour is the only Test of Gravity; and Gravity, of Humour. For a Subject which could not bear Raillery was suspicious; and a Jest that could not bear a serious Examination, was certainly false Wit."

One of the greatest Geniuses of the last Age, has given us a Jest that cannot abide the Test of the above Touch-stone. To raise our Merriment, he entitles one of his Pieces, *The indispensable Duty of Cuckoldom.*[7] But to endeavour to raise our Merriment, by the greatest Injury a Man can suffer, is like attempting to gather Grapes from Thorns, or Figs from Thistles. An infallible Way of trying true Humour, is by translating it. Turn but *the indispensable Duty of Cuckoldom* into any other Language, and it is much what as witty as the *indispensable Duty of Martyrdom*. I cannot therefore apprehend, how this low Piece of Buffoonery is a Proof, that the most serious Thing in the World may be turn'd into Ridicule. And yet a certain Writer of great Literature, and no small Ostentation, affirms it set the whole Nation a laughing. Surely one would not imagine, by some Strokes in the divine Legation of *Moses*, that the Author had so great a Redundance of Risibility.

The Character of the present Age is rather foolish than wicked, rather absurd than immoral; and in the Application of our Remedies, we should consult the Nature of the Disease. A prudent Physician will not purge and blister for the Cure of a Wart, or a Freckle.

I know a Set of Men equally remarkable for the Grimness of their Aspect, and the Austerity of their Writings: These have long waged War against Wit, as a Foe to Religion. Themselves, 'tis true, are not chargeable either with the Guilt of Humour, or good Breeding. Sometimes indeed they endeavour to be pleasant, but their Gaiety soon degenerates into simple Burlesque. Theirs is an illiberate kind of Wit that smells of the Lamp, and will sooner create a Surfeit than a Laugh. For a Pedant to rally with a good Grace, is much as feasible as for a Porter to make a Leg *a-la-mode*. They shew themselves serious even while they are aiming to be jocose, and amidst all their Pretences to Raillery, discover themselves to be really in earnest; for they set their Razors in Oil, not to shave but to cut Throats. A Clown is the more awkard for assuming the Gentleman; and a Pedagogue striving at the Language of the Court, the more consummately pedantic. But the Facetiousness of an Author, who betrays an Inclination of using his Adversary in a very different Manner, is like stabbing a Man with a smiling Countenance. 'Tis imitating the *Roman* Senators who dispatched CÆSAR with a friendly Salutation. But instead of being diverted with the Pleasantry of an Inquisitor, methinks I should hear him in sober Sadness. His counterfeit Drollery would scarcely exhilarate my Mind, while I apprehended his preparing a Rack to torture my Body. There is no Wit at all in a bloody Knife, and where is the Jest of being butchered for Heresy?

When a Writer of this Complexion begins with a Farce, depend upon't he concludes with a Tragedy. His affected Wit will soon terminate in his natural Scurrility. Nor treat they one another with greater Delicacy. Their controversial Writings are replete with Spleen, Ill-Nature, and Ribaldry. Nay, I have met with Language in their polemical Labours beneath the Character of a Porter. I would even venture that a Carman, or a Chimney-Sweep, of a glib Tongue and ready Memory, might make a Collection from those Magazines of Slander, sufficient to out-scold, out-rail, or even out-curse his whole Fraternity.

When these Gentlemen, find Subjects of Importance handled with the Frankness of Humour, they are instantly in Arms. They long to wield the Sword of the *Lord*, and of *Gideon*, and would fain suppress the Laugh by plain Suffocation or Strangling. Religion, say they, is shaken to its very Foundations; and the Humourist beyond all Controversy, an Infidel. Every Thing sacred, every Thing valuable is attacked and insulted. The Clergy in particular are the meditated Victims. For how can Religion subsist without its reverend Teachers? But does not this argue a Diffidence of their Cause? Is it not a Concession that some of their Pretensions cannot abide the Test? Whence else so great a Consternation at a little Drollery? So general an Alarm at a Piece of Banter? Can any Man be witty on the Claims of an Ambassador, who has his Credentials in his Pocket? 'Tis impossible: Nor can one help being so, on him that should demand the Rights of Embassy, without being able to produce his Testimonial, which is frequently the Case of some of the Order. But it being once laid down for a Postulate, that Religion, and their venerable selves, are inseparable, who can ridicule the one, without levelling at the other. When the Apostle was pleasant on the wooden Deities of *Ephesus*, the Temple of DIANA totter'd to its Basis. The established Idolatry could not bear Ridicule. Besides, it was an indecent Way of treating a Worship that had the Law in its favour. Accordingly it failed not to raise a Mob, and in Truth it was Blasphemy against the great Goddess, whom all *Asia*, and the whole World adored. It was making merry with Priests, who are too solemn a Subject to be handled with Levity. The Apostle, however, vouchsafed them

348

not a single Proof of the Unity and Incorporeity of the divine Essence. He contents himself with laughing at their Idols. *They are no Gods* says he, *that are made with Hands*. The severest Satire he could have uttered. One of the Prophets is also extremely facetious with such Divinities, as were beholden for their existence to a Statuary, and for their Adoration to a Band of Priests. But what is all this to Religion? Is a Man to prove in Mood and Figure, that a Marble Statue is not omnipotent; or, that an Image carved Yesterday, existed not from Eternity? And why should he be obliged to frame Syllogisms, to disprove that Grace inheres in a starched Band, or that a ministerial Beaver necessarily covers Wisdom and Sanctity? How then does he endanger Religion, which resides neither in Bands nor Hats? Indeed, all the Ridicule in the World cannot affect Religion. Truth, which is immutable, and Revelation, which is worthy of God, may safely defy the keenest Wit in the Universe. He that throws Dirt against Heaven, may expect to have it return on his own Head; but surely it will not tarnish the Radiance of the celestial Luminaries. He may betray the Folly and Darkness of his own Mind, but the Sun will shine as bright as ever. It is far otherwise, with the superstitious Trumpery, that shelters itself under the venerable Name of Religion. Imposture cannot stand the Shock of Wit. Mimickry and Grimace naturally dread Banter, as their most formidable Enemy; and methinks it is some Proof of the Usefulness of Banter, that it's generally thought to be so formidable an Enemy to many of the Claims of a certain Order of Men.

To reason against the Merit of a grim Phiz, or antic Habit, would sooner make the Reader nod, than put the Monk out of Countenance. But run a Parallel between a Priest at Mass, and a Monkey dancing the Rope, and you will at the same Time set the Muscles in Motion, and expose his Reverence.

There is another Reason for which the Gentlemen in black, will ever oppose the bringing their austere Dogmatas and absurd Practices, their formal Gravity, their devout Grimace, and ostentatious Trumpery, to the Test of Ridicule. Their *jus divinum* is in Truth founded, not on the Authority of Heaven, but in a Delusion of the Vulgar: Nor can they support their exorbitant Influence, any longer than while the Laity, are silly enough to believe there is something sacred in their Persons, To support and propagate this Error in weaker Minds, they should, if possible, keep themselves entirely out of the Reach of Raillery: But they are too fond of their ecclesiastical Fopperies to lay them open to Derision. They are sensible that their venerable Lumber, might justly be rendered the Object of Ridicule, by holding it in a proper Light. Besides which, just Raillery has a natural Tendency to excite Laughter, even in the most injudicious Persons; and produces that muscular Motion, almost as mechanically as the Vibration of a Pendulum, acts upon the Wheels of a Piece of Clock-Work. A well-conceived Joke would, therefore, produce that Effect, even in their most implicit Devotees; and at the same Time that it gratified the Humour of the Satirist, would set their most zealous Adorers a laughing. And as Laughter thus excited, is generally attended with a Contempt of the Object, should the Mirth of the Vulgar be raised too often, it would be productive of an habitual Contempt of those Things which, tho' despicable in their Nature, have been ever held in the highest Veneration by the ignorant Laity.

The Truth is, the Character and Claims of an Ecclesiastic, which are really just, evangelical and rational, are not proper Objects of Raillery; and the Man who attempts to divert himself with them, immediately subjects his own Person to Contempt and Ridicule. On the other Hand, to treat the ridiculous Fooleries of Priestcraft, with serious Argumentation, is such a Prostitution of the Art of Reasoning, as is to the highest Degree criminal and unpardonable.

He must be of an odd Turn truly, who would formally confute the Holiness of a sweeping Cloak, or the Religion of a canonical Robe; and very much resembles a Clergyman who, in the Fervor of his Zeal, exclaimed vehemently against the heinous Sin of wearing Patches. But instead of working the Reformation of his Parishioners, he procured himself the Nick-Name of *Parson Patch*. He attack'd with Gravity what should have been laugh'd at with Humour. The Foible of the Girls was not a Subject for an elaborate Argument in the Pulpit. Instead of being treated as a

Crime, it should have been rallied as a Folly. And if that was un-
becoming the Gravity of the Preacher, he should have resigned the
Field to the Humourists of the Age; which would, perhaps, have
been the first Time of an Ecclesiastic's delivering the Laity to the
secular Arm for their real Benefit.   Z.

1. The quotation should read: *Quamquam ridentem dicere verum quid
vetat?* "What prevents one from telling the truth while he laughs?" Horace,
Satires, I, 1, 24.

2. Most of the essays in the *Spectator* (1711–1712) were by Joseph Addison (1672–1719) and Richard Steele (1672–1729).

3. The weekly periodical edited by Thomas Gordon (d. 1750) and John
Trenchard (1662–1723) between 1720 and 1721. It was as intensely anticlerical as the *Independent Reflector*.

4. William Law (1686–1761), English clergyman, author of *Serious Call
to a Devout and Holy Life, The Spirit of Prayer,* and *The Spirit of Love.*

5. Isaac Ambrose (1604–1663?), a Puritan divine whose sermons were
characterized by deep feeling and earnest piety.

6. Anthony Ashley Cooper, 3rd Earl of Shaftesbury (1671–1713), essayist
and philosopher.

7. The subject of cuckoldry was a common theme in French literature
from Rabelais to Molière.

Number XLII

THURSDAY, SEPTEMBER 13, 1753

The Importance of the Office of a Justice of Peace, with the Qualifications necessary for its due Discharge [1]

> —————With an equal Scale,
> He weighs th' Offences betwixt Man and Man;
> He is not sooth'd with Adulation,
> Nor mov'd with Tears, to wrest the Course of Justice
> Into an unjust Current, t' oppress th' Innocent;
> Nor does he make the Laws punish the Man,
> But in the Man the Cause.   SWENAM [2]

THERE is scarce any Office in the Kingdom more ancient or extensive than that of a Justice of the Peace. It may at least be traced as far back as the Time of King EDWARD III. But there were Officers in the Nature of Justices of the Peace, called Conservators of the Peace, long before that Prince's Reign.

Their Jurisdiction is so various, and extends to such a Multiplicity of Cases, as to fill many Folios, of a certain Profession equally famous for their Volubility of Tongue, and voluminous Writings. They have in particular, as Justices of the Peace, a very ample Jurisdiction in all Matters concerning the Peace. And hence it has been held by some of the long Robe, that not only Assaults and Batteries, but Libels, Barratry, and common Night-walking, haunting Bawdy-Houses, and the like Offences, which have a direct Tendency to cause Breaches of the Peace, fall within their Cognizance, as Trespasses within the proper and natural Meaning of the Word.

It is evident, that a Magistrate of such extensive Jurisdiction, may, by the due Exercise of his Office, diffuse his beneficial Influence far and wide, or do the Public unknown Mischief, by not discharging it aright.

JUSTICE OF THE PEACE

The Poets tell us, that DEUCALION and PYRRHA,[3] re-peopled the World after the Deluge, by throwing Stones over their Shoulders, which instantly sprang up into Men and Women. I could wish that modern Times would either not mimick, or could successfully imitate the Fable. But I have often been a Witness to the *Elevation* of insensible *Stocks*, which yet did not make them *reasonable Creatures*.

It must needs administer a sublime Pleasure to every honest Breast, that this flourishing Province affords no Instance of this Nature: Such is our public Virtue, and the Care, Capacity and Reputation of our Magistrates.

It cannot, however, be denied, that a Weight and Influence with the Vulgar, do not immediately qualify a Man for a Justice of the Peace. For my Part I humbly conceive (saving the Judgment of my Superiors) that the said fashionable Qualifications might be dispens'd with, without any Detriment to the Country, for those more rustic and ungenteel Ones, of being a Man of *Conscience, Learning, Impartiality* and *Resolution*.

I am sensible some Persons will expect an Apology for my making *Conscience* a necessary Ingredient in the Character of a Justice of the Peace, when it is so rarely insisted upon in Officers of greater Distinction. But as I have the Misfortune to be a little singular in my Opinions, I am not absolutely convinc'd, that a conscientious virtuous Justice, would, barely upon that Account, do any considerable Mischief to the Publick. It might, I own, make him appear a little singular, and perhaps create him the Ill-Will of those of his Brethren who esteem'd it an Infringment on their Prerogative; but then he might easily assuage their Anger, by shewing that it was originally an Appendant of his Office, and by that Means rescue himself from the Charge of Innovation, and the greater Guilt of Integrity and a good Conscience.

So great a Veneration had the ancient *Greeks* for a Man of Virtue and Piety, that altho' no Person's Rank or Condition exempted him from bearing public Offices, yet his Course of Life and Behaviour did.* For if any Man led a loose and dissolute

* *Lysiæ Orat. in Evandr. Æschines contra Timarchum.* [Lysias, *Oration against Evander*; Aeschines, *Against Timarchus*]

Life, he was thought unworthy of the meanest Employment in the State; it being conceived improbable, that a Person incapable of behaving himself so as to gain Reputation in private Life, should be able to demean himself prudently in a public Station; or that he who had neglected his own Concerns, or failed in the Management of them, should be capable of undertaking public Business, and providing for the Common Wealth. For this Reason, before any Man was admitted to a public Employment, he was obliged to give an Account of himself, and his past Conduct, to certain Judges in the *Forum*, which was the Place appointed for his Examination. Nor was this alone thought sufficient: For tho' at this Time they Pass'd the Trial with Credit, yet the first *ordinary* Assembly after their Election, they were a second Time brought to the Test; when, if any Thing scandalous was made out against them, they were deprived of their Honours.†

Without an inviolable Regard to the Voice of Conscience, an Officer's Respect will naturally be bounded by his own personal Interest; or, if he prefers Honour to Riches, instead of extending his View to the public Emolument, he is wrapt up in the Contemplation of his own Grandeur. He is in Post, and that flatters his Ambition; or, hurried away in the Pursuit of his own Elevation, he tramples upon the Happiness of those whose Interests are intrusted to his Care. Your queer conscientious Fellow, on the Contrary, is ever and anon ruminating on his Duty. He cannot sacrifice the Public to his private Interest, without disturbing his inward Tranquility and Repose. He inviolably observes the noble Precept of PLATO, *so to watch the Safety of the People, as to aim all his Actions to that Mark, while he forgets his own Advantage.* Hence it is, that Friends and Foes meet with the same Treatment, and he acts as tho' he were utterly void of natural Affection. Nay, he thinks it his Duty to divest himself of himself; and to immolate his own Inclinations on the Altar of the Law. He considers himself a Terror to Evil-Doers; and on the least Suggestion of Partiality in favour of an old Friend, or a Bottle Companion, his Oath sounds dreadful in his Ear. He is, in fine, a stubborn, inflexible, incorruptible Creature, that will not perjure himself for Love

† Demosthenes *in Theocr.* [Demosthenes, *Against Theocrines*]

nor Money, notwithstanding all the Precedents that might be produced in his Justification. It affects me with singular Delight that we can boast so great a Number of Magistrates of this amiable Character.

The Want of a *competent Education* in a Magistrate, is an incredible Prejudice to the Community. *Ignorantia mater erroris,*[4] said an eminent Lawyer. A Man may really intend well, and exert his utmost Efforts for the public Good; but still, if he be unacquainted with his own Power and Duty, fruitless and unavailing are his most generous Wishes, and in the Language of the Apostle, *He bears the Sword in vain.* A Sense of his Incapacity renders him timorous and diffident, and frequently deters him from proceeding right, thro' an Apprehension that he is going wrong. It moreover debases the Grandeur of his Function, and subjects it to popular Odium and Contempt. Mankind have a strong Aversion against submitting to Persons of inferior Capacity, and a riveted Notion that their Superiors ought to surpass them as well in Knowledge as in Authority.

A Magistrate ought at least to have a general Idea of the Laws of his Country, and a more particular Acquaintance with those relating to his own Office. With such a Stock of Knowledge he will be able, as well as willing, to assert his Prerogative, nor suffer an Offender to escape, for fear of becoming criminal himself. The Sight of an illiterate Magistrate, never fails to put me in mind of Mr. GAY's Monkey with his Sword and Perriwig.[5] But how great is our Happiness, that all our Justices can both read and write, either in their proper Persons, or by their Proxies, their Spouses!

Impartiality is another essential Ingredient in the Character of a Magistrate. For if he follows any other Rule than that of his own Reason and Judgment; or suffers himself to be blinded by Favour or Animosity, how precarious our Property, how defenceless our Persons! The most salutary Laws may be perverted thro' his Prejudice, and the strongest Bulwark of our Liberty thrown down, or leap'd over. On the Contrary, a Man acting from impartial Motives, will so take Care of the whole collective Body, as not to serve the Interest of one Party, to the Prejudice or Neglect of the rest. But it is beyond Expression fatal to a Community, to have the

Administration of Justice committed to Men sway'd by Prejudice, and resigning those Guides which Nature has given them for their Direction, to their own intemperate Zeal, or the Dictates of a Party. A Man acting in the Capacity of a Judge, ought to divest himself of all Bias, and, as it were, to annihilate his own Passions. His Oath, his Honour, his Country, demand impartial disinterested Justice. He ought to drop the Man whenever he assumes the Judge, and know nothing of the Persons litigant, but that they are Parties to the Controversy before him. To pervert Justice, which like the liberal Light of Heaven ought to shine equally on all, for the Gratification of a personal Pique, is the utmost Degradation of human Nature, and the most villainous Revenge that can be conceived.

Without *Resolution and Intrepidity*, all other Qualifications will be of little Avail. A Man may be *honest, wise*, and *impartial*; but if he is fearful and pusillanimous, he will lie dormant and inactive, when there is the greatest Necessity for exerting himself. Some Magistrates, tho' honestly disposed, have neglected their Duty for fear of being traduced by malignant Calumniators. I will not mention those who stand in more Awe of a Band of Carmen, than of an armed Host; because that proceeds not so much from natural Timidity, as a more political Reason. But Men, who voluntarily screen themselves from useful Offices, or neglect their Duty, to avoid the Reflections that may be cast upon them by vulgar Tongues, should consider, that the Duty we owe our Country, is not to be dispens'd with thro' Fear of a little undeserved Reproach. They should disdain thus to bury their Talents, for the sake of passing their Days in a Kind of living Death; or to resign the Prize of Glory, in the Service of the Common Weal, for a cowardly Indolence, and the insipid Joys of soft Retirement, and a selfish Repose.

> —————————— *An empty Form,*
> *Vain is the Virtue, that amid the Shade*
> *Lamenting lies, with future Schemes amus'd,*
> *While* Wickedness *and* Folly, kindred Powers,
> *Confound the World.*

A Man of Resolution will spring into Action, and check the

Torrent of Vice and Licentiousness, in Defiance of Reproach and Infamy. Slander in such a Case is real Glory, and Aspersion and Opposition present Renown and immortal Fame.

It is a Kind of Tribute which every Man must expect to pay for his Integrity. It is a fiery Purgatory thro' which the best of Men must pass; but then it refines their Characters, and augments the Lustre of their Names. For in the End, they must be triumphant. When FABIUS would not come to a Battle with HANNIBAL, but endeavoured to weary him out by Delays, he was abused by his Countrymen, reproached with Cowardice, and called *Cunctator*, the Delayer. But afterwards, his Conduct, which Experience evinced to be equally admirable and successful, procured him universal Commendation. Thus, Intrepidity and Perseverance in our Duty, will at last disarm Malice itself, and stop the venomous Mouth of Envy. Our greatest Traducers will applaud our Resolution, and blush that ever they were our Enemies. Besides, Integrity is a constant Support of Courage; and the Testimony of a good Conscience, the best Cordial for the Wounds of Obloquy.

> *Justum et tenacem propositi Virum,*
> *Non civium ardor prava jubentium;*
> *Non Vultus instantis Tyranni*
> *Mente quatit solida.* HOR.[6]
>
> Z.

The Author is greatly obliged to the Occasional Reverberator,[7] *for his generous Design of giving him and his Friends an Opportunity of being heard in his Paper; and to extend its Influence and Circulation, has given Leave to his Printer to advertise the Times of its Publication in this Paper. I thank that Gentleman for the polite Offer of his Correspondence, and shall chearfully exert my utmost Abilities in assisting to maintain so catholic an Undertaking.*

1. Justices of the peace presided over the lowest common law courts in the colony, trying cases involving £5 or less. Livingston's criticism of these courts in the *Reflector* was oblique, but he and Smith made more direct attacks elsewhere. A letter in the *Gazette*, April 1, 1751, unsigned, decried the "utterly illiterate, and sometimes notoriously flagitious" persons who sat as justices in the rural districts. The sentiments were unmistakeably those of

the *Reflector's* editors. In his *History* (I, 310) Smith charged that many of the justices could "neither write nor read." And when the act for granting the justices' courts authority to try cases up to £5 came up for renewal in 1758, Livingston and Smith fought hard but unsuccessfully against it, unwilling to trust such causes to "poor, mean, ignorant and unworthy Persons." (Dorothy R. Dillon, *The New York Triumvirate* [New York, 1949], pp. 55–56; David Jones to Robert Charles, April 26, 1760, "Draft of Protest agt. the Act to continue the £5 Act," n.d., both in William Smith Papers, Nos. 191, 197, New York Public Library.)

2. An obscure and incorrect reference to a comedy, *SWETNAM, the Woman-Hater, Arraigned by Women* (London, 1620), by an unknown playwright, in response to Joseph Swetnam's *The Arraignment of Lewde, Idle, Froward and Unconstant Women* (London, 1615), a coarse and violent attack on women. The lines quoted by Livingston are spoken by Iago in Act I, scene 3, where the last two appear as:

> "Nor do's he make the Lawes
> Punish the man, but in the man the cause."

I am indebted to Miss Celene Idema of the Department of Library Science, University of Michigan, for locating the source of the quotation.

3. In Greek mythology, Deucalion and Pyrrha were the only survivors of a great flood sent by Zeus to punish mankind for its wickedness. From their son Hellen descended the Hellenic peoples.

4. "Ignorance is the mother of error."

5. John Gay (1685–1732), English playwright. The allusion is to his satiric fable titled "The Monkey Who Had Seen the World."

6. "The man who is tenacious of purpose in a righteous cause is not shaken from his firm resolve by the rage of the people urging him to do wrong, nor by the countenance of the threatening tyrant." Horace, *Odes*, III, 3, 1.

7. It appeared on September 7. See above, No. XL, notes 1 and 4.

Number XLIII

THURSDAY, SEPTEMBER 20, 1753

The Vanity of Birth and Titles; with the Absurdity of claiming Respect without Merit [1]

Omne animi vitium tanto conspectius in se
Crimen habet, quanto major qui peccat
Habetur. ————————   JUVENAL [2]

  I was born with Greatness;
I've Honours, Titles, Power, here within:
All vain external Greatness I contemn.
Am I the higher, for supporting Mountains?
The taller for a Flatterer's humble bowing?
Have I more Room for being throng'd with Followers?
The larger Soul for having all my Thoughts,
Fill'd with the Lumber of the State Affairs?
Honours and Riches are all splendid Vanities,
They are of chiefest Use to Fools and Knaves.   CROWN [3]

THE great Variety of Powers, Characters and Conditions, so obvious in Human Life, is an illustrious Proof of the Benignity and Wisdom of the supreme Governor of the Universe. From this vast Diversity naturally result Superiority and Pre-eminence in some, and Dependence and Subjection in others. To this *natural* Difference of Character, Society has introduced the additional Distinction of a *political* Disparity, by conferring on various of its Members, a Variety of Honours and Privileges in a gradual Subordination from the chief Magistrate, to the least dignified of his Subjects. Hence we owe a becoming Regard to those who are advanced by the Wisdom of the common Wealth, in Proportion to their Elevation, unless they forfeit it by their Demerit. But an indiscriminate Respect for Men in conspicuous Stations, barely on Account of their extraneous Advantages, tho' they abuse and pervert them, degenerates into a Vice, and is introductive of the

359

most pernicious Mischiefs. Real Dignity and Worth are personal and intrinfic. They cannot be derived from Princes, nor entailed on Titles. A Knave distinguished with Honours and Affluence, is only a more conspicuous and mischievous Knave. I have known an humble Husbandman of eminent Merit, and an exalted Favourite, that deserved the Gallows. Wealth and Preferment may exhibit a dazling Exterior, while the Heart continues the Receptacle of the most execrable Impurities. Blood cannot adorn the Mind, but the Mind enobles the Blood. 'Tis more honourable, infinitely more honourable to live great, than to be greatly descended. A Man of Virtue is a Name of Honour for the most illustrious Potentate, nor can the Splendor of a Throne compensate the Loss of solid Greatness.

A despicable Wretch loaded with Preferment, is the more contemptible by being placed in a stronger Point of Light. The heedless Multitude may be struck with the Glitter of Wealth and Titles; but the considerate Part of Mankind will distinguish between the specious Appearance, and the glorious Reality. They reluct at revering Titles misplaced, which are only like Sails swollen with Wind, that oversets every Vessel better rigged than balasted.

> *I look down on him*
> *With such Contempt and Scorn, as on my Slave*
> *He's a Name only, and all Good in him*
> *He must derive from his great grand Sire's Ashes:*
> *For had not their victorious Acts bequeathed*
> *His Titles to him, and wrote on his Forehead*
> *This is a Lord, —— he had liv'd unobserv'd*
> *By any Name of Mark, and died as one*
> *Amongst the common Rout.*

A virtuous Life is the most august Title in the World. Our Births are our Ancestors, but our Merit is our own. Greatness of Soul resides not in the Trappings of State, nor hath the least Connection with Names and Pedigree. Where there is no Difference in Men's Actions, Titles are Jests. A Fool or a Rogue arrayed with the Badges of Honour, is a more droll Figure than a Monkey drest in Purple.

A wise Man will admire Goodness, wherever he finds it. Whether it be cloathed in Rags, or attir'd in Ermine, it attracts his Esteem, and commands Veneration. He considers it as that which alone can give Distinction to Men, and without which, all their adventitious Honours are but like empty Pictures, to supply the Absence of inward Excellence.

'Tis a noble Character which the Poet gives of a Prince, who preferred Men according to their Merit;

> *No future Titles swell'd him; in his Sight,*
> *The worthy Man seem'd greater than the Knight;*
> True Honour *he to* Merit *chain'd, and found*
> *Desert the* Title *gives, Kings but the* Sound." LLEUELLIN [4]

'Twere to be wish'd, that all Monarchs, and their Representatives, would imitate the Example of this judicious Sovereign. 'Tis true, the Introduction of such a Custom, would, in some Countries, create a little Confusion. How many stately Personages would be remanded to their original Obscurity? And what a Number of brilliant Figures, when stripp'd of their external Dignities, would be reduced to their native Meaness and Insignificancy? But then this Disorder would be fully compensated, by the superior Advantages flowing from so wise an Establishment. It would doubtless be found the fittest Expedient that could be devised, for advancing the Happiness of Society, as well as promoting the most sublime and generous Virtue.

But Honours are seldom dispens'd according to Merit. Sometimes the meer Caprice of the Prince, raises a Man to the highest Offices of the State. At other Times a Minion is magnificently rewarded for his great Dexterity, in ruining a People to replenish the Royal Coffers. *Philip Comines*,[5] tells us, that at the Battle of *Mont'hery*, fought between LEWIS XI of *France*, and CHARLES, Duke of *Burgundy*, some lost their Offices for flying, which were bestowed on others who fled ten Leagues beyond them.

I have long observed, that the Way of Eminence is not always open to personal Worth. There is a more direct Road to Advancement, which it were easy to point out, did I not decline offending my Betters. But an antient Story I hope I may relate without giving Umbrage to any. When *Euripides*'s Father told him, he was knighted, he smartly replyed, *Good Father, you have that which every Man may have for his Money.* I believe this Remark has been often verified since the Days of *Euripides*. But I deem it my peculiar Happiness, that it is not applicable to the Province in which I live.

A Fool, says an Author, has great need of a Title. It teaches Men to call him Count and Duke, and to forget his proper Name of Fool.

I have often been pleased with the Answer of a *Spartan*, to a Man who asked him what Titles and Distinctions they had in his Country? "Only such," reply'd he, "as are made by Merit. We mind not Blood, not a vain Title floating on that Stream: Amongst us, great Actions only beget great Sounds. Your high-sprung Blood will be lost in *Sparta*, where you must give Place to aged Matrons, whose greatest Riches are their hoary Heads." The *Spartan* had a just Idea of the rational Claim to Esteem and Reverence. But I remember a mighty Potentate, who is of Opinion, that a Catalogue of swelling Titles, is peculiarly efficacious to awe and humble his Subjects. The King of *Bisnegar*, in the *East-Indies*, has honoured himself with the following Titles: "The Husband of good Fortune; God of great Provinces; King of the greatest Kings, and God of Kings; Lord of all Horse Forces; Master of those who know not how to speak; Emperor of three Empires; Conqueror of all that he seeth, and Keeper of all that he conquers; Dreadful to all the eight Coasts of the World; the Vanquisher of *Mahometan* Armies; Ruler of all the Provinces which he hath taken; Taker of the Riches and Spoils of *Ceylon*; which far exceeds the most valiant Men; which cut off the Head of the invincible *Viravalalan*; Lord of the East, North, South, and West; Hunter of Elephants; which liveth and glorieth in Virtue military; who reigneth and governeth the World." [6] Now, if amidst all this pompous Nonsense, his *Bisnegarian* Majesty is rapacious and tyrannical, despoiling his Subjects, and delighting in human Miseries, is it possible for any rational Creature to love and reverence him? Of what Avail is it to his Subjects, whether he be stiled *The Husband of good Fortune*, while they groan under Bondage and Misery? Can his fancying himself the *God of great Provinces*, mend the Matter, while his spacious Territories, are a spacious uncultivated Wilderness, and the dismal Theatre of Penury and Horror? Are his People the better for having their Monarch, entitled, *King of the greatest Kings*, while he exceeds all the imperial Wolves of antient *Rome* in Tyranny and Rapine? Wherein consists the mighty Blessing of his being *the Lord of all Horse Forces*, while he is enslaving the human Race, and depopulating his Kingdom? Is he a proper Object of Love and Complacency, while he makes himself *dreadful to all the World*? Or is he the more to be venerated for *hunting of Elephants*, if, at the same Time, he imitates NIMROD, and makes Man his Prey?

There is, perhaps, not a more dangerous Error, than to believe that we are bound to reverence Men for the Offices they sustain, without any Regard to their virtuous Qualities, or useful Actions. It is a Doctrine propagated by those, who, sensible of their Wickedness or Folly, endeavour to derive Honour from their Rank; and to varnish their Demerit with the external Gloss of an elevated Station. Utterly destitute of solid Glory, they would constrain the Homage of the People by the Splendor of their Office, and make their Quality secure that Veneration which they daily forfeit, or rather, were never entitled to, by their Conduct. As in Matters of Religion, nothing is more common with some, than to substitute Forms and Ceremonies, Holy-Days, and Fastings, in the Room of inward Holiness, and the substantial Duties of Morality: So in civil Life, nothing occurs more frequently, than to see an eminent Knave demanding the popular Esteem on Account of his Elevation. This ridiculous Respect paid to Men of superior Rank, without any Regard to their moral Character, is the Source of the most pernicious Consequences. It abates the generous Zeal of the true Patriot, when he observes the most abandoned, tho' dignified Miscreant, receiving the Homage of the Multitude, while himself is either despised or forgotten. It encourages the splendid Villain to continue in his Crimes, while he receives the Applause due to the most refulgent Virtues. Whereas a Contempt proportionate to his Demerit, might shame him out of his Vices, and work his Reformation.

Again, were Men only respected in proportion to the real Dignity of their Characters, greater would be the Number of those who had Merit. But when every worthless Wretch is reverenc'd on account of his Birth or Station, what Wonder is it, to find real Desert so great a Rarity?

To see a Man claiming Reverence for a Name or a Title without doing Good, nay, often, while he is playing the Rogue, is the most impudent and absurd Demand that can be conceived. A Magistrate who promotes the public Welfare, and studies the Happiness of the Community, is entitled to high Esteem, and can scarcely miss it. But if he does no Good; with all his Opportunities to do it, who can help despising him? — Are we to subvert the Reason of Things, and admire what we ought to hate? Are Weakness, or Pride, or Knavery, the Objects of Admiration, because they reside in a Person loaded with Preferments? Is it rational to bow down to a Colossus, because it is made to straddle and look big, tho' within, it is all Mortar or Lead? Are we to sanctify Wickedness, and pay Obeisance to Iniquity, because they are pompously lodged, and decorated with a fair Outside? In a Word, are we to sacrifice the indisputable Rights of Mankind, resulting from their natural Equality, to accidental and precarious Advantages, which have no real Merit in them? Men in Office are to be reverenced for their public Services, and their Usefulness to the Common Wealth. But when they are of no Service to the Community, or abuse the Trust reposed in them; how can I respect them for neglecting their Duty, and doing what deserves Dislike and Aversion? Surely Respect is neither annexed to Names nor Power. I have known the greatest Names commit the most infamous Actions; and as for Power, the Devil has more of it than any Man.

There is scarce any Thing, in which our Esteem is more misplaced, than in that common Instance of toasting Healths. If there be any Sense in Toasts, they were, doubtless, intended to express a peculiar Regard for the Person toasted. But if we practise them without any Discrimination, between the best and the worst of Men, we destroy the very Design of the Thing, and are guilty of the greatest Absurdity. And yet, how often is a Person in Company, obliged to drink a sorry Fellow, barely to avoid a Quarrel with the Gentleman who toasts him? And how often doth a Man become a reigning Toast, for accidentally jumping into a Fortune, tho' every Man in Company knows him to be one of the greatest Scoundrels in the Community? — I shall conclude this Paper with an excellent Paragraph from CATO's *Letters*.[7] "We must deserve Reverence before we claim it. If a Man occupies an honourable Office, civil or sacred, and acts ridiculously or knavishly in it, do I dishonour that Office, by contemning or exposing the Man who dishonours it? Or ought I not to scorn him as much as I reverence his Office, which he does all he can to bring into Scorn? I have all possible Esteem for Quality; but if a Man of Quality acts like an Ape, or a Clown, or a Pickpocket, or a profligate, I shall heartily hate and despise his Lordship, notwithstanding my great Reverence for Lords. I honour Episcopacy; but if a Bishop is a Hypocrite, a Time-server, a Traitor a Stock-jobber, or a Hunter after Power, I shall take Leave to scorn the Prelate, for all my Regard for Prelacy. It is not a Name however awful, nor an Office however important, that ought to bring or can bring Reverence to the Man who possesses them, if he acts below them, or unworthily of them. Folly and Villany, ought to have no Asylum; nor can Titles sanctify Crimes, however they may sometimes protect Criminals. A right honourable, or a right reverend Rogue is the most dangerous Rogue, and consequently, the most detestable."

Z.

1. Though apparently paradoxical for the scion of one of New York's aristocratic families to derogate birth and titles, Livingston's position was consistent. He had early confided to Welles that the world's "many alluring Charms" were "in reality but guilded [*sic*] trifles, and varnished nothings that please for a moment, and terminate in remorse." (April 5, 1744, JFP, Yale.) In 1746 he incautiously aired his views by attacking the wife of James Alexander, with whom Livingston was then serving his clerkship, on the basis of gossip that she had rebuffed a young man's attentions to her young daughter because she considered him, an organist at Trinity Church, beneath the girl's station. Livingston rushed to the young man's defense in an anonymous spoof, "Of Pride, arising from Riches and Prosperity," in the *New-York Weekly Post-Boy*, March 3, 1746. The imprudent diatribe caused his peremptory dismissal from Alexander's office, but the affair did not alter his sentiments,

the product of conviction, not the affectations of a literary *poseur*. From youth to manhood, he expressed constant irritation with "high life," with the "fobberies of Dress, and the airy Diversions of the gay world," and with the "vain formality of fools." See, for example, Livingston to Miss [Susanna] F[rench], August —, 1744, Letter Book, 1744–1745, Sedgwick Papers, Massachusetts Historical Society; to Peter R. Livingston, November 10, 1755, Letter Book A, 1754–1770, Livingston Papers, Massachusetts Historical Society; to Sarah Jay, October 7, 1779, *Proceedings of the New Jersey Historical Society*, n.s., LII (1934), 145. The theme appears frequently in Livingston's poem, *Philosophic Solitude* (1747).

2. "Every offence of the spirit is the more marked, the higher the rank of the person who commits it." Juvenal, *Satires*, VIII, 40.

3. John Crowne (1640?–1712?), English dramatist of the Restoration period, playwright to the Court of Charles II. The quotation is from *The Ambitious Statesman* (1679).

4. Llewellyn is the name of two Welsh princes of the thirteenth century who refused to recognize the sovereignty of the English kings and fought several bloody wars to maintain the liberties of Wales.

5. Philippe de Comines (c. 1447–c. 1511), French historian and courtier, author of *Mémoires sur les règnes de Louis XI et de Charles VIII*.

6. Livingston's slipshod reference is to Vijayanagar in Mysore, India, the seat of a flourishing Hindu empire from 1336 to 1565. Italian and Persian travelers marveled at the wealth and splendor of the capital, later sacked and destroyed.

7. On *Cato's Letters* see Introduction, p. 21 and Appendix III.

Number XLIV

THURSDAY, SEPTEMBER 27, 1753

The Arguments in support of an ecclesiastical Establishment in this Province, impartially considered, and refuted [1]

Eripe turpi
Colla jugo: Liber, liber sum, dic age.   HOR.[2]

WHETHER the Church of *England* is equally established in the Colonies, as in the Southern Parts of *Great-Britain*, is a Question that has often been controverted. Those who hold the Affirmative, have drawn a long Train of Consequences in favour of the *Episcopalians*, taking it for granted, that the Truth is on their Side. The *Presbyterians, Independents, Congregationalists, Anabaptists, Quakers*, and all those among us, who in *England* would fall under the general Denomination of *Dissenters*, are warm in the Negative. I beg Leave, therefore, to interpose in the Debate; and as I promised in the Introduction to these Papers to vindicate the religious, as well as civil Rights and Privileges of my Countrymen, I shall devote this Paper to a Consideration of so important a Point; to which I am the more strongly inclined, because such Establishment has often been urged against the Scheme I have proposed for the Constitution of our College. My Opinion is, that the Notion of a general religious Establishment in this Province, is entirely groundless. According to the strict Rules of Controversy, the *Onus probandi*, or the Burden of the Proof, lies upon those who affirm the Position; and it would, therefore, be sufficient for me barely to deny it, till those who advance the Doctrine of an Establishment, have exhibited their Proofs to maintain it. I shall, nevertheless, waive the Advantage of this Rule of the Schools, and, as becomes an impartial Advocate for Truth, proceed to state the Arguments, which are generally urged in support of an Establishment. I shall then shew their Insufficiency, and conclude with the particular Reasons upon which my Opinion is founded.

They who assert, that the Church of *England* is established in this Province, never, that I have heard of, pretended that it owes its Establishment to any provincial Law of our own making. Nor, indeed, is there the least Ground for such a Supposition. The Acts that establish a *Ministry* in this, and three other Counties, do not affect the whole Colony; and therefore can, by no Means, be urged in support of a general Establishment. Nor were they originally designed to establish the *Episcopalians* in Preference or Exclusion of any other Protestants in those Counties to which they are limited.[3] But as the Proposition is, that the Establishment of the Church of *England*, is equally binding here as in *England*; so agreeable thereto, the Arguments they adduce are the following:

First, That as we are an *English* Colony, the constitutional Laws of our Mother Country, antecedent to a Legislature of our own, are binding upon us; and therefore, at the planting of this Colony, the *English* religious Establishment immediately took Place.

Secondly, That the Act which established the Episcopal Church in *South-Britain*, previous to the Union of *England* and *Scotland*, extends to, and equally affects all the Colonies.

These are the only Arguments that can be offered with the least Plausibility, and if they are shewn to be inconclusive, the Position is disproved, and the Arguments of Consequence must be impertinent and groundless. I shall begin with an Examination of the First: and here it must be confessed for undoubted Law, that every new Colony, 'till it has a Legislature of its own, is in general subject to the Laws of the Country from which it originally sprang; But that all of them without Distinction, are to be supposed binding upon such Planters, is neither agreeable to Law nor Reason. The Laws which they carry with them, and to which they are subject, are such as are absolutely necessary to answer the original Intention of our entering into a State of Society. Such as are requisite in their New-Colony State, for the Advancement of their and the general Prosperity; such, without which they will neither be protected in their Lives, Liberty nor Property: And the true Reason of their being considered even subject to such Laws, arises from the absolute Necessity of their being under some Kind of Government, their supporting a Colony Relation and Dependence, and the evident Fitness of their Subjection to the Laws of their Mother Country, with which alone they can be supposed to be acquainted. Even at this Day we extend every general Act of Parliament which we think reasonable and fit for us, tho' it was neither designed to be a Law upon us, nor has Words to include us, and has even been enacted long since we had a Legislature of our own. This is a Practice we have introduced for our Conveniency; but that the *English* Laws, so far as I have distinguished them, should be binding upon us, antecedent to our having a Legislature of our own, is of absolute unavoidable Necessity. But no such Necessity, can be pretended in favour of the Introduction of any religious Establishment whatsoever; because, it is evident that different Societies do exist with different ecclesiastical Laws, or which is sufficient to my Purpose, without such as the *English* Establishment; and that Civil Society, as it is antecedent to any ecclesiastical Establishments, is in its Nature unconnected with them, independent of them, and all social Happiness compleatly attainable without them.

Secondly, To suppose all the Laws of *England*, without Distinction, obligatory upon every new Colony at its Implantation, is absurd, and would effectually prevent the Subjects from undertaking so hazardous an Adventure. Upon such a Supposition, a thousand Laws will be introduced, inconsistent with the State of a new Country, and destructive of the Planters. To use the Words of the present Attorney General, Sir DUDLEY RYDER, "It would be acting the Part of an unskilful Physician, who should prescribe the same Dose to every Patient, without distinguishing the Variety of Distempers and Constitutions." According to this Doctrine, we are subject to the Payment of Tythes, ought to have a spiritual Court, and impoverished as the first Settlers of the Province must have been, they were yet liable to the Payment of the Land Tax. And had this been the Sense of our Rulers, and their Conduct conformable thereto, scarce ever would our Colonies have appeared in their present flourishing Condition; especially if it be considered, that the first Settlers of most of them, sought an Exemption in these *American* Wilds, from the Establishment to which they were subject at Home.

Thirdly, If the Planters of every new Colony, carry with them the established Religion of the Country from whence they migrate, it follows, that if a Colony had been planted when the *English* Nation were Pagans, the Establishment in such Colony must be of Paganism alone: And in like Manner, had this Colony been planted while Popery was established in *England,* the Religion of Papists must have been our established Religion; and if it is our Duty to conform to the Religion established at Home, we are equally bound, against Conscience and the Bible, to be *Pagans, Papists* or *Protestants,* according to the particular Religion they shall please to adopt. A Doctrine that can never be urged but with a very ill Grace indeed, by any protestant Minister!

Fourthly, If the Church of *England* is established in this Colony, it must either be founded on Acts of Parliament, or the Common Law. That it is not established by the First, I shall prove in the Sequel; and that it cannot be established by the Common Law, appears from the following Considerations.

The Common Law of *England* properly defined, consists of those general Laws to which the *English* have been accustomed from time, whereof there is no Memory to the Contrary; and every Law deriving its Validity from such immemorial Custom must be carried back as far as to the Reign of RICHARD I whose Death happened on the 6th of *April,* 1199. But the present Establishment of the Church of *England,* was not 'till the fifth Year of Queen ANN.[4] And hence it is apparent, that the Establishment of the Church of *England,* can never be argued from the Common Law, even in *England*; nor could be any Part of it, since it depends not for its Validity, upon Custom immemorial. And therefore, tho' it be admitted, that every *English* Colony is subject to the Common Law of the Realm, it by no Means follows, that the Church of *England* is established in the Colonies; because, the Common Law knows of no such religious Establishment, nor considers any religious Establishment whatever, as any Part of the *English* Constitution. It does, indeed, encourage Religion; but that, and a particular Church Government, are Things entirely different.

I proceed now to a Consideration of the second Argument insisted on, to prove an episcopal Establishment in the Colonies, founded on the Act which established the Church of *England*, passed in the fifth Year of Queen ANN, recited and ratified in the *Act for an Union of the two Kingdoms of* England *and* Scotland.[5] And that this Act does not establish the Church of *England* in the Colonies, has been so fully shewn by Mr. HOBART,[6] in his *second Address to the episcopal Separation in* New-England, that I shall content myself with an Extract from the Works of that ingenious Gentleman, which, with very little Alteration, is as follows:

The Act we are now disputing about, was made in the fifth Year of Queen ANN, and is entitled, *An Act for* securing *the Church of* England, *as by Law established.* The Occasion of the Statute was this: The Parliament in *Scotland,* when treating of an Union with *England,* were apprehensive of its endangering their ecclesiastical Establishment. *Scotland* was to have but a small Share in the Legislature of *Great Britain,* but forty five Members in the House of Commons, which consist of above five hundred, and but sixteen in the House of Lords, which then consisted of near an Hundred, and might be increased by the Sovereign at Pleasure. The *Scots,* therefore, to prevent having their ecclesiastical Establishment repealed in a *British* Parliament, where they might be so easily out-voted by the *English* Members, passed an Act previous to the Union, establishing the Presbyterian Church within the Kingdom of *Scotland,* in Perpetuity, and made this Act an essential and fundamental Part of the Union which might not be repealed, or altered by any subsequent *British* Parliament; And this put the *English* Parliament upon passing this Act for securing the Church of *England.* Neither of them designed to enlarge the Bounds of their ecclesiastical Constitution, or extend their Establishment further than it reached before, but only to *secure* and *perpetuate* it in its then present Extent. This is evident, not only from the Occasion of the Act, but from the charitable Temper the *English* Parliament was under the Influence of, when they pass'd it. The Lords NORTH and GREY offered a Rider to be added to the Bill for an Union, *viz.* That it might not extend to an Approbation or Acknowledgment of the Truth of the Presbyterian Way of Worship, or allowing the Religion of the Church of *Scotland* to be what it is stiled, *the true protestant Religion.*

But this Clause was rejected. —— A Parliament that would acknowledge the Religion of the Church of *Scotland*, to be the true protestant Religion, and allow their Acts to extend to an Approbation of the Presbyterian Way of Worship, tho' they might think it best to secure and perpetuate the Church of *England* within those Bounds wherein it was before established, can hardly be supposed to have designed to extend it beyond them.—

The Title of the Act is exactly agreeable to what we have said of the Design of it, and of the Temper of the Parliament that passed it. 'Tis entitled, *An Act* not for enlarging, but *for securing the Church of* England, and that not in the *American* Plantations, but *as it is now by Law established*; which plainly means no more than to perpetuate it within its ancient Boundaries.

The *Provision* made in the Act itself, is well adapted to this Design; for it enacts, That the Act of the 13th of ELIZABETH,[7] and the Act of Uniformity, passed in the 13th Year of CHARLES II [8] and all and singular other Acts of Parliament then in Force for the Establishment and Preservation of the Church of *England*, should remain in full Force forever; and that every succeeding Sovereign should at his Coronation, take and subscribe an Oath to maintain and preserve inviolably, the *said Settlement* of the Church of *England, as by Law established*, within the Kingdoms of *England* and *Ireland*, the Dominion of *Wales*, and Town of *Berwick* upon *Tweed*, and the Territories thereunto belonging. This Act doth not use such Expressions as would have been proper and even necessary, had the Design been to have made a new Establishment, but only such as are proper to ratify and confirm an old One. The Settlement which the King is sworn to preserve, is represented as existing previously to the passing this Act, and not as made by it. The Words of the Oath are, *to maintain and preserve inviolably the said Settlement*. If it be asked, *What Settlement?* The Answer must be, a Settlement heretofore made and confirmed by certain Statutes, which for the greater Certainty and Security are enumerated in this Act, and declared to be unalterable. This is the Settlement the King is sworn to preserve, and this Settlement has no Relation to us in *America*; for the Act which originally made it, did not reach hither, and this Act which perpetuates them, does not extend them to us.

It is a Mistake to imagine, that the Word *Territories* necessarily means these *American* Colonies. "These Countries are usually in Law, as well as other Writings, stiled Colonies or Plantations, and not Territories. An Instance of this we have in the Charter to the Society for *promoting Christian Knowledge*." [9]

And it is the invariable Practice of the Legislature, in every Act of Parliament, both before and after this Act, designed to affect us to use the Words *Colonies* or *Plantations.* Nor is it to be supposed, that in so important a Matter, Words of so direct and broad an Intent would have been omitted. "The Islands of *Jersey* and *Guernsey*, were properly Territories belonging to the Kingdom of *England*, before the Union took Place; and they stand in the same Relation to the Kingdom of *Great Britain* since. The Church of *England* was established in these Islands, and the Legislature intended to perpetuate it in them, as well as in *England* itself; so that as these Islands were not particularly named in the Act, there was Occasion to use the Word *Territories*, even upon the Supposition, that they did not design to make the Establishment more extensive than it was before this Law passed." Further, in order to include the Plantations in the Word *Territories*, we must suppose it always to mean, every other Part of the Dominions not particularly mentioned in the Instrument, that uses it, which is a Construction that can never be admitted: For, hence it will follow, that those Commissions which give the Government of a Colony, and the *Territories thereon depending in* America (and this is the Case of every one of them) extend to *all* the *American* Colonies, and their Governors must of Consequence have reciprocal Superintendencies; and should any Commission include the Word *Territories* generally, unrestricted to *America*, by the same Construction the Governor therein mentioned, might exercise an Authority under it, not only in *America*, but in *Africa* and the *Indies*, and even in the Kingdom of *Ireland*, and perhaps, in the Absence of the King, in *Great-Britain itself.* Mr. HOBART goes on, and argues against the Establishment from the Light in which the Act of Union has, ever since it was passed, been considered.

Dr. BISSE, Bishop of *Hereford,* (says he) a Member of the Society, preached the annual Sermon, *February* 21, 1717, ten Years after the Act of Union took Place, and he says, it would have well become *the Wisdom wherewith that great Work* (the Reformation or Establishment of the Church of *England*) *was conducted in this Kingdom, that this foreign Enterprize* (the Settlement of Plantations in *America*) *also should have been carried on by the Government, in the like regular Way.* But he owns the Government at home did not interpose in the Case, or establish any Form of Religion for us. *In Truth,* (says his Lordship) *the whole was left to the Wisdom of the first Proprietors, and to the Conduct of every private Man.* He observes, that of late Years the Civil Interest hath been regarded, and the Dependance of the Colonies, on the Imperial Crown of the Realm, secured: But then, with regard to the Religion of the Plantations, his *Lordship* acknowledges, that *the Government itself here at Home, sovereign as it is, and invested doubtless with sufficient Authority there,* hath not thought fit to interpose in this Matter, *otherwise than in this charitable Way: It hath enabled us to ask the Benevolence of all good Christians towards the Support of Missionaries to be sent among them.* Thus Bishop Bisse thought as I do, and that the Act of Union, nor any other Law prior thereto, did extend the Establishment to the Plantations: And if the *Society* had not been of the same Opinion, they would hardly have printed and dispersed his Sermon. Neither did the Civil Rulers of the Nation, who may justly be supposed acquainted with its Laws, think the Act of Union, or any other Law, established the Church of *England* in *America.* This is plain from the Letter of the *Lords Justices* to Governor *Dummer,*[10] in the Year 1725, almost twenty Years after the Union, wherein they say, *there is no regular Establishment of any national or provincial Church in these Plantations.*

If it be urged, that the King's Commission to the late Bishop of *London,* proves an ecclesiastical Establishment here, it is sufficient to answer, that his *Lordship* was remarkable for Skill in the Laws, so far as they relate to ecclesiastical Affairs, as appears from his *Codex:* And he was of the contrary Opinion; for in his Letter to Dr. Colman,[11] of *May* 24, 1735, he writes thus: *My Opinion has* always *been, that the religious State of* New-England, *is founded in an equal Liberty to all Protestants; none of which can claim the Name of a national Establishment, or any Kind of Superiority over the rest.* This Opinion the Bishop gave, not only since the Act of Union, but even seven Years after he had received his Commission, and surely it must be admitted, that as he had Time enough to consider it, so he of all others best understood it.

Thus far Mr. Hobart. With Respect to the Act of Union, I beg Leave only to subjoin, that it is highly probable the *Scotch* Parliament believed the *English* intended to establish their Church only in *England;* for in the Close of the Act by which they had established the *Presbyterian* Church in *Scotland,* it is declared in these express Words, *That the Parliament of* England *may provide for the Security of the Church of* England, *as they think expedient, to take Place within the Bounds of the said Kingdom of* England. And whatever Latitude the Word *Kingdom* has in common Speech, it in a legal Sense is limited, to *England* properly so called, and excludes the Plantations.

Nor can we suppose, that the Church of *England* is established in these Colonies, by any Acts prior to the Act of Union above considered: For besides the several Opinions against such Supposition already adduced, 'tis unreasonable to imagine, that if there was any such Establishment, King CHARLES II in direct Repugnancy thereto, should have made the Grant of *Pennsylvania*, and given equal Privileges to all Religions in that Province, without even excepting the Roman Catholicks; and that the Colonies of *Rhode-Island, Connecticut*, and the *Massachusetts Bay*, should be permitted to make their provincial Establishments, in Opposition to an antecedent Establishment of the Church of *England*, especially as the Laws of the *Massachusetts Bay* Province, are constantly sent Home, and the King has the absolute Power of repealing every Act he should think improper to be continued as a Law. Whoever, therefore, considers this, and that the King is sworn to preserve the Church of *England* Establishment, must necessarily conclude, that whatever Sentiments may obtain among the Episcopalians in *America*, our Kings, and their Councils, have always conceived, that such Establishment could by no Means be extended to us. As to *Connecticut*, all the Episcopalians of that Colony, and even their Ministers, were legally compellable to contribute to an annual Tax for the Support of the Congregational Clergy, 'till of late they were favoured with a Law which grants them a Privilege of Exemption from that iniquitous and unreasonable Burden. But whether they are subject to the like unchristian Imposition in the other Colonies above mentioned, I am not sufficiently acquainted with their Laws to determine.[12]

A.

1. Livingston was diverted to this topic by his Anglican critics on the college issue. One of them had argued in the *Mercury* (July 30, 1753) that since the Church of England was established in the province, it merited

preferential status in the proposed college. Livingston in the *Reflector* and Smith in No. IV of the *Occasional Reverberator* pursued the subject. Livingston's essay, with errors acknowledged in the next issue, appears to have been hurriedly composed and printed.

2. "Rescue your neck from the yoke of shame. Go say: 'I am free, free.' " Horace, *Satires*, II, 7, 91.

3. The Ministry Act of 1693 provided for public support of "a good sufficient Protestant Minister" in the counties of New York, Queens, Westchester, and Richmond. (*Colonial Laws of New York*, I, 328–331.) Elected vestries of six parishes were empowered to levy local taxes for this purpose. Although the intention of the Assembly had not been to establish the Episcopal Church by this plan, the interpretation of successive royal governors produced that effect. When the Anglican Trinity Church in New York City received its charter in 1697, it enjoyed the exclusive benefits of the Ministry Act in the county of New York, and its minister was supported by public taxation. See R. Townsend Henshaw, "The New York Ministry Act of 1693," *Historical Magazine of the Protestant Episcopal Church*, II (1933), 199–204; Charles C. Tiffany, *History of the Protestant Episcopal Church in the United States of America* (New York, 1895), pp. 165–166; Morgan Dix, *A History of the Parish of Trinity Church in the City of New York*, 4 vols. (New York, 1898), I, 80–88, 91–92.

4. Act of 5 Anne, c. 5 (1707).

5. Act of 5 Anne, c. 8 (1707).

6. Noah Hobart (1706–1773), Congregationalist minister at Fairfield, Connecticut, had stirred up a brief pamphlet war with the Anglicans in 1746 by the sermon he preached at the ordination of Noah Welles. Answered by James Wetmore, he responded; other Anglicans joined in; and the printing presses poured out a minor flood of polemical tracts on the validity of presbyterian as against episcopal ordination. Welles sent Livingston the pamphlets as they appeared. Not surprisingly, Livingston found Hobart "a masterly Reasoner, and . . . a severe Satyrist," capable of saying "the most galling things with an air of good humor, and . . . sharp without Virulence." Wetmore, by contrast, he disparaged as "a profusion of Scandal, Ribaldry, and Billingsgate." (Livingston to Welles, February 18, 1749, JFP, Yale.) The long extract given in this number is from Hobart's *Second Address to the Ministers of the Episcopal Separation in New-England* (Boston, 1751). On the Hobart-Wetmore controversy, see Arthur Lyon Cross, *The Anglican Episcopate and the American Colonies* (New York, 1902), pp. 140–144; and William S. Perry, *History of the American Episcopal Church*, 2 vols. (Boston, 1885), I, 279–282.

7. 13 Eliz., c. 12 (1570).

8. 13 and 14 Charles II, c. 4 (1662).

9. The Society for the Promotion of Christian Knowledge, founded in England in 1699 to promote the spread of the Episcopal faith, conducted schools, established libraries, opened missions, and printed and distributed religious books. From it sprang the Society for the Propagation of the Gospel in Foreign Parts, later the Church of England's missionary arm in the American colonies.

10. William Dummer, Lieutenant Governor of Massachusetts, 1716–1723, and 1729–1730, defended Congregationalist ministers from the Anglican charge that they were not true clergymen because they lacked episcopal ordination.

11. Benjamin Colman (1673–1747), minister of the Brattle Street Church in Boston, received the degree of Doctor of Divinity from Glasgow in 1731.

12. Since 1727 Connecticut's Episcopalians were permitted to transfer their church taxes to a minister of the Church of England if they lived close enough to attend his services. Massachusetts made similar provision that year, though the communicant must live within five miles of the Episcopal minister to whom his church taxes were to be transferred. New Hampshire exempted non-Congregationalists from supporting the establishment only if they could prove regular attendance at another church. Anglicans do not appear to have profited heavily from this exemption. Rhode Island had no compulsory church taxation. W. W. Manross, *History of the American Episcopal Church* (New York, 1935), pp. 99, 105; Sanford H. Cobb, *The Rise of Religious Liberty in America* (New York, 1902), pp. 234, 270–271, 292.

Number XLV

THURSDAY, OCTOBER 4, 1753

A Catalogue of sundry Grievances, which require immediate Redress

Ab ovo
Usque ad Mala. Hor.[1]

I SHALL, in my present Speculation, beg Leave a little to deviate from my usual Method of treating my Subject, and instead of alloting a whole *Reflector*, to one Inconvenience, throw several Grievances into a single Paper. Indeed, the Mischiefs I shall offer to the public Consideration, are so evident, that they could not, separately considered, compose so many distinct Papers. They are glaring and conspicuous, and want nothing more to excite Compassion, and engage the Friends of Liberty in their Redress, than a plain and unembellished Enumeration. Arguments, in support of self-evident Truths, are idle and impertinent. I shall, therefore, without farther Proem or Preface, proceed to a Detail of the Grievances, under which several of the good People of this Province have long laboured, and that without any Attempt for their Removal.

The first I shall mention, is, that which several honest Gentlemen have suffered an Account of *Rotten Row* [2]: For it is to be remembered, that not long since, many of the worshipful Members of the Corporation, out of the Exuberance of their Liberality, were disposed to make a Present of it to the People, who had Lots bordering upon it. So generous an Intention one would have thought, ought not to have met with any Opposition: and yet we all know what a Clamour was raised about it. They were even reproached with a Design of squandering the publick Money, and their disinterested Munificence, was represented in an odious Light, tho' the very Objection urged against their disposing of it *Gratis*, was a cogent Argument in their Favour. For if they were offered five thousand Pounds by a Gentleman (who by the bye could have no Right to it, because he lived remote from it) the greater was their intended Charity in granting it, thro' *special Grace* and *meer Motion*. Now, as Generosity is one of the noblest, and most disinterested Virtues, there cannot be a great Grievance than to be obstructed in its Exercise; for which Reason, I hope, that whenever they renew their generous Offer, it will not meet with so absurd an Opposition.

The Custom-House is evidently aggrieved by the want of a Law to establish and enforce its supernumerary Perquisites. We all know, that there is at Present no Provision for *extraordinary Dispatch,* for which it is nevertheless equitably entitled to an extraordinary Gratuity. But such Gratuities not being enforced by Law, are liable to be daily controverted, and are sometimes, by sordid and avaricious Spirits, absolutely refused. Nor is this all. By the pious Genius of the *British* Constitution, a considerable Portion of the Year, is set a Part and dedicated to the Contemplation of the Lives and Actions of illustrious Saints and Martyrs, which has a happy Tendency to inspire us with an Emulation of their Virtues, and enliven the lamentable Decay and Languor of Religion. In such consecrated Seasons it is evident, that no Man of real Piety can consent to relinquish his devout Meditations for secular Employments, without a suitable Recompence. And yet, for Services done even on those Days, the Officer must entirely depend on the Generosity of his Employer, without any Certainty of an adequate Reward, to compensate the Loss of those holy Exercises. I had like to have forgot the Necessity for adding a Clause to the Act proposed, prohibiting the Comptroller of the Customs, for the Time being, from giving any Change for Money to be hereafter received for Services done and performed in the said Custom-House; or at least that it shall and may be lawful, to and for the said Comptroller, to retain and keep in his Hands, any Sum of Money not exceeding Eight Shillings, for any Debt accruing as aforesaid, of Nine Pence, or under, without being accountable for the Surplus to any Person or Persons whatsoever.

A certain Civil-Law Court in this Province, has long laboured under prodigious Difficulties, and is still as remote from Redress as ever. It has been most unjustly traduc'd, and its Impartiality called in Question, without Hesitation or Reserve. Now, as Truth and Righteousness always appear in brighter Colours after an impartial Scrutiny, it is to be wished, its most inveterate Adversaries would vouchsafe it an Opportunity of vindicating its immaculate Probity, and wiping off the malevolent Calumnies that have been thrown upon it. A public Acquittal would be a public Confutation of its Enemies, and remain on Record to the Confusion of the Slanderer, and its own immortal Honour.

Some of our thrifty Bakers, who have deserved well of their Country, by endeavouring to introduce brown Bread, which is much cheaper, as well as more wholesome, than white, cannot prosecute their laudable Scheme, without great Jealousy and Clamour. This I take to be the greater Grievance, as the Flour which they bake into such Bread, cannot by the Act, be exported for fine Flour,[3] and consequently would be so much clear Gain to the City, could they once persuade their Customers to the commendable Frugality of a home Consumption.

Amidst my Enumeration of public Evils, the tardy Progress of our College, occasioned by the Scrupulosity of irresolute Men, is not to be passed over in Silence.[4] Its Management has been presumptuously represented, as equally appertaining to all the various Denominations of Christians in the Province; and as tho' the Authors and Abettors of such detestable Heresies, were bent on the utter Extirpation of Religion, they have, with unexampled Temerity, rejected the Introduction of spiritual Rulers, as baneful to the Growth and Propagation of true Science. Nay, they have not even had the Breeding, humbly to offer our ecclesiastical Establishment the Preference; when no impartial Thinker, can either doubt the Reality of such an Establishment among us, or the Equity of the Claim consequent thereupon, in as much as both the one and the other, have been publicly asserted in a weekly News Paper that was never yet detected of Forgeries. The Perplexity about the Constitution of the College, purposely created by these restless Spirits, did lately, in the Opinion of many, prevent its final Settlement, at a Time when it was conceived to be just on the Crisis of being delivered up, to those who alone have hitherto produced a rational Claim for it. The postponing, therefore, the said Claim to be canvassed and misrepresented by Fanatics and Infidels, may be attended with insuperable Obstructions to the laudable Design of fixing it on a pure and orthodox Bottom. Had the Assembly, on the contrary, ran Headlong into the public-spirited Proposal of excluding Presbyterians, Dissenters, Enthusiasts, and Deists, from any Share in the Administration of the Academy, as they were publicly advised to do, we had already beheld the Dawnings of Literature, and should soon have been sensible, that none but the Episcopalians, from their never-failing Lenity and Indulgence, were deserving of so grand and important a Trust.[5]

Many of our young Gentlemen also labour under no small Difficulty, in that they cannot, as the Law now stands, profane the Name of God without either incurring a Fine, or a very ungenteel Punishment. This I take to be the greater Hardship, as the prohibiting them from taking the Name of God in vain, puts it out of their Power to give any Proof that they believe his Existence. For this Reason I have long wished to see this rigorous Act repealed; but on second Thoughts, I conceive there is no absolute Necessity for it, because some of our Magistrates, charitably considering the said Hardship, take especial Care not to be too rigid in its Execution.

Our Corporation has, for some Years past, labour'd under a first-rate Grievance, by the audacious Attempt of some evil disposed Persons, to introduce into the Common Council, Men of Sense and Distinction. Several Gentlemen of this Character, have actually been chosen, but still their Worships endured the Evil with a Christian Patience. The factious Spirits, however, not content with having a few Persons of Fortune and Capacity in that Office, seem, of late, resolved to use their Interest, to have the whole Corporation composed of Gentlemen; than which, I conceive, there cannot be a more violent Invasion of their ancient and undoubted Privileges.

The next I shall take Notice of is a Grievance, beneath which our Batchelors have long groaned, without any Prospect of Relief. It is well known, that by our Laws no Person is obliged to marry; and it is equally true, that whenever a Man suffers an Inconvenience, for not doing what by Law he is not obliged to do, such Inconvenience must be a Species of Persecution, and a more artful Method of disguising his Slavery under the Cloak of Liberty. Now this I take to be the very Case of the Batchelors. The Law doth not compel them to contract Matrimony, and yet denies their Issue the Privileges of Children born in lawful Wedlock; which is, in Reality, only a more sly and indirect Method of forcing them to marry: For while they remain single, they are still punished in the Scandal and Disadvantages of their Offspring. This must necessarily be a great Impediment to the Propagation of Bastards, and consequently, extremely injurious to a new settled Country, in want of People for the Cultivation of its Lands. To remedy this Inconvenience, and encourage the Multiplication of the Species, I would propose, that Bastardy for the future, be esteemed honourable; and natural born Children, equally capable of inheriting the Estates of their putative Ancestors, with a legitimate Issue. The most plausible Objection against this Proposal is, that it will diminish the Revenue of the Clergy in the Article of Marriage: But this would be abundantly compensated, by the greater Generation of Children, and consequently the greater Number of Christenings, as well as of Deaths; the latter of which must proportionably augment the Fees arising from Burials. Should I, notwithstanding, be over-ruled, I still hope, that in Compassion to the unhappy Sufferers themselves, some public Officer may be appointed to prevent all Possibility of increasing their Calamity, by qualifying them (sweet Ladies with your Favour) to divert you with more melodious Voices.

Another Grievance is, the Clergy's being most unreasonably abridged in their Power and Authority. For tho' they are beyond Controversy the Ambassadors of Heaven, they are often treated with less Ceremony than the Plenipotentiaries of earthly Sovereigns. Some People even carry their Disrespect, to the Length of preferring their own Judgment to that of their spiritual Overseers, and insist on a Liberty of thinking for themselves, in Matters so momentous as Religion and Government. To what an

Inundation of Irreligion and Profaness this must necessarily expose us, is a Topic, too Melancholy to dwell on. But to the Redress of this Calamity, I hope I shall myself not a little contribute, by representing their indubitable Claims, in some of my future Speculations, in a true Light, and illustrating the temporal Grandeur of their Function, to the utter Confusion of Deists and Libertines.

The last Mischief I shall mention is, the *Independent Reflector* himself. This presumptuous Writer has exerted his utmost to introduce universal Confusion and Disorder. A Man in a public Station cannot act awry, but he has the Assurance to pry into his Conduct, and without Favour or Compassion, expose him to open View. He regards neither Rank nor Quality, but impudently animadverts on the Actions of his Superiors without Timidity or Reserve. He has already disconcerted several Projects of the most eminent Personages amongst us; and audaciously attempts to disappoint those to whom Men much better than himself, submit with implicit Obedience. The Establishment of our College he has hitherto retarded by diabolical Instigation and Malice prepense. His abominable Opinions concerning Election-Jobbers, and the Heads of Parties, are enough to ruin half the Politicians in the Province. With respect to Religion he is truly detestable: For he examines with boundless Freedom into the Truth of Opinions, which the Generality of his Countrymen take for granted, and steels his Bosom against the Sanction of Authority. The very Tenets which his Grand Mother taught him in his Infancy, he has now the Confidence to unravel and scrutinize, according to the carnal Reasonings of his own Mind.[6] It would be endless to enumerate the Grievances of which he is the Author; but as they are all in my own Power to remove, I promise the Public they shall not remain Matter of Complaint, after those above-mentioned have been fully redressed.   Z.

To the INDEPENDENT REFLECTOR

SIR,

You have in your N° XXVII. clearly shewn the pernicious Consequence of our continuing to receive Copper Pence, for more than their real Value. The Force of your Reasoning upon that Subject, I was in Hopes, would long e'er now have open'd the Eyes of our Countrymen, and made them unite their Endeavours, to put a Period to so growing a Mischief, by executing the Plan you proposed for that Purpose. But in many Things Mr. REFLECTOR, you have the ill Fortune of CASSANDRA, whose Predictions were never regarded 'till their Accomplishment rendered all remedy fruitless.

I now beg Leave to inform you, that another Evil of a more destructive Nature relating to Copper Pence, is increasing upon us, and which, unless seasonably prevented, must in a short Time sink many Thousand to the Community. You have undoubtedly heard, that upwards of £40,000 Sterling, in counterfeit Pence, has lately been made in *Europe*, in Imitation of good Copper Half-Pence; vast Quantities of which have been purchased at 7d per Weight, and sent to *America*. Of these we have already a very considerable Number passing amongst us. It is not long since we had an Instance in this City, of a Bag of *Ten Pounds* being passed in Payment, which upon Complaint seized by a Magistrate, and another of *Forty Shillings*, all of the counterfeit Sort.

How great must be the Profit to the Villains who import them, is easily calculated, when they can purchase for *Two Shillings and Eleven Pence* Sterling, as many as pass here for *Twenty Shillings* Currency. Nor is it to be forgot, that the Composition of which they are made is such a Mixture, that their real Value is inferior to that of Iron, if they be of any Value at all. Yet I am persuaded, from my own Observation, that those Counterfeits already make Two *per Cent* of all the Pence passing in this Province.

In order to prevent this ruinous Evil, I would earnestly recommend it to my Countrymen, and particularly to the Merchants of this City, to count and examine all they receive, and return every one that is not genuine. It is easy to distinguish the false from the true, the former being cast and rough, and the latter milled and smooth. Nor would it perhaps be improper for Magistrates and Grand Juries, from time to time, to make diligent Enquiries for the Detection of the Delinquents who import them, that their being speedily brought to condign Punishment, may prevent their future Offence, as well as deter others from amassing Fortunes by ruining their Country.

If the Public will, after this Notification, remain insensible of the Mischief, I have for my Part, discharged my Duty, by imparting to them this Intelligence, as you will do in publishing these well-meant Hints of

Your real Friend,

SHADRECH PLEBIANUS.

384

CATALOGUE OF SUNDRY GRIEVANCES

1. "From the eggs to the apples," i.e., from soup to nuts. Horace, *Satires,* I, 3, 6.

2. "Rotten Row" was a term applied in reproach to Hunter's Key, a street extending along the East River from Old Slip to Wall Street. The name first appears on maps of 1754 and 1755. Residents of the area complained at about this time that a once desirable residential site was becoming a "Very Great nuisance" because of "the Filth that floats there" and "the putrid Stench, arising from that Sink of Corruption." A protracted conflict developed between commercial interests and residents over the area's future, whether to grant the adjacent water lots to residents or non-residents and whether to reserve the area for private use or for a public market. The issue was compromised in 1767. For the earliest maps showing Rotten Row, see I. N. Phelps Stokes, *The Iconography of Manhattan Island,* 6 vols. (New York, 1915–1928), I, 275 and Plate 34; and David T. Valentine, *History of the City of New York* (New York, 1853), map between pp. 304 and 305. On the water-lots issue, see Stokes, I, 619, 718, 769, 783–784. The *Reflector* favored public improvement of the site, with a portion of the land for a public market. See No. LII.

3. For the provisions of this act, see *Reflector,* No. XXIV, note 3.

4. Livingston's essays in March and April and the subsequent press warfare had increased public awareness of the Anglican character of the proposed college. Three earlier developments came into sharper focus when viewed through the *Reflector's* hostile lenses: (1) of the ten trustees appointed under the 1751 act to manage the lottery funds, seven were Episcopalians, two were of the Dutch Reformed Church, and the tenth was Livingston himself; (2) the only proposal the lottery trustees had received for locating the college was from Trinity Church, which on March 3, 1752, offered to give part of its King's Farm property "for the erecting and use of a Colledge"; and (3) William Smith, the young Anglican who headed the team of penmen assembled to counteract the *Reflector,* had published, in April, 1753, a blatantly partisan plan for the college, providing for an Anglican clergyman as both college head and rector of Trinity Church, and for the Anglican liturgy in its public prayers. (*Ecclesiastical Records of the State of New York,* Hugh Hastings, ed., 7 vols. [Albany, 1901–1916], V, 3220; [William Smith], *A General Idea of the College of Mirania* [New York, 1753], pp. 65–66, 85–86; *New-York Gazette, Supplement,* November 7, 1752; *New-York Mercury,* November 6, 1752.)

Whatever hopes the Anglicans may have cherished for speedily terminating the college affair and organizing it along church lines were dashed by the *Reflector's* crusade. When the Anglican managers of the scheme presented an informal request to Governor George Clinton, sometime in the fall of 1753, for a charter of incorporation, he turned them down; and when two new bills for raising additional funds for the college were introduced into the Assembly during the summer of 1753, several members expressed their suspicions of the composition of the board which was administering the lottery monies. Disappointed because the bills passed the house nevertheless, Livingston was pleased that his literary labors had opened the eyes of the dissenting sects and that the partiality of the lottery trustees was exciting "the Jealousy of every unbiassed mind." (*Independent Reflector, Preface,* pp. 15–17; Livingston to Welles, February 1, 1754, JFP, Yale; *Colonial Laws of New York,* III, 899–910; *Assembly Journal,* II, 337, 345, 350–351.)

5. In less sarcastic vein Livingston disclaimed responsibility for having delayed establishment of the college. "The erection of a College on a generous bottom I never opposed. . . . Against a free College . . . I have written not a word . . . nor does any man more ardently long for so excellent an establishment . . . [but] If my adversaries mean by the charge, that I have prevented the execution of the . . . little dirty contracted party project . . . I wish I had . . . reasons to flatter my self, with being the instrument of such extensive utility to my country. . . . But at their door lies the slow prosecution of this momentous affair: For had they not attempted to engross its Government into their hands, there would have been no ground for the opposition I excited." *Independent Reflector, Preface,* p. 15.

6. Ten years earlier Livingston had written to Noah Welles to congratulate him on having burst "the Schackles of Tyrant Custom" in his free "unfetter'd" choice of a sectarian attachment: "Every man has an indisputably [*sic*] right, and it's absolutely his duty, when he arrives at the years of maturity, to set aside the prejudices of youth (which make a lasting impression) to examine the Religion of his Country, and judge for himself." (April 5, 1744, JFP, Yale.)

Number XLVI

THURSDAY, OCTOBER 11, 1753

Of Creeds and Systems, together with the Author's own Creed

Credat Judæus Apella.　　　　　　Hor.[1]

Our spiritual Directors have not only an indisputable Right to auricular Confession, but also to exact an Account of every Man's Faith, to see whether he be an orthodox Believer, or a pernicious Heretic. The former, indeed, is at present, in protestant Countries, most lamentably neglected, being almost entirely engrossed by the Church of *Rome.* Yet whoever impartially considers the singular Advantages thence accruing to the external Splendor of Religion, and the Power and Influence of the Priesthood, cannot but seriously bewail so fatal an Omission. 'Twere therefore to be wished, that the Clergy would use their pious Endeavours to re-introduce the above wholesome Discipline, which could not fail of adding new Weight and Importance to their ecclesiastical Dignity. But tho' the Neglect of so necessary a Part of the ministerial Function as auricular Confession, must unavoidably affect every good Man with undissembled Sorrow, yet we may gather some Consolation from the unspeakable Benefit resulting from Creeds and Systems, in which the *Romish* Church hath not the Impudence to exalt herself above us. The Advantages of thus giving an Account of our Faith, by subscribing or assenting to Creeds, are not more evident, than is the Reason and Propriety of the Thing. No one can object against making an open Declaration of the Religion he professes, nor ought any Man to be ashamed of his Principles. It is true, it may by Men of carnal and deistical Turns, be objected, that as the Laity in all protestant Countries are possess'd of the Bible, their Belief of the Holy Scriptures, is sufficient without any particular Creeds thence extracted, or pretended to be so. But this is a Piece of Sophistry pregnant with

Absurdity and Deism. For although the whole revealed Will of God is worthy of equal Credit, as alike proceeding from the immutable Source of Light and Truth, yet every Part of his Revelation doth not equally merit the Distinction of an Article of Faith: That is to say, tho' it is all to be believed, it is not to be believed with an equal Assent, and one Truth may be more true than another. What ought therefore to be considered as an Article of Faith, or, in other Words, to be embraced with a stronger Faith than the rest, is impossible to be known by the illiterate Laity, 'till it be drawn out and ranged in the Form of a Creed by some Council or Convocation, which Extraction and Arrangement give it that Pre-eminence and Superiority above any other Part of the inspired Oracles.

There is another Objection in which Men of Libertine and Latitudinarian Principles, may expect to triumph. They may urge, that if Creeds are wholly collected from the Scriptures, then our believing the latter, renders the former altogether useless and impertinent: If, on the Contrary, they contain any Thing repugnant to Scripture, they ought undoubtedly to be rejected. But these pertinacious Disputants do not consider that such Creeds, being agreeable to holy Writ, is no Argument against their Utility and Importance. For it is well known, that many Things of absolute Necessity to Salvation, are delivered in Scripture, in Expressions metaphorical and figurative, which, when reduced to Creeds, are either expressed or expounded in modern Language; and to argue against the Use of Creeds, because they contain nothing contrary, nor in Addition to the Word of God, would equally militate against the Use of preaching, which is also agreeable to the Word of God. Besides, for us to determine what Creeds are agreeable or repugnant to Scripture, is in Reality claiming a Right of private Judgment; when by the very Supposition, to *judge for us*, is the Prerogative of our ghostly Directors. And where *in the Name of Common Sense*, is the Absurdity of supposing some Things delivered in the lively Oracles, in Terms ambiguous and parabolical, on purpose to display the Necessity of an uninterrupted Succession of Teachers, in a more glaring and incontestible Light.

It may again be objected, that admitting a Necessity for making such a Collection of the most fundamental Truths of our holy Religion, yet as Religion is a personal Thing, no Council or Convocation can arrogate a Right of making any Creeds that shall be binding on the Consciences of Christians: But this Objection, besides having already been obviated in Part, may receive this further Reply, that since in Roman Catholic Countries, it has by woful Experience been found fatal to the Church, and introductive of numberless Heresies, to entrust the Laity with the Scriptures; what damnable Errors are not to be apprehended from suffering every Man, besides reading the Bible, to collect particular Articles of Faith, in direct Opposition to the established Orthodoxy! Surely every Man has not sufficient Abilities to understand the Scriptures. The making Creeds, and composing Systems, are therefore absolutely requisite to maintain an Uniformity of Faith of Doctrine. For, was every Man left to himself in religious Matters, he might run the Hazard, either of esteeming some Parts of Scripture *fundamental*, which nevertheless for wise Reasons have not been thought proper to be inserted in any Creed; or he might believe nothing but the Bible; either of which might eventually prove prejudicial to the Cause of Orthodoxy. Besides, was every Individual to follow his particular Humour in Matters of Faith, it might create as many different Opinions as there were Men; and then, small indeed would be the Revenue of the Clergy, for every particular Man could not maintain a Priest of his own.

Moreover, without such a Collection of the most essential Articles of the Christian Religion, as we term a Creed, it might often happen, that a very good Man might have a very bad Faith; in which Case, neither the inward Sincerity of his Heart, nor his outward Christian Deportment could be of any Avail to his future Happiness. Whereas the yielding a firm Assent to Creeds composed by proper Authority, will atone for numberless Peccadilloes, and entitle the Believer to the divine Acceptance, notwithstanding the external Irregularities of his Life and Conversation.

It is further evident, that tho' all the various Systems of Christians are to be regarded as *Christianity regulated and methodized*;

yet as different Sects in such Regulation and Disposition, make use of different Terms to express the same Idea, such Terms must necessarily furnish Occasion for Disputation and Controversy, and by that Means exhibit fresh Proofs of the Use and Necessity of Expositors for the Interpretation of their true Meaning and Import. Nor would it be possible, without knowing People's Principles, to argue against them; which would in a great Measure retrench the Learning of Divines, as well as curtail the Number of polemical Writings.

Thus, the Use of Creeds, which is the Construction of the Clergy upon the Scriptures, and as it were, the Compendium of the essential Doctrines of Revelation, is clearly demonstrated: So that I should think myself sufficiently justified, for making public Profession of my Belief, could I assign no other Reason for it, that what is included in, or may be fairly inferred from, the above Arguments. But I have a stronger Inducement to lay before the Publick the Articles of my Faith. The Success of my weekly Reflections, depends in a great Measure, upon the Knowledge of my Principles. For the same Things published by Persons of different Persuasions, ought undoubtedly to meet with a very different Reception: Nay, the clearest Truths delivered by an Heretic, are more pernicious than the grossest Falsehoods published by a Writer of sound and orthodox Principles. It will morever save some of my reverend Friends a good deal of Trouble, in attempting to discover my religious Opinions. It is well known, that some have represented me as an Atheist, others as a Deist, and a third Sort as a Presbyterian. My Creed will shew, that none have exactly hit it. For all which Reasons, I shall chearfully lay before them the Articles of my Faith: But, *Know all Men by these Presents*, that I intend neither to burn nor pistol any Man alive, for not swearing to them, especially if he is predetermined to perjure himself.

I

I believe the Scriptures of the Old and New Testament, without any foreign Comments, or human Explications but my own; For which I should doubtless be honoured with Martyrdom, did

I not live in a Government which restrains that fiery Zeal which would reduce a Man's Body to Ashes for the Illumination of his Understanding.

II

I believe that many an honest Man has worn a red Coat, and many a Rogue a black One.

III

I Believe there is no Merit in pretending to believe what is impossible to be believed; and that Mysteries, tho' not incredible, are incomprehensible, and that whoever attempts to explain or illustrate them, proves himself an illustrious Blockhead.

IV

I Believe, that when our Saviour said, they teach for Doctrines the Commandments of Men, he did not intend to confine the Charge to the Pharisees.

V

I Believe that the Word *Orthodoxy*, is a hard equivocal priestly Term, that has caused the Effusion of more Blood than all the Roman Emperors put together.[2]

VI

I Believe that the Quakers have a good deal of Religion, and not a single Priest.

VII

I Believe, that to defend the Christian Religion is one Thing, and to knock a Man in the Head for being of a different, is another Thing.

VIII

I Believe, that if the whole Kingdom professed one Religion, it would be of no Religion; and that the Variety of Sects in the Nation, are a Guard against the Tyranny and Usurpation of one over another.[3]

IX

I Believe, that whatever Persuasion hath the Power of the Secular Arm on its Side, may be enabled to oppress others, or abridge them of their natural Rights; while the latter tho' more numerous and opulent are incapable of injuring the former, or worrying each other, having nothing to defend their own Cause, but the paltry unavailing Weapons of Reason and Argument.

X

I Believe the Transubstantiation of the Elements into Flesh and Blood, by the Mouth of a Romish Priest, to be equally possible with the Transmutation of Sinners and Numskulls into Saints and Scholars, by the Hands of a protestant Priest.

XI

I Believe, that he who feareth God and worketh Righteousness, will be accepted of him, even tho' he refuse to worship any Man, or order of Men, into the Bargain.

XII

I Believe, that Archbishop WHITGIFT [4] spoke Truth, when he said, that Archbishops are neither divine nor apostolical, but [a] human Institution, and since the Apostles' Time.

XIII

I Believe, that Riches, Ornaments and Ceremonies, were assumed by Churches for the same Reason that Garments were invented by our first Parents.[5]

XIV

I Believe, that a pious and charitable, a wise and benevolent Divine, will conciliate the Affection, and attract the Esteem of every good Man, and that scarcely too much Respect can be paid to a Character so amiable, meritorious and uncommon.

XV

I Believe, that a Man may be a good Christian, tho' he be of no Sect in Christendom.[6]

OF CREEDS AND SYSTEMS

XVI

I Believe, that, bating ROBERT BARCLAY'S [7] Enthusiasm, his Apology contains more of primitive Christianity, than one half of the theological Systems extant.

XVII

I Believe, that our Faith like our Stomachs may be over-charged, especially if we are prohibited to chew what we are commanded to swallow.

XVIII

I Believe, that Religion doth not consist in black Coats, or black Cassocks, in Hats ros'd or unros'd, in Bands or Surplices, in cant Phrases or demure Looks, but in loving God and keeping his Commandments.[8]

XIX

I Believe, that a luxurious Parson may as well play the Glutton upon Plum-Pudding and dry'd Cod, as upon roast Beef and Mutton.

XX

I Believe, that there is more Iniquity committed under the Robe, than is repented of under the Gallows; and that in one Sense a black Petticoat is like Charity, often *covering a Multitude of Sins.*

XXI

I Believe, that some People will curse me for believing so.

XXII

I Believe, that some of the Priesthood greatly impose on the Credulity of the Vulgar, and that *by this Craft they get their Wealth.*

XXIII

I Believe, that some Men appear in Sheep's Cloathing, who inwardly are ravenous Wolves.

XXIV

I Believe, that when two Clergymen damn one another, neither of them abounds with Christian Charity.[9]

XXV

I Believe, that swearing and lying for the Church, is a Heterodoxy in Practice seldom exclaimed against by Ecclesiastics, and that no Falsehoods or Calumnies, however incredible and contradictory in themselves, are not chearfully believed and published when they make for the Advancement of the Cause.

XXVI

I Believe, that a certain worthy and charitable Society for the *Promotion of Christian Knowledge,* are frequently and scandalously abused, by Accounts transmitted from the *American* Plantations, notoriously false and chimerical.

XXVII

I Believe, that where one Clergyman enters into Orders for the Abolition of the Kingdom of Darkness, being moved thereunto by the Holy Ghost, there are fifty who assume the Gown by the Instigation of Mammon, and to allay the Insurrection of their Stomachs.

XXVIII

I Believe, that *Jacob's* Prophecy, that the Tribe of *Levy* would be Instruments of Cruelty, is verifyed every Day in the Year.

XXIX

I Believe, that if the Sentence of the Clergy was ratifyed in Heaven, the Laity would be obliged to pay very dear for not going elsewhere.

XXX

I Believe, that I shall believe that the Clergy are more pious than other Men, when I see good Reason to believe it.

OF CREEDS AND SYSTEMS

XXXI

I Believe, that to the Composition of Sermons, Knowledge and Study are two essential Requisites; and that to preach, or rather read other Men's Performance, is a Proof either of Ignorance or Laziness.

XXXII

I Believe, that when a certain King was canoniz'd, there was an extraordinary Scarcity of Martyrs.

XXXIII

I Believe, that a Nursery of Learning, may be a Blessing or a Bane to the Society in which it is erected.

XXXIV

I Believe, that since the last Session of our General Assembly, some sanguine Expectations have been frustrated, and some elevated Hopes repressed.

XXXV

I Believe, that if some Magistrates held their Offices for Life, they would not be afraid of offending every low-liv'd Fellow among their Constituents, nor be terrified at the Threats of a Carman or Cobbler.

XXXVI

I Believe, that if the Surveyor of our public High-Roads was weighed in the Balance, he would be found wanting; and that the Corporation's not cashiering him in *February* last, tho' another offered to keep them in Repair for fifty Pounds a Year, cannot easily be reconciled with that Regard for the public Interest with which they are known to be inspired.

XXXVII

I Believe, that was it in the Power of some Gentlemen I could name, the INDEPENDENT REFLECTOR had long ago been crop'd and pilloried.

XXXVIII

I Believe, that the Virulence of some of the Clergy against my Speculations, proceeds not from their Affection to Christianity, which is founded on too firm a Basis to be shaken by the freest Enquiry, and the divine Authority, of which I sincerely believe without receiving a Farthing for saying so; but from an Apprehension of bringing into Contempt their ridiculous Claims, and unreasonable Pretensions, which may justly tremble at the slightest Scrutiny, and which I believe I shall more and more put into a Panick, in Defiance of both Press and Pulpit.

XXXIX

I Believe, that this Creed is more intelligible than that of St. *Athanasius*; and that there will be no Necessity for any Bishop to write an Exposition on the Thirty Nine Articles of *my* Faith.[10]

Z.

1. "Let the Jew Appella believe it," i.e., only the credulous or superstitious will believe it. Horace, *Satires*, I, 5, 100.

2. On orthodoxy Livingston had written some years earlier: ". . . when we consider that truth is comprised in a small compass, but that error is infinite, we shall not be so positive and dogmatical, to set up for infallibility, and anathemize those of a contrary opinion. . . . all [Christians] have an equal right to think themselves the best; and if they are heretical in some tenets, in others they are confessedly orthodox" (to Rev. James Sprout, September 22, 1744, Letter Book, 1744–1745, Sedgwick Papers, Massachusetts Historical Society); and "it's unaccountable to me that a person of any reason should reproach another for differing from him in principles, when in fact this differs no more from that than that does from this, and Athens has always been as far from Lacaedemon, as Lacaedemon from Athens" (to Welles, April 5, 1744, JFP, Yale).

3. "The very Deists contribute to our Happiness as Christians, by giving us an Opportunity of vindicating our holy Religion, and proving its divine Authority. . . ." *A Letter to the Freemen and Freeholders . . .* (1750), p. 3.

4. John Whitgift (1530?–1604), Archbishop of Canterbury under Elizabeth and an uncompromising foe of Puritanism.

5. This theme appears as early as 1747 in Livingston's poem *Philosophic Solitude*.

6. Which permitted Livingston to say a few months later: "I am no sectary. . . . I am a sincere professor of the religion of Jesus; and consider the several distinctions among Protestants as more or less convenient, but [in] no ways essential." *Independent Reflector*, Preface, p. 31.

7. Robert Barclay (1648–1690), Scottish defender of the Society of Friends and author of *An Apology for the True Christian Divinity, as . . . Preached by the People Called, in Scorn, Quakers* (1676).

8. "As I have always professed a religion, consisting solely in the pure and unadulterated revelation of *Jesus,* I give myself no concern at the rage and resentment of those, who preach for *doctrines, the commandments of men." Independent Reflector, Preface,* p. 3.

9. Years later Livingston expressed his sorrow that so many disputants on theological subjects had been so embroiled in "scholastic subtleties and metaphysical profundities" that they "sacrificed that brotherly love, and that tenderness for the religious sentiments of others . . . which is so distinguishing a characteristic of a truly Christian temper." Livingston to Rev. James Pemberton, May 28, 1783, Gratz MSS, Historical Society of Pennsylvania.

10. Philip Schuyler, visiting New York City from Albany, was delighted with the satiric tone of this parody of the Thirty-Nine Articles. To a friend he wrote: "I send you the forty-sixth number of the *Independent Reflector,* which is making a notable stir here. The clergy, and all churchmen, are in arms against it, and our friend, Will. Livingston, who is the principal writer, is thought by some to be one of the most promising men in the province. I esteem the Church and its liturgy, but I believe he is right in opposing the ridiculous pretentions of the clergy, who would make it as infallible as the Popish Church claims to be. I wish liberty of conscience in all things, and I believe our friend is right. . . ." Quoted in Benson J. Lossing, *The Life and Times of Philip Schuyler,* 2 vols. (New York, 1872), I, 78.

Number XLVII

THURSDAY, OCTOBER 18, 1753

Of Credulity

O Credulity—————————
Security's blind Nurse! The Dream of Fools,
The Drunkard's Ape, that feeling for his Way,
E'en when he thinks in his deluded Sense,
To snatch at Safety, falls without Defence.   MASON [1]

THE Infidelity of the present Age, is a common-place Topic with those whose Office it is to rally the Vices and Follies of human Nature. It is an Opinion too generally received, that Man is led into all the Crimes and Extravagancies he commits, thro' Unbelief: And no Wonder this Doctrine, false as it is, should be so vigorously inculcated by Men whose Interest consists in a Depression of the rational Faculties. To lead a moral Agent hood-winked, while his Capacities exert themselves with Vigour and Unrestraint, is a perfect Solecism: And to enfeeble or bind them in the Fetters of Credulity, is the only Method to obtain the great End aim'd at by many Divines and Politicians, *to wit*, an universal absolute Dominion over the Minds of Men. The Sophistry they use is plainly reducible to this. Infidelity is of such a Nature, as to lead Mankind into vicious and irregular Practices; therefore all the Vices and Irregularities that Men commit, are the natural, the inevitable Consequences of a Principle of Unbelief; that is, to speak in Terms of Art, they deduce an *universal* Consequence from a *particular* Premise. The Falsity of such Reasonings is easily detected. For tho' Infidelity is undoubtedly productive of Vice, it may still be argued, that most of the Enormities of human Nature, proceed not from Infidelity, but its Opposite; I mean, a fond and implicit Confidence in the Opinions of others. A Position that may easily be maintained against a whole Host of civil and ecclesiastical Tyrants. Such being therefore the Art and Chicanery of some, my Sentiments upon the grand Causes of our Depravity, will, doubtless, incur the Charge of Novelty and Libertinism. I cannot, however, help thinking, that most of the Excesses so natural and congenial to our Species, are to be deduced from that Source.

If we turn our Attention to that Sort of Knowledge which is built upon the Observation of human Life, we may readily perceive, that an immoderate Credulity is the principal Cause of all the Lapses and Irregularities of our Conduct. Strongly of this Opinion was a judicious Author, who thus delivers himself upon the Subject, "Give me but half a dozen Persons, whom I can persuade that it is not the Sun which makes our Day Light, and I should not despair of drawing whole Nations to embrace the same Belief." Nor, strange and impossible as this Doctrine may seem, do we want Instances to convince us, that Positions, equally absurd, have, by Numbers, been assented to as unquestionable Truths. Our most darling Tenets, should they be tested by the Rules of cool deliberate Reason, would often turn out mere Creatures of the Authority of a Nurse, a Parent, a Priest, or some other Person to whose Judgment we pay a most unreserved Deference. The Matter may be carried still farther; for so great is Man's Credulity, that frequently a Fact or Proposition not only derives its Authority from its Fitness to deceive, but even from the Unintelligibleness of its Nature, powerful Arguments are successfully drawn to command our Assent. To verify this Observation, we need only reflect upon the vast Abuse of *Faith*, the grand Hinge upon which turns the whole System of Christianity. This cardinal Virtue, where it in Reality implies a bare Assent to the Truth, either of a Fact or a Doctrine, built upon rational Evidence, is generally perverted into that absurd and detestable Kind of Credulity, that with insatiate Gluttony swallows the most palpable Absurdities, the most incoherent Dogmas, the most mysterious and inconsistent Nonsense. So that, in short, under this Notion of Faith, he is the best Christian who discovers the greatest Avidity for an unrestrained Belief of Impossibilities and Falsehood. The Truth of these Things shall hereafter be exemplified in the clearest and most indisputable Manner. That Christianity requires any other Belief of the Truth of a Fact or Proposition, than such as is supported by rational Testimony, I challenge every vigorous Assertor of implicit Faith to prove: [2] And yet that the most palpable Absurdities are daily recommended to us, as proper Objects of Christian Faith, whoever is the least acquainted with *Priestianity* can have no Room to doubt.

But to return. The Talk I have proposed to myself is very easy, it being barely to shew, from the following simple Reflections, that we commit more Errors in the Conduct of Life upon a Principle of Credulity, than its Opposite.

In order to do this, it will be expedient, precisely to define what I mean by *Credulity*, and what by *Infidelity*. Credulity is a Belief of the Truth of a Fact or Proposition *unsupported* by rational Evidence: Infidelity (where it signifies Incredulity) is the Disbelief of the Truth of a Fact or Proposition *supported* by rational Evidence. And it may be observed as a farther Explanation, that a Fact or Proposition in itself true, is to the Person believing it upon insufficient or no Evidence, as tho' it were not true, since it would, upon the same Kind of Evidence, or without any at all, be productive of a credulous Assent, even were it false. Whence it is evident, that the Belief of all Facts or Propositions, whether true or false in themselves, are to the Person who believes them without rational Evidence, imputable as tho' they were false: For, as to the Person believing, the Belief of a Fact or Proposition without Evidence, tho' the Nature of it will admit of sufficient Evidence to support the Truth, is equal to the Belief of it when its Nature will admit of no Evidence to support it, that is, when 'tis false. The Reason of this is plain: For as the Truth is only such to the Believer upon proper Evidence, he who gives Credit to what is really true without such Evidence, would as readily believe a Falsehood; since to the Person believing in a particular Case without Evidence, it does not appear that the Thing he believes can possibly have any Evidence in its Support.

From the above Considerations, this fair and undeniable Consequence may be drawn, that all Facts or Propositions, whether true or false in themselves, shall indifferently be charged upon the Person believing them, whether they believe upon insufficient

Evidence, or without Evidence, as direct Falsehoods; insufficient Evidence and no Evidence, being equally inconsistent with Truth.

It is therefore apparent, that the whole System of a credulous Person's Faith, whether in Matters purely Christian, or Moral, or Civil, even tho' entirely consistent with Truth, will no more denominate him good and virtuous, than if he had exercised it in the Behalf of palpable Falsehoods. But if this be the Case, what becomes of the credulous Man's Religion? Tho' it be true, it shall not be imputable to him as such, it being unsupported by rational Evidence: Is it false, he shall be accountable for it; because he ought never to give his Assent to any Thing that is not recommended to him with sufficient Evidence. Does his Religion break out into Acts, he labours under the lamentable Disadvantage of never doing good, while he is continually subject to the Commission of Evil.

On the Contrary, the Man who doubts or disbelieves, notwithstanding a Sufficiency of Evidence, tho' his Disbelief is imputable to him as a Fault, yet he is exempt from the Charge of Infidelity, whenever he disbelieves what is false. The Infidel in Theory, as he will not be sway'd by sufficient Evidence, cannot *a fortiori* be supposed to believe what is false, or in other Words, what is necessarily unsupported by Evidence, and consequently inconsistent with his lukewarm Faith. The Unbeliever, and the Credulous Man, are equally chargeable with Guilt, the one in disbelieving when there is sufficient Evidence to warrant an Assent, the other for believing without Evidence. Besides which, the latter is continually inclinable to believe the greatest Untruths with the same Relish that he assents to Truth; because Evidence or no Evidence, the grand Criteria of Truth and Falsehood, are never a Question with him. But to continue the Parallel: Thus much may be admitted in favour of both, that no Person can possibly be supposed so thorough-paced an Infidel, as to disbelieve all Truth: Neither is the credulous Man so entirely devoted to implicit Faith, as absolutely to believe every Thing he meets with. They both err in a Degree. Yet so much the more subject to Error are the Credulous than the Unbelieving, that these are equally imposed upon, both with Truth and Falsehood, Reality and

Fable, while the Fault of those lies only in disbelieving the Truth.

But to be convinced how much more we are in Danger of precipitating ourselves into Guilt, thro' a fond Credulity than from a Principle of Unbelief, we need only consider the former Vice in one of its particular Tendencies. As great a Paradox as it may seem to reconcile Opposites, and reduce Things that are in their Nature incompatible, into a Subserviency to each other, it may safely be maintain'd, that nothing opens a wider Door to Infidelity than implicit Belief. For First, as he that is remarkable for a steady and invariable Attachment to Truth, is undoubtedly at the farthest Remove from Infidelity. So on the other Hand, the credulous Man is continually exposed to be lured from the Truth, and may be drawn into a Desertion of his Principles, by every *Wind of Doctrine*. Should he happen to believe what is in itself true, yet the Manner of his believing entirely discredits his Faith, while at the same Time he is as guilty in changing his Opinion, as if he had believed upon proper Evidence. Nay, farther, as he has in Reality no Principles, he will be ready to change what he calls such, as often as new Ones have an Opportunity of making an Impression on his fluxile Understanding. He is, therefore, likely to prove the greatest Infidel imaginable; because, even when he is so fortunate as to meet with Truth, he is not able to adhere to it.

Secondly, If the Reasoning above advanced, is just, the credulous Man cannot possibly escape falling into Infidelity. Nay, by being credulous, he actually proves himself an Infidel: For, to apply the Argument to Christianity, there are certain Doctrines revealed to us from Heaven, the Evidence of which is so clear and obvious, that the meanest Understanding may, in the Use of proper Means, attain to the Knowledge and Belief of them. And it is further necessary to save a Person from Infidelity, that he believe them as Truths, that is, upon proper Evidence; because they can never be true to him, or any one living, except they carry Evidence with them sufficient to evince themselves such. But the Man who believes them upon improper Evidence, believes them not because they are true; he never having sought after such Evidence as is necessary to ascertain their Truth, and therefore does not believe them, in the proper Sense of Faith, for Truths. Whence it plainly follows, that if a Belief of the Truth of those Doctrines, is necessary to save a Man from Infidelity, the credulous Man, who does not believe them upon such Evidence as is requisite to ascertain their Truth, must, by a fatal Necessity, be an Infidel. And here a Word of Advice might be given to some miss-judging Clergymen, which, should they deign to accept, would doubtless prove more efficacious in destroying the Kingdom of Darkness, than their vociferous Declamations against Infidelity in general, by which, in reality, is too often meant, the Privilege of thinking for ourselves. A Man, with them, who thinks freely, is an Infidel, because his Faith clashes with their Notions of Orthodoxy. Tho' in Truth, such a Difference is far from proving him to be an Infidel. That Word, in its proper and abstract Sense, means no more than the Disbelief of what sufficiently appears to be true. It has, however, been found convenient for many, to give it a relative Meaning. But the Person to whom it is applied, must be oddly circumstanced, since he may either be a sound Believer, or an Infidel, as often as he shall think proper to change Countries or Climates.   B.

The Letter subscribed Common Sense, *is come to hand, and with the Liberty of a few Alterations, may be inserted in a future Paper.*

The Author is obliged to the Gentleman who styles himself LAICUS, *and thinks he cannot better acknowledge the Favour of his friendly Rebuke, than by inserting his Letter the first Opportunity; and in the mean Time wishes the Continuance of his Correspondence.*

The Letter dated at South-Hampton, *in* Suffolk *County, contains too many just Remarks on our future College to be buried in Oblivion.*

1. Rev. William Mason (1724–1797), Vicar of St. Trinity Hall in Yorkshire, author of a number of odes, elegies, and dramatic poems.

2. The objection he raised ten years earlier against the doctrines of the "New Light" preachers of the Awakening was that their "mean Ideas" of the dignity of human nature "clashes [*sic*] with sense and cannot bear the touchstone of reason." Livingston to Welles, May 27, 1742, November 14, 1743, JFP, Yale.

Number XLVIII

THURSDAY, OCTOBER 25, 1753

Of the WASTE *of* LIFE

I am obliged to an ingenious but sparing Correspondent for
the following Paper.

> ------*Amusement reigns, Man's great Demand:*
> *To trifle is to live. As* ATLAS *groan'd*
> *The World beneath, we groan beneath an Hour,*
> *And cry for Mercy to the next Amusement,*
> *Yet when Death kindly tenders us Relief,*
> *We call him cruel; Years to Moments shrink,*
> *Ages to Years.------*   Night Thoughts

> *Preteriunt et Imputantur.*[1]

Time is justly esteemed by the wisest and best of Men, a golden
Treasure: And he may properly be stiled a virtuous Niggard, who
is the most sedulous to preserve and improve a Treasure so
inestimable and sacred. But into such an Abyss of Degeneracy is
human Nature plunged, that in the very Instance where Avarice
would be transform'd into the noblest Virtue, Mankind almost
universally become extravagant and prodigal. Strange Absurdity
of human Conduct! always bewailing the momentary Duration of
their Existence, yet lavishly wasting its present Moments; and
longing impatiently for the Conclusion of every Period of it. "We
are for lengthening the Span in general, but would fain contract
the Parts of which it is composed."

What can be a more glaring Evidence of the Folly and In-
consistency of Mankind, than to see those very Persons, who
complain of the Shortness of Life, wasting it in a supine Indolence
and Inactivity; or which is equally criminal, spending it in a dull
round of Amusements and Diversions, while they remain dead to
all the important and valuable Ends of living.

OF THE WASTE OF LIFE

How often do we behold, even Persons in the elevated Stations of Life, who pique themselves on their good Breeding, and imagin'd Superiority of Understanding above the lower Class of their Fellow-Creatures, using all the Arts they are able to invent, to make *Time*, which lies too heavy upon their Hands, steal away imperceptibly, and to no Purpose! The Variety of Games, too many to be enumerated, to which Mankind are so generally and fondly attached, are all of them but ingenious Contrivances to *kill Time*, as the *French* most emphatically express it. These are now become the reigning Employments of the Age, and with regret I mention it, of too many of my Fellow Citizens of both Sexes; among those especially who call themselves the Polite and Well-bred. Hours, Days and Months, are sordidly wasted in one continued Circle of such trifling Amusements. The Mind, that superior Part of Man, evidently designed by the wise Author of Nature, for more excellent and sublime Pleasures, is suffered to lie idle, and contract a Rust which can scarce ever be worn off.[2]

> *Ah how unjust to Nature and himself,*
> *Is thoughtless, thankless, inconsistent Man!*
> *Like Children babbling Nonsense in their Sports,*
> *We censure Nature for a Span too short;*
> *That Span too short, we tax as tedious too;*
> *Torture Invention, all Expedients tire,*
> *To lash the ling'ring Moments into Speed;*
> *And whirl us (happy Riddance!) from ourselves.*

The fond Humour of being caressed by the Gay and the Fashionable, is what too often betrays even Men of Sense into the Practice of these *annihilating* Amusements. I call them *annihilating*, because I cannot but look upon them, as the artful Inventions of the stupid Part of our Species, to bring down Men of superior Knowledge to a level with themselves. During the Progress of a Game, the greatest Genius is upon a Par with one of the meanest Understanding: The Knowledge of the former lies dormant, and the Ignorance of the latter is concealed: The wise Man and the Fool appear in a Point of Light equally advantageous; for when the Game begins, Conversation ends. This simple Consideration, methinks, might be sufficient to dissuade Men of Sense from giving

405

into such degrading Amusements. "Let the *Theban* Youth pipe," said ALCIBIADES, "for they know not how to discourse: But we *Athenians* have MINERVA for our Patroness, and APOLLO for our Protector." [3]

I happened the other Evening to fall into the Company of five or six Persons of both Sexes. The Gentlemen, in Compliance with the polite Taste, accepted the Invitation of the Ladies to a Card-Table: Upon which all the Springs of Discourse were immediately shut up; and except the frequent Repetition of a few Game-Phrases, a profound Silence ensued. I, who never had the Honour of being instructed in the genteel Exercise, was left to entertain myself with my own private Reflections. I could not but call to Mind a Story I had somewhere met with, of the celebrated Mr. LOCKE. Being invited to dine with the Lords HALIFAX, ANGLESEY, and SHAFTESBURY, immediately after Dinner the Cards were called for. Mr. LOCKE retiring to a Window, and writing some time in his Pocket-Book, was interrupted by My Lord ANGLESEY, who desired to know what he was writing, "Why, My Lord," answered he, "I endeavour to improve myself as much as I can by your good Company, and having waited with Impatience for the Honour of being present at a Meeting of the most ingenious Men of the Age, I thought it best to write your Conversation, and have accordingly set down the Substance of what has been said within this Hour or two." There was no need for Mr. LOCKE to read much of this Dialogue: The noble Lords perceived the Banter, and throwing aside their Cards, enter'd into a Conversation more befitting their Character. Glad would I have been, if by any Artifice I could have disengaged my Male Companions from the enchanting Diversion; but the Dread of being branded with the odious Appellation of ill-bred and un-polite, I well knew must render all such ineffectual. Accordingly I framed the best Excuse I was able for my not staying, and left them to the undisturbed Enjoyment of their empty Soliloquies.

Surely, did a Stranger to human Nature take but a superficial Survey of the Beau-Monde, and behold that Labyrinth of vain and childish Amusements, or that State of Indolence and Inaction, into which they are dissolved, without the remotest Surmise of any future Existence; he would doubtless be inclined to think they were a Race of Beings, whom the Author of Nature had placed upon the Earth, beyond the Verge of his Jurisdiction, to spend a transitory Duration in an unremitted Pursuit of every sensual Gratification, and to retire at last to their original Nonentity.

But the Creator of the Universe was too wise to form his Creatures for such insignificant Purposes. No Man can pretend a Charter of Indulgence for a Life of absolute Ease and Inactivity. He designed every Individual to move in a certain Sphere, and to accomplish the Duties of a certain Station. Even a heathen Moralist could tell us, that we are but Actors of a certain Part, which the Director of the Drama has allotted us; and so ought to act well and handsomely the Part which falls to our Share. And it must be the highest Impeachment of the divine Wisdom, to imagine he can, as an unconcerned Spectator, behold us wasting the contracted Span of Life, in a State of inglorious Indolence, or in a Series of no less inglorious Amusements.

If we look around us, we see not only the whole material Universe in Motion, but the whole Animal System of the Universe incessantly active. Shall Man then who claims an Alliance with those sublime Intelligences above, who are Activity itself, by a Life of Idleness and Sloth, defeat the Intention of his and their common Creator? Must he not thereby expose himself to the Displeasure of the latter, and to the everlasting Scorn and Derision of the former?

> *And is there in Creation, what, amidst*
> *This Tumult universal, wing'd Dispatch*
> *And ardent Energy, supinely yawns?*
> Man *sleeps;* and Man *alone;* and Man, *for whom*
> *All else is in Alarm: Man the sole Cause*
> *Of this surrounding Storm! and yet he sleeps,*
> *As the Storm rock'd to rest.*[4]

One of the Roman Emperors, on his Death Bed, demanded of his Attendants, whether they thought he had performed in a becoming Manner, the Part which was assigned him upon the Theatre of Life; and having received a Reply, suitable to his real Worth, cry'd out, "Let me then retire from this Stage with your

Approbation and Applause." Would we, like him, make our Exit, at the Close of this earthly Scene, amidst the Eulogies of our Acquaintance, let us seriously reflect upon the Figure our Conduct here will make in that important Hour: Whether we have acted well the Part allotted us, and how gracefully it will appear in the View of Mankind: In short, whether our Behaviour has accorded with our Dignity, as rational intelligent Beings, and has been such, as will tend to advance our Felicity in a State of future Existence.

T. T.[5]

The following Letter appears to be wrote by one of the People called QUAKERS, and contains so much good Sense, that I shall lay it before the Reader without a farther Apology, or adding any Reflections of my own upon the Subject Matter.

To the Author of the INDEPENDENT REFLECTOR

Flushing, *the Place of my Pilgrimage, the* 12*th Day of the Month called* October, *in the Year,* 1753

FRIEND,

I HAVE read many of thy weekly Sayings, and perceive that thou art much set against that Yoke of spiritual Bondage, which neither we nor our Fathers were able to bear; for verily it is a Yoke heavy and cumbersome, wherewith, according to the Exhortation of the Apostle PAUL, we desire not to be again entangled. Therefore I have rejoiced with Gladness of Heart that thou goest on valiantly, and hast none to make thee afraid. But I must reprove thee for mingling so much carnal Mirth with thy most serious Meditations. For this I praise thee not, seeing that all Things ought to be done in Order, and thou shouldest remember, that the primitive Christians were Men of Gravity, and an Ensample to all succeeding Generations of that comely Virtue. But as I give thee Reproof where Reproof is meet, so will I also render thee all deserved Laud and Commendation. For thou seemest in Truth to think for thyself, and rather to follow the Light within, and to hold fast the Form of sound Words, than to be led by those who have no Right to the Guidance of thy Reason, seeing that to thyself thou standest or fallest. I can also say Yea and Amen to thy Cogitations concerning the Vanity of long Garments, for as much as the Fashion of this World passeth away, and that true and undefiled Religion consisteth not in the external Cloathing, but abideth in the

408

inward Man. Nay, I have marked that thou hast made seemly mention of ROBERT BARCLAY, in thy Creed so called, howbeit he was not of thy Way. But thou hast moreover accused him of Enthusiasm, which peradventure is more than thou knowest.

I will not glory in aught among the Friends, nor be puffed up with spiritual vaunting; for what have we that we have not received? Nevertheless, as I have found it on my Spirit to send thee this Epistle, thou wilt not I trust, accuse me of carnal boasting, for telling thee that we have no Perils of priestly Enthraldom, so long as we hold that every Man, yea and every Woman, hath a Call to do all the Good they can, and that if they should withhold their Gifts for the Lack of filthy Lucre, it would savour of worldly Mindedness. So that the Words *Benefices* and *Revenues*, with other antichristian Sounds, and alien from the lively Oracles, are not so much as named among us; but we look steadfastly (and oh! that we did so more and more) unto the Recompence of the Reward which awaiteth the faithful Dispensers of Truth, not in this World, but in that which is to come.

I also find, that thou maintainest that every one should be persuaded in his own Mind, and withstandest those to their Faces who gainsay thee in that Matter. In which I will furthermore bear thee Testimony. For verily every Man ought to be in Subjection unto that Light which enlightened every Man that cometh into the World. And why should we not say unto the Man that would bring our Consciences into Captivity, even as the Egyptian spake unto MOSES, *Who hath made thee a Judge?*

But albeit that there be no Contentions amongst ourselves concerning fleshly Rule, yet cannot I speak thus of those who are not content with the Wages of their proper Flock, but do furthermore demand Tribute of us; which seemeth a Matter of greater Marvel, in as much as GEORGE, King of *Great-Britain*, hath declared, that none of his Subjects should suffer Persecution in his Reign. How then are we brought into the Bondage of giving Part of our Substance unto those that appertain not unto us, yea, and verily profit us Nothing?

Thou also speakest my Mind, that no Man ought to be grieved in his Body or Substance for committing Folly, but should rather be exhorted by the Church, and if he will not hear them, he should be as an Heathen and a Publican. And even then we should rather make Supplication for his Renewal to him that can reclaim at the eleventh Hour, than use the Weapons of the Flesh to the Perdition of his Body.

But that in which above all Things I wish thee to prosper, is in thy worthy Labours to bring to nought, that Abomination of Desolation which still seeketh its own to the Downfall of others' Welfare. I mean that unchristian League of making the School intended for the Edification of our little Ones, a Gin and a Snare to bereave us of our Liberty. Against this proud Imagination thou hast uttered manifold Sayings, which thy Adversaries have not been able to gainsay. And I hope that Friend J——— [6] will well ponder the Matter before he agreeth to put a Chain about our Necks, seeing that the Men of this Country who have raised him on high, can also enter into a Covenant against him, if he should shut his Ears to their Cries, and do foolishly to find Favour with the great Ones of the Earth.

For as much, therefore, as there seemeth no Evil in thy Thoughts, but that which above all Things thou proposest to thy self, is to declare and defend the Truth; I bid thee go on and prosper. And in this Confidence I have meditated this Epistle, comprehending briefly the chief Principles wherein I think thee of a right Mind, to the Intent to bear Testimony to the Truth; and not so much cumbering myself about the Excellency of Speech and enticing Words of Man's Wisdom, as desiring that Truth may abound in its greatest Efficacy and Operation. My Daughter PHÆBE, and DEBORAH the Wife of my Bosom, salute thee. Receive also the Salutation of

Thy Sincere Friend,

J. F.

1. A condensation of three groups of lines from the second part of *Night Thoughts*, by Edward Young (1683–1765), published 1742–1745. The Latin paraphrases Martial, *Epigrams*, V, 20: "They [the days] pass and are charged against us."

2. As a young man Livingston had expressed to Welles his annoyance with most of the female company New York City offered. They spent their "golden hours in midday Slumbers and inglorious trifles," their bedrooms filled with "boxes, oyntments, powders, combs, vials, curling-tongs, perfumes, Drugs, brushes, pins, . . . rings, [and] Jewells," and their amusements consisting of "paint, play-books, cards, ballads, clasps, buckells — and diamonds. . . . in a perpetual circulation of Dress and undress they spend their valuable hours till Death conveys them to the silent Tomb." (November 14, 1743, JFP, Yale.)

3. "Minerva has a few votaries among this ignorant generation," Livingston had complained to his former tutor shortly after he arrived in New York City from Yale, "tho' Bacchus and the Queen of Love own the greater number." Livingston to Chauncey Whittelsey, August 23, 1744, Letter Book, 1744–1745, Sedgwick Papers, Massachusetts Historical Society.

4. Livingston has dropped three lines from the original passage in *Night Thoughts*.

5. "T.T." was obviously fictitious. The sentiments he expressed were too much Livingston's own for mere coincidence. In addition to the similarities already indicated above, compare the last paragraph with his letter to his fiancée years earlier: "I never had a meaner opinion of earthly grandeur than after having read the conquests of some of the celebrated heroes of an-

tiquity . . . [and] consider them in their dying hour, when, notwithstanding their . . . immense treasures . . . they must . . . breath[e] out their souls without the least gleam of certainty whether they will triumph in immortal happyness or sink into intolerable misery." Livingston to Miss [Susanna] F[rench], August —, 1744, Letter Book, 1744–1745, Sedgwick Papers, Massachusetts Historical Society.

6. James De Lancey, New York's Lieutenant Governor.

Number XLIX

THURSDAY, NOVEMBER 1, 1753

Of human Nature, the Immortality of the Soul, and whether it can exist without thinking

——————— In doubt to act, or rest,
In doubt to deem himself a God, or Beast;
In doubt his Mind or Body to prefer,
Born but to die, and reas'ning but to err,
——————————
Created half to rise, and half to fall;
Great Lord of all Things, yet a Prey to all;
Sole Judge of Truth, in endless Error hurl'd:
The Glory, Jest, and Riddle of the World,
POPE'S *Essay on Man*

MAN, considered in different Lights, is of all Creatures the most base and abject, the most noble and august. As in one View he has the Mortification to call Corruption his Father; he may, in another, claim Kindred with Angels, and triumph in the Immortality of his Being. He is informed with an intelligent Something that makes Excursions beyond the Stars; and he lies immersed in Matter, and is absorb'd in Impurities. The Lord of the Creation is a Slave to his own Passions; and he who grasps at Eternity, an Heir of Putrefaction. He is endowed with Reason, and surrounded with Darkness. His Grandeur and Wretchedness are alike conspicuous. He may without Vanity reflect on himself, as capable of a Participation of the Divinity; and without Error rank himself with the meanest Reptile. He is in short, an infinite Insect, and a despicable Immortal.

'Tis the Inattention to this Contrariety in Man to which we are to ascribe all the false and imperfect Representations of human Nature. Those who have only considered it in the bright

Part of its Character, have exaggerated its Dignity, and declaim'd on its Perfection and Glory, without the least Notice of its Infirmity and Vileness. Others on the Contrary, strangers to its Excellence, but conscious of its Meaness, have degraded and vilified the Species; and represented Man as utterly abominable, and the Object of Horror.

It is, perhaps, no inconsiderable Proof of the Truth of Religion, that amidst the insuperable Errors which bewildered the Philosophers in their Contemplations of human Nature, it is Revelation alone which hath dispelled the Darkness, and at once discovered the indelible Characters of our Grandeur, and the deplorable Fountain of our Corruption. It represents Man as originally happy and innocent, and still retaining, amidst all his adventitious Impurity, some of the shattered Rays and pompous Ruins of his primitive Lustre. It reveals the Origin of his double Nature, in unfolding his Desertion from God, by aiming at Independence; and presuming to make himself the Centre of his own Happiness. And hence his present Degradation and Abasement.

Nor less perplexed were the heathen Sages about the Immortality of the Soul. SOCRATES, indeed, seems to have had comfortable Hopes of a future happy Existence. Nothing less than such an animating Prospect, could have enabled him to quit the Stage of Life, with so triumphant an Exit. CICERO wishes, doubts, considers, believes and doubts again: And PLATO himself concludes his *Phaedon*, with declaring that his best Arguments amount only to raise a Probability.[1] Probable Conjectures were the utmost they could arrive at, and this Probability was clouded and obscured with unanswerable Objections. 'Tis true, the Nature of the Soul itself, and particularly its Immateriality, furnishes no insignificant Proof of its eternal Duration. Its Love of Existence, its Horror of Annihilation, its Capacity for endless Improvements, and consequently its perpetual Progress towards Perfection, are all pleasing Speculations, and corroborating Circumstances. The Triumphs of Vice, and the Sufferings of Virtue, are inexplicable Paradoxes in the moral World, upon any other Hypothesis than that of a future State of Existence, and a more equitable Retribu-

413

tion. The Absurdity of supposing our Appetite for Being, to be totally extinguished by Death, strongly intimates a nobler Existence, where all our Talents will be exerted, and all our Capacities gratified. The present World appears only in the Light of a probationary Scene to introduce us into another; or a Nursery whence we are to be transplanted into a friendlier Climate, to grow and spread and flourish thro' indeterminable Ages. Our Thoughts can wander beyond the Confines of the Creation, and tower above the remotest Star. And shall the Existence of a Creature be circumscribed by Time, whose Thoughts are boundless and illimitable?

The Belief of the Immortality of the Soul, imparts an unutterable Dignity to human Nature. It inspires us with sublime Sentiments of our future Grandeur, and affords the strongest Incitements to great and glorious Actions. The Hope of Annihilation, on the contrary, is the Disgrace of our Species, sordid, dastardly, and infamous. These are some of the Probabilities that the Soul will survive the Funeral of the Body. But either as to its Duration or Happiness, what can Reason determine with Certainty? We reluct at the Extinction of our Being, and contemplate the unbounded Prospect of Eternity, *but Shadows, Clouds, and Darkness rest upon it.*

That we feel within us, a certain intelligent, spiritual and conscious Principle, that depends not on the Body for its Existence, but doth itself impart Life and Animation, Impulse and Direction to the whole animal Frame, is beyond all reasonable Question. But to infer from thence, that the Soul is incapable of existing without Thought, after the Dissolution of its Companion, or even that it is incapable of absolute Non-Existence, is an unconsequential Deduction. We observe in Brutes, Life, Animation, Direction and Design, and yet no one that I know of, has professedly maintained the Immortality of their Spirits. On the other-hand, DESCARTES has advanced several Propositions to prove them perfect Machines, which, of the two, is doubtless the most improbable Supposition. To talk of Brutes acting by Instinct, may be a more specious Way of concealing our Ignorance, but removes not a single Difficulty. Their Instinct is as independent on

Matter as the Soul of Man, and Matter as such, equally incapable of the Contrivance observable in the animal, as in the rational Kingdom. Nay, I question whether the Soul of an ARCHIMEDES, lodged in the Body of a Fox, could furnish stronger Proofs of its Ingenuity, than are daily exhibited by that sagacious Animal, without troubling his Head about such abstruse Erudition.

To form a clear Idea of Spirit without Thought, is I own, impossible. But it is equally beyond our Power, to frame a just Conception of Spirit with Thought. The Truth is, we have no adequate Idea of Spirit at all. The Impossibility, therefore, of distinct Conceptions of an uncogitative Soul, either proves nothing, or too much. It is sufficient to our Purpose, that Thought is not essential to our Spirits. And this is evinced by constant Experience; for we find that we can pass whole Hours without it. It may, indeed, be objected, that this arises from the present Union of Soul and Body. But that the Body prevents the Cogitation of the Soul, is difficult to demonstrate. If the former has any Influence on the latter in Sleep, it must cause it to exert its Activity, and throw it into Reflection. For that it should operate on the Soul, without occasioning Consciousness, is utterly unintelligible: And if it be wholly unoperative, then the Soul is entirely left to itself, and as free to prosecute its Speculations, as if it were disembodied. And yet how many Hours of the Night do we pass without a single Thought? Cogitation is therefore rather a Property, than of the Essence of the Soul. It is an accidental Mode that doth not constitute its Nature, nor is necessary to its Existence. The Soul can think, and it can exist without thinking, as a Body can move and exist without Motion. And if it can exist one Moment without Thought and Reflection, who can determine how long it may so exist? We are not conscious that our Souls reflected antecedent to, or coeval with their Union to our Bodies. Nor is it probable that the Soul of a Foetus, before the Organization of the Body, hath any Thought. Nay, it may be traced, how Children by gradual Steps, attain to the Faculty of reasoning. And if the Soul could exist without Thought, previous to, or any Time after, its Conjunction with the Body, what Reason can be assigned against its existing without Thought, after its Separation from it?

Again, it appears that all our Ideas are either received by the external Organs, or compounded of those, by the internal Operations of the Mind. The former are called Ideas of Sensation, the latter of Reflection. Hence it is that in our Dreams, when the Body has the least Effect on the rational Faculties, the Soul never starts any new Ideas, but only jumbles together those we have already received in either or both of the Ways just mentioned. It may therefore be demanded, upon what Objects the Soul in its future Existence, supposing it always to think, will employ its Cogitations. Whence will it derive a new Fund of Ideas? Will it only busy itself in recollecting its former Images, or will it receive new Impressions without the Channel of bodily Organs? Will a new Set of Perceptions be impressed on a Spirit incorporeal and impassive? Ideas of Sensation it cannot obtain, for want of external Inlets; nor can it create fresh Ideas of Reflection, but out of those it formerly received by Sensation. In what, therefore, will consist its Pleasure or Pain, is not easy to conceive, except it be the Consciousness of its Guilt, or Rectitude, while in Conjunction with the Body. This, and this alone, is all the Notion we can frame of its Happiness or Misery. The rest is shrouded in impenetrable Darkness.

Add to this, that human Nature is visibly stained and polluted with brutal, nay, with diabolical Passions. It is, in short, too corrupted and depraved to have thus proceeded out of the Hands of the all-perfect and all-bounteous Creator. To suppose that the Almighty originally created our Souls with the Passions of Envy and Malice, and joined them to Bodies subject to innumerable Pains and Infirmities, is a Reflection on the Author of our Beings, whose Works are all harmonious and compleat. To pretend that we are punished for the Transgression of a federal Head whom we did not elect, and felled by an Agent whom we did not delegate, and who appears in fact to have been unfit to be so impowered, by abusing his own Liberty, is a Doctrine easier swallowed than digested. To insist that our Souls derive their Impurity from Traduction of spiritual Generation, is supposing them to consist of Parts, and for that Reason, absurd and unphilosophical. A State of Pre-Existence, seems therefore the most probable Method of accounting for our present Degeneracy, and vindicating the divine Conduct, by supposing the actual Defection and Lapse of every Individual. Upon this Supposition our Proclivity to Evil, and the Misery of Infants, without any Crime committed in the Body, is clearly accounted for, and the divine Providence eternally vindicated. This being the Case, it evinces not only the Possibility of the Soul's Existence without Thought for an Hour or a Night, but for a Number of Years, sufficient to obliterate all its former Perceptions. And so total an Oblivion of its primitive Felicity, is doubtless a benevolent Contrivance of infinite Wisdom, to prevent its reflecting on the exalted Station whence it was degraded to do Penance in the Body. From whence it follows, that the only Objection to this Hypothesis, admits the very Truth I contend for. I mean, that we are incapable of recollecting our original Rectitude, and the Time and Reason of our Degradation. This Objection, instead of overthrowing the Reason I have assigned for the present Condition of human Nature, shews the Possibility of the Soul's existing without perceiving. Nay, he that will endeavour to recollect his Thoughts during the first two Years of his Life, must own the Possibility of his existing a Thousand, without being able to recall a single Idea.

Nor does this reasoning against the Soul's being necessarily and essentially conscious, in the least affect its endless Duration. A Man does not deny the Existence of a Globe, by denying it to be in Motion. No more doth he disown the Immortality of the Soul, by disbelieving its eternal Consciousness. Nor will the Annihilation or Mortality of the Soul necessarily follow, even from a Denial of its Immateriality. It is incumbent on those who deny the Possibility of the Almighty's superadding Thought to Matter, to prove the Position; because a Negation against Omnipotence, ought to be clearly demonstrated.

Moreover, as it is impossible to shew, that the supreme Being cannot render Matter conscious, so neither can it be proved, that he cannot make Matter as well as Spirit, immortal. For whatever is not self-existent, but created and finite, may cease to exist. Hence it must be the divine Agency, and the Power of the Father of Spirits, that will continue and uphold the Soul's eternal Duration. And the same Agency and Power may infinitely perpetuate the Existence of Matter.

It is therefore to REVELATION alone, that we are indebted for the Discovery of the Soul's eternal and conscious Existence. It is this that has brought to Light not only *Immortality*, but an Immortality of *Life*, Perception, and Felicity.[2]   Z.

1. *Phædo* [*or, On the Soul; Ethical*], one of Plato's dialogues dealing with Socrates' death; its theme, the immortality of the soul. Livingston's reference is to 114 d.

2. This essay was obviously written to counteract the repeated charges of atheism directed against Livingston in the *New-York Mercury*. It reveals much of his unsystematic, latitudinarian religion. His view of Deity, omnipresent, anthropomorphic, and immanent, placed him outside the camp of the Deists, whose theology he had disparaged as early as 1751. Yet his conception of God as "clock-maker" and his acceptance of nature and the harmony of the universe as the perfect revelation of divine handiwork had much in common with Deism. Confirmed Deists, however, would have found completely unacceptable Livingston's confusion of the natural with the supernatural in his defense of immortality, the scriptural allusions with which he filled his kingdom of nature, the natural justifications he offered in defense of Scripture — "the Doctrine of the New Testament will appear most admirably to harmonize with Nature" (to Welles, January 13, 1746, JFP, Yale) — and his belief in the "pure and unadulterated religion of Jesus." Livingston was never very troubled by the inconsistencies in his religious system. As for immortality, Livingston had long ago decided that "the office of Death is but a passage into Life." (to Welles, January 5, 1747, JFP, Yale.)

Number L

THURSDAY, NOVEMBER 8, 1753

The Advantages of Education, with the Necessity of instituting Grammar Schools for the Instruction of Youth, preparatory to their Admission into our intended COLLEGE [1]

> My SPIRIT pours a Vigour thro' the Soul,
> Th' unfetter'd Thought with Energy inspires,
> Invincible in Arts, in the bright Field
> Of laurel'd Science, as in that of Arms.
>
> THOMSON, *Liberty*

To enumerate all the Advantages accruing to a Country, from a due Attention to the Encouragement of the Means of Education, is impossible. The happy Streams issuing from that inexhaustible Source, are numberless and unceasing. Knowledge among a People makes them free, enterprizing and dauntless; but Ignorance enslaves, emasculates and depresses them. When Men know their Rights, they will at all Hazards defend them, as well against the insidious Designs of domestic Politicians, as the undisguised Attacks of a foreign Enemy: But while the Mind remains involved in its native Obscurity, it becomes pliable, abject, dastardly, and tame: It swallows the grossest Absurdities, submits to the vilest Impositions, and follows wherever it is led. In short, irrefragable Arguments in favour of Knowledge, may be drawn from the Consideration of its Nature. But it is sufficient barely to observe its Effects. He must be a Stranger to History and the World, who has not observed, that the Prosperity, Happiness, Grandeur, and even the Strength of a People, have always been the Consequences of the Improvement and Cultivation of their Minds. And indeed, where this has been in any considerable Degree neglected, triumphant Ignorance hath open'd its Sluices, and the Country been overflowed with Tyranny, Barbarism, ecclesiastical Domination, Superstition, Enthusiasm, corrupt Manners, and an irresistible confederate Host of Evils, to its utter Ruin and Destruction. While *Egypt* was the School of the Ancients, her martial, was not inferior to her literary, Glory. The successful Defence of the Greeks, against the powerful Invasions of *Persia*, is to be imputed, rather to their Art than to any other Cause. And when *Rome* had compleated the Conquest of the World, she triumphed over it as much in Science as in Power and military Valour.

But as necessary and advantageous as the Education of Youth is to a Country, it has often been remarked, that of all the Provinces on the Continent, not one has been so culpably inattentive to this important Article as ours. I wish it was in my Power, to disprove the Truth of the Observation. We are not only surpassed by several of our Neighbours, who have long since erected Colleges for publick Instruction, but by all others, even in common Schools; of which I have heard it lamented, that we have scarce ever had a good One in the Province. It is true, we had a Law which declared in its Preamble, that the Youth of this Province, were not inferior in their Geniuses to those of any other Country: But against this it is to be observed, that the Law is long since expired, and probably our natural Ingenuity abated, and even tho' this was not our Case, I can by no Means agree, that the natural Fertility of our Geniuses, is a sufficient Reason for the total Neglect of their Cultivation.[2]

It is with Joy I observe the present Disposition of our Legislature, to remove the Scandal of our former Indolence, about the Means of Education, in the Measures we are pursuing for the Establishment of a College. That important Design must flourish under the Care of the Public. Our Province is growing and opulent, and we are able to endow an University in the most splendid Manner, without any Burden upon the People. Scarce any Thing at present but the Nature of its Constitution demands the Study of the several Branches of the Legislature. And that alone is a Subject worthy their utmost Vigilance and Attention. A College in a new Country, and especially in a Province of such scanty Limits as ours, will necessarily make a vast Alteration in our

Affairs and Condition, civil and religious. It will, more or less, influence every Individual amongst us, and diffuse its Spirit thro' all Ranks, Parties and Denominations. If it be established upon a generous and catholic Foundation, agreeable to the true Nature and End of a Seminary for the Instruction of Youth in useful Knowledge, we and our Posterity will have Reason to bless its Founders, and long will it continue the Fountain of Felicity to the Province. But should it unhappily be made the Engine of a Party in Church or State — should it be constituted with any Badge of religious Discrimination or Preference, we have no Reason either to believe or wish its Prosperity. Such an impure Source must necessarily poison us with its infected Streams, endanger our precious Liberties, discourage our Growth, and be obstructive to the public Emolument. But this Matter I have fully considered in some of my former Papers on the College. The laudable Generosity which our Assembly have already exhibited in their Sentiments relating to its Constitution, have procured them the most general Applause, and inspired the People with a Confidence that they will faithfully guard their Privileges sacred and political.

Whoever has been at a College, is not ignorant, that the Youth at their Initiation, must be considerably instructed in the Latin and Greek Tongues; their first Exercises there, consisting in reading the principal Authors that have written in those Languages.[3] Hence it is plain, that good Grammar Schools are absolutely necessary in a Course of Education, to the Growth and Prosperity of our College, where, instead of studying the Rudiments of those Languages, after only one Year's Exercise in them, the Youth enter upon sublimer Employments in Logic, Philosophy, Ethics, *etc.* in which it is impossible for School Boys, thro' the Immaturity of their Judgments, to make any valuable Proficiency. At the same Time, therefore, that we institute a College, we should by no Means neglect the Encouragement of Schools, without which it will be thin and unprosperous. To what Purpose shall we rear a vast and costly Edifice, and raise an expensive Fund for the Support of Instructors, but for the Benefit of the Students? And to supply the latter without good Schools throughout the Province, will be impossible, unless the College itself be made one, which will be a Scheme both unexampled and absurd.[4]

With Submission therefore, to my Superiors, I would propose, that an Act be passed for building and establishing two Grammar Schools in every County, and enabling the Inhabitants, annually to elect Guardians over them, and Impowering the Assessors to raise Fifty Pounds per Annum, as a County Charge, for the Support of each Master, to be nominated and paid by those Guardians.[5]

This Step is, in my Opinion, not only feasible, but free from all the Objections which lie against a Grammar School Education in the College, and will, besides, be attended with very good Consequences.

First: Two Schools in a County will probably, for many Years, be more than sufficient for the Instruction of the Children to be sent from it to the College, and both of them may be raised at a very inconsiderable Sum. In the Colonies to the Eastward, they are built upon the Commons, contain but one Room, are tight and warm, and not more costly nor larger than a common Log Cottage. The Master suits himself with a Lodging in the Village, and so do his Pupils generally at a very cheap rate. The Masters among them are such as have been graduated at their Colleges, and for want of Estates, stoop to this Employment, till they have more fully prosecuted their Studies; and having but just finish'd their collegiate Education, are perhaps better fitted for that Business, than Persons of riper Years, who have worn off their academical Learning, and are determined upon some particular Office or Occupation. I make no doubt therefore, but that it will be easy to supply our Schools with Preceptors, at Fifty Pounds per Annum each, since there are many such in those Colonies who are glad to take up with a more inconsiderable Sum. But as it seems agreed to fix the College in this City, the Salaries of the same Officers, if Grammar Schools be supported in the College, must be vastly augmented, because their additional Expences in Diet and Dress, must be very much enhanced; and perhaps it will be no easy Matter to provide a Fund for the College, sufficient to sustain the continual Charge of so many Masters.

Secondly: Supporting the Youth at those Schools in the Country, will be but a Trifle compared with the prodigious Expence of maintaining them in the City, which probably will prevent many from bestowing upon their Children a publick Education.

Thirdly: It is worth Consideration, that as Boys at a very early Age may be fit for the Grammar School, the Tenderness or Weakness of Parents, may raise Objections against sending them to *New-York*, at the proper Time, for their Study of the Tongues; and in Consequence thereof, to their utter Ruin, prevent their ever passing thro' the College who might otherwise be constantly kept, during their Infancy, at a Country School, under the Care of their Parents, till they were in Age, and Capacity, prepared for entering the College. And, indeed, I cannot help thinking, but that this Objection alone would prove fatal to the Scheme of supporting Grammar Schools in the College; for where one Man would agree to put a Lad of Ten or Twelve Years of Age to School, Fifty or a Hundred Miles from him, many, rather than submit to it, would refuse giving their Children any Education at all, especially if it be also considered how susceptible tender Minds are of all Impressions, whether Good or Evil, and how necessary it is in forming their Morals, that they should be kept under the Eye of their Parents.

Fourthly: It is not to be supposed that, let a Boy's Genius be never so promising, he can be well-fitted for his Entrance into the College, in less than four Years. Nor will he thence carry off much Knowledge, unless he continues his Studies there, at least four Years more. So that, if he is sent to the College for his Attainment of the Tongues, his Absence from Home, and Residence in the City, will take up eight Years, where the Expence of his Tuition, extraordinary Dress and Diet, will perhaps exceed his Father's Purse, and for that insurmountable Objection, prevent his ever having the Means of an Education; when, if one Half of that Time was spent at no Charge for Tuition, and a very trifling Expence for his Board and Dress in the Country, his Talents might be cultivated to the Advantage of himself and the Public.

Fifthly: At these County-Schools it will be in the Power of

423

those Parents to have their Children taught Latin and Greek, who are neither able nor inclined to give them an academical Education, from which they will be deterred by the Expence of maintaining them four Years in *New-York*. Nor, tho' they should not intend them so ample an Education as they would receive in the College, would it in many Cases be improper to let them pass thro' the Grammar Schools. I have known many Men, without any other Assistances in Education than what they received at such Schools, make a very agreeable and useful Appearance in Life: And it is, perhaps, principally to be ascribed to the Number and Cheapness of those little Country Seminaries, that the *Scotch*, in the Article of Literature, support the Reputation of exceeding in general, any other Nation in the World. Besides the Advantage of acquiring a Knowledge of those Languages sufficient to read and examine the Writings of the Ancients, the shortest Course that can be recommended for the Attainment of any considerable Accuracy in the Knowledge even of our own Language, is by a tolerable Acquaintance with the Latin and Greek Tongues. Whoever understands those Languages, and English, will find the latter vastly augmented and enriched by Derivatives from the former. The technical Terms, or Words of Art, are deduced almost entirely from those Fountains, as well as many others of Use, even in common Conversation. It would be an endless Piece of Work to be indebted to our Dictionaries (which by the Way are seldom to be depended upon, often unsatisfactory, and defective) for the Meaning of Words; which must always be the Case, when we are ignorant of the Languages from whence they are derived. Besides, Boys in the Study of the Languages, are employed in a Manner best suited to their Capacities. Plain Rules of Morality and History are generally the Subjects of the Books put into their Hands. Whatever they are designed for, there can be no Danger of an Excess in their Studies of these Things, and their Progress in them principally depends upon the Memory, a Faculty of the Mind which is generally exercised the first of any others in Youth. In a Course of Grammar School Learning, they are enured to Books and Attention, in a Manner the most easy and natural. Their Capacities gradually opened — their Curiosities raised —

their Powers strengthened — their Views extended, and their Minds familiarized to Inquiry: All which must be necessary and advantageous to them in any Employment in Life, even tho' they do not enter upon collegiate Exercises in a more deep and abstruse Course of Studies. It is Dr. SWIFT who says, *"The Books read at School are full of Incitements to Virtue, and Discouragements from Vice, drawn from the wisest Reasons, the strongest Motives, and the most influencing Examples. The very Maxims set up to direct modern Education, are enough to destroy all the Seeds of Knowledge, Honour, Wisdom and Virtue among us. The current Opinion prevails, that the Study of Greek and Latin is Loss of time."* [6]

Sixthly: It may be observed, that few, if any, of the Pupils in the Grammar School to be erected in the College, will be of an Age to admit of their living within its Walls. Their tender Years will render it necessary for them to board at private Houses in the City, for the Advantage of Nurses to exercise over them a Mother's Care, which will prevent the Masters from that narrow Inspection into their Conduct from which they cannot so well be exempted at a School in the Country, and at the same Time weaken the Support of a suitable Government in the College, where, unless the strictest Regimen is observed, the wildest Confusion and Disorder will take Place, to the absolute Ruin of the Students.

I only add, that no Instance can be assigned that Grammar-School-Learning was ever a Part of the Instruction in any College or University; and I conceive, for the Reasons before offered, it would be very improper for us to begin such an unprecedented Institution. The Encouragement of County Schools, will supply our College with Students, in a Manner best suited to our Circumstances; and if we neglect them, I think one may venture to predict, that the Academy will never rise to any considerable Fame, nor answer the general Expectations of the Province.

A.

1. This essay had appeared anonymously, in essentially the same form, in the *New-York Gazette,* December 11, 1752.

2. The "singular" preamble preceded a 1732 "Act to encourage a Public School in the City of New York for teaching Latin Greek and Mathematicks."

The passage, "Whereas the City and Colony of New York abounds with Youths of a Genius not Inferior to other Countries. . . ." afforded William Smith, Jr., author of this issue, much "merriment." The act provided for public support, out of municipal and provincial funds, for the school then being conducted in New York by Mr. Alexander Malcolm. The statute expired in 1737, was renewed for a year, and then died permanently. *Colonial Laws of New York*, I, 813–817, 973–977; Smith, *History*, II, 2–3.

3. Harvard's entrance requirements in 1655 demanded a reading knowledge of the "ordinary Classicall Authors," an understanding of Greek grammar, and skill in writing or speaking Latin prose and writing Latin verse. Yale's of 1726 were similar. For a recent discussion of the classics in the colonial colleges, see Robert Middlekauff, "A Persistent Tradition: The Classical Curriculum in Eighteenth-Century New England," *William and Mary Quarterly*, XVIII (1961), 54–67.

4. Samuel Johnson attested the prescient character of this observation a few years after he assumed office as president of King's College. "Our great difficulty is that our grammar schools are miserable." It became necessary to devote the first year of college to the "grammatical" education the student should have acquired before entrance. (Johnson to East Apthorp, December 1, 1759, *Samuel Johnson Writings*, IV, 56.) The complaint must sound astonishingly familiar to college presidents two hundred years later.

5. The 1732 act, precedent for this proposal, had provided for an annual salary of at least £40 for the master of the grammar school and established a Board of Visitors — the Justices of the Supreme Court, the Mayor, Recorder, and Aldermen of New York City, and the Rector of Trinity Church — to inspect the school, remove the master "in case of Misbehaviour or Neglect of his Duty," and appoint his successor. The salary was to come from the provincial license fees on hawkers and pedlars and from special municipal levies. The school was to provide free education for twenty scholars, nominated by the municipal officials of Albany and New York City and the justices of the peace in the rural districts.

6. *An Essay on Modern Education.* In the original the last two sentences precede the first and are separated from it by several pages.

Number LI

[On the College and the Clergy]

W HEN I consider, either the favourable Sentiments which the Author of the following Letter is pleased to entertain of some of my Reflections, or the Importance of the Subject he has chosen, and the masterly Manner in which he handles it, I think it would be an Injury, both to the Public and myself, to refuse it a Place in the REFLECTOR.

To the INDEPENDENT REFLECTOR

SIR,   *Philadelphia, October* 21, 1753.

T HO' we are unknown to each other, and my Residence is out of the Province, for which your Papers are more particularly calculated, I cannot restrain my Acknowledgments to an Author who inspired with an amiable Disinterestedness, so industriously aims at the Advancement of the Honour and Happiness not only of his own Country, but of universal Mankind. I heartily approve of your Papers in general; but of those on the Subject of the College, I have the highest Opinion. The Method you therein pursued is strictly accurate, and the Scheme you proposed for its Constitution and Government, judicious and wholesome. I do not remember to have heard any Man, who has impartially considered it, advance any material Objection against it. Nor do I believe, from what I know of the State of your Province, that a more advantageous Scheme can possibly be recommended to a People split into such a Diversity of religious Opinions. Yours not only obviates the Jealousy of each, but effectually secures all in the lasting Enjoyment of their Liberties. And in this View of your Sentiments on that important Subject, it has been Matter of Surprize to many Gentlemen among us, who heartily desire to fee Learning prevail in the Plantations, that, after the Plan you have drawn up and proposed, the Affair of the College should have so tardy a Progress. These Colonies have hitherto been too much despised by some British Politicians, whose Indifference has often exposed us to sundry political Disadvantages. The best Means for raising a Sense of our Importance, and in Consequence of it, an Attention to our provincial Interests, is, in my Opinion, to encourage the Education of Youth in all our Provinces. The Importation of Foreigners, and our own Growth, will, indeed, people our Country. Our Lands may be cultivated, and our Commerce enlarged; but our Reputation, and even our Strength, will principally depend upon able Councillors, sensible Representatives, and Officers of Judgment and Penetration. But, how shall we preserve those Rights of which we are ignorant? How introduce Measures necessary for our general Prosperity, but with great Art and Address? Tho' we are entitled to all the Rights of Englishmen, we have not an equal Security with those of our Fellow Subjects, who enjoy the Happiness of living under the immediate Protection of our gracious Sovereign. The Infancy of our Country, necessarily exposes us to many Defects which are not to be found in a State grown perfect and compact by Time and Experience, Our political Frame must attain its full Maturity by Steps gradual and slow. Nor shall we ever behold this happy Period, 'till we apply our Thoughts to the Consideration of our Condition, Interest and Relations. There are doubtless some Instances of Persons of that Turn among us: A few will, however, but little avail us: Their Influence will be no wider than their Sphere. Such a Spirit must become general, before the Advantages will be so; and of all the Methods we can pursue, there is none so likely to enkindle and diffuse it, as the Encouragement of Education, thereby furnishing our Colonies with Men of Sense and Literature, with enterprizing Heads, and Hearts inflamed with Patriot-Fire.

I assure you, *Sir*, I am deeply affected with the Indifference which prevails among some of you in the important Undertaking of erecting a College; and I think the Opposition to your Scheme, as it retards that useful Design, a Shame to your Adversaries. Such a *Seminary* would not only be advantageous to your Province, in the View I have before considered it, but would attach to it many of our Youth. Our Academy is only intended to teach the lower Kinds of Knowledge; and, indeed, in that Respect, will, undoubtedly, be of admirable Service. But if the College of *New-York*, is established upon the free Bottom you proposed, by which all the Students, of whatever Protestant Denomination, will be received upon, and admitted to a perfect Parity of Privileges, it cannot but prosper, and invite Pupils from all our Colonies, as it will, in Reality, be preferable to the public Seminaries of all of them, each savouring more or less of religious Party.[1] Nor has the Catholicism of your Plan been less happy in obviating the Objections which the Gentlemen of the *West-Indies*, have hitherto raised against most of our Northern Colleges.

The Contention about introducing the *English* Liturgy, tho' I profess myself a Churchman, has, in my Opinion, had more Regard paid to it, than ought to be allowed to any Thing that impedes so good a Design. You, indeed, have insisted, that no Form used by any Church in your Province should be introduced, lest a Discrimination of one Sect enkindle the Jealousy of the Rest, to the Prejudice of the College. I concur with you in Opinion, if a Form could be agreed upon free from the Objection: But you'll admit it a great Pity, that such a trifling Dispute, should retard so glorious and beneficial an Undertaking. The Form of Prayer you proposed as a Model, tho' ingenious, will, I believe, never be consented to, because I do not suppose your Assembly will ever think proper to give themselves the Trouble of preparing a Set of Forms. In Favour of the Liturgy of the Church of *England* it is urged, that the Nation has approved it; but it must be confessed, that tho' it is very well suited to the State of a Church, it will require a considerable Alteration, to adapt it to the State of such a Seminary: The Forms of the *Dutch* and *French* Protestant Churches are as good, and will require less Alteration and Addition; and if it should not be thought proper to introduce them, rather than the Contention about Forms should impede that noble Design, the Prayers, I think, should be left to the Discretion of the President, with the Trustees, to whom it should be committed, to draw up a Formulary, to be laid before your Legislature for their Approbation and Establishment.

These, Sir, are my Sentiments of the Matter, and upon your Promise to correct them, you have Leave to give them a Place in your Paper. I hope, at your next Session, something definitive will be done in this Affair. May God inspire your Legislature with a generous Regard to the Liberties of their Countrymen, and assist them in establishing the College upon such a Foundation, as that it may continue a perpetual Blessing to your Province, and of general Utility to Mankind. I *am, etc.*

A.

I shall very chearfully insert the following Letter, as my judicious Correspondent so handsomely exposes an Absurdity long complained of, and yet repeatedly practised. Nor shall I scruple, considering the Humour and Good Sense with which the Gentleman writes, to acknowledge the Favour of his future Letters.

THE INDEPENDENT REFLECTOR

To the Author of the INDEPENDENT REFLECTOR

SIR,

As you seem to write with an Intention to reform all Abuses, whether of a civil or religious Nature, I take the Liberty to present you with my Complaint against the Minister of the Parish to which I belong. Our View in calling this Gentleman, was to instruct us in all the important Truths of Christianity, and to enforce the Practice of substantial Virtue, and evangelical Holiness. But these, I am sorry to say, are Things about which he seldom troubles his Head. On the Contrary, his Sermons are rather calculated to make one a Critic or Pedagogue, than a good Man or a Christian. He consults his own Humour much more than the State of his Audience; and seems to take greater Delight in displaying his Literature, than in augmenting the Number of his Converts. His Sermons are so replete with abstruse Erudition, that if I affirmed they were unintelligible to forty-nine in fifty of his Congregation, I should speak within Compass. There is not a single Critic or Commentator, who has animadverted on his Text, that can escape him. No, his Hearers must be teaz'd with all the discordant Sentiments of perhaps, twenty Expositors: And after having given us the Construction of *Euthemius, Ambrose, Gaudentius, Theophilactus, Austin, Basil, Hieronymus, Beza, Anastatius, Ryertus, Maldonatus, Voetius, Horenbeck, Cocceius, Witsius, Zwinglius, Woolfgangus, Amesius, Van Maestricht, Mauritius, etc.* he gravely delivers his own, which generally differs from them all. Nay, I have heard him discant for above half an Hour on the various Readings of an Hebrew Word; which after all matter'd not a Groat, nor in any wise tended to the Edification of his People.[2] For what is all the cabalistical Nonsense of the Jewish Rabbins, or Popish Monks, or modern Schoolmen, to us? And of what Service can it be to his Congregation, to be teazed, as it often happens, for an Hour at a Time, with the idle Definition of the Ornaments of the Temple, which after all cannot be truly represented? Or of fifty other Things in common Use, and known to every Body? We want to have the most essential Doctrines of our holy Religion, clearly illustrated, and the immutable Duties of a virtuous Life enforced by the strongest Motives: And above all, the Vices and Irregularities most prevalent amongst us, severely reprehended, and their opposite Virtues as warmly inculcated. But as to the Shape of St. PETER's Sword, or the Size of the Carbuncle in the Temple of JERUBBABEL, with many other theological Curiosities of the same Consequence to Religion, *who hath required it at his Hands?* If he is our Shepherd, pray let him feed his Flock. But can we live on the airy Diet of chimerical Rhapsodies, that afford us no spiritual Nutriment?

430

Or is he in a likely Way to advance the Practice of Virtue and Piety, who bewilders himself and his Hearers, in the intricate Mazes of scholastic Distinctions, and metaphysical Whimsies,? If this be not a prefering the enticing Words of Man's Wisdom, to that Demonstration of the Spirit mentioned by St. PAUL, I must own I am at a Loss for the Apostle's Meaning. Surely he either thinks it fit to disbelieve, or improper to obey another Observation of the same inspired Pen-Men, with respect to such unintelligible Preaching. *If I know not the Meaning of the Voice, I shall be unto him that speaketh a Barbarian, and he that speaketh shall be a Barbarian unto me.*[3] Nay, if he had adapted a judicious Wish of St. AUSTIN, instead of all the scholastic Trumpery he so frequently collects from him, I should have no Occasion to trouble you with this Complaint. *I had rather* (says that Father) *that the Grammarians should cavil, than that the People should not understand.*

Another Thing for which he is highly to blame, is his unchristian Acrimony against those of different Persuasions: For instead of leveling his Thunder at Vice and Immorality, it is generally aim'd at those he is pleased to term Hereticks; and such with him, are all they that differ from him. The ancient Sect of the *Gnostics,* and fifty other Heresies now extinct, live only by his Spleen: *Arius, Socinus, Luther,* and *Arminius,* he classes with the spiritual Enemies of King DAVID, and for that Reason very devoutly curses them in the Language of Scripture every Sabbath Day. In short, he scarce ever preaches a Sermon, in which he does not take Occasion to lug in by Head and Shoulders, all the different Sects he can enumerate, in so much, that I have often wondered to find him content himself, with spending the whole of his Rage upon the modern Heresies, such as *Arminianism, Moravianism, etc.* without, moreover, superadding all the — *Isms* of the Old Testament, and shewing us the damnable Error of *Perizzitism, Jebuzitism, Hivitism, etc.* which would be equally conducive to the Edification of his People.

Some Persons will doubtless think this Method of handling his pastoral Labours, both uncharitable and heretical; and that it is inconsistent with the profound Submission we owe to the Clergy, thus to depicture his Reverence in the Exercise of his apostolical Functions. But if that *Labourer is unworthy of his Hire,* who, instead of being assiduous in the Duties of his Calling, wastes the scanty Moments of his public Appearance, in an empty and unprofitable Display of his Talents; to be told of his Error in such a Manner as to enforce his Notice, is the least Resentment he can possibly expect. But should he hereafter be determined to aim at informing the Consciences, and correcting the Morals of his Audience, rather than fatigue their Attention with that *which profiteth Nothing,* he will as surely command the Applauses of his Hearers, as he has hitherto justly deserved a public Reprehension.[4]

Z.

1. Of the existing colonial colleges in 1754 Harvard (1636) and Yale (1701) had been founded under Congregationalist auspices, William and Mary (1693) under Anglican, and the College of New Jersey (1746) — later Princeton — under Presbyterian sponsorship. The Philadelphia Academy (1740) was non-denominational, but it was not elevated to collegiate status until 1755.

2. The model for this unflattering description may have been the Reverend Joseph Noyes, minister of the New Haven church Livingston was compelled to attend at Yale — notorious for his long-winded sermons. When Thomas Clap, the college president, remonstrated with Noyes, the minister is reported to have defended himself, saying "You do not know what an ignorant people I have to preach to." To which Clap is supposed to have responded tartly: "Yes I do, and I know that as long as you preach to them in this way, they always will be ignorant." George P. Fisher, *A Discourse Commemorative of the History of the Church of Christ in Yale College . . .* (New Haven, 1858), pp. 8, 45 note.

3. I Cor. 14:11.

4. This "communication" was undoubtedly Livingston's own composition. Almost every idea in it and a good deal of the language appear elsewhere in his writings, public and private.

Number LII

THURSDAY, NOVEMBER 22, 1753

The Consideration of the natural Advantages of New-York, *resumed and concluded* [1]

> *Lo! swarming o'er the new discover'd World,*
> *Gay Colonies extend; the Calm retreat*
> *Of undeserv'd Distress, the better Home*
> *Of those whom Bigots chase from foreign Lands:*
> *Not built on Rapine, Servitude and Woe,*
> *And, in their Turn some petty Tyrant's Prey;*
> *But bound by social Freedom, firm they rise;*
> *Of Britain's Empire the Support and Strength.*
> THOM[SON], *Lib*[*erty*]

THO' Boasting in general be a Foible worthy of Contempt, yet when our Country is the Subject, our warmest Commendations are, methinks, neither illaudable nor disgraceful. So early do we receive this patriot Passion, and so intimately are we concerned in that Object of our Affections, that the Praises we bestow upon the Place of our Nativity, tho' often repeated, justly admit of Apology, and even of Excuse. For my own Part, to dwell upon so interesting a Theme, affects me with singular Pleasure; and the Evidences which appear in my Papers of an unfeigned Regard to this Province, I esteem their greatest Ornament. My Countrymen at least can have no Reason to repine at the Continuation of this Subject. The Public Weal is my only Aim, and I flatter myself that the Display of our superior Advantages naturally tends to advance it. I proceed, therefore, according to my Promise, to resume the Detail, and make it the Subject of another REFLECTOR.

With regard to our Situation in respect of foreign Markets, *New-York* is to be preferred to any of our Colonies. It lies in the Center of *North-America,* and is therefore most happily situated for supporting a Trade with all the Plantations from *Georgia* to

Halifax. Connecticut on the East, and *New-Jersey* on the West, are fertile and well cultivated Colonies, and thro' natural Necessity, must always contribute their Aids in rendering this City a plentiful Mart, because their Exports cannot with equal Ease and Safety be conveyed to any other Port of considerable Traffick. The Projection of *Cape Cod* into the Ocean, renders the Navigation from *Connecticut* to *Boston*, at some Seasons, extremely perilous. Nor is it uncommon for their Coasters to be driven off the *Cape*, and obliged to winter in the *West-Indies*. But their Vicinity to us affords them a safe and easy Conveyance to *New-York* thro' the Sound. *Philadelphia*, indeed, joins *New-Jersey* on the West; but it is well worth remarking, that the Lands adjacent to the River *Delaware*, on the *New-Jersey* Shore, below *Philadelphia*, are unprofitable Barrens, and the River navigable but a few Miles above it; and that a Voyage from the eastern Part of *New-Jersey* to *Philadelphia*, exposed to the open Sea on one Side, and a hazardous Coast on the other, and then to a dangerous Navigation in *Delaware*, is a Circuit of not less than Three Hundred Miles; while four Rivers, rolling from the Heart of that Colony, disembogue within a few Miles of our City. And thus two Provinces, both capable of the highest Improvements, from their natural Situation conspire to aggrandize *New-York*, almost as effectually as if they were part of this Colony. Not one of the Provinces has a River so far navigable into the Country as ours; whence it is that the Indian Trade from those vast Territories on the North, determines its Course to *Albany*, and thence down *Hudson*'s River to *New-York*, as naturally as a Stream gliding in its proper Channel.[2]

Our Harbour, or rather Road, is as safe as others generally are, most of them being subject to important Objections, and often indebted for their Security to very expensive Improvements of Art. The mooring Ground is good, free from Bars, and not incommoded by Rocks, the Water of an equal and convenient Depth, and the Shore bold to the very Edges; and but for floating Cakes of Ice in the Winter, our Shipping would be entirely exempted from Danger. Nor is it difficult perfectly to secure them from that Inconvenience. The Place called *Rotten-Row*,[3] has hitherto been their only Asylum, tho' unhappily of late, it annually becomes less and less fit for that Purpose: The Scheme I propose to perpetuate, or rather increase its former Usefulness, is both simple and cheap. The whole Length of this Opening should be filled up to the Extent of One Hundred Feet, and from each End of it a strong open Pier carried out into the River; between which, our Shipping will have all proper Security and the greatest Conveniency for lading, unlading, and careening, that can either be expected or desired. The free Passage of the Tides under the Bridges of the Piers, will always preserve a sufficient Depth of Water. The Part proposed to be filled up will be very spacious, and being at an equal Distance from the two Extremes of the Town, the fittest Place for erecting a large Market-House, very advantageous to the adjacent Inhabitants, as well as ornamental and convenient to the whole City. By this Alteration also, the putrid Stench, arising from that Sink of Corruption, so prejudicial to the Healths and Lives of the People, will be effectually prevented. The continual Evacuations of the Sewers at the Slip and Meal Markets, as well as the main Stream of the River, have already rendered *Rotten-Row* much shallower than it was, and will make it in Time, incapable of screening our Ships from the Ice: But this Project will always protect them from that Hazard and Damage.

The City of *New-York* consists of about Two Thousand Five Hundred Buildings. It is a Mile in Length, and at a Medium not above half that in Breadth. On the South it forms a Point into a large Bay. The East Side lies on a Streight [Strait], which at eighteen or twenty Miles eastward, opens to the Sound. It adjoins to *Hudson*'s River on the West; and such is its Figure, its Center of Business, and the Situation of its Buildings, that the Cartage in Town from one Part to another, does not at a Medium, exceed one Quarter of a Mile: The prodigious Advantage of which, to a trading City, is more easily conceived than expressed. It facilitates and expedites the lading and unlading of Ships and Boats, saves Time and Labour, and is attended with innumerable Conveniencies to its Inhabitants.

The City of *Philadelphia* is situated along a fresh Water

River, at the Distance of near two hundred Miles from the Sea. The Navigation up to it is tedious, and, as I said before, difficult and dangerous. During the Severity of Winter, it is locked up from all marine Correspondence with the rest of the World, and thus, necessarily for several Months every Year, exposed to an almost total Stagnation of Trade. Numberless must be the Inconveniences resulting from this their melancholly Imprisonment — Commerce groans — a listless constrained Inactivity prevails, and an unprofitable Consumption devours the Fruit of their Labours, 'till the returning Spring takes off the Embargo, unlocks their River, and again opens the Theatre of Business and Profit. But the Trade of *New-York* boasts an Exemption from such Embarassments — No Season prevents our Ships from launching into the Ocean and pursuing their Traffick — The Depth of Winter scarce obstructs our Commerce, and during its greatest Severity, an equal unrestrained Activity runs thro' all Ranks, Orders and Employments. Even then our Merchants exult in the Return of their Ships, while our Neighbours of *Philadelphia* wait for Intelligences they are unable to improve, or concert Schemes which it is beyond their Power to execute.

Tho' we abound in no one Kind of Fish sufficient for a Staple, yet such is our Happiness in this Article, that not one of the Colonies affords a Fish-Market of such a plentiful Variety as ours. *Boston* has none but Sea Fish, and of these *Philadelphia* is entirely destitute, being only furnished with the Fish of a fresh Water River. *New-York* is sufficiently supplied with both Sorts. Nor ought our vast plenty of Oysters to pass without particular Observation: in their Quality they are exceeded by those of no Country whatsoever. People of all Ranks amongst us, in general prefer them to any other Kind of Food. Nor is any Thing wanting, save a little of the Filings of Copper, to render them equally relishing even to an English Palate, with the best from *Colchester*.[4] They continue good eight Months in the Year, and are, for two Months longer, the daily Food of our Poor. Their Beds are within View of the Town, and I am informed, that an Oysterman industriously employed, may clear Eight or Ten Shillings a Day. Some Gentlemen a few Years ago were at the Pains of computing the Value of this Shellfish to our Province in general. The Estimate was made with Judgment and Accuracy, and their Computation amounted to Ten Thousand Pounds per Annum. Their Increase and Consumption are since every much enhanced, and thus also their additional Value in Proportion. I confess it has often given me great Pleasure to reflect, how many of my poor Countrymen are comfortably supported by this Article, who without it could scarcely subsist, and for that Reason beg to be excused for the Length of this Reflection on so humble a Subject, tho' it might justly be urged to the Honour of our Oysters, that, considered in another View, they are serviceable both to our King and Country.

It is generally believed, that this Province abounds with a Variety of Minerals. Of Iron in particular we have such plenty, as to be exceeded by no Country in the World of equal Extent. It is a Metal of intrinsick Value beyond any other, and preferable to the purest Gold; the former is converted into numberless Forms for as many indispensible Uses, the latter for its Portableness and Scarcity is only fit for a Medium of Trade: But Iron is a Branch of it, and I am persuaded will, one Time or other, be one of the most valuable Articles of our Commerce. Our annual Exports to *Boston*, *Rhode-Island*, and *Connecticut*, and since the late Act of Parliament, to *England*, are far from being inconsiderable. The Bodies of Iron Ore in the Northern Parts of this Province are so many, their Quality so good, and their Situation so convenient, in respect of Wood, Water, Hearth-Stone, proper Fluxes, and Carriage, for Furnaces, Bloomeries, and Forges, that with a little Attention we might very soon rival the *Swedes* in the Produce of this Article. If any *American* Attempts in Iron Works have prov'd abortive, and disappointed their Undertakers, it is not to be imputed either to the Quality of the Ore, or a Defect of Conveniences. The Want of more Workmen, and the Villainy of those we generally have, are the only Causes to which we must attribute such Miscarriages. No Man who has been concerned in them will disagree with me, if I assert, that from the Founder of the Furnace to the meanest Banksman or Jobber, they are usually low, profligate, drunken and faithless. And yet under all the innumerable

Disadvantages of such Instruments, very large Estates have, in this Way, been raised in some of our Colonies. Our Success, therefore, in the Iron Manufactory, is obstructed and discouraged by the Want of Workmen, and the high Price of Labour, its necessary Consequence, and by these alone: But 'tis our Happiness that such only being the Cause, the Means of Redress are entirely in our own Hands. Nothing more is wanting to open a vast Fund of Riches to the Province, in this Branch of Trade, than the Importation of Foreigners. If our Merchants and landed Gentlemen, could be brought to a Coalition in this Design, their private Interests would not be better advanced by it, than the public Emolument; the latter in particular, would thereby vastly improve their Lands, increase the Number, and raise the Rents of their Tenants. And I cannot but think, that if those Gentlemen who are too inactive to engage in such an Enterprize, would only be at the Pains of drawing up full Representations of their Advantages for Iron Works, and of publishing them from time to time in *Great-Britain, Ireland, Germany* and *Sweden,* the Province would soon be supplied, with a sufficient Number of capable Workmen in all the Branches of that Manufactory.[5]

Of the Fertility of our Soil there needs no other Proof, than the vast Quantity of Flour and other Produce we annually export, by which alone we have been enabled to bear up under our late prodigious and expensive Importation of dry Goods from *Europe.*[6] The Province is well watered, and abounds with Timber and other Materials for naval Stores, and is capable (as hath been said) to raise annually Forty Thousand Tons of Hemp. Whenever our Husbandmen are driven to a greater Attention to Agriculture than is necessary at present, it will be found that we are most happily supplied with a Variety of Manure, adapted to the different Genius of the Soil in various Parts of the Province. In those near the Sea, where the Ground is light and yielding, the Shore is cover'd with a Sea Weed, by which it may be exceedingly enriched. The Land along *Hudson's* River, is in general colder and tough, but Lime, which is its natural Cure, may be every where obtained: Hills of Lime-Stone being plentifully found on both Sides of the River.

I might enlarge this Detail, with the Enumeration of many

other Marks of the exuberant Bounty, and peculiar Favour of Providence to us, beyond any other Province on the Continent; but the Limits I have prescribed to my Papers forbid a more ample Display. A. & X.

I am greatly obliged to Mr. CHRISTOPHER SOWER, *Printer, in* Germantown, *for the Book which he has been pleased to send me as a Present.*[7]

1. A continuation of No. VIII.

2. In his *History* (I, 280–281), Smith, the author of this number, conceded that the fur trade had by this time been "much impaired by the French wiles and encroachments." By establishing posts among the western tribes and employing *coureurs de bois* — French traders who lived with the natives — France had impaired the monopoly that Albany once held in the Indian trade. See Peter Wraxall, *An Abridgment of the Indian Affairs*, C. H. Mc Ilwain, ed. (Cambridge, Mass., 1915), introd.; Ruth L. Higgins, *Expansion in New York: With Especial Reference to the Eighteenth Century* (Columbus, Ohio, 1931), chap. 4; and Arthur H. Buffinton, "The Policy of Albany and English Westward Expansion," *Mississippi Valley Historical Review*, VIII (1922), 327–366.

3. Hunter's Key. See *Reflector*, No. XLV, note 2 above.

4. Colchester, on the Coine River in Essex, England, has been celebrated for its oysters since the reign of Elizabeth I. The mineral content of the water there gives its oysters a distinctively copper flavor. New Yorkers would presumably achieve this flavor artificially.

5. New York's only iron works at this time were those at Ancram, on the Livingston Manor, constructed between 1741 and 1743. Early operations were curtailed by the shortage of skilled workers of which Smith complained here. Slaves, unsuccessfully employed for a time, were ultimately replaced by foreign craftsmen. Ancram ore was considered so excellent, the entire output was committed before it even reached the market. See Harrington, *op. cit.*, pp. 149–150; A. C. Bining, *British Regulation of the Colonial Iron Industry* (Philadelphia, 1933), pp. 23–24; Irene D. Neu, "The Iron Plantations of Colonial New York," *New York History*, XXXIII (1952), 3–24; Edmund B. O'Callaghan and others, eds., *Documents Relative to the Colonial History of the State of New York*, 15 vols. (Albany, 1853–1887), VII, 335–336.

6. "Our importation of dry goods from England is so vastly great, that we are obliged to betake ourselves to all possible arts to make remittances to the British merchants. It is for this purpose we import cotton from St. Thomas's and Surinam; lime-juice and Nicaragua wood from Curacoa [*sic*]; and log-wood from the bay [of Honduras], . . . and yet it drains us of all the silver and gold we can collect." Smith, *History*, I, 281.

7. Christopher Sauer (1693–1758) conducted the German-language press at Germantown, Pennsylvania, one of the most active of all colonial presses. From it came a large number of devotional and theological tracts, a German newspaper, and an edition of the Bible in German (1743), the first in the American colonies in a European tongue.

APPENDIX I

PLANNED ADDITIONAL NUMBERS OF THE
INDEPENDENT REFLECTOR

In the *Preface* to the *Reflector,* which appeared early in 1754, Livingston offered "the following List of subjects" on which he had written and intended to write "had not the fears of my enemies and the spite of malignants, frustrated my designs, by bereaving me of the liberty of the Press."

LIII. On the excellency of Trials by Juries, with the qualifications of jury men, and some directions for the better judging of written evidence, and the testimony of witnesses.

LIV. A Letter to the speaker of the general Assembly, on the importance of a free College; and the necessity of its immediate institution.

LV. An enumeration of sundry articles, to be inserted in an act, for the amendment of the law in this colony.

LVI. Further reasons on credulity.

LVII. A Dissertation on political trimmers in general; with an evolution of the little arts to gain popularity, practised by those of this province in particular.

LVIII. Remarks on the XXXIX Article of the instructions, to his late Excellency Sir Danvers Osborn. [This article dealt with the question of payment of salaries to royal officials and legislative control of disbursements. By 1752, the Assembly had developed the precedent of voting appropriations for salaries on an annual basis only and also of voting the salaries to individual office-holders by name. Osborne, who arrived in October, 1753, was sternly commanded in this article of his royal instructions to reverse the process, regain control of disbursements, and secure a permanent grant of funds for salaries. Leaders of the anti-gubernatorial party saw to it that this obnoxious article was published in the newspapers. See *New-York Mercury,* November 12, 1753; also Smith, *History,* II, 159–160.]

441

APPENDIX I

ing lay-overseers of the conduct of their missionaries; to transmit accounts of their stations and conduct, agreeable to truth, and exempt from all priestly forgeries.

LXXIII. A brief view of our public buildings; with a panegyric on our exquisite taste respecting architecture.

LXXIV. Of informations by the Attorney General; with the necessity of an act of Assembly for their regulation and restraint.

LXXV. An essay on the nature, relations, and rights of colonies among the Antients.

LXXVI. The right of this colony to be represented in an assembly, or provincial parliament.

LXXVII. The necessity of an established colony-constitution.

LXXVIII. Reflections on the extent of English and British acts of Parliament.

LXXIX. The equal rights of British subjects in the plantations, to the privileges enjoyed by their fellow subjects in Great Britain, asserted and vindicated.

LXXX. The extent of the power of the legislatures of the colonies.

LXXXI. Remarks on the legislative councils in the plantations.

LXXXII. The slavish and pestilent principles contained in a pamphlet, entitled *An Essay on the Government of the Colonies,* examined and refuted; with the propriety of calling the author to an account, for aspersing all the Assemblies on the continent; and endeavouring to undermine the very fundamentals of our constitution and liberties. [This publication appeared in 1752 and was authored by Archibald Kennedy, the provincial Customs Collector and Receiver-General and a member of the Governor's Council. It was a strong plea for maintaining the prerogatives of the Crown against the encroachments of the Assembly — an extreme royalist position proudly asserted by one who considered himself a "mighty Governor's Man." On this publication, see Lawrence C. Wroth, *An American Bookshelf: 1755* (Philadelphia, 1934), pp. 29–31, 118–119, 122–126.]

LXXXIII. Of Incredulity.

LXXXIV. The dangerous effects of an exorbitant popularity; with reflections on the wisdom of the *Ostracism* amongst the Greeks, during their democratical state.

443

APPENDIX I

444

APPENDIX I

APPENDIX II

THE PROBLEM OF AUTHORSHIP OF THE
INDEPENDENT REFLECTOR

The identity of the authors of the individual essays in the *Independent Reflector* has been one of the minor mysteries of the literary and political history of colonial New York. The alphabetical signatures employed by the editors and writers are unrevealing; the pseudonyms used by contributors and letter-writers in the journal — *Philalethes, Shadrach Plebianus,* "Timothy Freeheart" — are tantalizingly obscure. The manuscript originals of only a few of the printed essays have survived, and positive identification of each of the authors at this date is virtually impossible. Nevertheless, at least three latter-day literary detectives have had their appetites sufficiently whetted by the mystery to undertake a solution.[1]

The William Smith Papers in the New York Public Library provide the most useful basis for this detective work. Among Smith's manuscripts are the drafts of several numbers of the *Reflector.* One, the essay on "New York in its natural advantages shortly considered," is in Smith's own hand. When published, the paper bore the signature "A."[2] The draft of another number, written by Livingston, bears the notation in Smith's handwriting, "Perused, 26 May 1753 — A."[3] Further corroboration of A's identity is contained in a key to the *Reflector's* authorship prepared by a contemporary reader, James Kinsey of New Jersey, who served with Livingston in the First Continental Congress. Kinsey identified A as Smith.[4] On this evidence, Smith may be credited with sole authorship of ten essays published over the signature A and with joint authorship of four others.[5] Next to Livingston, Smith was the heaviest contributor to the *Reflector.*

John Morin Scott's contributions are more difficult to verify. The draft of the article on New York's natural advantages which Smith wrote was "Examined and amended by X." The handwriting of this notation appears to be Scott's, but few other samples of his writing at this time are available to substantiate this opinion. Scott's role is obscured further by Kinsey's contemporary key, which identifies X as William Alexander. In any case, X was not a large contributor to the *Reflector,* penning only three whole essays and sharing in two others.[6] Whatever Scott's particular contributions were, there is no doubt that he aided in the production of the *Reflector*: he publicly confessed as much.[7]

Livingston's own essays were usually signed Z. The manuscript

446

of No. XLIII on "The Vanity of Birth and Titles," reposing in the William Smith Papers, is in Livingston's hand. When published, the essay bore the signature Z. The draft of the article on the natural advantages of New York written by Smith and amended by X was also indorsed: "Perused and approved by Z, Nove. 13, 1752." This indorsement, too, is in Livingston's hand. In addition, those numbers of the *Reflector* which announced the editor's purpose and replied to the journal's public detractors were all signed Z. Finally, Kinsey's contemporary key identifies Z as Livingston. Over this signature, then, Livingston wrote twenty-two whole essays and co-authored five others.[8]

Two issues of the *Reflector*, Nos. XXXVI and XXXVII, comprise a single essay in two parts. The first is signed Z; the second, B. In reply to some criticism directed at *the authors* of the two articles, Livingston replied that the critic was quite mistaken: "the *Independent Reflector* . . . I assure you, Sir, never conceived himself to consist of a *Duality* of Persons." [9] If Livingston was not dissembling, then he wrote over the signature B as well as Z, which would make him responsible for ten more essays and a share in one other.[10]

To recapitulate, of the 54 essays in the *Reflector* (Nos. VIII and XXIV each containing two), Livingston may be credited with 33 whole essays and co-authorship of 4 others.[11] Smith and Scott together wrote 13 whole essays and shared in 6 others. The three remaining essays, signed M, N, and O, were the work of other hands, as were the letters from various correspondents which filled portions of twenty of the *Reflector's* issues. The task of identifying these additional contributors is virtually insuperable. Some of the "letters to the editor" which appeared in the paper were undoubtedly the fabrications of the editors; others were genuine.[12] Noah Welles contributed at least one, for which he received Livingston's warm thanks.[13] The most regular of these correspondents was SHADRACH PLEBIANUS, who was responsible for no less than four letters and whose assistance Livingston later recalled with "peculiar veneration" and "the warmest gratitude." Kinsey's key credibly identifies him as William Peartree Smith.

One can only guess at the identities of the triumvirate's other literary assistants. Anglican critics charged that James Alexander was "father" to the *Reflector* coterie and William Smith, Sr., its spiritual "uncle"; but it is unlikely that either of these gentlemen contributed.[14] Other more likely candidates for this honor are William Alexander; Robert R. Livingston, William's cousin and the father of the future Chancellor; Reverend Aaron Burr, President of the College of New Jersey; and Reverend Alexander Cumming, assistant pastor of the First Presbyterian Church in New York City.[15]

APPENDIX II

The Reflector was largely the handiwork of William Livingston. There is little doubt that his was the driving force behind its inception and its publication, that the journal was essentially his in design and execution, and that the roles of his coadjutors, even the principal ones, were secondary. Their contributions were always subject to his own editorial scrutiny.[16] When critics assailed the paper, Livingston wrote the responses of the *Reflector*; and when the journal ceased publication, he wrote the *Preface* which constituted the paper's public *apologia*. The *Independent Reflector* essays always bespoke his own sentiments; and when his assailants alluded publicly to *the* Reflector, it was always William Livingston they had in mind.

1. The three most exhaustive analyses of the problem of authorship are those of Richardson, *Early American Magazines*, pp. 78–82; Dillon, *New York Triumvirate*, pp. 34–35 note; and Harold W. Thatcher, "The Social Philosophy of William Livingston" (unpublished Ph. D. dissertation, University of Chicago, 1935), pp. 18–19.

2. William Smith Papers, No. 212, New York Public Library; *Independent Reflector*, VIII, LII.

3. "The vanity of birth and titles," William Smith Papers, Box 198–206, New York Public Library.

4. Kinsey's key is in the Henry E. Huntington Library (San Marino, California) copy of the *Reflector*, item 107797.

5. Richardson's conclusion differs from the above in crediting Smith with only nine whole essays. Dillon accepts this figure. Thatcher credits Smith with ten. The difference arises from varying interpretations of No. XVI. This is a long letter signed "Publicus," but it is introduced and concluded with remarks by A. Richardson excludes this number from Smith's contributions; the present analysis includes it.

6. Richardson, Thatcher, and Dillon are in agreement on X's contributions.

7. *New-York Mercury*, September 3, 1753.

8. Richardson credits Z with only twenty-one essays, including No. XLVIII, which consists of two letters to the editor. Since the whole issue is signed Z, it is included among Livingston's contributions in the present analysis.

9. *The Occasional Reverberator*, II, September 14, 1753.

10. Richardson, Thatcher, and Dillon all accept Livingston's explanation and credit him with the essays signed B. An element of confusion is introduced, however, by the issue (No. VI) which is signed Z *and* B. Moreover, Kinsey's contemporary key identifies B as Scott.

11. Richardson credits Livingston with 32 in whole and 5 in part; Thatcher's tally is 32 whole and 4 shared; Dillon's is 31 whole and 4 in part. The variations arise from differences in crediting Livingston with essays signed by him but containing letters from others. The present analysis credits Livingston with every issue signed Z or B irrespective of its contents.

12. One, which was received by the editors but not published, is signed

APPENDIX II

"H. W." It is in the William Smith Papers, No. 205, New York Public Library.

13. This was either the letter in No. XIII or the one in XV. On this, see *Reflector*, XIII, note 7.

14. *Samuel Johnson Writings*, I, 187, IV, 15.

15. For the suggestion of Cumming's contribution, see *ibid.*, I, 167; Livingston to Welles, January 17, 1753, JFP, Yale; and Webster, *Presbyterian Church*, p. 615; for the others, see New York Historical Society *Collections*, 1 Ser., III (1821), 366; Isaiah Thomas, *History of Printing in America*, 2 vols. (Worcester, 1810), II, 317; Richardson, *Early American Magazines*, p. 82; Mott, *American Magazines*, p. 48.

16. The essay on New York's natural advantages (Nos. VIII and LII) was published not under the title originally selected by Smith but under that subsequently inserted by Livingston. Smith, on the other hand, urged Livingston to add to his article on the vanity of birth and titles (No. XLIII) "Something . . . on the abuse of toasts," but the printed essay appeared without the insertion.

APPENDIX III

THE *INDEPENDENT REFLECTOR* AND THE *INDEPENDENT WHIG*

Livingston's admiration for the English radicals, Thomas Gordon and John Trenchard, is disclosed explicitly by a long quotation from *Cato's Letters* in No. XLIII of the *Reflector* and his sponsorship, with Smith and Scott, of the republication of Gordon's anticlerical tract, *The Craftsmen*;[1] but the real measure of their influence is the frequency with which the *Reflector* copied the sentiments of the *Whig* and often its language. The striking similarity between the first *Reflector* and the first and second issues of the *Whig* has already been noted.[2] Eight other numbers of the *Reflector* were similarly patterned after essays in the *Whig*.[3] Livingston's phraseology, at times, almost duplicated that of the *Whig*. Thus, where Gordon and Trenchard described orthodoxy as a "hard, equivocal, priestly Word, [that] has done more Mischief to Mankind, than all the Tyrants that ever plagued the Earth," Livingston spoke of it as "a hard equivocal priestly Term" that "has done more Mischief to Mankind than all the Tyrants that ever ravag'd the Globe."[4] On other occasions, the phraseology was changed but not the meaning.

The following parallels are significant:

Independent Whig	*Independent Reflector*
. . . no Man living desires to pay a more true and affectionate Esteem and Reverence than my self to those Clergymen . . . whose Lives and Manners grace and adorn their Professions and Doctrine. (No. II)	No Man on Earth has a greater Regard for the virtuous Clergy than myself. (No. XXXIV)
As it is therefore impossible to shew too much Respect to virtuous Clergymen, so the corrupt Part of them cannot be too much expos'd. (No. II)	No greater Honour can be paid to the Priesthood, than by exposing those who are its Reproach and Blemish. (No. XXXIV)
In this everlasting Scuffle and Civil War, they [priests] had so mangled Truth, and muffled it up, that few could distinguish it from the false Images they had made of it. (No. II)	. . . the plain and amiable religion of Christ, hath by the voluminous rubbish . . . of ecclesiastics been so mangled . . . that it is at present no where to be found pure and genuine, save only in the volume of inspiration itself. (*Preface*, p. 4)

450

They are no sooner discharged from the Nurse and the Mother, but they are delivered over to Spiritual Paedagogues, who have seldom the Capacity . . . to venture at a *Free Thought* . . . . From thence they are sent to the Universities . . . and . . . Their Business afterwards is not to find out what is Truth, but to defend the received System, and to maintain those Doctrines which are to maintain them. (No. V)

Let but a Nurse or a priest implant the seeds of superstition in a tender mind, and 'tis great odds, but they take root beyond . . . power . . . to eradicate. . . . Academies . . . are seldom Places of candid Inquiry. . . . The System of the College is generally taken for true, and the sole Business is to defend it. Freedom of Thought rarely penetrates. . . . (*Preface,* p. 1 and No. XVII)

. . . the Christian Religion, most easy and intelligible in it self, and adapted to the meanest Capacities. (No. VIII)

. . . Christianity . . . is so clear and obvious, that the meanest Understanding may . . . attain to . . . [its] Knowledge and Belief. (No. XLVII)

Youth is the great Opportunity of Life, which settleth and fixeth most Men either in a good or bad Course; and the Impressions, especially bad Impressions, then made, are usually lasting. (No. XVII)

The Principles . . . implanted in the Minds of Youth, grow up and gather Strength with them. . . . when once the Impressions are . . . incorporated with the intellectual Substance, they are obliterated with the greatest Difficulty. (No. XVII)

When they go into Holy Orders, they profess, that they are inwardly mov'd by the Holy Ghost . . . tho' . . . many are inwardly mov'd by the Prospect of Power and Wealth. (No. XVII)

But when [he] . . . jumps into Commission with a Lye in his Mouth, that he is mov'd by the Holy Ghost, when his highest Aim is a fat living. . . (No. XXXIV)

There is therefore no Authority but two, Scripture and Reason. The Scripture is our Rule of Faith; and Reason . . . is our Rule for understanding the Scripture. (No. XXVII)

. . . Christianity requires . . . no other Belief of the Truth of a Fact or Proposition, than such as is supported by rational Testimony. (No. XLVII)

Religion is a voluntary Thing; it can no more be forced than Reason, or Memory, or any Faculty of the Soul. (No. XXXIV)

. . . as Religion is a personal Thing, no Council or Convocation can arrogate a Right of . . . binding . . . the Consciences of Christians. (No. XLVI)

. . . there is but one Article of Faith . . . namely, that Jesus is the Messiah. . . . (No. LIII)

All the Faith it requires is, that Christ was the promised Messiah. . . . (No. XXXI)

APPENDIX III

Neither a Man's Mind, nor his Palate can be subject to the Jurisdiction of another; and whoever takes upon him to regulate one's Throat and Stomach, and direct one how much to swallow. . . . (No. XXXIV)

. . . our Faiths like our Stomachs may be overcharged, especially if we are prohibited to chew what we are commanded to swallow. (No. XLVI)

1. See Introduction, p. 31 and note 60.

2. See Introduction, pp. 27–28.

3. Compare *Whig* III and *Reflector* XXXIV, *Whig* V and *Reflector* XVII, *Whig* VI and *Reflector* XLVI, *Whig* XXI and *Reflector* VI, *Whig* XXIX–XXX and *Reflector* XVII, *Whig* XXXIX and *Reflector* XLI, *Whig* IX–XLVII and *Reflector* XXXI, *Whig* XLIX and *Reflector* XLIV.

4. *Independent Whig* (1721), p. xlvi; *Independent Reflector*, VI and XLVI.

Index

INDEX

INDEX

INDEX

INDEX

Psychology, sensationalist, 416
Public office, in New York City, 381; qualifications for, 359–365; sale of, 30
Pyrrha, 353

Quakers, 206n10, 211–212, 275, 391, 397n7, 408–410
Queen Street (N.Y.C.), 152
Queens County, New York, 42–43
Queen's Farm, 35
The Querist, 43n109
Quintilian, quoted, 173; 174
Quitrents, 124, 152, 153

Rationalism, 398–403, 406–408, 409
The Reflector, 28
Religion, 90, 162–163, 295, 363, 383, 388, 396n3, 418n3; creeds in, 387–396; establishment of, 181, 367–375, 392; orthodoxy in, 90, 91, 92–93, 130, 276, 389, 391, 396n2; reason and, 334n1, 334n2, 330–331, 386n6, 399–403, 409; tyranny in, 79, 90, 91, 161, 220, 292–297, 309–310, 316, 317. *See also* Christianity; Clergy; Episcopacy; Freedom of religion
Revolution, American, 48
Republicanism, 56
Rhode Island, 239, 240, 437
Richard I, 370
Ridicule, defense of, 345–351
Rochester, Earl of, 327n8
Roman Catholic Church, 24, 78, 91, 130, 176, 272, 287, 370, 375, 387, 389. *See also* Papacy
Roman Empire, 257, 347, 407–408; decline of, 328; elections in, 279–280; heroes of, 79; patriotism in, 215–216; public honors in, 113–114; road repair system, 71, 73; sale of offices in, 115; scientific achievements of, 420
Romulus, 125
Roosevelt, Jacobus, 127n3
Roosevelt, John, 127n3
Rotten Row, *see* Hunter's Key
Rutgers, Cornelia, 127n3
Ryder, Dudley, 369

Sacheverell, Reverend Henry, 320
Sacket, ———, 121, 152
Sallust, 111, 115, 191
Scipio, 79
A Scheme for the Revival of Christianity, 31, 277

Schuyler, Philip, 397n10
Scotland, 368, 371–372, 424
Scott, Reverend John, 17
Scott, John Morin, 5, 13, 14, 16, 17–18, 343n1, 344n5, 446, 447
Scriptures, 90, 91, 92, 95n2, 102n3, 110n5, 127n2, 157, 176, 240, 271, 274, 277n5, 296, 308, 325, 348–349, 387, 388, 389, 390, 418n2; quoted, 131, 135, 136, 204, 235, 242–249, 263, 270, 309, 319, 355
Seabury, Reverend Samuel, 206n7, 277n1
Separation of church and state, 307–308, 312–316, 318nn5,7, 367–375, 391–392
Sharpas, William, 121
Shaftesbury, Earl of, 346, 406
Shakespeare, William, 132
Shaw, Peter, 28n72
Shower, Bartholomew, 138
Sidney, Philip, 49
Smallpox, 85
Smith, William, Sr., 7, 16, 18, 44
Smith, William, Jr., 5, 13, 14, 16–17, 22, 26, 31, 39, 43n109, 48, 95n1, 134n3, 163n4, 305n10, 343n1, 344n5, 357n1, 376n1, 426n2, 439n2, 446, 447
Smith, Reverend William, 1n2, 36, 40, 276n1, 385n4
Smith, William Peartree, 13, 14, 16, 447
Smith family, 12
Smollett, Tobias, 284n5
Society for the Promotion of Christian Knowledge, 372, 376n9, 394
Society for the Promotion of Industry (Boston), 107
Society for the Promotion of Useful Knowledge (New York), 14, 18–19
Society for the Propagation of the Gospel in Foreign Parts, 26, 27, 376n9
Social attitudes, 30, 257–261, 359–365, 365n1, 404–408, 410nn2,3.
Socinians, 272
Socrates, 413
Sons of Liberty, 47
South Sea Bubble, 21
Sower, Christopher, 439
Sparta, 114, 198n2, 362
The Spectator, 3, 13, 20, 28, 344n5, 345
Spurius Melius, 279–280
Spuyten Duyvil, 75n1
Squire, Francis, 31, 277n1
Stanley, Sir William, 323
Steele, Richard, 3, 20, 351n2

459

THE JOHN HARVARD LIBRARY

*The intent of
Waldron Phoenix Belknap, Jr.,
as expressed in an early will, was for
Harvard College to use the income from a
permanent trust fund he set up, for "editing and
publishing rare, inaccessible, or hitherto unpublished
source material of interest in connection with the
history, literature, art (including minor and useful
art), commerce, customs, and manners or way of
life of the Colonial and Federal Periods of the United
States . . . In all cases the emphasis shall be on the
presentation of the basic material." A later testament
broadened this statement, but Mr. Belknap's interests remained constant until his death.*

*In linking the name of the first benefactor of
Harvard College with the purpose of this later,
generous-minded believer in American culture the
John Harvard Library seeks to emphasize the importance of Mr. Belknap's purpose. The John Harvard
Library of the Belknap Press of Harvard University
Press exists to make books and documents
about the American past more readily
available to scholars and the
general reader.*